Financial Advisor Series

ESSENTIALS OF LIFE INSURANCE PRODUCTS

C.W. Copeland
Glenn E. Stevick, Jr.

THE AMERICAN COLLEGE PRESS

FA257.04.1

270 S. Bryn Mawr Avenue
Bryn Mawr, PA 19010
(888) AMERCOL (263-7265)
www.theamericancollege.edu
Library of Congress Control Number 2014942121
ISBN-10: 1-58293-163-1
ISBN-13: 978-1-58293-163-0
Printed in the United States of America

FINANCIAL ADVISOR SERIES

Sales Skills Techniques

Techniques for Exploring Personal Markets

Techniques for Meeting Client Needs

Techniques for Prospecting: Prospect or Perish

Women and Money—Matters of Trust

Product Essentials

Essentials of Annuities

Essentials of Business Insurance

Essentials of Disability Income Insurance

Essentials of Life Insurance Products

Essentials of Long-Term Care Insurance

Essentials of Multiline Insurance Products

Planning Foundations

Foundations of Estate Planning

Foundations of Retirement Planning

Foundations of Financial Planning: An Overview

Foundations of Financial Planning: The Process

Foundations of Investment Planning

THE AMERICAN COLLEGE

The American College® is an independent, nonprofit, accredited institution founded in 1927 that offers professional certification and graduate-degree distance education to men and women seeking career growth in financial services.

The Solomon S. Huebner School® of The American College administers the Chartered Life Underwriter (CLU®); the Chartered Financial Consultant (ChFC®); the Chartered Advisor for Senior Living (CASL®); the Registered Health Underwriter (RHU®); the Registered Employee Benefits Consultant (REBC®); the Chartered Healthcare Consultant™, the Chartered Leadership Fellow® (CLF®); and the Retirement Income Certified Professional (RICP®) professional designation programs. In addition, the Huebner School also administers The College's CFP Board—registered education program for those individuals interested in pursuing CFP® certification, the CFP® Certification Curriculum.

The Richard D. Irwin Graduate School® of The American College offers the Master of Science in Financial Services (MSFS) degree and several graduate-level certificates that concentrate on specific subject areas. It also offers the Chartered Advisor in Philanthropy® (CAP®) and the Master of Science in Management (MSM), a one-year program with an emphasis in leadership. Additionally, it offers the Doctoral Program in Financial and Retirement Planning. The National Association of Estate Planners & Councils has named The College as the provider of the education required to earn its prestigious AEP designation.

The American College is accredited by **The Middle States Commission on Higher Education**, 3624 Market Street, Philadelphia, PA 19104 at telephone number 267.284.5000.

The Middle States Commission on Higher Education is a regional accrediting agency recognized by the U.S. Secretary of Education and the Commission on Recognition of Postsecondary Accreditation. Middle States accreditation is an expression of confidence in an institution's mission and goals, performance, and resources. It attests that in the judgment of the Commission on Higher Education, based on the results of an internal institutional self-study and an evaluation by a team of outside peer observers assigned by the Commission, an institution is guided by well-defined and appropriate goals; that it has established conditions and procedures under which its goals can be realized; that it is accomplishing them substantially; that it is so organized, staffed, and supported that it can be expected to continue to do so; and that it meets the standards of the Middle States Association. The American College has been accredited since 1978.

The American College does not discriminate on the basis of race, religion, sex, handicap, or national and ethnic origin in its admissions policies, educational programs and activities, or employment policies.

The American College is located at 270 S. Bryn Mawr Avenue, Bryn Mawr, PA 19010. The toll-free number of the Office of Professional Education is (888) AMERCOL (263-7265); the fax number is (610) 526-1465; and the home page address is theamericancollege.edu.

CONTENTS

PREFACE

The purpose of this book is to develop your professionalism as a financial advisor counseling prospects and clients about life insurance. We intend to do this by teaching you about the needs of clients and the benefits of life insurance to shape your performance as a successful advisor. By gaining a deeper understanding of the life insurance contract and the economic needs it satisfies, you will be better able to help clients meet their life insurance requirements. This book will review the principles of life insurance and the various types of life insurance products. It will analyze the technical aspects of life insurance policies and ways of comparing them. It will also review life insurance policy provisions, taxation, marketing ideas, and ethics for financial advisors. This information will be accompanied by a review of the selling/planning process applied to life insurance. It is our hope that this book has the right blend of technical knowledge and practical information to accomplish our mission.

While much of the material presented will be new to you, some will, no doubt, refresh knowledge you acquired in the past. In either case, all of the material is both valuable and necessary if you aspire to be successful in the life insurance marketplace. The benefits you gain from studying the material will be directly proportional to the effort you expend. So, read each chapter carefully and answer both the essay review questions and multiple-choice self-test questions for the chapter (preferably before looking in the back of the book for the answers); to do less would be to deprive yourself of a unique opportunity to become familiar with life insurance and to learn more about selling it.

This book includes numerous educational features designed to help you focus your study of life insurance. Each chapter of this book includes the following:

- an overview identifying learning objectives
- a chapter outline
- examples, figures, and lists
- key terms and concepts
- review questions (essay format)
- self-test questions (multiple-choice format)

The back of the book includes a glossary, answers to the questions, and an index.

Finally, all of the fine individuals noted on the acknowledgments page made this a better book, and we are grateful. However, despite all the help we received, some errors have undoubtedly eluded us. For these we are solely responsible.

C.W. Copeland / Glenn E. Stevick, Jr.

ACKNOWLEDGMENTS

Thanks to the following practicing advisors and home office experts who gave editorial assistance in revising this edition:

- Ralph Adamo
- Alex Edmisten
- Alan Gay
- Susan Martin
- Chris Mendoza
- Sterling Raskie
- Dave Romagosa
- Maxwell Schauweker
- Cleveland H. Watkins
- J.L. Wilson

We would also like to thank John Whitham, Librarian of The American College's Knowledge Center, and his staff (especially Maryanne Adler) for their assistance in researching industry information in updating this textbook.

Very special thanks to previous authors for their expertise in creating this book. Much of the manuscript was adapted from *McGill's Life Insurance*, Edward E. Graves, editor.

For their valuable contribution to the development of this book, appreciation is extended to Travis Meister for production assistance, and Todd Denton and Jane Hassinger for editorial assistance.

To all of these individuals, without whom this book would not have been possible, the college expresses its sincere appreciation and gratitude.

C.W. Copeland
Glenn E. Stevick, Jr.
The American College

ABOUT THE AUTHORS

C. W. Copeland, Ph.D., is an assistant professor of insurance at The American College of Financial Services. His responsibilities at the college include developing materials for and coordinating the FSCP Program. Additionally, Dr. Copeland conducts scholarly research in Behavioral Economics and teaches professional/graduate-level courses in insurance and financial planning at The College. He is the author of *Financial Services Overview: The Practicum* published by The American College. He has been a regular guest on radio and television shows across the country where he addresses audiences on financial planning strategies on a regular basis. Dr. Copeland also writes articles for *Advisor Today,* a national magazine for the financial services industry.

Prior to joining The American College, Dr. Copeland served for 13 years as an adjunct professor in the School of Business at Clark-Atlanta University and 16 years as an instructor with R.S. Thomas Training Associates providing pre-licensing training, continuing education, and business development advice for financial services professionals. Dr. Copeland has more than 17 years of industry experience as a financial planner where he coordinates the efforts of attorneys, tax advisors, employee benefits coordinators, estate and business planners, and pension managers for the benefit of his clients. He holds numerous licenses and registrations (Georgia, Missouri, New Jersey, North Carolina, South Carolina, and Tennessee) in the areas of investments and insurance.

Dr. Copeland earned his B.S. degree from Tuskegee University, his M.S. degree from Georgia Tech, and his Ph.D. degree from the University of Georgia.

Glenn E. Stevick, Jr., LUTCF, CLU, ChFC, is an adjunct professor of insurance at The American College of Financial Services. His responsibilities at The College include writing and preparing text materials. He also teaches insurance and financial planning courses at The College.

Mr. Stevick is co-author of *Essentials of Long-Term Care Insurance, Techniques for Exploring Personal Markets, Essentials of Life Insurance Products*, and *Foundations of Financial Planning: The Process*; he is author of *Techniques for Meeting Client Needs, Essentials of Business Insurance, and Essential of Estate Planning*. All of these books are published by The American College. Mr.

Stevick also writes articles for *Advisor Today*, the national magazine distributed to members of NAIFA.

Before joining The College, Mr. Stevick worked for New York Life as a training supervisor for 15 years in its South Jersey office. He also served as an agent with New York Life for more than 2 years. Prior to his insurance industry experience, Mr. Stevick taught psychology at the college level and worked in various educational and mental health programs.

Mr. Stevick earned his BA degree from Villanova University and his MA degree from Duquesne University.

SPECIAL NOTES TO ADVISORS

Text Materials Disclaimer

This publication is designed to provide accurate and authoritative information about the subject covered. While every precaution has been taken in the preparation of this material to insure that it is both accurate and up-to-date, it is still possible that some errors eluded detection. Moreover, some material may become inaccurate and/or outdated either because it is time sensitive or because new legislation will make it so. Still other material may be viewed as inaccurate because your company's products and procedures are different from those described in the book. Therefore, the authors and The American College assume no liability for damages resulting from the use of the information contained in this book. The American College is not engaged in rendering legal, accounting, or other professional advice. If legal or other expert advice is required, the services of an appropriate professional should be sought.

Caution Regarding Use of Illustrations

The illustrations, sales ideas and approaches in this book are not to be used with the public unless you have obtained approval from your company. Your company's general support of The American College's programs for training and educational purposes does not constitute blanket approval of the sales ideas and approaches presented in this book, unless so communicated in writing by your company.

Use of the Term Financial Advisor or Advisor

Use of the term "Financial Advisor" as it appears in this book is intended as the generic reference to professional members of our reading audience. It is used interchangeably with the term "Advisor" so as to avoid unnecessary redundancy. Financial Advisor takes the place of the following terms:

Account Executive
Agent
Associate
Broker (stock or insurance)
Financial Consultant
Financial Planner
Financial Planning Professional
Financial Services Professional
Life Insurance Agent
Life Underwriter
Planner
Practitioner
Producer
Property & Casualty Agent
Registered Investment Advisor
Registered Representative

Health Underwriter
Insurance Professional
Senior Advisor

ABOUT THE FINANCIAL ADVISOR SERIES

The mission of The American College is to raise the level of professionalism of its students and, by extension, the financial services industry as a whole. As an educational product of the college, the Financial Advisor Series is central to accomplishing this mission. Because knowledge is key to professionalism, a thorough and comprehensive reading of each book in the Series will help the practitioner-advisor better service his or her clients; a task made all the more difficult as the typical client becomes ever more financially sophisticated and demands that his or her financial advisor be knowledgeable about all the latest products and planning methodologies. By providing practitioner-advisors in the financial services industry with up-to-date, authoritative information about various marketing and sales techniques, product knowledge, and planning considerations, the books of the Financial Advisor Series will enable many practitioner-advisors to continue their studies and develop and maintain a high level of professional competence.

When all of the books in the Financial Advisor Series are complete, the Series will encompass 16 titles spread over three separate subseries, each with a special focus. The first subseries, *Sales Skills Techniques,* will focus on enhancing the practitioner-advisor's marketing and sales skills, but will also touch on product knowledge and planning considerations. The second subseries, *Product Essentials,* will focus on product knowledge, but will also delve into marketing and sales skills, as well as planning considerations. The third subseries, *Planning Foundations,* will focus on the various planning considerations and processes that form the foundation of a successful career as a financial services professional. When appropriate, many of the books in this subseries will also touch upon product knowledge and sales and marketing skills. Current and forthcoming titles are listed earlier in this book.

OVERVIEW OF THE BOOK

Essentials of Life Insurance Products is an adaptation and selection of topics from *McGill's Life Insurance*.

This book is organized around the selling/planning process and covers the fundamentals of the life insurance product. It begins with the basics of life insurance, including insurance principles, product design, and the economic value of a human life. The course covers the two most basic forms of life insurance, term and whole life, then expands into interest-sensitive and variable insurance products, which represent the great array of products sold in today's markets. Additional topics include the personal and business uses of life insurance, methods of determining life insurance needs, today's life insurance buyers, comparing costs between policies, policy illustrations, policy provisions, settlement options, life insurance taxation, marketing ideas and ethical issues facing the financial advisor. Throughout the text is a discussion of the selling/planning process as it applies to life insurance.

To accomplish all of the above, chapter 1 covers the economic basics of life insurance, with emphasis on the human-life-value approach and identifying a family's needs for its use. The concepts covered include risk pooling, how the premium is determined, and personal life insurance needs. Chapter 2 provides an in-depth look at methods of determining life insurance needs of individuals and businesses, and how to determine the amount of life insurance needed by an individual. Term insurance policies and provisions are explained in chapter 3, and chapter 4 examines whole life insurance in detail. Chapter 4 also presents the pros and cons of the term versus permanent debate. Chapter 5 looks at variable and universal life and the specific product features and issues associated with these products. Chapter 6 examines the methods available to fairly compare policy costs, and discusses critical components of policy illustrations, many of which most of the public, and even some advisors, are unaware or simply overlook. Chapter 7 studies the policy provisions that define the life insurance contract and how the contract operates. Lastly, chapter 8 covers the topics of life insurance income, estate and gift taxation, life and viatical settlements, life insurance marketing ideas, and ethical principles for financial advisors.

BASIC PRINCIPLES OF LIFE INSURANCE 1

Learning Objectives

An understanding of the material in this chapter should enable you to

1. Define the basic principles of life insurance.
2. Explain the concept of risk pooling and the law of large numbers.
3. Explain how mortality, interest, and expense serve as the building blocks of life insurance.
4. Explain how the premium for yearly renewable term is determined.
5. Describe how the level premium insurance concept works.
6. Explain the concept of human life value and how it relates to the need for life insurance.
7. Identify and explain the expenses commonly associated with death and settling the deceased's estate.
8. List and explain the income needs of family survivors.
9. Explain the post-death cash needs of survivors.
10. Explain the steps in the selling/planning process.

This chapter explores the concept of risk pooling and other principles of life insurance. It defines how life insurance is structured. The human life value concept as the underlying economic principle for the need for life insurance is explained and the basic needs for life insurance are outlined. The chapter ends with a discussion of the selling/planning process applied to life insurance.

Basic Principles of Life Insurance

Life insurance is based on several basic principles that apply to all types of insurance, and that form the foundation of the insurance contract. Understanding these principles will help us better understand how life insurance works as we begin our study of life insurance products. The purpose of this course is to give you a much deeper understanding of life insurance products and related concepts that will help you, as a financial advisor, work with prospects and clients on ways to protect their families against the risk and financial impact of death. It will accomplish this by reviewing the basic principles of how life insurance works, the different financial needs that life insurance can address, the various types of life insurance, ways of comparing policies, the advantages and disadvantages of life insurance illustrations, life insurance policy provisions, the taxation of life insurance and some marketing and ethical concepts applicable to selling life insurance.

The information in this course is largely to educate you, not your clients. You will not necessarily discuss much of this material with clients, since it is largely technical and not relevant to the consumer, but it is important for you to understand it so you can appreciate the concepts and benefits of life insurance, how they work, and explain them correctly and with confidence to others.

The financial advisor can have a significant role in helping individuals and families establish a firm foundation of financial security. They should be able to address the fundamental financial needs and reasons for owning life insurance. He or she should be able to help prospects and clients recognize and accept their financial needs, and encourage them to act to take care of those needs. People face many financial challenges, and the ability to plan and save for the future is often put off for the pressures and pleasures of today.

This is clearly seen in recent research published by LIMRA, a research, consulting and professional development organization that helps insurance and financial services companies increase their marketing effectiveness. A recent LIMRA study (Household Trends in Life Insurance Ownership study, LIMRA, 2010, LL Global, Inc.) found that only 44 percent of U.S. households have individual life insurance, representing a 50-year low in individual life insurance ownership. The number of U.S. households with no life insurance whatsoever is growing. Today, 30 percent of households (35 million) have no life insurance coverage, compared to 22 percent of households in 2004. Despite high unemployment, the study reveals a continuing increase in the proportion of insured households that have only group insurance. Among households with children under age 18, which arguably have the greatest need for life insurance, 11 million have no coverage. Today 77 percent of husband-wife families with children under 18 have life insurance coverage, compared with 90 percent in 2004. As families have less to fall back on financially in the economic downturn, more families are living on the edge, without the safety net that life insurance provides.

Many Americans say they have not bought more life insurance because they have other financial priorities right now. Among households with children under 18, four in ten say they would have immediate trouble meeting everyday living expenses if the primary breadwinner died today. Another three in 10 would have trouble keeping up with expenses after several months. Half of households feel they need more life insurance than they have—the highest level ever. According to LIMRA's study, life insurance beat out all other sources of financial assets or income that Americans expect to use to help pay bills and to maintain their lifestyle in the event of the primary wage-earner's death. On average, households say they should have enough life insurance to replace their incomes for 6.2 years, but in reality they own enough to replace the household's income for only 3.5 years. Almost eight in 10 U.S. households currently do not have a personal life insurance agent or broker to turn to and most of them say they never did. These facts represent an enormous opportunity as well as a challenge to the life insurance industry and insurance producers.

The Role of the Financial Advisor

There is much to learn to be a competent financial advisor. You must master the core skills of your business including marketing, prospecting, selling, business organization, planning and management, communications, technical and product knowledge, and financial acumen. To be effective, you must know how to help people structure their financial goals. To become a professional and trusted advisor, you must help prospects and clients recognize and accept their financial needs, and encourage them to act to take care of those needs. That is rarely an easy job.

People expect more from financial advisors today than they did in the past. There have been serious violations of trust from financial institutions and those who work for them, and this situation is especially acute today. As an advisor, you are expected to act professionally and give accurate and valuable advice, based on your knowledge, skill and experience.

Financial advisors assist people who are facing the challenges of life such as retirement, disability, long-term care needs, or death. We help people address the problems these life events inevitably create. These are tough issues. Our task is to focus on these issues, the needs and dreams of our prospects and clients, and to devise the best ways to fulfill their goals and dreams. When we do this, our relationships with clients become meaningful to them and us, and we all benefit.

The financial services industry is very competitive. As you progress in your career, you must develop your knowledge and skills. This must become the difference between you and the competition in some meaningful way. You must ask yourself, how well do you understand your client's financial problems and goals? What ideas do you have to help him or her address them? How skilled are you at carrying out the selling and planning process? You must know your products and how they relate to other financial products that your clients will be offered. How deeply do you believe in the value of your products?

However, just because you want to help people does not mean that they want your help. Many people think they do not need your help because they are "do-it-yourselfers," or they do not recognize or accept that they have a financial need. You may not have been able to establish a relationship of trust with a prospect that will enable you to start this discussion. Many of those that need your help do not have the money or willingness to pay for it. Success will depend on finding people who want and need your help, and are willing and able to pay for it.

Most people are not looking for help. Most people engage advisors in the midst of or after triggering life events—not proactively, but reactively. Research studies and our own experience point out that people do not like to think about or discuss these topics. Retirement, death, divorce, having children, paying for college, layoffs and unemployment, long-term care events, and disability are critical triggers for prospects to either seek or accept professional financial help. Get ahead of this fact with targeted marketing, and seek prospects and markets where you can address these issues with prospects.

How many people you see will determine how successful you become, not how much you know. Knowledge supplements a successful practice; it does not create it. Activity is the key to staying in the business and eventually becoming successful. Make two appointments everyday for some time in the future. Having two appointments every day for the foreseeable future is the path to success.

Selling is a complex, psychological use of questions and statements that motivate people to make a decision and take action. It is neither simplistic nor devious, if done well and professionally. People fail to act in their own best interest and tend to stay put, regardless of their discomfort, unless motivated by a fear of loss or hope of gain that is greater than the cost of a solution or doing nothing. No amount of professional knowledge will make a bit of difference to this critical process unless you have someone to talk with. Expertise is useless until the prospect is engaged in the process. Most new advisors will need four or five strategic and repetitive marketing activities to be successful. With time and experience, these activities may be reduced to one or two core activities discovered through actual results over time. Quality comes from experience, and experience comes from repeated activity and many failures.

Insurance Defined

Insurance can be defined from many different points of view. For example, from an economic viewpoint, insurance is a system for reducing financial risk by transferring that risk from a policyowner to an insurer. The social aspect of insurance involves the collective bearing of losses through contributions by all members of a group to pay for losses suffered by some group members.

From a business viewpoint, insurance achieves the sharing of risk by transferring risks from individuals and businesses to financial institutions specializing in risk. The insurer is not in fact paying for the loss. The insurer writes the claim check, but is actually transferring funds from individuals who as part of a pool, paid premiums that created the fund from which the claims are paid.

Lastly, from a legal standpoint, an insurance contract (policy) transfers a risk (the possibility of a loss), for a premium (consideration), from one party (the policyowner) to another party (the insurer). It is a contractual arrangement in which the insurer agrees to pay a predetermined sum to a beneficiary in the event of the insured's death. By virtue of a legally binding contract, the possibility of an unknown large financial loss is exchanged for a comparatively small certain payment. This contract is not a guarantee against a loss occurring, but a method of ensuring that payment is made for a loss that does occur.

The Financial Planning Process

financial planning process

The financial advisor uses a planning approach to marketing insurance and financial products. This course emphasizes life insurance, but the skills and processes covered can apply to all financial product sales. Financial planning is a process that accomplishes both of the following:

- determines the client's financial problems and/or financial goals
- develops a plan to solve the client's problems and/or achieve the client's goals

Although some people may benefit from comprehensive financial planning, the process of addressing all aspects of one's financial life at one time, most people do not require this approach, and even if they do, they are unwilling to spend the time and money it requires. It is difficult to deal with the totality of one's financial problems and goals all at once. This is also challenging for the financial advisor, who needs specialized education, experience and training to take on this challenging task. In most cases, you will be addressing only one or a few of the most important financial needs for the prospect or client at the initial and subsequent meetings.

At the foundational level of the financial plan, the advisor and client should focus on providing protection against life's uncertainties, those events, such as the death of an income producer or parent, that could have a devastating effect on the financial well being of an individual and his or her dependents. This is the fundamental purpose of life insurance. Life insurance will also be involved in the financial planning process as financial objectives such as wealth accumulation and wealth distribution come into focus.

Life insurance was once considered an isolated financial product designed to protect policyowners from the financial consequences of premature death. Little attempt was made to integrate life insurance planning with the complete array of products sold by all types of financial institutions. In recent years, it has become increasingly difficult to view insurance products in isolation from a comprehensive financial planning process. This is due in part to the growing popularity of the financial planning approach and in part to the integration of the financial services industry, where a broad range of financial products are being made available within one financial services organization.

Risk Management

risk management

Life entails risk, which is defined as the probability of loss. People generally seek security and avoid uncertainty. The risk of death is unavoidable, and is especially an economic threat if premature, when an individual may be exposed to heavy financial responsibilities, yet has not had the time to accumulate enough savings to offset the financial needs of survivors. Life insurance provides a tool for *risk management*, a process for dealing with the risk of loss of life.

Insurance substitutes certainty for uncertainty, through the pooling of groups of people who share the risks to which they are exposed. Uncertain risks of individuals are combined, making the possible loss more certain, and providing a financial solution to the problems created by the loss. Small, certain periodic contributions (premiums) by the individuals in the group provide a fund from which those who suffer a loss are compensated. The certainty of losing the premium replaces the uncertainty of a larger loss. Life insurance thus manages the uncertainty of one party through the transfer of a particular risk (death) to another party (the insurer) which offers a restoration, at least in part, of relatively large economic losses suffered by the insured individual and his or her dependents.

indemnity

The essence of insurance is the principle of *indemnity*, that the person who suffers a financial loss is placed in the same financial position after the loss as before the loss occurred. He neither profits nor is disadvantaged by the loss. In practice, this is much more difficult to achieve in life insurance than in property insurance. No life insurance company would provide insurance in an amount clearly exceeding the estimated economic value of the covered life. Limiting the amount of life insurance sold to reflect economic value gives recognition to the rule of indemnity. Additionally, only persons exposed to the potential loss may legitimately own the insurance covering the insured's life.

Risk Pooling

risk pooling

Life insurance is based on a concept called *risk pooling,* or a group sharing of losses. People exposed to a risk agree to share losses fairly or on an equitable basis. They transfer the economic risk of loss to an insurance company. Insurance companies collect and pool the premiums of thousands of people, spreading the risk of losses across the entire pool. By carefully calculating the probability of losses that will be sustained by the members of the pool, insurance companies can equitably spread the cost of the losses to all the members. The risk of loss is transferred from one to many and shared by all insureds in the pool.

EXAMPLE

The simplest illustration of risk pooling involves providing insurance for one year, with all members of the group the same age and possessing roughly similar prospects for longevity. The members of this group agree that a specified sum, such as $100,000, will be paid to the beneficiaries of those members who die during the year, with the cost of the payments being shared equally by the members of the group. In its simplest form, this arrangement might involve an assessment upon each member in the appropriate amount as each death occurs. In a group of 1,000 persons, each death would produce an assessment of $100 per member. Among a group of 10,000 males aged 35, 21 of them could be expected to die within a year, according to the 1980 Commissioners Standard Ordinary Mortality Table (more on this later). If expenses of operation are ignored, cumulative assessments of $210 per person would provide the funds for payment of $100,000 to the beneficiary of each of the 21 deceased persons.

Examples of Risk Pooling

Homeowner's Insurance

Of 1,000 houses, each worth $200,000, assume only one house per year is destroyed by fire. Each homeowner could contribute $200 per year into a pooled fund that could pay out the full $200,000 value to the homeowner of a destroyed home. Such pooling transfers the risk of bearing the full impact of a potential $200,000 loss by an owner.

Life Insurance

Ten thousand males aged 35 contribute to a life insurance pool. Twenty-one of them are expected to die this year (based on 1980 CSO Mortality Table). The mortality charge is $2.10 per $1,000 of benefit. If each of the 10,000 contributes $210 to fund death benefits (ignoring costs of operation), a death benefit of $100,000 could be paid for each of the 21 expected deaths.

Members of the group pay premiums that are measured to be individually and collectively fair based on the risk they impose on the company and the pool. (Each class of policies should pay its own costs.) If all insureds contribute a fair amount to the mortality fund held by the insurance company, there will be sufficient dollars in the fund to pay the death benefits of those insureds that die in the coming year. Individually, we do not know when we will die, but statistically, the insurer can predict with great accuracy the number of individuals that will die in a large group of individuals. The insurance company has taken an uncertainty on any individual's part, and turned it into a certainty on their part.

The Law of Large Numbers

For a plan of insurance to function, the pricing method needs to measure the risk of loss and determine the amount to be contributed to the pool by each participant. The theory of probability provides such a scientific measurement.

Probabilities for life insurance are represented in a mortality table. The *mortality table* is very versatile, developing probabilities of dying over the entire life span. Life expectancy at any age is the average number of years of life remaining once a person has attained a specific age. It is the average future lifetime for a representative group of people at any given age. The probable future lifetime of any individual, of course, will depend on his or her state of health, among other things, and may be much longer or shorter than the average.

law of large numbers

The statistical group that is observed for purposes of measuring probability must have mass—that is, the sample must be large enough to allow the true underlying probability to emerge. The *law of large numbers* states that as the size of the sample (insured population) increases, the actual loss experience will more and more closely approximate the true underlying probability. This means that the insurer's statistical group must be large enough to produce reliable results, and that the group actually insured must be large enough to produce results that are consistent with what probability predicts.

Insurance relies on the law of large numbers to minimize the speculative element and reduce volatile fluctuations in year-to-year losses. The greater the number of exposures (lives insured) to a peril (cause of loss/death), the less the observed loss experience (actual results) will deviate from expected loss experience (probabilities). Uncertainty diminishes and predictability increases as the number of exposure units increases. It would be a gamble to insure one life, but insuring 500,000 similar persons will result in death rates that will vary little from the expected.

A peril is a cause of a loss. In life insurance, the event against which protection is granted, death, is uncertain for any one year, but the probability of death increases with age until it becomes a certainty. If a life insurance policy is to protect an insured during his or her entire life, an adequate fund must be accumulated to meet a claim that is certain to occur.

Some people claim that insurance is a gamble. Insurance is actually the opposite of gambling. Gambling creates risk where none existed. Insurance transfers an already existing risk exposure and, through the pooling of similar loss exposures, reduces financial risk.

The Building Blocks of Life Insurance—Mortality, Interest, and Expense

All life insurance products are actuarially created by calculating the relationships of mortality, interest, and expense, and the financial values resulting from each based on time. The assumptions made concerning these three factors will determine the premium at which a policy is sold, the structure of the policy, and over time the performance of the policy and the profitability and solvency of the life insurance company. All life insurance policies, regardless of type, are based on these same elements.

mortality

interest

expense

Mortality rates project the cost of covering death claims as they occur. *Interest* earnings reflect the income the company expects to receive from the investment of premiums over time that will be added to the reserves, held aside to pay future claims. *Expenses* include the cost of creating, offering, and maintaining the product to pay all promised benefits. These factors must also provide profit to the insurer.

Different products apply these factors in different ways. Term insurance has a pay-as-you-go structure. Premiums increase as mortality increases and the policy does not build cash value. Interest earnings have a smaller impact on the premium than in permanent policies and expenses are largely covered by the policy fee.

In permanent whole life insurance (WL), the policyowner pays premiums in advance, paying a higher, or excess, premium that can be "reserved," so that premiums can remain level throughout the insured's life. This higher premium level builds cash value the policyowner can access through loans or cash surrender of the policy. In WL, these factors are "bundled," meaning they are not itemized or disclosed separately.

On the other hand, in universal life (UL), the costs are unbundled, meaning the components of mortality, interest, and expense in the policy are identified and the values and charges for each are itemized in regular reports to policyowners. Mortality charges are identified as cost of insurance (COI), which are monthly charges based on the insured's issue age, attained age, net amount at risk, gender, and underwriting class. Interest is paid each month on the cash value at the current crediting rate. Administrative expenses are charged monthly. All of these elements have a current rate, and are subject to maximum and minimum guaranteed charges or interest crediting as stated in the policy.

Because of the unbundled nature of policy costs, UL works like an investment account with term coverage. The mortality charges are similar to those of term, and the interest rates reflect the current market and adjust to changing market conditions. The policyowner accepts more of the investment and mortality risk, with a minimum guaranteed interest crediting rate, and maximum mortality and expense charge guarantees.

Variable universal life (VUL) contains death benefits and cash values that vary with the performance of the subaccounts selected. The death benefit and cash value are not guaranteed, and can fluctuate according to market performance. The life insurance aspect of VUL is essentially the same product as UL with the same features and specifications for the most part. The main difference between UL and VUL is that VUL allows the policyowner to allocate the premiums and cash value of the policy among a group of variable subaccounts.

Mortality

To price insurance products, and ensure the adequacy of reserves to pay claims, actuaries use mortality tables to project the number and timing of future insured deaths. Actuaries study the incidence of deaths in the recent past, and develop expectations about how these events will change over time, allowing them to develop an expectation of the timing and number of such events in the future. A safety margin is built in that increases the mortality rates above what is expected. In participating policies, savings created by these conservative assumptions can be returned as dividends. In nonparticipating policies, the safety margins must be smaller in order for the premium rates to be competitive.

A *mortality table* shows the mortality experience used to estimate longevity and the probability of living or dying at each age, and thus determine the premium rate. Mortality tables may include the probability of surviving any particular year of age, remaining life expectancy for people at different ages, the proportion of the original birth cohort still alive, and estimates of a group's longevity characteristics. Life mortality tables today are constructed separately for men and women, and are created to distinguish individual characteristics such as smoking status, occupation, health histories, and others.

2001 CSO Mortality Table

With significant improvements in mortality over the last 20 years, mortality rates are decreasing. One resulting change is the extension of the life span in the *2001 CSO (Commissioners Standard Ordinary) Mortality Table* to attained age 120 (compared with age 100 in the 1980 CSO table). The CSO mortality tables represent the most widely used estimates of expected rates of death in the United States based on age. The data used for the CSO tables is taken from data developed by the American Academy of Actuaries, and adopted by the National Association of Insurance Commissioners (NAIC). The CSO mortality tables are used to calculate reserves and minimum cash values for state regulatory purposes, as well as life insurance premiums. Larger insurance companies use their own morality statistics to calculate their pricing of products, based on their own selection and underwriting practices. Because 1980 CSO mortality represents the vast majority of in-force policies, it is, and will be, relevant for years to come, even though newly issued policies will be using 2001 CSO rates. As of January 1, 2009, all new products must use the 2001 CSO table to calculate nonforfeiture and reserve values for state regulatory purposes.

Interest

Insurers invest the premiums they receive and accumulate them for future claims and other obligations, such as policy loans and surrenders. Life insurance company portfolios are traditionally long-term and emphasize safety of principal and predictable rates of return, to accommodate their long-term obligations. Typically, two-thirds or more of this capital is invested in bonds and mortgages, which meet the above criteria. A smaller percentage is invested in common stocks, due to their volatility. Today, common stocks represent less than 10 percent of the average life insurer's general account portfolio.

Since recently issued policies have low claims experience as a whole until years later, there is an adjustment in the calculation of the premium for the *time value of money* (compound interest). If the investment results exceed the guaranteed minimum, policyowners benefit from either participating dividends or excess interest crediting to the policy's cash value.

Expense

Life insurance companies incur acquisition and administrative expenses in the course of doing business. Acquisition expenses include the costs incurred in obtaining business and placing it in force, such as advertising and promotion fees; commissions; underwriting expenses; costs associated with medical exams and attending physicians' statements, inspection report and credit history fees; home office processing costs; and an addition to the insurer's reserve, surplus, and profits. Administrative expenses include the costs associated with collecting premiums and distributing dividends, continuing producer compensation, investment expenses, and home office overhead. Any costs the insurer incurs must be recovered through mortality savings, expense charges, and (or) reduced interest crediting.

Determining the Premium

The 1980 CSO Mortality Table lists different rates for men and women of different ages. The rate per $1,000 of benefit for women aged 35 is $1.65 in the 1980 CSO table. Companies that issue policies to only the healthiest applicants will have rates significantly lower than those in the CSO tables. Even insurance companies issuing policies to applicants in average health usually offer rates lower than those listed in the CSO tables.

yearly renewable term (YRT)

To demonstrate how the tables are used, we will first examine how the premium for a *yearly renewable term (YRT)* insurance policy is calculated. YRT is the simplest form of insurance offered by life insurance companies. It provides insurance for a period of one year and allows the policyowner to renew the policy for successive periods of one year each, paying just the mortality charges and administrative expenses for one year at a time, and no more. The interest component is minimal.

The mortality charge for YRT insurance is determined by the death rate for the attained age of the individual involved. Each premium purchases only one year of insurance protection. Each group of policyowners of a given age is considered to be a separate class for premium purposes; each group must pay its own death claims, with the burden shared equally by the members of the group. Because the death rate increases with age, the premium for yearly renewable term insurance normally increases each year.

EXAMPLE

For a group of 100,000 women aged 25

- The average mortality rate, according to the 1980 CSO Mortality Table, is 1.16 per 1,000.
- Expected deaths from the group for the year are 116.
- A $1,000 death benefit per deceased results in $116,000 in claims.
- Each woman contributes $1.16 to cover the death benefits (ignoring costs of operation).

Because premiums are paid to the life insurance company in advance, the cost of the anticipated death claims would be distributed pro rata over the 100,000 policyowners, and a premium of $1.16 would be collected from each policyowner. Note that:

- the premium is precisely the same as the death rate applicable to those insured
- those policyowners who, according to the mortality projection, will die during the year, contribute on the same basis as those who will survive

Each policyowner pays a share of his or her own death claim. This is a principle that underlies all life insurance contracts. The proportion, however, varies with the type of contract, age at issue, and duration of the protection.

If the 99,884 survivors of the original group of 100,000 policyowners was insured for another year, they would be exposed to the death rate for persons aged 26, or 1.19 per 1,000, which would theoretically produce 119 deaths and claims totaling $119,000. That sum divided equally among the 99,884 participants would yield a premium of $1.19 per person. If the 99,765 women who survived the first and second year should desire insurance for another year, provision would be made for $122,000 in death claims, requiring a premium of $1.22 per person.

For the first several years, the premium would continue to increase slowly, being $1.35 at age 30, $1.65 at age 35, and $2.42 at age 40. Later, however, the premium would rise sharply, reaching $3.56 at age 45, $4.96 at 50, $7.09 at 55, $9.47 at 60, and $14.59 at 65. If the insurance is continued beyond age 65, the cost becomes prohibitive, soaring to $22.11 per $1,000 at age 70, $38.24 at 75, $65.99 at 80, and $116.10 at 85. The premium at 90 would be $190.75 per $1,000; at 95, it increases to $317.32. Finally, if a woman aged 99 should want $1,000 of insurance on the YRT basis, she would have to pay a premium of $1,000, since the 1980 CSO table assumes that the limit of life is 100 years and that a person aged 99 will die within the year, or at least the policy period will end.

Level Premium Plan

Level premium insurance is a plan of insurance under which premiums do not increase from year to year but remain constant throughout the premium-paying period. It does not imply that the policyowner must pay premiums as long as he or she has insurance protection, only that all premiums required will be of equal size.

If premiums that increase each year are leveled out, the premiums paid in the early years of the contract will be more than adequate to meet current death claims, while those paid in the later years will be insufficient to meet incurred claims. This is a simple concept, but it has many consequences and far-reaching significance.

reserve

With the level premium technique, the excess premiums in the early years of the contract create an accumulation fund that is held by the insurance company for the benefit and to the credit of the policyowners. This is not a trust fund in the legal sense, which would require the insurance company to establish separate investment accounts for each policyowner and render periodic accountings. This accumulation is called a *reserve*, which is an amount that must be accumulated and maintained by the insurance company to meet definite future obligations.

legal reserve

Because the manner in which the fund is to be accumulated and invested is strictly regulated by law, the reserve is usually referred to as the *legal reserve*. The reserve is a composite liability account of the insurance company, not allocated to individual policies, but an aggregate of individual accounts established to the credit of the various policyowners. In practice, each policy is credited with a cash value or surrender value, which is not the same as the reserve, but is based on the excess premiums paid during the early years.

Term Policies

From the standpoint of an individual policy, the excess portions of the premiums paid in the early years of the contract are accumulated at compound interest and subsequently used to supplement the inadequate premiums of the later years. This process can be explained most simply in connection with a contract that provides protection for only a temporary period, as opposed to one that provides insurance for the policyowner's whole life.

Figure 1-1 shows a level premium term policy issued at age 25, remaining in force to age 65, based on the 1980 CSO female table with an interest assumption of 4.5 percent. It is assumed, in calculating the level premium, that the reserves are invested at 4.5 percent, and that the YRT (Yearly Renewable Term) premiums earn 4.5 percent each year before being disbursed for any death benefits paid. In this example, for the sake of simplicity, no allowance is made for expenses, which makes it easier to understand.

Figure 1-1
Annual Premium Comparison Level Term to Age 65 and Yearly Term

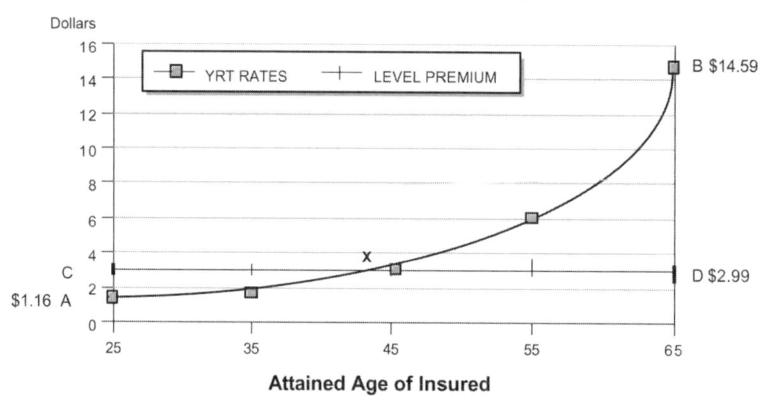

In Figure 1-1 the curve *AB* represents the premiums at successive ages that would be required to provide $1,000 of YRT insurance from age 25 to age 65. The premium ranges from $1.16 at age 25 to $14.59 at age 65. The line *CD* represents the level premium that would be required to provide $1,000 of insurance from age 25 to age 65 on the *level (premium) term* basis. The level premium to be paid each year through age 64 is $2.99. This amount exceeds the premiums that would be required on the YRT plan prior to age 44, but is smaller than those payable thereafter.

The area *AXC* represents the excess portions of the level premiums paid prior to age 43; the area *BXD* represents the deficiency in premiums after that age. The second area is much larger than the first. The disparity in the size of the two areas is attributable to the fact that the sums represented by the area *AXC*, which represent the reserve under the contract, are invested at compound interest, and the interest earnings are subsequently used along with the principal sum to supplement the premium deficiency in the later years.

The reserve is completely exhausted at age 65 (the end of coverage), having been used to pay the policy's share of death claims submitted under this group of policies. The reserve, including the investment earnings derived from them, is gradually used up after age 44 in the process of supplementing the deficient level premium. The reserve under this particular contract—term to 65, issued at age 25—reaches its maximum size at age 53, diminishing thereafter at an accelerating rate until exhausted at the expiration of the policy.

Ordinary Life Policies

The functioning of the level premium plan is even more striking when applied to a WL policy. A comparison of the level premium required under an ordinary life policy (WL) with that required on the YRT basis is presented below. An *ordinary life policy* is a type of WL for which level premiums are paid until the insured's death, or the policy termination date of age 100 or 120 (the end of the mortality table used), whichever comes first. The terms ordinary life and WL are interchangeable. Today we more commonly use the term whole life (WL).

The age of issue is 25 and the premiums are based on the 1980 CSO female table and 4.5 percent interest, with no allowance for expenses. In this case, an annual level premium of $6.09 per $1,000 paid as long as the insured lives would be the mathematical equivalent of a series of premiums on the YRT basis, ranging from $1.16 per $1,000 at age 25 to $956.94 at age 99.

The 1980 CSO Female Table assumes that everyone who survives to age 99 will die during the year, producing a net premium on the yearly renewable term basis equal to the face of the policy, less the interest that will be earned on the premium during the year. In the figure, line *CD* bisects the curve *AB* between the ages of 53 and 54.

The disparity between the areas *AXC* and *BXD* is very much greater in this case than in the previous figure. Excess premiums (area *AXC*) in the early years of an ordinary life contract (or for any type of level premium insurance contract) will offset the deficiency in the premiums of the later years when the term premium is in the hundreds of dollars. With the aid of compound interest, the policy will accumulate a reserve equal to the policy face amount by the time the insured reaches the policy maturity (termination) date.

Figure 1-2
Annual Premium Comparison Whole Life and Yearly Term

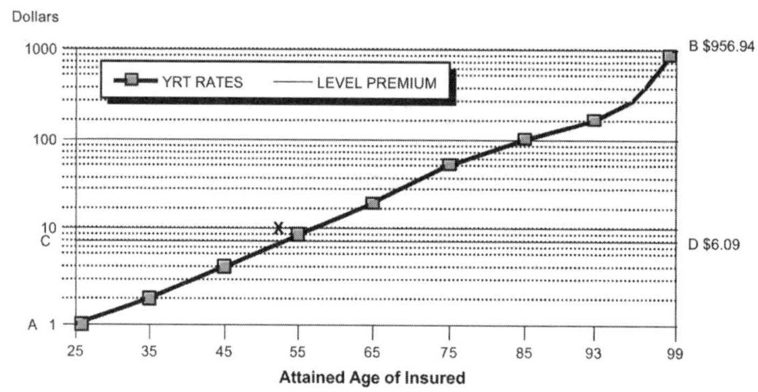

This is in contrast to the level premium term contract, under which the reserve is completely used up at the expiration of the contract (maturity date). The difference is because the risk (probability of occurrence) under a whole life contract providing protection for the life of the insured is one "converging into a *certainty*," while the risk under a term policy is a mere *contingency*—one that may or may not occur. Under a whole life contract, provision must be made for a death claim that is certain to occur, the only uncertainty being the time it will occur.

Yearly Term versus Level Premium for Life

Female Aged 25

- Annual level premium of $6.09 per $1,000 of coverage
- Exceeds yearly term cost of $1.16 per $1,000 coverage at age 25
- Level premium exceeds the yearly term premium until the insured reaches her mid-50s
- Beyond age 55, the level premium of $6.09 per $1,000 of coverage is less than the cost of yearly term coverage per $1,000
- By age 99, the yearly term premium of $956.94 per $1,000 of coverage greatly exceeds the $6.09 cost per $1,000

By the time an insured has reached 99, the reserve under his or her policy must have accumulated to an amount that will equal the face amount of the policy, supplemented by the final annual premium and the interest on the combined sums for the last 12 months of the contract. A whole life contract will either pay a death claim, or it will endow at the maturity date and the policyowner will receive the face amount. This must be the case if each class of policyowners is to be self-supporting, meaning there are no other funds for the payment of the claims of the last members to die. In effect, such policyowners pay off their own death claims, in addition to paying their share of the death claims of all other members of the group.

Net Amount at Risk

amount at risk

Under a level premium contract, the accumulated reserve becomes a part of the face amount payable upon the death of the insured. From the standpoint of the insurance company, the effective amount of insurance is the difference between the face amount of the policy and the reserve. This is called the *amount at risk*, and is the amount the insurer must be able to collect from the reserve to pay the claim. As the reserve increases, the amount at risk decreases. The significance of this relationship is that as the death rate increases, the amount at risk (the effective amount of insurance) decreases, producing a *cost of insurance* within practical and affordable limits.

Table 1-1 Influence of the Reserve on COI

Year	Attained Age at Beginning of Year	Reserve End of Year Even Dollars	Net Amount at Risk	Death Rate per 1,000	Cost of Insurance
1	25	$ 5	$995	1.16	$1.15
5	29	22	978	1.30	1.27
10	34	55	945	1.58	1.49
20	44	139	861	3.32	2.86
30	54	252	748	6.61	4.94
40	64	397	603	13.25	7.99

cost of insurance

The *cost of insurance* is an actuarial term referring to the sum obtained by multiplying the death rate at the insured's attained age by the *net amount at risk*. This is the amount of actual insurance and determines the amount a policyowner must pay for protection. It is the sum that each policyowner contributes as his or her share of death claims in any particular year. This process is illustrated in the table above.

net level premium

The *net level premium* is the premium based on mortality and interest, and disregards expense. For example, the net level premium for an ordinary life contract on a female issued at age 25, based on the 1980 CSO table and 4.5 percent interest, is $6.09. Since the death rate at age 25 is 1.16 per 1,000, about $5 of the first premium is excess and goes into the policy reserve. If the policyowner should die during the first year, the company would use the $5 in settling the claim and would have to draw only $995 of the $1,000 face amount from the premiums contributed by the other policyowners in the age and policy classification of the deceased. This would mean that each member's pro rata share of death claims in the first year would be only $1.15 (1.16 × 0.995), instead of $1.16, the YRT premium for $1,000 of insurance at age 25 (with no allowance for interest).

By the end of the 5th year, the reserve, or accumulation of excess payments, will have increased to $22 per $1,000, which sum would be available for settlement of a death claim under the policy. The net amount at risk would have decreased to $978, which would necessitate a contribution from the other policyowners (and the deceased) of only $1.27, instead of the YRT premium of $1.30. The reserve will have grown to $139 per $1,000 by the end of the 20th year, which would reduce the cost per $1,000 from $3.32 to $2.86. By the time the insured reaches 65, the reserve under the policy will have accumulated to $397, and the actual amount of protection will have shrunk to $603.

A death claim in the 40th year of the contract would be settled by payment of the $397 in the reserve and $603 from the current year's premium payments (of all the policyowners). The pro rata share of each policyowner for all death claims during the year would be only $7.99, as compared to $13.25 if no reserve had been available. The influence of the reserve on the COI is even more significant at the advanced ages.

Under the level premium plan, a $1,000 policy does not provide $1,000 of insurance. The company is never at risk for the face amount of the policy—even in the first year. The amount of actual insurance is always the face amount, less the policyowner's own accumulated excess payments. The accumulation is the reserve for insurance company purposes, and it is the cash value (slightly less in early years) for policyowner purposes. Because the excess payments may be withdrawn by the policyowner at any time through the cash surrender or loan privileges, they may be regarded as a savings or accumulation account. Thus, a level premium policy does not provide pure insurance but a combination of decreasing insurance and increasing cash values, so that in any year their sum is equal to the face amount of the policy. This is illustrated below for an ordinary life policy of $1,000 issued at age 25, based on the 1980 CSO Female Table and 4.5 percent interest.

Figure 1-3
Proportion of Protection and Savings Elements in Ordinary Life Contract, Issued at Age 25; 1980 CSO Female Table and 4.5 Percent Interest

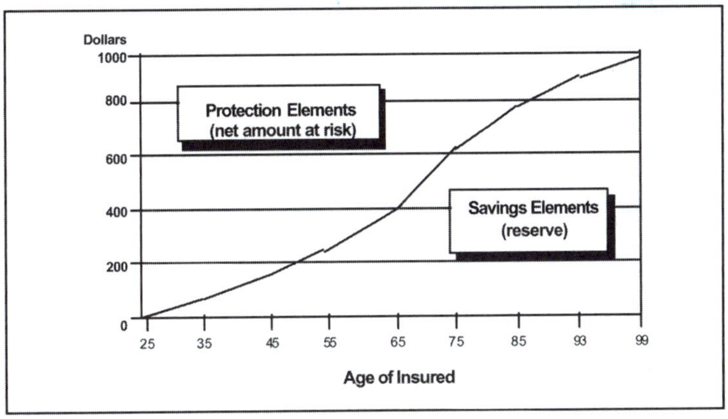

The area below the curve represents the reserve under the contract or the policyowner's equity in the contract. The area above the curve represents the company's net amount at risk and the policyowner's amount of protection. As the reserve increases, the amount of protection decreases. At any given age the two combined will equal the face amount of the policy. By age 95, the protection element of the contract has become relatively minor, and by age 100—the end of the contract—it has completely disappeared. At age 100, the policyowner will receive $1,000, composed entirely of the cash value element.

This combination of protection and accumulated cash values is characteristic of all cash value plans. Fundamentally, one contract differs from another only in the proportion in which the two elements are combined. This basic truth should be kept in mind as you study the types of life insurance polices.

Yearly term insurance is all protection and has no cash value, while single premium life insurance is at the other end of the spectrum with the highest cash values and lowest proportion at risk. Accumulated cash values should be thought of as some degree of prefunding. Single-premium policies are fully prefunded, and lower-premium policies that develop cash values are only partially prefunded. The shorter the premium-paying period, the higher the proportion of cash value to death benefit, and the higher the premium.

The impact of the level premium plan effects all operations of a life insurance company. The investment of these funds has presented the life insurance industry with one of its most challenging problems, but at the same time has enabled insurance companies to contribute to the dynamic expansion of the American economy.

The level premium plan underlies the system of cash values and other surrender options that has made the life insurance contract one of the most flexible and valuable contracts in existence. The greatest significance of the plan is that it is the only arrangement under which it is possible to provide insurance protection to the policyowners at life expectancy ages and beyond without the cost becoming prohibitive.

Human Life Value

The economic values of a human life are the basis for the need for life insurance, and can help determine the amount of life insurance needed by an individual or a family. A human life has an economic value only if some person(s) or organization depends upon or expects to receive some monetary benefit through that life. The following discussion explains how human life value is determined, and lists and describes the specific needs for life insurance. The methods used to calculate the amount of life insurance needed by individuals and families are discussed later.

The Concept of Human Life Value

A human life possesses many values, most of them irreplaceable and not easily measured. These values are founded on religious, moral, and social relationships. From a religious standpoint, for example, human life is regarded as immortal and endowed with a value beyond the comprehension of mortal man. In a person's relationship with other human beings, a set of emotional and sentimental attachments is created that cannot be measured in monetary terms or supplanted by material things.

Such values, however, are not the foundation of life insurance. Although not oblivious to these values—in fact, life insurance has strong moral and social overtones—life insurance is concerned with the human life value, or the economic value of a human life, which is derived from its earning capacity and the financial dependence of others on that earning capacity.

The Economic Value of the Human Life

In terms of its physical composition, the human body has a limited dollar value. In terms of earning capacity, however, it may be worth millions of dollars. Yet, earning power alone does not create an economic value that can logically serve as the basis of life insurance. A human life has an economic value only if some other person or organization expects to receive an economic advantage through its existence.

If an individual is without dependents and no other person or organization depends financially on that person, either now or in the future, then that life, for all practical purposes, has no monetary value that needs to be insured. Such an individual is rare. Most income producers either have dependents or can expect to acquire them in the normal course of life. Even those income earners with no family dependents often provide financial support to business or charitable organizations. In either case, a basis exists for life insurance.

Preservation of Family's Economic Security

In many cases, an income producer's family is completely dependent on his or her personal earnings for survival and the comforts of life. In other words, the "potential" estate, or the earnings and savings that may be received and accumulated in the future, is far more substantial than the existing estate—the savings that the family has been able to accumulate. The family's economic security lies in the earning capacity of each income earner, which is represented by his or her "character and health, training and experience, personality and power of industry, judgment and power of initiative, and driving force to put across in tangible form the economic images of his mind," said Solomon Huebner in 1950.

Over time, this economic potential are gradually converted into income, a portion of which is devoted to self-maintenance, a portion to support of dependents, and if the income is large enough, a portion to savings to meet future needs and contingencies. If the individual lives and stays in good health, the total income potential will eventually be realized, for the benefit of the family and others who receive benefits from his or her efforts. If an income earner dies or becomes permanently and totally disabled, the unrealized portion of his or her total earnings potential will be lost, and in the absence of other measures, the family will soon find itself destitute or reduced to a lower income than it previously enjoyed.

This need not happen, however, since there are life insurance contracts that can create a fund at death to at least partially, and possibly fully, offset the lost income of the insured. By means of life insurance, an individual can ensure that the family will receive the monetary value of those income-producing qualities that lie within him or her, regardless of when death occurs. By capitalizing this life value (creating a fund large enough to generate investment income approximating the salary or wages of the individual) , an income earner can leave the family in the same economic position that they would have enjoyed had he or she lived.

These concepts are the basis of a sales presentation that was commonly used 30 years ago, and is still valid today, called “live, quit or die”. The concept was that life and disability insurance can protect the economic values of a working person, and that in a way one cannot lose by purchasing these insurance contracts. Only one outcome can ultimately occur in life. A person will

- live, and the cash values of the life insurance policy will be available as living benefits
- die, and the death benefits will provide for survivors
- surrender the policy (quit), and much if not all of the premiums paid can be recovered

An additional condition was sometimes added—become disabled—to demonstrate the waiver of premium provision, or the use of a disability policy, that can provide income in the case of disability.

The Moral Obligation to Provide Protection

Most people assume major responsibility for the support and maintenance of their dependent children during their lifetime. In fact, they consider it one of the rewarding experiences of life. In any case, the law attaches a legal obligation to the support of a spouse and children. Thus if there is a divorce or a legal separation, the court will normally decree support payments for dependent children and possibly alimony for the dependent spouse. In some cases such payments, including alimony, are to continue beyond the provider's death, if the children are still dependent or if the alimony recipient has not remarried. In such event, the parent and ex-spouse are required to provide life insurance or to set funds aside in trust.

It takes a high order of responsibility for a parent to voluntarily provide for continuation of income to dependents after his or her own death. It virtually always involves a reduction in the individual's own standard of living. Yet, few would deny that any person with a dependent spouse, children, or parents has a moral obligation to provide them with the protection afforded by life insurance, as far as his or her financial means permit.

In his book *Life Insurance*, Dr. Solomon Huebner said the following concerning the obligation to insure:

> From the family standpoint, life insurance is a necessary business proposition that may be expected of every person with dependents as a matter of course, just like any other necessary business transaction which ordinary decency requires him to meet. The care of his family is man's first and most important business. The family should be established and run on a sound business basis. It should be protected against needless bankruptcy. The death or disability of the head of this business should not involve its impairment or dissolution any more than the death of the head of a bank, railroad, or store. Every corporation and firm represents capitalized earning capacity and goodwill. Why then, when men and women are about to organize the business called a family should there not be a capitalization in the form of a life insurance policy of the only real value and goodwill behind that business? Why is it not fully as reasonable to have a life insurance policy accompany a marriage certificate as it is to have a marine insurance certificate invariably attached to a foreign bill of exchange? The voyage in the first instance is, on the average, much longer, subject to much greater risk, and in case of wreck, the loss is of infinitely greater consequence.
>
> The growth of life insurance implies an increasing development of the sense of responsibility. The idea of providing only for the present must give way to recognition that a person's responsibility to his family is not limited to the years of survival. Emphasis should be laid on the "crime of not insuring," and the finger of scorn should be pointed at any man who, although he has provided well while he was alive, has not seen fit to discount the uncertain future for the benefit of a dependent household. . . . Life insurance is a sure means of changing uncertainty into certainty and is the opposite of gambling. He who does not insure gambles with the greatest of all chances and, if he loses, makes those dearest to him pay the forfeit.

The Many Uses of Life Insurance, The Swiss Army Knife of Financial Products
You can use life insurance to: • Provide a death benefit • Provide income to survivors • Secure a line of credit • Fund a buy-sell agreement • Guarantee future insurability • Equalize an inheritance • Pay estate taxes • Create an estate • Give to charity • Supplement college, retirement, and other expenses • Pay funeral and last expenses • Pay mortgages and debts • Provide an employee benefit • Protect a business from financial loss

Diminishing Nature of the Human Life Value

The economic value of an income earner tends to diminish with the passage of time. His or her earning level may continue to increase for a certain period or indefinitely, but with each passing year, the remaining period of income production becomes shorter. Each year of income that is realized means that there is one year less that remains to be earned. Because an individual's economic value is the unrealized earning capacity represented by his or her ability and skills, his or her economic value must diminish as potential income is converted into actual income. This principle is illustrated by the diagram below.

The line *AB* represents the lifetime of an individual born at point *A* and dying at point *B*. The line *AB* also represents the cost of maintenance and, during his or her productive years, the individual's income tax liability. The arc *CD* represents earning capacity. During the period *A to C*, there are no earnings, but there are costs of maintenance represented by the triangle *AEC*. Earnings commence at *C*. The area of arc *CD* that extends above arc *AB* represents earnings in excess of taxes and the cost of self-maintenance. Point *D* marks the age of retirement, and the area *DFB* symbolizes the second major period in the individual's life, during which the cost of self-maintenance exceeds his or her income.

Figure 1-4
Hypothetical Illustration of Economic Value of a Human Life

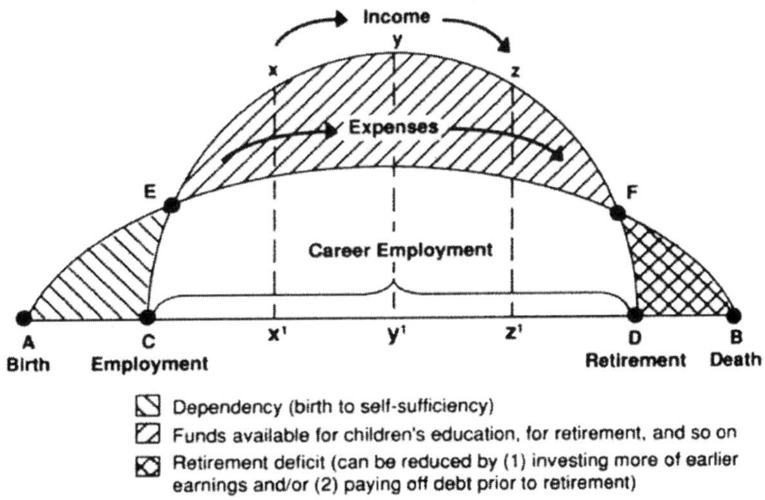

The monetary value of the individual is at its peak at point *E* when net earnings are just beginning. At the point where xx^1 intersects the arcs, the earnings rate has increased, but potential future earnings have declined. The earnings potential shows further decreases at yy^1 and zz^1 ; at point *F*, it has shrunk to zero.

The previous figure is illustrative and conceptual. Neither earnings nor maintenance expenses follow a symmetrical curve. For example, the childhood period starts with a highly unsymmetrical outlay for maternity costs. Income is also likely to commence earlier than at point C, and is unlikely likely to decline so gradually to the age of retirement. In most occupations people reach their maximum earnings in their 40s and 50s, and earnings increase or decline only slightly to retirement, when they terminate abruptly. The following figure shows a typical pattern of earnings among clerical and professional groups.

Figure 1-5
Typical Pattern of Earnings

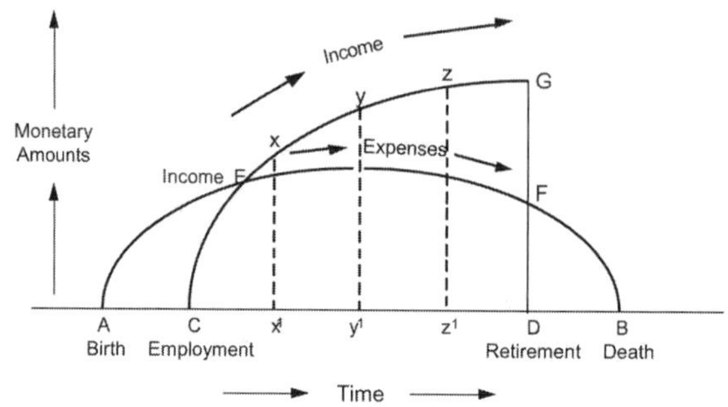

Life Cycle of Life Insurance Needs

These diagrams roughly illustrate the economic foundation of three broad categories of life insurance. The first is childhood, represented by the area *AEC*. During this period, an individual's needs are met by the parents or other persons responsible for their care. If the child dies before becoming a producer, the investment in nurturing, maintenance, and education is lost. This can be a sizable sum, especially if the child has been educated at private schools. Various studies have shown that the cost of rearing a child to age 18 ranges from 1.5 times to 3.25 times the parents' average annual income. At today's prices, those cost are even higher. While most parents regard these expenditures as one of the duties and privileges of parenthood, and resist labeling them as an investment to be recovered in the event of the child's death, such costs do create a substantial insurable value. This value can logically serve as one of the bases for juvenile insurance, or insurance on children.

The second category of insurance is portrayed by the area EGF in Figure 1-5. The surplus earnings in this area are the source of support for the individual's dependents and a broad measure of the economic loss to the family if the producer(s) should die. A portion of these earnings will go toward insurance premiums, and for both spouses' retirement needs, but the share that is needed for the care and maintenance of the family should be capitalized and preserved for the family through life insurance.

Finally, the individual's retirement needs are represented by the area *DFB*. Although the income vacuum may be partially filled by federal Old Age, Survivors, and Disability Income (OASDI or Social Security) benefits, pension plans and other tax-qualified plans (such as profit sharing, income deferral, and thrift or savings), and individual investments, the most realistic sources of funds to cover any income shortage are through investment income, life insurance and annuities. This remaining need can be satisfied with group life insurance through employment and/or a personal insurance program. For long-term planning purposes, however, individuals should not rely on group life insurance for any more than the funds that can—and will—be kept in force after an unforeseen job loss. Individuals should check their employer's plan to find out how much of the group life insurance they can convert to individual insurance after termination of employment.

Life Insurance Needs

Why have life insurance? Ben Baldwin gets to the heart of this question in his book, *The Complete Book of Insurance* (Irwin Professional Publishing, 1996). Mr. Baldwin says to answer this question, a person needs to ask two more questions. The first is, "In the event of my death, will anyone experience an economic loss?" If the answer is yes, then the second question is, "Do I care?" If the person does not have anyone who will experience a financial loss at his or her death, or if he or she does not care that those people will experience an economic loss, then that person is not a prospect for life insurance.

This comment beckons a few axioms from the archives of life insurance selling. The first is that "life insurance is sold, it is not bought". Because so many people find reasons not to take the initiative to purchase life insurance, or in many cases do not understand the need for life insurance, the insurance advisor takes the initiative to discuss this important risk management tool.

As suggested by Mr. Baldwin's approach, an old axiom in the life insurance business says that life insurance is only sold when somebody loves somebody. As the Life and Health Insurance Foundation for Education (LIFE) advises, "Life insurance isn't for the people who die. It's for the people who live." This is a major shift of perspective for many prospects. (It's about them, not you.) The following discussion addresses the needs that may result from the death of a breadwinner and should be your foundation for educating a prospect regarding the needs for life insurance.

human life value approach

needs analysis approach

The *human life value approach* produces a value for a person's economic worth at a given point in their life. This method does not anticipate actual dependent needs that may arise with the death of a person. An estimate of these needs is obtained through a needs analysis approach, which addresses the question: How much life insurance is enough? The *needs analysis approach* is a way to determine how much life insurance a person should carry by analyzing the needs his or her family and other dependents would experience if that individual died.

It would be difficult, if not impossible, to prepare a list of all needs that might possibly arise after the death of an income producer. Family circumstances differ, and a list of needs that would be appropriate for one family might be quite unsuitable for another. Even within any particular family, the needs picture changes from time to time.

Life insurance is the best way to address the financial impacts of death, regardless of when or why it occurs. Life insurance benefits individuals, families, businesses, and their communities, because it delivers tax-free money without administrative hassles and settlement costs. It does so from the inception of coverage until its eventual fulfillment. The following section outlines the general categories of needs that are likely to be found in a typical family situation.

Cleanup Fund (Final Expenses)

cleanup fund

A *cleanup fund,* or funds for final expenses, is a fund set aside for those expenses associated with the death of an individual. Burial or cremation expenses are by no means the only expenses associated with death. The final expenses depend very heavily on the individual circumstances of each death. Some people undergo a lengthy period of hospital treatment and incur large medical bills. Home or convalescent care is rarely covered by private insurance and Medicare offers limited coverage for those over 65. Prolonged medical care and rehabilitative treatment may leave a family's finances devastated even before death occurs. Following death there are usually substantial bills, including funeral expenses, transportation expenses, and cemetery or mausoleum charges.

Many of the expenses associated with a death occur after the funeral. The costs of settling financial and property matters in closing the deceased's estate are examples. Also included are court fees related to the appointment of an executor or administrator to manage and settle the estate, fees charged by the executor or administrator, attorneys' fees, and court costs for probate.

Managing the estate prior to final property disposition may be extremely complex. This may require the services of specialized investment and/or real estate managers to safeguard the property until it is sold or distributed. The provisions of the will and the nature of the property involved may require a long period of management before the estate is closed. Some assets may be hard to sell due to prevailing economic conditions following death. The terms of the will may require the establishment of trusts and other legal work that may be expensive as well as time consuming. Even the task of locating heirs or other beneficiaries of the estate may require a lengthy search to obtain death certificates for potential recipients who predeceased the insured or are estranged from the family. The longer this process takes, the more costly it becomes.

The administrator or executor has responsibility for settling the outstanding debts and closing the financial affairs of the deceased. These duties include filing tax returns and paying tax liabilities. This process is much more easily addressed when there is adequate cash available, life insurance policy proceeds often being the only source of funds. It is usually not advisable to have life insurance proceeds payable directly to the estate. Rather, they should be paid to a trust or to an individual with an interest in the estate. Cash can then be made available by purchases of assets from the estate or loans to the estate.

The size of the estate and the nature of the assets it contains heavily influence the optimal planning strategies for minimizing taxes and accomplishing individual objectives. Paying policy proceeds directly to the estate is less of a problem for small estates with no federal estate or gift tax liability than it is for large estates. The most important point is that any planning must be done prior to death to achieve the best results. For sizable estates in which there are transfers of life insurance policyownership, it is better if the planning is done at least 3 years prior to the death. Tax treatment will be governed by policyownership, beneficiary designations, and trusts in effect at the time of death. The estate may be subject to greater expenses in the absence of proper planning. Even if an administrator or executor knows how to minimize taxes, his or her hands will be tied unless assets have been properly positioned and the necessary documentation, trusts, and other instruments are in place before the insured's death.

The death of an insured family member usually terminates an income stream that the family has relied upon. The costs of daily living for survivors, final expenses for the deceased, emergencies, repairs, and replacements, death taxes, and the cost of estate administration create an immediate need for funds. Mortgages might well be included in the list, but in view of their size and the special problems associated with them, they are usually treated as a separate need.

One of the goals of good planning is to make sure the emergency fund is adequate to meet the survivors' needs until life insurance proceeds and other potential sources of funds become available. Families having an adequate source of emergency funds in liquid holdings, such as money market funds, mutual funds, bank balances, cash management accounts, and life insurance cash values may easily meet any need for immediate cash following the death. However, the need for additional funds becomes urgent if the family does not have an emergency fund or has depleted it prior to the death.

Estate Clearance Fund

estate clearance fund

An *estate clearance fund* represents money needed to pay any administrative and estate settlement costs, such as attorney and executor fees, appraisers and accountant fees, probate expenses, and state and federal inheritance and estate taxes. Individuals who acquire a sizable net worth during their lifetime may be subjected to taxes on that net worth at their death. The tax is progressive in nature with a lower rate applicable to smaller estates, increasing to 35 percent for large estates. With the estate tax credit set at five million dollars in 2011 and 2012, estates of wealthy individuals will be subject to the federal estate tax. These estate tax rates and exemption amounts can be expected to change as the political climate changes.

Federal estate taxes must normally be paid within 9 months of the owner's death. This presents a real problem for individuals or families whose most important and largest assets are illiquid forms of investment, such as family-owned businesses and investment real estate. Often, these assets cannot be quickly converted to cash without a significant decrease in value. In some cases, the family would prefer to retain the asset and its future income-generating potential. Life insurance proceeds can provide the necessary cash to pay the tax liability and to preserve the assets being taxed for the benefit of family survivors.

Federal gift taxes can also be a sizable tax liability at death. The rates are the same as those for federal estate taxes. They apply to all nonexempt gifts on a cumulative basis. In other words, the aggregate amount of gifts made since 1976 is taken into consideration in determining the applicable gift-tax rate for the gifts currently being taxed. For donors in the highest tax brackets the gift tax can equal 35 percent of the value of the gift itself.

The gift tax triggered by the donor's death often involves gifts that were completed because of that person's death. Examples include jointly owned property after one of the joint owners dies, and life insurance proceeds under some policyownership and beneficiary designation situations. Settlement of the estate may also result in gift taxes due on gifts made shortly before death.

Most states impose death and/or inheritance taxes in addition to the federal estate taxes. These taxes, like the federal taxes, are due within a relatively short period after death and must be paid with liquid funds. Careful planning is required to provide for these state and federal taxes, especially if life insurance is to be the funding mechanism. If they are not properly structured, the policies themselves may be subject to the tax, further increasing the tax liability of the estate. Good estate planning can avoid unnecessary taxes, and provide the optimal tax-saving strategy for the heirs of the decedent.

Income Needs

income needs

Surviving family members will be faced with the financial demands of maintaining the household and meeting the needs of household members. There will be continuing costs for food, transportation, and utilities. Mortgage payments may have to be continued, and even if they are insured, will have to be paid temporarily. It often takes time for the survivors to determine if there is current life insurance on the mortgage and to file a claim if coverage exists. In the absence of coverage, the surviving family members will have to continue making mortgage or rent payments. *Income needs* are the ongoing needs for income of the surviving dependent family members that continue until those members are self-supporting. They include readjustment period income, dependency period income, and income for the surviving spouse and other dependents.

Readjustment Income

readjustment income

The surviving family members often, at least temporarily, continue their established lifestyle and experience the same level of expenses they incurred prior to the supporting wage earner's death. This means a continuation of bills for cable TV services, magazine subscriptions, newspapers, club memberships, entertainment, and miscellaneous costs. *Readjustment income* is an amount closely equivalent to the family's share of the income producer's earnings at the time of his or her death.

If the surviving family members are aware of their financial situation and they have planned for the death contingency, they will know whether they can afford to maintain the same standard of living or if cost cutting will be necessary. Even if the household budget does have to be trimmed, it is unrealistic to expect the survivors to cut back on their expenses immediately after the death. Changes in a family's living standard are usually accomplished through a certain amount of trial-and-error adjustment over a period that often exceeds one year.

Few individuals are able to leave an estate, including life insurance, substantial enough to fully replace the standard of living that their dependents enjoyed while the income earner was still alive. This means that an adjustment will have to be made to the family's standard of living following the wage earner's death. To cushion the economic and emotional shock, however, it is desirable to postpone that adjustment for a period following the income earner's death. The length of the period depends largely on the magnitude of the change that the family will have to make in living standard. If the surviving spouse must refresh or acquire skills to gain employment, a longer period may be needed. Whatever the duration, the income during this readjustment period should be approximately equivalent to the family's share of the deceased's earnings at the time of his or her death.

Life Insurance Shoppers' Motivations for Buying Insurance	
Final Expenses	48%
Income Replacement	53
Mortgage protection — pay off mortgage	21
Transfer wealth	21
Pay estate taxes or estate bills	8
Replace another life insurance policy	14
Supplement employer-provided life insurance	9
Children's education — college funding	11
Tax savings	8
Business purposes	2
Charitable gift	2

The above table presents the results of a LIMRA survey (2011 Buyer's Study, LIMRA International, Inc.), taken to establish prospects' motivations for purchasing life insurance.

The emotional turmoil following the death of a close family member usually lasts about one year. As survivors cope with the death, the grieving process often distracts them from concentrating on financial issues. They may forget to pay important bills, which could worsen their financial position. Creditors who insist on being paid immediately can be an additional source of emotional stress at this time. Survivors who are able to convince these creditors that adequate life insurance will be available are usually not pressed for collection until proceeds have been received.

Dependency Period Income

dependency period income

After the expiration of the readjustment period, *dependency period income* should be provided in a reduced amount until the children, if any, are able to support themselves. Two concepts are involved: how much income should be provided and for how long. As a minimum, there should be sufficient income to allow the family to remain intact, and to allow the surviving spouse to devote adequate time to the care and guidance of the children during their formative years.

The financial needs of family survivors do not end at the closing of the deceased's estate. Minor children and other dependents may need support for a lifetime or at least for many years until they become self-supporting. Life insurance and other accumulated assets can provide that necessary financial support. With proper planning, a surviving spouse can be supported during this dependency period as well, rather than being forced to prematurely enter the labor market. If the surviving spouse lacks training, or is disabled, reentering the workforce may not be an option.

When planning the income needs for surviving family members, it is important to include all persons who depend on the income of the person to be insured. Such planning is important for each member providing income to the family unit. This often includes both husband and wife, and it could include children living at home who contribute income to support the family.

In today's world of multiple marriages and divorces, it is common to have more than one group of minor children to be supported. The husband and wife may have children from previous marriages, in addition to the children of the current marriage. This situation could involve the finances of three or more separate households, if all of the dependent children do not live in the same household with the newly married husband and wife. The sources of support available to children from previous marriages obviously affect the children's financial needs. The income needs of the youngest children—usually the children of the current marriage and those with the longest remaining period of dependency—should be given top priority.

The most important determinants of the duration of the income needed are the present ages of the insured's children and the type of education they will receive. Generally, income should continue until the youngest child is 18. If there are several children, the income can be reduced somewhat as each reaches the age of self-sufficiency. If the children are to receive a college education, income will have to continue for a longer period. For planning purposes, the immediate death of the income producer is assumed. The needed income is projected for a period equal to the difference between the present age of the youngest child and the age at which the child is expected to become self-supporting.

Children with physical disabilities or mental impairments that will prevent them from ever becoming self-supporting may need lifelong financial support. Their dependency can continue many years beyond the deaths of both parents. Planning for the financial support of children with special needs can be very complex. Severely handicapped children may require institutional care, which can be extremely expensive in private facilities. Care for handicapped children may be available through public institutions only if the family withdraws financial support, allowing the child to qualify for welfare programs. In some states this is very difficult, because minor and disabled children are deemed to be "forced heirs." Any inheritance, asset or trust established for the support of these children must be very carefully structured. The rendering of public institutional support often gives the government the right to be reimbursed from assets inherited by, or set aside for the benefit of the child receiving the institutional care. In some cases, the government has even been able to invade trusts.

Life Income for Surviving Dependent Spouse

After the children have become self-sufficient, the widow(er) may still require an income for support. If the surviving spouse is a full-time homemaker until the children finish at least part of their education, he or she may subsequently be able to obtain employment. However, the surviving spouse's earning power will likely have declined substantially as the result of having been out of the workforce for a period of time. After the birth of children, for example, a wife sometimes gives up her job. As the years pass, she may lose many of the occupational skills she once possessed and would have to return to the labor market as a middle-aged woman with deficient skills. Under such circumstances, employment opportunities are limited. Many individuals feel a moral obligation, therefore, to provide their spouses with incomes that will continue throughout the remaining years of their lives. The income may be modest, but it can be the difference between complete dependency on welfare services and reasonable self-sufficiency.

EXAMPLE
The death of a nonincome-earning spouse can greatly increase the costs of the surviving household. A single parent has to pay for essential services, such as childcare, transportation, and domestic chores that were previously performed by the deceased spouse and cannot be done by the survivor.

Parents and Other Dependents

Other family members who may have a period of dependency are the husband and/or wife's parents. The financial demands of providing parental support can be minimal—providing room and board in the home for example. At the other end of the spectrum, support of a parent in an institution can be very expensive. Care for an elderly parent in an upscale institution often costs more than two times the median family income.

EXAMPLE
Elderly parents can instantly loose their independence and self-sufficiency by means of an accident or sudden change in health. They may be hospitalized after a fall or a stroke and never be able to live by themselves again. Adult children are often overwhelmed by the demands of seeking or providing care for a parent.

The voluntary assumption of financial support for another individual often implies a willingness to provide that support as long as it is needed. That need may extend beyond the death of the supporter. Careful planning and adequate amounts of life insurance can assure extended parental support even if the supporting child predeceases that parent. Otherwise, the supporting child's death may force the parent to drastically change living arrangements and lower his or her standard of living.

Financial dependence is not restricted to children, spouses, and parents. In some cases, distant relatives and current or ex-in-laws may have to be supported for one reason or another. Some families take in foster children and develop emotional bonds that are as strong as those between natural parents and their children. Many of these foster parents extend financial support beyond that required by the foster parent program.

Cash Needs

cash needs

Cash needs require some amount of money be set aside to pay an obligation in a lump sum, or as another ongoing income need, depending on family circumstances and preferences.

Funds to Repay Debt

Many personal debt agreements have a clause specifying that the full remaining balance will become due and payable upon the death of the debtor. This clause may be present whether or not there is any credit life insurance covering the loan agreement. Although lending institutions regularly offer credit life insurance at the time the loan is initially created, such coverage is not mandatory and is often refused by the borrower. When credit life insurance is in force, the remaining loan balance will be repaid to the lender by the credit life insurance company when a death claim is filed. However, there is always the possibility that credit life insurance benefits will not be collected if the survivors, executor, or administrator are not aware of the insurance. Credit insurance information, therefore, should always be noted in files pertaining to the insured's debt.

Credit life insurance is not the only way of repaying debts that become due and payable at death. All types of life insurance policies provide death benefits that are suitable for repayment of debts. A single large policy can provide enough funds to liquidate many or all debts. Moreover, the standard types of individual life insurance policies may be lower in costs than credit life policies.

There are some debts that do not become due and payable upon the death of the borrower. This is more likely to be the case when both husband and wife are liable for the debt. Adequate amounts of individual life insurance will give the survivor the option of either paying off the debt or continuing to repay it according to schedule. That option is not available under credit life insurance, because benefits automatically cancel the debt once a claim has been filed and approved for payment.

Mortgage Redemption Needs

Homeownership is usually burdened with a mortgage and it is highly probable that a balance will still be outstanding upon the death of a person with dependent children. In some cases, of course, the widow(er) may want to sell the house and move into a smaller one or into an apartment. Assuming the house can be sold for an amount that exceeds the remaining mortgage balance, it may not be essential to provide funds for the liquidation of the mortgage. In many cases, however, it is preferred that the survivors will continue to occupy the family residence, and funds to pay off the mortgage may be needed. If the family can remain in the home, free of a monthly mortgage payment, the family's income need will be greatly reduced.

Educational Needs

The income provided for a surviving spouse during the period when the children are dependent should normally be adequate for secondary school expenses, as well as for general maintenance. However, if a college education for one or more of the children is a goal, additional income will be needed. A college or professional education is beyond the means of many dependent children who lose an income-earning parent.

Minor children need uninterrupted support for their education—from their first day in the classroom to young adulthood. The funding requirements for educating children vary widely from one family to another. A public school education that ends at high school has relatively modest costs compared to the costs of a private school education including preschool, prep school, private university, and professional school. The factors influencing parents' educational goals and decisions for their children involve a complex mixture of family history, family philosophy toward education, family income, and the abilities and personality of the child. Planning for an ivy-league education, for example, will be for naught if the child does not have adequate financial resources to enable him or her to attend a school of that caliber.

For very young children, the planning horizon for education may exceed 20 years. Adjustments for inflation must be made for educational costs to be incurred more than a decade into the future. Choosing the appropriate inflation factor involves estimation, but it is safe to assume that the rate will be as great or greater than general inflation. Some authorities on the subject recommend a planning assumption of 7 percent to 8 percent annual inflation in education costs.

Educational needs of the family are not restricted to the children. A surviving spouse may need further education to increase future income potential to help support the family. The spouse may need a refresher course or training to return to a prior occupation. On the other hand, the spouse's need may be extensive, such as to prepare to enter the job market for the first time or to upgrade to a higher-paying career.

One important consideration in providing education or training to the surviving spouse is whether the survivor will be able to earn any income while pursuing his or her education or training. Funding spousal education on a full-time basis usually requires prefunding family support while the spouse is a full-time student and prefunding the educational or training costs as well.

In some cases, the surviving spouse may be able to pursue the education on a part-time basis while he or she is employed in the workforce. This is an emotional and challenging avenue for a surviving spouse who is now also a single parent. Pursuing education on a part-time basis may greatly lengthen the period needed to complete the educational program. This will delay any significant increases in earned income for the surviving spouse and family members. If the potential increase in income because of further education is large enough, it may actually be less costly to prefund a full-time educational program.

Emergency Needs

From time to time in the life of a family, unforeseen needs for money arise because of illness, surgery, major dental work, home repairs, or many other reasons. It is unrealistic for the family income providers to leave only enough income for the family to subsist if everything goes well and not to plan for unusual expenditures. Therefore, a liquid fund should be set up from which additional income can be provided if and when it is needed. Some financial planners suggest that the emergency fund often warrants a higher priority than income for dependents. The actual setting of priorities is properly the responsibility of the income earner(s). A 3 to 6 month fund of average spending amounts is normally suggested, but this will vary by family.

Funding Trusts at Death

Trusts are contractual arrangements for the ownership and management of assets by a trustee according to the trust agreement. The trustee manages trust assets on behalf of and for the benefit of the trust beneficiaries. There are many different motivations for the establishment of a trust. One is to get professional management from a corporate entity, such as a trust company or a bank trust department, so that the trustee will not predecease any of the trust beneficiaries. Tax considerations may also justify the creation of a trust.

Life insurance is often an integral part of the trust funding. The trust itself often owns life insurance on the grantor, who names the trust as beneficiary of that insurance. Trusts can also be beneficiaries of insurance policies not owned by the trust. Those insurance proceeds provide the funds necessary for the trust to carry out its objectives. Some trusts are set up specifically for the purpose of funding life insurance premiums and receiving proceeds. If estate tax minimization is the objective of the trust, the trust is subject to more stringent requirements that can change many times during the existence of the trust.

Trusts have always been an important means of extending family financial management by the parents beyond their lifetime. In these arrangements, the trust is often used to distribute funds periodically rather than in a lump sum. The objective is usually to protect a child from spending funds frivolously. By spreading out the distribution, the child is unable to get access to and squander the entire sum immediately after the parents' death. Final distribution from such trusts is often based on the beneficiary's attainment of a specified age and is usually the parents' decision as to when the child will be mature enough to handle the funds responsibly.

Trusts can be set up for the benefit of children with mental impairments or other problems that would prevent them from ever becoming capable of managing their own finances. The nature of the trust depends very heavily on the type of care being provided to such children, especially on whether the care is private or public.

Trusts
• Contractual agreement created by trustor • Managed by trustee • For benefit of trust beneficiaries, such as child or spouse • Can own and manage assets • Can be funded with life insurance • Can own life insurance policies

Trusts can also be an important tool for keeping assets from a spouse to prevent the assets from being directed to a stepchild or to an unforeseen family member if the surviving spouse were to remarry after the insured's death.

Life insurance and trusts are often combined in creative ways to fund charitable gifts. Sometimes the entire arrangement is for the exclusive benefit of the charity. In other arrangements, the trust is set up for a combination of family objectives and gifts to charitable institutions. Such arrangements usually involve a stream of income payments and subsequent distribution of the trust corpus. The charity or the family member can be the recipient of the income payments, the corpus, or both.

Charitable Donations

Life insurance policies are often used to increase the value of gifts to charities. This can be accomplished either by giving the policy itself to the charitable organization or by naming the charity as the beneficiary on the existing life insurance policies. Where federal estate tax considerations are important, a new life insurance policy may be purchased by the charity itself at the request of the donor, who would give the necessary permission and information to complete the policy application and would provide the funds for premium payments.

Life insurance can also be used for charitable giving even if the charity is not a beneficiary of the insurance policy. The donor can use adequate amounts of life insurance to fund the needs of surviving family members and thereby free up personal property and other assets for lifetime gifts to the charities.

Gift tax and estate tax considerations are often strong motives for making charitable gifts. Because tax laws can—and probably will—change, tax planning should be carefully coordinated by a knowledgeable tax adviser.

Funding for Gifts to Individuals

The use of life insurance is not limited to benefiting family members and related trusts and charities. Life insurance can be used to benefit anyone the donor specifies. The motivation could be friendship, long-term loyalty, respect for another's accomplishments, support of a common endeavor, or any other commitment about which the individual feels strongly. The intended recipient can be made beneficiary of a life insurance policy or a beneficiary of a trust funded by life insurance proceeds.

One of the important factors favoring life insurance policies is that the proceeds do not generally go through probate and are not a matter of public record. The proceeds are payable quickly and directly to the beneficiary. Complications of settling or managing the estate have no bearing on nor do they delay the payment of proceeds under a life insurance policy unless the proceeds are payable directly to the insured's estate. In estates large enough to have a federal estate tax liability, therefore, it is generally not a good idea to have life insurance proceeds payable to the insured's estate.

Funding Home Health Care or Nursing Home Care

The cash values of life insurance policies can be used for home health care or nursing home care if that is deemed desirable or necessary. Access to the cash value is available through policy loans, partial withdrawals of the cash value, or outright surrender of the policy.

Long-term-care riders are available with some life insurance policies to provide for home health care or nursing home care needs. In some cases, the rider is available without any additional charge; in other cases, there is a nominal charge. In essence, these riders make a portion of the death benefit, usually 1 percent or 2 percent of the face value of the policy, available each month that the insured qualifies for the benefit. The subsequent death benefit payable is reduced dollar-for-dollar for each accelerated benefit payment made under these riders. Their pre-death benefit payments are usually subject to an aggregate limitation of 50 percent of the face value of the policy, although a few insurance companies have increased the aggregate limitation to 70 percent or 80 percent of the policy face value.

Retirement Needs

Retirement is a planning need that the financial advisor must anticipate. This contingency determines the type of insurance the prospect should purchase. If the family needs are met with cash value life insurance (assuming adequate funds for premiums), the cash values under this insurance can supplement other retirement income sources to take care of the postretirement needs of the insured and his or her spouse.

Life insurance policies can be an important source of supplemental retirement income funds for the insured and for the surviving spouse. These funds can supplement any other source of retirement income available from corporate pensions, IRAs, qualified plans, investments, and Social Security. This can be accomplished by utilizing the cash value of the life insurance prior to the insured's death. Some policies, such as UL policies, allow partial withdrawals of cash value amounts without terminating the policy. Under any life insurance policy having a cash value, the policyowner can always gain access to the funds by either taking out a policy loan or surrendering the policy for the entire cash surrender value. Surrendering the policy, of course, terminates any death benefit protection.

I AM A LIFE INSURANCE POLICY

I am a piece of paper, a drop of ink, and a few pennies of premium.

I am a promise to pay.

I help people see visions, dream dreams, and achieve economic immortality.

I am education for the children.

I am savings.

I am property that increases in value from year to year.

I lend money when you need it most, with no questions asked.

I pay off mortgages so that the family can remain together in their own homes.

I allow people to dare to live and to die responsibly.

I create money where none existed before.

I am the great emancipator from want.

I guarantee the continuity of a business.

I conserve the employer's investment.

I am tangible evidence that a man is a good husband and father, and that a woman is a good wife and mother.

I am a declaration of financial independence and economic freedom.

I am the difference between an old man or woman and an elderly gentlemen or lady.

I provide cash if illness, injury, old age, or death cuts off the breadwinner's income.

I am the only thing that can be bought on the installment plan that a family doesn't have to finish paying for.

I am protected by laws that prevent creditors from assessing the money I give to loved ones.

I bring dignity, peace of mind, and security to the family.

I supply investment capital that makes the wheels turn and the motors hum.

I guarantee the financial ability to have happy holidays and the laughter of children—even though father or mother is not there.

I am the guardian angel of the home.

I am life insurance.

The Selling/Planning Process for Life Insurance

There are two sides to every purchase—something is bought and something is sold. In the professional selling/planning process, it is essential that the advisor understand the buyer's side of the situation. Because of the intangible nature of life insurance and a general aversion to the concept of personal mortality in our society, the advisor typically takes the initiative in the sales process. But sales do not happen without the buyer's cooperation and participation. In the client-focused sales process, the buyer's realization and acceptance of his or her needs and goals is of utmost importance. By understanding the buying cycle, the advisor can appreciate the process the buyer is going through, and how the buyer views the process. Empathy and client-focused behavior on the part of the advisor play a key role.

The Selling/Planning Process

A thorough understanding of the selling and buying process will help you achieve sales success and produce satisfied clients. Working with the prospect means guiding that person through each step of the selling/planning process. If any step is omitted or inadequately completed, the result will be that a sale is not made, or the sale will be on an unstable foundation that may end in disappointment. By following the selling/planning process systematically, better results will be obtained for both the client and the advisor, because a more complete process will be achieved. If the sale is not successful, it provides you with an opportunity to analyze what took place between you and the prospect, and identify the areas that need strengthening and improvement.

selling/planning process

The *selling/planning process* involves eight steps that move a prospect through a procedure that culminates in satisfying the needs and wants of the buyer. These needs and wants must be matched with the appropriate product or service. This matching, plus your own creativity, may convince the buyer to act and buy now to fill the needs.

The American College has adopted the phrase, the selling/planning process, to emphasize that financial services advisors need sales skills, that the client-advisor relationship typically involves a selling process, and that financial advising and counseling have sales elements. On the other hand, the financial planning movement has gained prominence in recent years and has influenced the client/advisor relationship. This has advanced client-focused selling and the total-needs approach to selling. The industry and the public recognize the comprehensive nature of our financial lives and the need to take an integrated approach to planning our financial security.

The Eight Steps of the Selling/Planning Process

1. ***Identify the prospect.*** Identify whom you are going to approach and why. Effective selling begins with getting in front of prospects who have a probable need for your products and who can afford them. They appreciate you and your services and may be a source for repeat business and referrals. You need a system to consistently find potential clients in target markets. The key to successful selling is prospecting and marketing.

2. ***Approach the prospect***. Contact the prospect by telephone, by mail, or face to face and ask for an appointment, stating the reason why you are interested in meeting. As telemarketing and direct mail become less effective, referral prospecting is becoming more critical than ever.

3. ***Meet the prospect***. In the initial interview, establish rapport and explain your business purpose. Make positive statements about yourself, your company, and the services you offer. Ask thought-provoking and challenging questions, and encourage agreement to proceed with the gathering of relevant information about the prospect. Impress upon the prospect what makes you different from other advisors and what you offer that is of added value. Establishing the prospect's interest in pursuing solutions to uncovered needs is essential for the selling/planning process to proceed.

4. ***Gather information and establish goals***. Using a fact-finder, ask questions that will help you gain information about the prospect's situation. These questions should seek to uncover information about goals, attitudes, and priorities, in addition to facts about the prospect's personal and financial life. Ask the prospect what his or her expectations are for your relationship. What results does he or she want? This will help you understand what you should plan to deliver and how to deliver it.

Information is required to define the prospect's current situation, determine what his or her desired future situation is, and when it is to be achieved. Establish what the prospect is willing and able to do to achieve these goals. This information must be accurate, complete, up to date, relevant, and well organized. Financial plans based on erroneous or incomplete information, will be deficient, inappropriate, inconsistent with the prospect's other goals, and perhaps even dangerous to his or her well being.

Goal setting is important to creating a successful financial plan. By guiding the prospect through the goal-setting exercise, the advisor not only helps to establish reasonable, achievable goals, but also sets the tone for the entire selling/planning process and the advisor-client relationship.

5. ***Analyze the information.*** Once the relevant information about the prospect has been gathered, organized, and checked for accuracy, consistency, and completeness, you need to analyze the prospect's present financial situation. The objective is to identify where the prospect is now in relationship to the goals that were established in the previous step. You must identify real problems and needs to which your products and services will provide real solutions.

Although the prospect's situation may reveal a number of strengths, more than likely your analysis of the prospect's present situation will reveal a number of weaknesses, or conditions that are preventing achievement of the prospect's goals. The prospect may have excellent fringe benefits at work, including good life, medical, and disability insurance benefits. He may have just recently updated his will and installed a living will that includes provisions that legally carry out his wishes in the case of death or catastrophic illness. On the other hand, the prospect may be using debt unwisely, amassing credit card and other debt, paying unnecessarily high federal income taxes, or be inadequately insured. A prospect's investment portfolio may be inconsistent with her investment objectives or risk tolerance.

It may be that the prospect cannot realistically attain the goals stated, and they need to be revised. For example, the prospect's income and resources may prevent reaching a specified retirement income goal or retirement starting age. In this case, the advisor should help the prospect revisit the goal and revise it, or discuss what needs to be done to achieve that goal. Postponing retirement, saving more money, seeking higher returns, or deciding to deplete principal during retirement are four possible ways to help the prospect achieve the retirement goal. Presented as alternatives, the advisor can help the prospect restate the original goal in terms that will make it more achievable.

6. ***Develop and present the plan.*** After the information has been analyzed and the objectives to be achieved confirmed, and if necessary revised, the next step is to devise a realistic plan for bringing the prospect from his or her present financial position to the attainment of those objectives. A good plan must reflect the prospect's needs, attitudes, and goals. The plan must be the prospect's plan, not the advisor's plan.

It is not likely that any individual advisor can maintain an up-to-date familiarity with all the strategies that may be available and appropriate for a given prospect's situation. Based on his or her education, experience, training and specialization, the advisor is likely to rely on a given number of proven strategies and products that typically work when encountering similar prospect circumstances. When additional expertise is needed, the advisor should always consult with another advisor who is a specialist in the field in question.

There is usually more than one way to achieve a prospect's financial goals. When this is the case, the advisor should present alternative strategies for the prospect to consider and should explain the advantages and disadvantages of each strategy. Your presentation should provide an answer to the problems and needs discovered in your analysis of the prospect's situation. You support the decision to buy now because your product is the best available solution. Of course, your prospect must agree with this conclusion. You want to anticipate client concerns and provide answers for them.

After the plan is presented and reviewed with the prospect, the "moment of truth" arrives. The advisor must ask the prospect to approve the plan, or some compromise alternative, and commit to purchasing any products that may be part of the plan's implementation. Planning involves selling, and good selling is based on good planning.

7. ***Implement the plan.*** You must motivate the prospect to act and help him or her acquire the financial products necessary to put the plan into action. You must answer concerns that may prevent him or her from implementing the plan. Then, you must support the decision to buy the products you recommend. Complete the application(s) and all required forms, explain the process to the prospect, and verify that everything that is being done is understood. Perform or order all field underwriting requirements as needed. If the plan is limited in scope or complexity, it may be within the advisor's ability to implement the plan entirely. Otherwise, it may be necessary to call upon additional specialized professional expertise where needed. For example, legal instruments, such as wills and trusts, may need to be drawn up and executed. It is typically part of the advisor's responsibility to motivate and assist the prospect in completing each of the steps necessary to implement the plan.

8. ***Service the plan.*** This may be the most important step in preserving your hard work and expanding on it. Deliver the policy and reaffirm the decision to buy, citing the problems that can be solved by having this product. Restate the benefits you are providing. Get referrals. Service will help you build your long-term career as a financial services professional. Through service, you enhance and cement your relationship with each new client, make additional sales, and set the stage to obtain quality referrals to new prospects.

The relationship between the advisor and client should be ongoing. Normally, the advisor meets with the client once a year, or more or less frequently as agreed upon, to review the performance of the vehicles selected to implement the plan. The advisor should also review the client's personal and financial situation, as well the tax and financial environment around him or her, to establish if anything has changed that would warrant making changes to the plan.

Figure 1-6
Steps of the Selling/Planning Process:

Chapter One Review

Key terms and concepts are explained in the glossary. Answers to the review questions and the self-test questions are found in the back of the book in the Answers to Questions section.

Key Terms and Concepts

financial planning process
risk management
indemnity
risk pooling
law of large numbers
mortality
interest
expense
2001 CSO Mortality Table
yearly renewable term (YRT)
reserve
legal reserve
amount at risk
cost of insurance
net level premium
human life value approach
needs analysis approach
cleanup fund
estate clearance fund
income needs
readjustment income
dependency period income
cash needs
selling/planning process

Review Questions

1. Define the basic principles of life insurance. [1]
2. Explain the concept of risk pooling and how it relates to life insurance. [2]
3. Explain how mortality, interest, and expense serve as the building blocks of life insurance. [3]
4. Explain how the premium for Yearly Renewable Term (YRT) is determined. [4]
5. Explain how the level premium insurance concept works. [5]
6. Explain the concept of human life value and how is relates to life insurance. [6]
7. Identify and explain the expenses commonly associated with a death and settling the deceased's estate. [7]
8. List and explain the income needs of surviving family members. [8]
9. Explain the post-death cash needs of survivors. [9]
10. Explain the steps in the selling/planning process. [10]

Self-Test Questions

1. The newest mortality tables introduced by the NAIC are called the
   - (A) 1980 CSO Tables
   - (B) 2001 CSO Tables
   - (C) 2003 CSO Tables
   - (D) 2007 CSO Tables

2. In a level premium ordinary life policy, the net amount at risk
   - (A) increases each year
   - (B) decreases each year
   - (C) remains the same over time
   - (D) could increase or decrease based on investment returns

3. Which of the following is a characteristic of an ordinary life (WL) policy?
   - (A) It is the most expensive form of cash value insurance.
   - (B) It matures at age 65.
   - (C) It has an increasing cash value and decreasing risk amount.
   - (D) Both the cash value and amount at risk increase annually.

4. The reserve is
   - (A) a plan of insurance under which premiums do not increase from year to year
   - (B) the same as the policy cash value or surrender value
   - (C) an amount that must be accumulated by the insurer to meet definite future obligations
   - (D) an asset of the company allocated to individual policies

5. The step in the selling/planning process where you establish rapport, explain your purpose, ask some questions, and get agreement to proceed is called
   - (A) meeting the prospect
   - (B) analyzing the situation
   - (C) presenting the solution
   - (D) selecting the prospect

6. At the end of the term period of a term life insurance policy, if death has not occurred, the company will
   - (A) pay a living benefit
   - (B) pay a refund on premiums
   - (C) pay a portion of the death benefit
   - (D) pay no benefit as premiums are considered fully earned

7. Which of the following statements is (are) correct about level premium insurance plans?

   I. The $1,000 policy does not provide $1,000 of pure insurance.
   II. The company is never at risk for the face amount of the policy.

   (A) I only
   (B) II only
   (C) Both I and II
   (D) Neither I nor II

8. Which of the following statements concerning the readjustment period for survivors after a wage earner's death is (are) correct?

   I. The length of the period should be less than one year, ideally 3–6 months.
   II. The income during this period should be approximately equivalent to the insured's earnings at the time of death.

   (A) I only
   (B) II only
   (C) Both I and II
   (D) Neither I nor II

READ THE FOLLOWING DIRECTIONS BEFORE CONTINUING

The questions below differ from the preceding questions in that they all contain the word EXCEPT. So you understand fully the basis used in selecting each answer, be sure to read each question carefully.

---

9. In calculating insurance needs, cash needs would include all of the following EXCEPT

   (A) income for a surviving spouse
   (B) education fund for children
   (C) emergency fund
   (D) cleanup fund or final expenses

10. All of the following statements concerning risk pooling are correct EXCEPT

 (A) It involves combing risks by persons exposed to loss from a particular source.

 (B) It involved sharing losses on some equitable basis.

 (C) It is one important element that must be present in any sound insurance plan.

 (D) It is used only when the insurance is issued by a mutual company.

LIFE INSURANCE NEEDS IN PERSONAL AND BUSINESS PLANNING

2

Learning Objectives

An understanding of the material in this chapter should enable you to

1. List and explain the methods used to determine the need for life insurance.
2. Apply the five-step process for estimating a person's economic human life value.
3. Explain how life insurance can enhance a business's credit.
4. Discuss briefly how life insurance is used in employee benefit planning, including group term life insurance and executive bonus plans (Sec. 162).
5. Explain the basic concepts of split-dollar life insurance plans and the two tax methods applied to these plans.
6. Explain deferred compensation and how life insurance is used in executive compensation planning.
7. Discuss how life insurance is used for key employee protection for a business.
8. Explain the basic concepts of buy-sell agreements and how life insurance is used in this type of planning.

This chapter defines the methods of analyzing personal and family needs for life insurance, and then reviews the needs and uses for life insurance for a business. The discussion of business life insurance needs addresses employee benefit plans, executive compensation plans and business insurance plans that can take advantage of tax provisions established in the Internal Revenue Code.

Life insurance is the top financial resource families would use to help them cope after the death of a wage earner, but they are somewhat naïve in their preparation for such an event. According to LIMRA's U.S. Life Insurance Ownership Study (last updated in 2010),

- Almost 6 in 10 households have less than $50,000 in financial investments (including retirement savings), and 1 in 3 households have less than $10,000.
- Half of U.S. households readily admit that they currently don't have adequate life insurance coverage.
- Three in 10 households have no life insurance coverage on anyone in the household.
- One in 4 households are covered only by group life insurance. These households are highly vulnerable to losing the only life insurance they have in an economy where employees continue to lose their jobs.
- The percentage of households owning individual life insurance is at the lowest level in 50 years. Only 44 percent currently have individual life insurance, down from 50 percent just six years ago
- A very short time after the death of a wage earner, two thirds of U.S. households would struggle just to cover everyday living expenses.

The need for what you do based on these statistics is considerable.

Approaches to Determining the Life Insurance Needs

Life insurance ownership in the United States is widespread, but inadequate. Seven in ten households own some type of life insurance, yet they admit they need more. Fifty-eight million U.S. households believe they do not have enough life insurance (Source: 2010 U.S. Life Insurance Study, LIMRA).

Determining the appropriate amount of life insurance to meet a client's need is one of the key services a financial advisor provides. We will now review four methods for accomplishing this task including the multiple-of-income method, the human life value approach, the financial needs analysis method, and the capital needs analysis method.

How Much Do I Need?

If a prospect asks you, "How much life insurance do I need?" you should explain that it is not easy to answer this question spontaneously, because insurance needs are complex and differ from person to person. Go on to explain that if he or she will tell you what they and their family would like to accomplish, you will be able to help them determine the best amount of life insurance for them.

Establishing how much life insurance a person should have requires a detailed analysis of the person' life circumstances. There is no blanket formula to determine this. The best approach is to look at the present and future financial needs of the family, identified through a financial needs analysis as discussed below.

A plan should be developed that can satisfy the agreed-upon need within the family budget. Sometimes, a combination of permanent and term life insurance is required to accomplish this. Occasionally, the client will purchase only part of the needed protection, aiming to supplement the plan with additional purchases in the future, if insurability permits. It may take years to complete the program. Often, it is never completed, but any insurance in force is better than little or none.

There are several ways to calculate the amount of life insurance needed, ranging from simple to complex. Some planning techniques can be done by hand and some may require a computer. One method is not necessarily better than another. Your choice should be based on how accurate and in-depth the calculation needs to be for the prospect and whether the prospect wants to preserve or consume the capital set aside for future needs.

Without establishing needs or a human life value, the prospect is left with a suggested amount of insurance that lacks rationale and explanation. To someone with less than $1,000 in the bank, a $250,000 life insurance policy may sound enormous. Without context, this large amount of money may seem excessive, even though the individual in question may have a human life value to his or her family in excess of $1 million.

Plan for Life by Planning for Death
Plan for life as though you will live forever; plan for death as though it will come today.

Assume Death Occurs Today

The cardinal rule in insurance planning is the assumption that the insured will die today. If there is no assumption of immediate death, it will be impossible to pinpoint the needs for insurance or the sources of available cash and income. You will only be able to make rough estimates. You must plan for circumstances as they exist today. In presenting your analysis, you might explain to the prospect what the situation would be had she or he died today. This is not intimidation. It allows the prospect to be realistic, focus on the present, and deal with the reality of life and death.

Dual-Income Families

Today, most families have more than one income earner. We need to consider both incomes and a variety of possibilities based on family preferences and goals in the event of an income earner's death. Total needs planning becomes more urgent when the circumstances are complicated by a variety of needs, such as survivor income, disability income, and retirement planning. The result is often two programs, each satisfying an appropriate share of the total needs of each income earner.

Considering Social Security

Social Security benefits give the advisor another planning tool. Social Security is typically either fully or partially calculated into the program, or set aside as a future inflation hedge. People have opinions about the future soundness of the program, and everyone hopes that they will have a Social Security income after paying the FICA taxes on their earned income over the years. However, many younger people are suspicious about what that amount will be when they retire.

When choosing the planning method to be used, the inclusion or exclusion of Social Security income must be considered. People who prefer not to use Social Security as part of their total-needs planning will want all future income needs to be provided for through their own resources. For others, Social Security can be figured into dependency income through the survivor's benefits and in retirement income calculations. Each step can be considered individually. Some prefer to include Social Security, feeling confident in the program, while others do not, preferring to allow Social Security to serve as a hedge against inflation, future reductions in benefits, and other unforeseen events.

Multiple-of-Income Approach

multiple-of-income approach

Financial journalists tend to prefer simplistic rules of thumb for determining the life insurance amount needed, such as the *multiple-of-income approach*, because it is easy to explain and requires few calculations. This method simply takes some multiple of annual income to determine the amount of life insurance a breadwinner should carry. What is most interesting about this approach is the large variation in the recommended multiple to be used, commonly ranging from 3 to 10 times (or more) annual income. Additionally, this simplistic approach ignores the financial and personal situation of the individual. It does not take into account the important differences in people's lives that actually determine what amount of life insurance they should have, such as family size, living expenses, and stage of life.

An attempt to determine life insurance needs that does not rely upon a fair amount of client information is of questionable worth. The multiple-of-income approach ignores information about assets the client has already accumulated and any external financial resources such as trusts and inheritances. The multiple-of-income approach can over-insure or under-insure the client. On the other hand, simplistic rules of thumb may work if they are the only approach that motivates the client to purchase needed insurance. Sometimes clients resist providing the information necessary for a thorough analysis of their needs and this is the only recourse.

Without establishing needs or a human life value, the prospect is left with a suggested amount of insurance that lacks rationale and explanation. To someone with less than $1,000 in the bank, a $250,000 life insurance policy may sound enormous. Without context, this large amount of money may seem excessive, even though the individual in question may have a human life value to his or her family in excess of $1 million.

Shortcoming of Multiple-of-Income Method
• It does not recognize accumulated assets.
• It does not recognize individual family circumstances or family objectives.

Human Life Value Approach

human life value approach

The human life value concept is important to determining the life insurance need and serves as its foundation. The *human life value approach* is based on the concept that a person should carry life insurance in an amount equal to the *capitalized value* of his or her net future earnings. This capitalized value should be large enough to yield, at an assumed rate of interest, an income equal to the family's share of those earnings. As an alternative, a person could capitalize this value at a figure large enough to yield an annual income equal to a specified percentage, such as 50 percent, of those personal earnings at the time of the provider's death. In response to inflation, some suggest capitalizing the worker's full income (or more) so that the income portion that would otherwise go to income taxes and the insured's self-maintenance can be used to offset general price inflation.

Human life value is measured daily in wrongful death lawsuits. The economic loss of the victim's human life value, or financial contribution to the family and other survivors, is the basis for determining monetary awards in these cases. When a wrongful death suit is filed, both sides routinely retain economists to evaluate the victim's human life value. Economic loss may also include nonwage income such as fringe benefits and services to the family that would need to be replaced if death occurs. When a car is destroyed, it can be replaced through auto insurance. With life insurance, when the insured dies, he or she cannot be replaced; only the financial contribution he or she makes to dependents is replaceable. Insuring human life value is the primary purpose of life insurance.

Computing the monetary value of a person involves an estimate of the individual's future earnings for each year from his or her present age to the date of retirement, taking into account the normal trend of earnings and inflation. From each year's income, the cost of self-maintenance, life insurance premiums, and personal income taxes are deducted. The remaining income for each year is then discounted at an assumed rate of interest.

present value

The sum of the discounted values for each year of potential income is the present value of future earnings, which represents the monetary value of the life in question. *Present value* is what money to be received in the future is worth today. It is equivalent to the actual sum to be received in the future, discounted (reduced) by an interest rate that represents the interest that could be earned on that money if it was received today instead of in the future. Ideally, this amount will be sufficient to permit the family to enjoy the same standard of living that it would have enjoyed had the provider(s) not died.

Five-step Procedure for Estimating Economic Value

A reasonably accurate estimate of a person's economic value for purposes of life insurance can be calculated by a simple method using a computer, a financial calculator, or compound-interest discount tables. There are five steps in this procedure:

1. Estimate the individual's average annual income over the remaining years of his or her income-producing lifetime.
2. Deduct federal and state income taxes, life insurance premiums, and the cost of self maintenance.

3. Determine the number of years between the individual's present age and the planned retirement age.
4. Select a reasonable rate of interest at which future earnings will be discounted.
5. Multiply (1) minus (2) by the present value of $1 per annum for the period determined in (3), discounted at the rate of interest selected in (4).

The first step projects the pattern of future earnings. It is difficult to accurately estimate the average annual income that can be expected. Inflation, technological change, and increased global competition are accelerating the rate of change and our society's economic volatility.

The costs in the second step are also difficult to estimate, but income taxes and the cost of self-maintenance can be approximated based on current tax rates (Congress can always change future tax rates). The purpose of step (2) is to discount the funds that serve purposes other than supporting one's dependents and to arrive at the family's share of the breadwinner's personal earnings. The determination of the income tax liability, life insurance premiums, and the cost of self-maintenance can be eliminated if the prospect can estimate the portion of personal earnings that currently go to the support of the family, typically about half of the provider's gross personal earnings. In the low-income brackets, the percentage is a little higher, but in no event more than two-thirds; in the higher-income brackets, the percentage might be lower than one-half.

Elements of Economic Value Estimates

- Average annual earnings estimate
- Taxes, self-maintenance costs, life insurance premiums
- Remaining years in workforce before retirement
- Estimated interest rate applicable to future working years

The purpose of step (3) is to determine how long the family can expect to receive the income projected in step (2), ignoring the possibility that the individual may die before reaching retirement age. The rate of interest selected in step (4) should be in line with the rate generally payable on short-term fixed-income investments, such as money market funds and Treasury bills.

Calculating Present Value

present value of $1 per annum

The *present value of $1 per annum,* the only new element involved in step (5), is obtained directly from a financial calculator or a computer using financial software. The present value of $1 per annum is the value today of a series of equal periodic payments made at the end of each period and discounted at an appropriate interest rate. It can also be taken from a compound discount table that shows the present value of a series of future income payments—specifically, $1 per annum—for various periods of time and at various rates of interest.

EXAMPLE

Examples of present values of $1 per annum

- Forty annual payments of $1 at the end of each year with an interest rate of 0 percent are equal to $40 today.
- Forty annual payments of $1 at the end of each year with an interest rate of 5 percent are equal to $17.16 today.
- Forty annual payments of $1 at the end of each year with an interest rate of 4.5 percent interest are equal to $18.40 today.

The entire process of computing the monetary value of a human life is illustrated with the following example:

EXAMPLE

Angus McDonald is a married male, aged 35, with gross annual earnings of $40,000 (expected level to retirement) and with an assumed $20,000 available annually to support his family. Angus plans to retire at age 65. The assumed interest rate is 5 percent. Thirty years of $1 payments has a present value of $15.37. Applying the five-step procedure produces the following results:

1. The average annual future earnings are $40,000.
2. The portion of the average annual future earnings available to the family per year is $20,000.
3. The number of years to retirement is 30.
4. The assumed interest rate is 5 percent.
5. The present value of future earnings to the family is calculated as follows:
   $40,000 — $20,000 = $20,000
   $20,000 x $15.37 = $307,400

Ideally, the life of each income earner should be insured for an amount equal to his or her full economic value, as measured by financial support to dependents. Upon the death of the income producer, the insured sum should then be liquidated, meeting the different needs as they arise and in the order of their importance. If the insured lives to retirement, the sums accumulated through permanent insurance cash values, except for amounts required for cleanup and other necessary purposes, can be used to supplement the postretirement needs of the insured and his or her spouse.

Attaining this ideal is difficult, even when death benefits available under Social Security and employer benefit plans are taken into account. The basic problem is that when both the economic value and the needs are at their maximum—at younger ages—the funds available for premium payments are at their minimum. In the lower income groups, almost all of the family income is spent on the necessities of life; very little is saved. As the family income rises, spending for consumer goods increase, but they make up a smaller percentage of total income. Thus, more money is available for insurance premiums and other forms of savings. By that time, however, the need for insurance may have declined.

More sophisticated approaches to determining needs are described below. These approaches translate the client's needs into estimated costs, then evaluate assets and existing coverage to determine how much of the funding is already in place. Any deficit between the intended goals and current financial resources is usually a candidate for additional life insurance.

Need Analysis Approach

In order to conduct the needs analysis approach, qualified prospects must be serious about their financial future and the financial advisor must establish enough trust for the information gathering and analysis process to proceed. Problem solving requires complete and accurate information about current income, potential future income, accumulated assets, investments, pensions, and other qualified plan holdings. In addition, it is important to develop the client's priorities for life and financial goals. A lot of time and energy is often spent in gathering the necessary information before this information can be analyzed and recommendations made.

financial needs analysis approach

In the *financial needs analysis approach,* a client's needs must be translated into estimated costs. A fundamental difference between the needs approach and the human life value approach is that two individuals may have similar human life values, yet one may have a mortgage and the other may not. Their debts may be totally different, and one may have no children to educate, while the other may have several. These costs must then be evaluated to determine how much of the funding is already in place. Any deficit between the intended goals and current financial sources indicates a need for life insurance. Life insurance provides a means of completing the financing of family goals that individuals work toward during their lifetime. The advisor and client must then decide on the trade-offs between the needs that the client wishes to protect and the cost of life insurance to provide that protection.

The term "leaving the family in their own world" is used to describe the ideal of this process. This is similar to the phrase, standard of living. That world consists of all the ways the family uses the family income. Financially, this means providing the same funds to support that standard of living after the insured's death as before. This is where the insurance need often grows to a substantial amount. Final expenses are actually a small part of the total need that clients do not anticipate.

There are producers who would advise against using the word "need", because it carries a negative connotation. For example, after the World Trade Center attack on 9/11/2001, the federal government established a relief fund for survivors of those killed that day, using an appraisal method that tried to determine the future economic loss associated with those deaths. It considered age, income and future earnings potential, not need—essentially the human life value method. Compensation amounts ranged from $250,000 to $7 million, with the average award for a death claim exceeding $2 million. The average claim valued the future earnings of the victim at nearly 16 times annual income. After life insurance and other offsetting factors, the future earnings value was more than 11 times income. The average victim had life insurance coverage of 2.9 times their income.

If a prospect can afford it, it is a luxury to have the maximum an insurer will issue. This may be 10–15 times annual income, which is more than many companies would issue. For many prospects, this is not an option and the needs analysis method provides a rationale for the amount of insurance a prospect should buy. Although Ben Feldman taught us that the premium is not the problem, but the solution to the problem, for many people the premium is perceived as a problem. The average U.S. household with life insurance owns enough to replace 3.5 years of income, a measure consistent across all income groups (LIMRA, 2010 U.S. Life Ownership Study). This is far from what anyone would consider a human life value solution.

Financial Needs Analysis

Life insurance needs are summarized below to introduce the financial needs and capital needs analysis methods. These methods are used to determine a prospects needs for life insurance, based on two broad categories—cash needs and income needs.

	Financial Needs Analysis—Amount of Insurance Needed
	Estimated economic value or amount needed to fund desires
–	Amounts already available (Social Security, investments, existing insurance and retirement benefits and so on)
=	Unfunded amount that can be made up with life insurance

Cash Needs. Cash needs analysis determines the amount of funding that needs to be set aside to pay expenses that the deceased would have otherwise paid in a lump-sum amount. Cash needs at death include: final expenses such as those associated with funeral, burial, or cremation, if applicable; estate taxes; probate expenses; attorneys' fees; unpaid costs of a last illness; and operating expenses for the survivors' household. An emergency fund and a child-care and educational fund can also be provided in this category.

Income Needs. Income needs analysis determines the needs for survivors' income. These amounts, together with the amount from the cash needs analysis, will provide the funding for the survivors' future lifestyle. If there is an income shortfall, this method determines the amount of life insurance needed to cover the shortfall, using either a capital conservation or capital distribution method (discussed next).

The need for survivor income becomes evident at the moment of death. These needs will continue until the surviving dependents become self-supporting. Depending upon a family's situation, this can be a short time, or it can last decades. In some families, surviving members may never become self-sufficient, and there is no intent that they do so.

It is common to classify survivors' ongoing income needs into four categories:

- *Readjustment income* covers the period immediately after death.

- *Dependency period income* is available until the youngest child becomes self-sufficient.
- *Blackout period income,* if needed, provides funds for a surviving spouse who is not eligible to receive Social Security income after the children have become self-sufficient (discussed further below).
- *Retirement income,* if needed, provides additional funds for the surviving spouse after eligibility for social security and any private pension benefits.

Guidelines for the Insurance Needs Assessment

Cash Needs

Final expenses/burial fund—costs of funeral expenses plus other costs associated with death, such as medical expenses for a last illness, estate settlement costs, property transfer costs, etc. The following questions can be used to determine final expenses:

- Have you ever thought about what a funeral costs?
- Are you aware of all of the costs that might arise immediately upon your death?
- How much do you think they would require?

Mortgage payment fund—amount required to pay off the balance of the mortgage on the family home to allow the family to keep it. If the family rents a home, calculate the annual rent times the number of years the fund will be needed. The following questions can be used to establish the mortgage payment fund:

- If you were to die tonight, would you want your family to be able to keep the house?
- How much do you think that would require?

Debt payment fund—amount required to pay existing debts that may become due immediately, such as car loans, credit cards, personal loans, etc. The following questions can be used to determine the size of the debt payment fund:

- Would you want your family to be able to pay off all your outstanding debts if you were to pass away?
- How much do you think that would require?

Education fund—amount needed in the future to help fund the children's higher education. The following questions can be used to determine the size of the education fund:

- How do you feel about education for your children?
- Is providing an education for your children a priority for you?
- How much do you think that would require?
- Where do you see them going to school?
- If you or your spouse were to die, do you think it would be harder for the remaining spouse to save for college?

Other/emergency fund—a fund set aside to meet the routine emergencies of daily living, such as car repairs, that are currently met with the help of the wage earner. The following questions can be used to determine emergency funds needed:

- Would your family be able to handle other emergencies, like major car repairs or home repairs, without you here to help?
- How much do you think should be set aside for emergencies?

Other immediate cash needs—list any other special needs identified by the prospect. Ask the prospect if there are any other obligations they can think of that their family might have difficulty meeting if they were to expire tonight.

Income Needs

Annual income fund—enter the amount of annual earned income from salaries, wages and regular bonuses for both the prospect and spouse. Have the following discussion with the prospect:

- If you were to die, your family would lose your earning power. How much of what you earn would they need to maintain their current lifestyle?
- How long would they need it?
- Your income probably increases annually. Would you want your family's income to increase as well?
- By what percentage?

Total family income need—annual amount needed is the amount of the prospect's income that would be required by the family to maintain its current lifestyle. Income from other sources, like Social Security, can be taken into consideration in determining the amount needed. The annual amount needed is multiplied by the number of years the amount is to be provided.

Income Sources

Savings and investments—Include all savings and investment programs, including personal retirement plans (IRAs), that would be available. Ask the prospect if his or her current resources would meet all of the needs just identified if they were to pass away tonight.

Company benefits—Include company-sponsored life insurance plans that would be available in the event of death. Also include any pension or other benefits the employer provides that would be available at death.

Family and friends—Include the amount that would be provided by other family members or friends.

Current life insurance—Include the total of all existing life insurance in force, excluding any provided through employment, which was included above.

Other—Include any other sources of cash that the prospect thinks would be available to provide income.

Calculation

Total all the available resources. Total the immediate cash needs and the family income needs. Subtract the available resource figure from the combined needs figure.

capital distribution method

The Capital Distribution Method. In the financial needs analysis approach, both principal and interest are used to provide income and capital for a certain period into the future, at which point all capital is spent. This is also known as the *capital distribution method* or *liquidating approach*, since all funds are expected to be distributed over time. Since the principal is used as income, this method requires a smaller amount of initial principal to provide the desired income than the capital conservation method, which preserves principal.

A serious shortcoming of the liquidating approach is that the fund may eventually be totally consumed. This strategy requires estimating the insured's likely maximum age at death and planning liquidation for that date or later. Any liquidation planning based on the beneficiary's death at an early age runs a high risk of liquidating the proceeds while the beneficiary is still dependent on them. This could leave survivors with limited income resources and may be unacceptable if the income is expected to last for the beneficiaries' lifetime. Although requiring a smaller amount of principal, this method leaves no room for contingencies, adjustment for inflation, or for any balance of principal to be passed on to other beneficiaries. They run out of money before they run out of time. Financial advisors are advised to plan for liquidation in such a way that the beneficiary is likely to run out of time before he or she runs out of money.

There are two ways to eliminate the potential problem associated with liquidating the principal sum over the beneficiary's lifetime. One approach is to use policy proceeds at death to provide a life income through policy settlement options or separate annuity contracts. These arrangements guarantee lifelong income payments regardless of how long the recipient lives. The other approach (nonliquidating) uses the creation of capital large enough that all the income benefits can be provided through investment income alone.

The amounts associated with each of these categories vary widely from one individual to another and from one family to another. Reliance on general guidelines rather than on individual evaluation will increase the likelihood that important and potentially costly needs may be overlooked or ignored, that the analysis will be inaccurate, and that the prospect may not buy-in to the analysis and proposed solution.

Because the purpose of life insurance is to fund the unfunded portion of these cash and income needs objectives, it is important to consider all existing funds that can provide part or all of these needs. For simplicity and efficiency, most planners suggest using some target percentage of the insured's current income as the target income level, rather than calculating a composite of each individual anticipated need component. It is often suggested that the survivor(s) will need about 70 percent of the pre-death income to carry on financially after a breadwinner's death.

Projecting future cash flow and deducting the existing sources of income are the first steps in determining the income deficit. The next step is to find the present value of all future income needs. This calculation can be done in many different ways and with many different levels of specificity. Often it is broken up into components, so that the income deficit will be the same throughout a particular component period. If the calculation is done this way, the final calculation of the total income need is the sum of the present values of each of the separate, individually calculated components.

Most financial advisors suggest that these components be kept to a minimum and that simplifying assumptions be made whenever possible to keep this estimation process from becoming too cumbersome and time consuming. It is important to remember that this is still an estimation process intended to simulate unknown future occurrences. The estimates are made without the benefit of knowing what future inflation rates and investment returns will be.

Some advisors suggest that all values should be done in current dollar amounts and with no discounting applied to future income periods. Such discounting merely complicates an imprecise estimation process; ignoring inflation may also help make the estimates more accurate. An inordinate amount of time and resources can be spent trying to precisely estimate future income flows. Just because a computer can produce numbers with four-decimal-place precision does not mean that those numbers will actually unfold in the future.

Within the life insurance industry, the liquidating approach is referred to as *financial needs analysis*, and a nonliquidating approach is referred to as *capital needs analysis*.

Financial Needs Analysis—The Liquidating Approach

- All investment income is distributed
- Part of the investment capital is distributed with each payment
- Intent is to nearly exhaust the investment fund at the end of recipient's life
- Requires estimation of the remaining lifetime of the recipient

Capital Needs Analysis

capital conservation method

The Capital Conservation Method. The capital needs analysis method uses the *capital conservation method,* where capital is preserved rather than spent. This method uses only the interest generated from investments to provide the desired income. Capital is not invaded, so the investment amount should not vary, if invested conservatively. The money is placed in a well-allocated and diversified portfolio, depending on risk/return characteristics suitable to that client. If the client can tolerate risk, the money can be invested more aggressively to increase potential growth. The goal is to produce an after-tax income from the interest to meet the beneficiary's income needs. The principal remains intact, to be used as a hedge against inflation and other contingencies, or to be passed on to the beneficiary's heirs.

The insurance need generated by capital conservation exceeds that created by the capital distribution technique illustrated earlier. The flexibility and the added advantage of preserving capital make the capital conservation method appealing to many prospects. Computer software is available to perform these calculations.

To apply this method, a simple financial statement is prepared which lists the prospect's cash and income goals, and assets and liabilities. In the example that follows, the prospect has existing life insurance of $100,000, and a net interest rate of 6 percent (the effective after-tax interest rate) is assumed. Using this information, an acceptable rate of return is determined.

Financial Statement for the Prospect Capital Conservation Approach	
Goals:	
Mortgage liquidation	$45,000
Final expense	15,000
Cash fund for emergency	8,000
Education guarantee fund	60,000
	$128,000
Income replacement (33%) at current rate of $833 per month without touching principal (6% return).	
($833 x 12 mos. = $9,996 ÷ 0.06 = $166,600)	$166,600
Total needed to fulfill goals	$294,600
Assets:	
Nonliquid assets (home, auto, furniture) are not considered working capital and will not be considered for investment.	
Liquid assets include:	
Life insurance	$100,000
Savings	
Liabilities:	
There are no outstanding debts except the mortgage.	
There is a capital shortfall of $194,600.	
($294,600 – $100,000 = $194,600)	$194,600
Recommendations:	
Make up the capital shortfall with additional life insurance.	
Start a savings program now for the future.	

Advantages of Capital Conservation. An insurance program built on the capital conservation concept has several advantages:

- First, life insurance proceeds can be invested at current interest rates, rather than placing them under more conservative contractual guaranteed rates normally found in settlement options.
- Second, capital conservation provides an opportunity to hedge the client's life insurance program against inflation. Income-producing principal is preserved and can be passed on to the prospect's heirs or used for other investment or business opportunities that may arise in the future.

- Third, it is designed to provide an income that a beneficiary will not outlive if the principal is not invaded and if the assumed interest rate is achieved.

Despite its advantages, however, capital conservation is not appropriate for all prospects. Since it assumes current, not guaranteed, interest rates, capital conservation offers no guarantee that the prospect's economic goals will be accomplished.

Capital Conservation Method
If • client needs/wants long-term security, • inflation is a primary concern, • survivors are young and dependent, • flexibility (liquidity) is needed, • Social Security is not to be used in determining needs **then** create interest-only income from a fixed pool of capital: 1. Determine present unfunded cash needs 2. Determine unfunded annual income needs 3. Agree on assumed net interest rate 4. Establish new capital required to solve income need 5. Divide unfunded annual income by assumed net interest rate 6. Add totals from item 1 and item 4 The result is the amount of life insurance required to create a capital pool to fund immediate cash needs and ongoing income needs without depleting capital.

Another advantage of the nonliquidating approach is the simplicity of calculating the needed capital fund. The desired income level is easily capitalized by dividing the amount of income by the applicable interest rate representing the after-tax investment return anticipated on the capital sum. For example, if $100,000 per year is desired, and the capital sum generating those income payments can realistically expect to generate a 5 percent return after taxes, a $2 million fund is needed. This is determined by taking the desired income amount and dividing into that the estimate of the after-tax investment return rate. In our example it was 0.05, or 5 percent. This division yields the $2 million capital fund amount needed. The lower the after-tax investment return rate, the higher the capital fund needed to produce the same amount of income. Similarly, higher marginal tax rates will lower the after-tax return rate and increase the size of the fund needed to generate the income.

Elements of Needs Analysis
• Final expenses • Readjustment income • Income during dependency period • Life income for surviving dependent spouse • Special needs • Mortgage redemption needs • Educational needs • Emergency needs

Comparing Needs Analysis and Human Life Value Approaches

We can now compare the monetary value of the above financial-needs approach with the human life approach computed earlier. For purposes of comparison, assume—as in the case of Angus McDonald—that the family head is a male aged 35, has gross annual earnings of $40,000, and devotes $20,000 per year to his family. Assume that he has a wife aged 30 and two children, ages 2 and 5, and that an income of $1,700 per month is to be provided during the first 2 years, $1,460 per month during the next 14 years, and $971 per month thereafter for the life of the surviving spouse.

In computing the present value of the foregoing series of income payments (*income needs*), it is advisable to treat them as a life income of $971 per month payable from the surviving spouse's age 30 with an additional income of $489 per month for 16 years and another $240 per month for 2 years. Based on annuity table values, a life income of $971 per month for a female, aged 30, with payments guaranteed for 20 years, has a present value of approximately $220,000. The present value on a 4 percent interest basis of $489 per month for 16 years is $69,263, and the present value of $240 per month for 2 years is $5,526. The present value of the family's income needs when the figures are rounded to the nearest hundred dollars is $294,800.

The total increases when the *cash needs* (cleanup fund, mortgage redemption fund, educational needs, and emergency needs) are added. Even if no provision is made for the children's college education, a cleanup fund of $20,000, a mortgage redemption fund of $80,000, and an emergency fund of $30,000 will increase the total to $424,800. If $80,000 is provided to each of the children for a college education, the total income requirements reach $584,800. The human life value approach results in a life insurance need of $307,400.

EXAMPLE

Married male aged 35, spouse aged 30, children ages 2 and 5		
Income needed first 2 years	$ 1,700	per month
Income needed next 14 years	$ 1,460	per month
Income thereafter for surviving spouse	$ 971	per month
Assumed interest rate	4%	
Cleanup fund	$20,000	
Mortgage redemption fund	$80,000	
Emergency fund	$30,000	
Education fund for children	$160,000	
Combined needs (rounding to nearest $100)	$584,800	

It is not likely that these needs will have to be met entirely through life insurance. If the individual in the example is covered under Social Security, with benefits approaching the maximum, nearly two-thirds of the income needed until the youngest child is 18 will be provided by the federal government (assuming the widow does not remarry and both children survive the period). This would reduce the personal insurance requirements by approximately $170,000.

If the husband had attained "fully-insured" status for Social Security at the time of his death, at age 62 the widow would become entitled to a life income of $800 per month, which would reduce the personal insurance requirements by another $29,600. The individual may also be covered by group life insurance, with benefits of possibly $150,000 or more. Therefore, it is possible that all the cash and income needs will be met in full with the purchase of $235,000 of additional life insurance.

The retirement needs of the husband do not require additional insurance. If the husband purchases $300,000 of whole life insurance (roughly the equivalent of the income needs) before age 35, it will have accumulated at least $125,000 in cash values by age 65. This will provide him with a life income with payments of more than $1,012 per month guaranteed for 10 years. If his wife is also alive and in need of retirement income protection, the accumulated sum could be converted into a joint-and-last-survivor annuity, which would provide a lower (7.5 percent to 14 percent reduction) income per month as long as either the husband or the wife survives. Such an income, supplemented by Social Security benefits and possibly retirement benefits from an employer pension plan, should meet their retirement needs.

Business Uses of Life Insurance

No well-run business entity can afford to operate without insurance covering its resources against loss. This is as true for the human resources of a business as it is for its buildings and equipment. Life insurance funds a wide variety of business needs; this section will briefly outline some of these.

Credit Enhancement

Life insurance can enhance a business's credit in two ways, by improving its general credit rating and by making collateral available.

The first credit function of life insurance is closely allied to key person insurance (discussed later). Anything that stabilizes a business's financial position improves its credit rating. Insuring the lives of key personnel not only assures banks and other lenders that the business will have a financial cushion if a key person dies, it also improves the firm's liquidity through the accumulation of cash values that are available at all times. As a result, the firm is able to command more credit and obtain it on better terms.

Another use of life insurance for credit purposes is pledging it for collateral. It can protect the lender against loss arising out of the death of a key person of the borrower, or it can provide protection against the borrower's unwillingness or inability to repay the loan.

An example of the key person situation is a firm that would like to borrow additional sums to take advantage of a business opportunity. If the bank has confidence in the business and feels that the only contingency to fear is the death of the business head or some other key person, it can extend the additional credit upon the borrower's assignment to the bank of a life insurance policy in an appropriate amount on the life of the proper key person. For this purpose, term insurance may be used. The security behind the loan is the earning capacity of the business and the integrity of its owners. The policy provides protection against the death of the person whose business acumen assures the loan's repayment. Loans secured by the assignment of a term insurance policy on the borrower's life are also found in personal or nonbusiness transactions. For example, consider an aspiring doctor who borrows money from a benefactor for medical school, repaying the funds after establishing a practice. In the interim, the benefactor is protected by a term insurance policy on the budding physician's life.

A loan based on cash values is in a different category. The basic security lies in the policy values; the amount of the loan, therefore, is always less than the cash value under the policy assigned to the lender. If the borrower dies before the loan is repaid, the lender recovers funds from the death proceeds, with the difference paid to the insured's designated beneficiary. If the borrower lives, but the loan is not paid at maturity, the lender—if also the policyowner or absolute assignee—can recover the funds by surrendering the policy for cash or by exercising the policy loan privilege. Life insurance policies are widely used for this purpose in both business and personal situations. Policyowners frequently borrow through the policy loan privilege, rather than through assignment to a bank or other lender.

Employee Benefits

Designing the compensation package for the owners and employees of a business is a critical step in the business planning process. In small, closely held businesses, the businessowner's needs will often dictate both the size and form of compensation provided to employees. In addition, nonowner key employees of closely held businesses must be adequately compensated or the businesses could lose their best employees to competitors. Finally, larger, publicly held corporations must compete for the services of valued executives, and employee benefits represent a significant portion of the total compensation package.

Employee benefit plans provide three broad types of benefits that can be financed through insurance: disability benefits, death benefits, and pension benefits. The plans that provide such benefits are usually referred to as group health insurance, group life insurance, and pensions. We will focus on the latter two areas in this chapter.

Group Term life Insurance Plans (IRC Sec. 79)

group term life insurance

Group term life insurance is a benefit plan provided by an employer to a group of participating employees. Such plans, also known as IRC Sec. 79 plans, allow the employer a tax deduction for premium payments on behalf of a participant, unless the premium amounts exceed the reasonable compensation limits.

If the coverage provided by the plan is nondiscriminatory, the first $50,000 of coverage is provided tax free to all plan participants. If the plan discriminates in favor of key employees, with respect to coverage or benefits, the actual premiums paid on behalf of such key employees are taxable as ordinary income. The taxable amounts of coverage (amounts above $50,000) are taxed according to a rate schedule, called Table I, provided by IRS regulations and are presented in the table below.

Table 2-1 Group Term Rates — Cost per Month per $1,000

5-Year Age Bracket	Table 1 Rates
Under 30	$0.06
30 to 34	0.08
35 to 39	0.09
40 to 44	0.10
45 to 49	0.15
50 to 54	0.23
55 to 59	0.43
60 to 64	0.66
65 to 69	1.27
70 and above	2.06

Requirements Under Sec. 79

Through a contract held directly or indirectly by the employer, coverage under a Sec. 79 plan must provide only death benefits excludible from income tax to a group of at least 10 employees, although special rules provide an exception for smaller groups. The insurance protection provided must prevent individual selection of the amount of coverage. The coverage can be based on formulas related to age, service, job classification, and compensation. For example, a plan that provides a death benefit five times the participant's annual salary prevents individual selection.

EXAMPLE
Suppose a retired executive has $150,000 of postretirement group term life coverage. Since $100,000 of this coverage is subject to tax, the executive would have to include $792 (12 x $0.66 x 100) in income annually at age 64. The annual taxable income incurred by the executive jumps to $1,524 at age 65, and $2,472 at age 70 (see previous table).

Executive Bonus Life Insurance Plans (Sec. 162)

executive bonus life insurance plan Sec. 162

In an *executive bonus life insurance plan Sec. 162,* business owners and executives apply for, own, and name the beneficiary on permanent life insurance policies covering their lives. The premiums for such policies are provided through a bonus payment by the business. The business either pays the premium directly to the insurer or gives the premium as a bonus to the employee, who is billed by the insurance company.

The income taxation of the plan is simple. The premium amount paid directly to the insurer (or to the employee, as a bonus) is treated as gross income to the employee and is subject to the employee's individual income tax rate. If the bonus, plus the employee's other compensation is "reasonable," the business deducts the amount of the bonus as an ordinary business expense. Although the tax burden of the plan is immediate to the executive, the bonus can be designed as a zero-tax bonus to reduce the executive's out-of-pocket costs. A zero-tax bonus is one large enough to pay the tax on the bonus.

The primary advantage of a business's adoption of an Sec. 162 plan is its exemption from the federal nondiscrimination and administrative reporting rules applicable to most other types of fringe benefit plans. The businessowners or board of directors of a closely held business or professional corporation can select the participants and limit the plan to those employees who want individual life insurance coverage. In addition, there are no discrimination rules with respect to benefit limits.

However, a business should use caution in providing unlimited coverage, since the business deduction for bonus payments to the plan is limited by the reasonable compensation rules. If the limit is exceeded, the business income tax deduction will be lost on any bonuses to employees that are deemed unreasonable, and the excess bonus will be treated as a dividend payment, rather than as compensation. The corporation should adopt the Sec. 162 plan by a board of directors' resolution and provide evidence in the minutes of the corporate purpose for establishing the plan, such as indicating the need to retain or attract key executives by offering the Sec. 162 plan as a benefit.

Split-Dollar Life Insurance Plans

split-dollar life insurance

Split-dollar life insurance is an arrangement of permanent life insurance to provide an executive benefit. The following discussion summarizes several forms of split-dollar arrangements. There are numerous variations within each arrangement.

Basic Concepts

Split-dollar life insurance plans split a life insurance policy's premium and benefits between two individuals or entities, typically an employer and employee. The two parties share the premium costs, according to an agreement. At the death of the insured or the termination of the agreement, the parties split the policy benefits or proceeds according to their agreement.

Split-dollar plans are used as a fringe benefit option because the plans can be limited to a select group of key personnel. The coverage amounts and terms of a split-dollar arrangement are not subject to the nondiscrimination rules that apply to qualified pension plans and other benefit arrangements. The purpose of these plans is to provide a life insurance benefit at a low cost and low outlay to key employees. Split-dollar plans are an alternative to other methods of providing death benefits (as a reward or incentive to selected executives), such as an insurance-financed, nonqualified, deferred-compensation plan or life insurance in a qualified plan (discussed later).

Split-dollar plans can also help provide business continuity, by providing funds for shareholder-employees to finance a buyout of stock under a cross-purchase buy-sell agreement (discussed later), or to make it possible for nonstockholding employees to affect a one-way stock purchase at an existing shareholder's death. This helps establish a market for what otherwise might be unmarketable stock, while providing an incentive for employees to stay with the company.

Generally, the employer's cost for a split-dollar plan is fully secured by the insurance contract. At the employee's death or termination of employment, the employer is reimbursed from policy proceeds for its premium outlay. The employer receives no tax deduction for its payments, but as a result of the reimbursement, the net cost to the employer for the plan is limited to the loss of the net after-tax income that could have been earned on the amount of premium paid during the period the plan was in effect.

Policy Ownership

Common methods of arranging split-dollar policyownership are discussed below.

endorsement method

Endorsement Method. In the *endorsement method*, the employer owns the policy and is responsible for paying the entire premium to the insurance company. The beneficiary designation provides for the employer to receive a portion of the death benefit equal to its premium outlay, with the remainder of the death proceeds going to the employee's designated beneficiary.

An endorsement to the policy is filed with the insurance company under which payment to the employee's beneficiary cannot be changed without consent of the employee (or a designated third person when the employee wishes to avoid incidents of ownership for estate tax purposes). Advantages of the endorsement method are as follows:

- greater control by the employer over the policy
- simpler installation and administration; the only documentation required is the policy and endorsement
- avoidance of any formal arrangement that might constitute a loan, for purposes of state and federal laws prohibiting corporate loans to officers and directors
- if the company owns an existing key employee policy on the employee, it can be used directly in the split-dollar plan without change of ownership. Using an existing policy may be important if the employee has developed health problems since the policy was issued.
- the plan will be taxed under the economic benefit rules, which may be more advantageous than the alternative loan treatment. (Participant reports income based on value of pure insurance coverage under Table 2001.)

collateral assignment method

Collateral Assignment Method. Features of the *collateral assignment method* of split-dollar policyownership are as follows:

- The employee (or a third party) is the owner of the policy and is responsible for premium payments.
- The employer makes loans of the amount of the premium the employer has agreed to pay under the split-dollar plan.
- This arrangement is treated for tax purposes as a series of loans.
- To secure the loans the policy is assigned as collateral to the employer.
- At the employee's death, the employer recovers its cumulative premium payments from the policy proceeds, as collateral assignee. The remainder of the policy proceeds is paid to the employee's designated beneficiary.
- If the plan terminates before the employee's death, the employer can be reimbursed out of policy cash values; the employee continues as the owner of the policy.

Some advantages of the collateral assignment method are as follows:

- It gives more protection to the employee and the employee's beneficiary.
- It is easier to implement using existing insurance policies owned by the employee.
- It is easier for the employee to keep the policy out of the estate for federal estate tax purposes. This is done by having the policy owned from the outset by a third party chosen by the employee, such as an *irrevocable life insurance trust* to pay insurance proceeds to the desired beneficiary.

Two Methods for Taxation

The regulations provide two mutually exclusive methods for taxing split-dollar life insurance arrangements. Ownership of the life insurance contract determines which method applies. By deciding on employee or employer ownership, the taxpayer decides whether to proceed under the economic benefit or loan regime.

1. Under the *economic benefit method,* the owner of the life insurance contract provides economic benefits to the nonowner of the contract. The value of the life insurance coverage or other benefit

provided to an employee under a split-dollar plan is valued and taxed to the employee as additional taxable income.

The economic benefit method essentially applies to an *endorsement-type* plan under which the employer is the owner of the life insurance contract and endorses a portion of the death benefit to the employee.

2. Under the *loan method,* the nonowner of the life insurance contract is treated as a lender for the premium payments to the owner. The loan treatment will apply to collateral assignment plans, in which the employee or the employee's trust or beneficiary is the owner of the contract.

Life Insurance in Deferred-Compensation Plans

Under a deferred-compensation plan, part of the employee's compensation over the employee's working years is deferred until a later period, such as at the employee's retirement. This deferral meets two goals. First, the deferred compensation will provide income for the employee during his or her retirement. Second, the deferred-compensation plan is tax-deferred until the income is received.

Deferred-compensation plans are either *qualified* or *nonqualified*. Qualified plans must meet federal nondiscrimination and compliance standards, which increase the cost, since a broad base of employees must be included, and significant administrative fees must be paid. However, the corporation gets an immediate income tax deduction for contributions to the plan while the employee's tax on plan benefits is deferred until the benefits are received. Qualified plans include pension plans, IRAs, profit-sharing plans, and Sec. 403(b) plans.

nonqualified deferred-compensation

Nonqualified deferred-compensation plans provide a similar deferral of the employee's receipt of ordinary income. However, nonqualified plans also cause a deferral of the employer's tax deduction until such benefits are paid. Since small businesses and closely held corporations often want to maximize the benefits for owners and discrimination is permitted in nonqualified arrangements, the goal of their retirement plans is to discriminate in favor of owners and key executives.

Life Insurance in Qualified Plans, IRAs, and 403(b) Plans

qualified retirement plans

Qualified retirement plans are employer sponsored retirement plans that are eligible for favorable tax status under the Internal Revenue Code. Examples include defined-benefit pension plans, cash-balance plans, money-purchase pension plans, target-benefit plans, profit-sharing plans, 401(k) plans, stock bonus plans, and ESOPs.

A qualified plan may provide a death benefit in addition to retirement benefits, even without using life insurance. In a defined-contribution plan, the participant's vested account balance will be paid to the participant's beneficiary if the participant dies before retirement or termination of employment. Defined-benefit plans, unless they use insurance, usually do not provide a death benefit other than whatever survivor annuity provision the plan provides.

A qualified plan must generally purchase life insurance to provide any substantial preretirement death benefit. This is particularly important in the early years of his or her employment when the amount contributed on the participant's behalf is still relatively small.

Although employees are generally not taxed on the promised benefits from a qualified plan until they are received, death benefits provided by life insurance are currently taxable. The current cost of "pure insurance" protection is subject to taxation, determined by the rates supplied by IRS Table 2001—One Year Term Premiums.

An insured preretirement death benefit can be provided in either a defined-benefit or a defined-contribution plan. Contributions to the plan by the employer may be used to pay life insurance premiums as long as the amount qualifies under the tests for incidental benefits.

In general, the IRS considers that nonretirement benefits—life, medical, or disability insurance—will be incidental and therefore permissible as long as the cost of providing these benefits is less than 25 percent of the cost of providing all the benefits under the plan. In applying this approach to life insurance benefits, the 25 percent rule is applied to the portion of any life insurance premium that is used to provide current life insurance protection. Any portion of the premium that increases the cash value of the policy is considered a contribution to the plan fund that is available to pay retirement benefits, and it is not considered in the 25 percent limitation.

The decision to include life insurance in a qualified plan depends on the plan's objective. The employer must first decide whether and to what extent it will provide death benefits to employees—under a group term or as an incidental benefit in a qualified plan. The death benefit should be designed to produce the lowest employer and employee cost for the benefit level desired.

Other Retirement Plans

A Keogh plan is a qualified plan available to a proprietor or one or more partners of an unincorporated business. Life insurance can be used to provide a death benefit for regular employees covered under the plan, and the rules discussed in this chapter apply. Life insurance can also be provided under the plan for a proprietor or partners, but the tax treatment for proprietors and partners is slightly less favorable.

Life insurance can also be used to provide an incidental benefit under a tax-deferred annuity plan (403b) on much the same basis as in a qualified profit-sharing plan. Covered employees will have Table 2001 death benefit costs to report as taxable income, as in a regular qualified plan.

Life insurance contracts are not permissible investments for an individual retirement plan (IRA). This means that an IRA cannot provide an insured death benefit. Similarly, a simplified employee pension plan (SEP) cannot purchase life insurance, since SEPs are funded with individual IRA contracts.

Types of Nonqualified Deferred-Compensation Plans

Nonqualified deferred compensation plans come in two general types, salary reduction arrangements and salary continuation plans.

Salary Reduction Arrangements

A salary reduction plan is an agreement between an employer and a participating employee to either reduce the employee's salary or to defer an anticipated bonus and provide that such amounts will be received in future tax years. These plans defer compensation that the employee would otherwise receive in cash, and generally provide an investment return on the amounts deferred.

Salary Continuation Plans

Most nonqualified plans fit into the broad category of salary continuation plans. Salary continuation plans can be designed to provide deferred-compensation benefits at the participant's death, disability, and/or retirement. These arrangements have no current cash option available to the employee. The death or disability benefits are a percentage of the employee's compensation and are provided to the employee or his or her beneficiary.

Financing a Nonqualified Deferred-Compensation Plan with Life Insurance

The employer can finance its obligation in a nonqualified plan through corporate-owned life insurance. This type of financing is attractive, since life insurance as a corporate asset is a good match for the type of liabilities created by nonqualified arrangements. The accumulation in an ordinary life insurance policy can be useful in the participant's retirement years in providing for any salary continuation benefits offered by the plan. The primary benefit of the life insurance financing is its ability to meet the employer's death benefit obligation should the participant die prematurely during the working years.

Nonqualified plan policies are owned by and payable to the employer. As such, they avoid the constructive-receipt or economic-benefit problems, because the general creditors have access to the funding policies. The premiums are nondeductible, but the cash surrender value builds up tax free, and the proceeds are nontaxable when received. The corporation receives a deduction when the benefits are actually paid to the participant, since the employee's benefit is taxable as income.

Key Person Life insurance

key person life insurance

The purpose of *key person life insurance* is to indemnify a business for the loss of earnings caused by the death of a key officer or employee. In many businesses, there is one person whose capital, technical knowledge, experience, or business connections make him or her a valuable asset of the organization and a necessity to its successful operation. This is more likely to be true of a small business. A manufacturing or mining enterprise may depend on one or several individuals whose engineering talents are vital to the business. An employee with unusual administrative ability or the ability to develop and motivate a sales organization may also be a key person. An educational institution or any organization that depends partly on charitable giving may regard a highly successful fund-raiser as a key person.

Elements of Key Person Valuation
• Profits directly attributable to person's efforts • Additional compensation necessary to replace the person • Recruiting and training costs to find or create a replacement

It is difficult to estimate the economic loss that the organization would suffer in the event of the key person's death. In most cases the loss is measured in terms of earnings, but occasionally it is based on the additional compensation that would have to be paid to replace the key employee. In some cases, the reduction in earnings is assumed to be temporary, while in other cases, a permanent impairment of earning power is envisioned.

The first step in handling this risk is to identify the key employees. Key employees have several characteristics that distinguish them from other employees:

- A key employee might have a specialized skill critical to the success of the business. Potential replacements may possess this skill, but may have to be recruited at higher salary levels.
- The employee has a large customer or client base and is responsible for attracting a significant amount of business.
- The key employee might be a source of capital if his or her loss would damage the closely held business's credit rating.

A business can purchase life insurance on the key employee to cover the risk of an income loss and/or increase in expenses resulting from the key employee's death. Ideally, some form of permanent insurance is purchased, and the accumulating cash values are reflected as an asset on the business's books. If key person protection is needed for only a temporary period or if the primary concern is the key employee's dollar value to the business, term insurance may be used. Decreasing term might be appropriate, because the loss to the business due to the key employee's death decreases as the insured approaches retirement and the business can expect to have his or her services for fewer years.

The business should be the owner and beneficiary of key employee life insurance. This should pose no insurable interest problems, since the business will suffer a financial loss at the death of the key employee. The premiums for key employee insurance will be nondeductible, while death benefits will be received income tax free.

Funding Buy-Sell Agreements with Life Insurance

The death of a businessowner has an immediate and drastic impact on a businessowner's heirs, the surviving businessowners, the business itself, and its employees. Without a well thought-out business continuation plan, all of these interested parties will face significant uncertainties and problems. Furthermore, they must face these uncertainties and problems without the guidance of the now deceased businessowner.

Buy-Sell Agreements for Partnerships. A general partnership terminates by operation of law at the death of a partner, unless the partnership agreement provides for continuation. Without planning, a deceased partner's interest in the partnership will have to be liquidated by the surviving partner(s). The surviving partners become responsible for paying the deceased's fair share of the business's value to his or her estate. Liquidation of a business almost invariably results in severe shrinkages of the business's assets. Accounts receivable yield only a fraction of their book value, inventory is disposed of at sacrifice prices, furniture and fixtures are sold as secondhand merchandise, and goodwill is lost completely. Liquidation deprives the surviving partners and employees of their means of livelihood, and family members of income.

Objectives of Buy-Sell Agreements

- Provide for transfer of deceased person's ownership interest
- Establish an agreed-upon method of valuing the interest
- Facilitate the continuation of the business despite the termination of the deceased person's participation and ownership
- Establish the desired method of financing the ownership-interest transfer(s)
- Provide an equitable method for terminating the interest of nonparticipating heirs

In the absence of a prior agreement among the partners, any attempt to avoid liquidation is beset with legal and practical complications. Even if the surviving partners can raise the cash to purchase the deceased's interest—an unrealistic assumption in most cases—they have to prove that the price paid for the interest is fair. It is seldom practical for the widow(er) or other heir to become a member of the reorganized partnership or to purchase the surviving partner's interests.

The goal of the surviving partners is to continue the business of the partnership without interruption. Certainly, they would like to keep liquidation payments to a minimum. Therefore, the surviving partners' goals conflict with those of the deceased partner's estate. Without a prearranged agreement, a dispute between the heirs and the surviving partners is nearly inevitable. The estate may be compelled to settle for far less than the fair market value of the business. If the surviving partners cannot make the required payments, the partnership may have to be sold or terminated—a result that generally benefits neither the heirs nor the surviving partners. The solution is a binding partnership buy-sell agreement.

Since there is more than one owner, the partnership buy-sell agreement must address the possibility that any of the partners will be the next to die. Therefore, the agreement contains mutual promises between the partners that provide for different purchasers and sellers depending on the circumstances. Each partner will bind his or her estate to sell if he or she dies. Each partner will agree to purchase the partnership interest held by the deceased partner's estate if he or she is among the surviving partners.

buy-sell agreement

In order to avoid this dilemma, members of a partnership can enter into a *buy-sell agreement*. Such an agreement binds the surviving partners to purchase the partnership interest of the first partner to die at a price set forth in the agreement and obligates the deceased partner's estate to sell his or her interest to the surviving partners. The various interests are valued at the time the agreement is drawn up, and revised from time to time thereafter. Each partner is insured for the amount of his or her interest, and either the partnership or the other partners own the insurance. Upon the first death among the partners, the life insurance proceeds are used by the partnership or the partners to purchase the deceased's interest. The business continues in operation for the benefit of the surviving partners, and the deceased's heirs receive the going value of his or her business interest in cash.

All parties benefit by the arrangement. After the first death, the surviving partners can enter into a new buy-sell agreement, or they can continue under the original agreement with the necessary valuation and insurance adjustments. Life insurance is uniquely suited to financing such agreements, since the very event that creates the need for cash also provides the cash.

Types of Partnership Buy-Sell Agreements. There are two basic approaches to arranging a buy-sell agreement—the entity approach and the cross purchase agreement.

entity plan

Entity Approach. Under the entity plan, the partnership is the purchaser in the buy-sell agreement. At the death of a partner, the partnership *liquidates* the interest held by the deceased partner's estate. Liquidation payments are divided into two components. The first component is a payment in exchange for the decedent's partnership interest. These payments are subject to capital-gain tax treatment. The remaining payments are ordinary income items that are taxable on the estate's income tax return, such as the deceased partner's share of partnership income and unrealized receivables. Under an entity buy-sell agreement both the partners and partnership are parties to the agreement providing for continuation of the partnership's business by the survivors.

cross-purchase agreement

Cross-Purchase Agreement. The *cross-purchase agreement* provides that the surviving partners are obligated to buy a prearranged share of a deceased partner's interest from his or her estate. The agreement is generally funded by life insurance policies owned by the individual partners. Each partner should purchase life insurance policies on the life of the other partners whose deaths will obligate the policyowner to purchase the decedent's partnership interest. Thus, the individual partners become owners, beneficiaries, and premium payers for life insurance policies covering the lives of the other partners. At the death of a partner, the surviving partners receive the death proceeds from the policies, which will be transferred to the deceased partner's estate in exchange for the partnership interest. Each partner should secure a policy with a death benefit equal to his or her share of the purchase price of a deceased partner's interest.

Although the surviving partners purchase the interest from a deceased partner's estate, the tax treatment of the purchase and sale is similar to the entity approach. Some portion of the purchase price will be treated as the exchange of a capital asset—the partnership interest. The remaining portion of the purchase payments will be treated as distributions of income to the deceased partner's estate.

The choice between the entity or cross-purchase approach is a complex one. Details such as the number of partners, the differences in income tax treatment, the cost basis of the different partners, and the financial considerations of the partnership will dictate the appropriate choice.

Generally, the partnership should adopt the entity approach if it is in a better financial position to make the premium payments than the individual partners. This will be true if some partners are younger and/or own smaller partnership interests. The partnership ownership of life insurance creates a pooling approach to fund the buy-sell agreement. The business might also adopt the entity approach, if there are a large number of partners entering into the agreement. Fewer individual life insurance policies are usually required if the partnership has more than two partners.

Corporate Buy-Sell Agreements. The same type of agreement is desirable for the stockholders in a closely held corporation. Although the death of a stockholder does not legally dissolve the corporation, the same practical difficulties may be encountered in any attempt to continue the business. These difficulties arise because stockholders of a closely held corporation are also its officers, earnings are distributed primarily in the form of salaries, and no ready market exists for the stock.

Upon the death of a principal stockholder in a closely held corporation, the surviving stockholders are faced with three choices (apart from liquidation), all of which may prove undesirable. They may

1. accept the widow(er) or other adult heir of the deceased into the active management of the corporation;
2. pay dividends, approximately equivalent to the salary of the deceased stockholder, to the widow(er) or other heir without any participation in management on the heir's part; or
3. admit outside interests to whom the deceased's stock have been sold into active management of the company.

The surviving spouse and/or heirs face the possibility of having to dispose of the deceased's stock at a sacrifice price, either to the surviving stockholders or to outsiders, neither of whom would normally be inclined to offer a fair price, or retain the stock and receive no dividends. These difficulties can be avoided through a binding buy-sell agreement financed by life insurance. Under such an agreement, the surviving stockholders will get the corporation's stock, and the widow(er) will receive cash for the business interest.

A corporation is a separate legal entity apart from its shareholders. As such, it provides limited liability to its investors and is a separate taxpayer with entirely different tax rates and rules than those applicable to individual taxpayers. Although the corporation as a separate entity has, potentially, a perpetual life, the continuation problems that plague other forms of closely held enterprises also apply to closely held corporations. From a practical standpoint, a closely held business, regardless of its form, cannot continue without the services of at least one key individual. In a closely held corporation, the key individuals usually include the shareholders. The death, retirement, or disability of these key individuals threatens the future of the corporation. For this reason, the closely held corporation and its shareholders should consider adopting a buy-sell agreement.

Types of Corporate Buy-Sell Agreements. In corporate buy-sell agreements, an entity plan can also be established as a stock redemption plan. The cross purchase arrangement is also available, as in partnerships.

Entity Buy-Sell Agreement (Stock Redemption). Under a *stock-redemption agreement,* a corporation is the "purchaser" of the stock at the death of a shareholder. Each shareholder subject to the agreement binds his or her estate to transfer the stock to the corporation in exchange for the required purchase price. The corporation redeems a deceased shareholder's stock in exchange for cash, and either retires the stock or holds it as treasury stock. This reduces the number of shares of stock outstanding in the corporation. From the surviving shareholder's standpoint, the percentage ownership held by each surviving shareholder increases proportionately when a deceased shareholder's stock is redeemed.

The tax treatment of a stock redemption can be extremely complex. A stock redemption is treated as a distribution of cash or property from the corporation to a shareholder. The redemption distribution may be treated as a taxable dividend to the redeemed shareholder, or as a sale or exchange subject to capital gains. It is essential to qualify the stock redemption as a sale or exchange to avoid disastrous tax consequences to the redeemed shareholder's estate.

Another tax problem associated with the stock-redemption agreement is the loss of income tax cost basis for the surviving shareholders. Since the corporation is the purchaser in the stock-redemption agreement, the surviving shareholders will not be treated as contributors to the purchase. Thus the surviving shareholders will not receive an increase in their income tax basis in their stock, as they do in the cross-purchase agreement, since the corporation, not the shareholders, provides the purchase price.

If life insurance is chosen as the funding mechanism, the corporation should be the applicant, owner, and beneficiary of the policies. Ownership of the policies is particularly important for a corporation that does not have an abundance of retained earnings. Under most state corporate laws, a corporation cannot make a distribution of any kind to a shareholder, including a stock redemption, unless the corporation has adequate surplus. The receipt of life insurance proceeds at a shareholder's death provides the necessary surplus to redeem the deceased shareholder's stock. The corporation should acquire life insurance on the life of each shareholder who becomes a party to the agreement. To ensure that the death proceeds will be adequate to meet the corporation's obligation, the agreement should be updated periodically to prevent the life insurance coverage from becoming inadequate as the value of the corporation rises.

Corporate Cross-Purchase Buy-Sell Agreements. The corporate cross-purchase agreement is similar to the partnership cross-purchase agreement discussed earlier. Each shareholder agrees to purchase a specified percentage of the shares of stock held by a deceased shareholder at the time of death, and to bind his or her estate to sell the stock owned at his or her death. The corporation is not a direct party to the buy-sell agreement. The corporation should, however, issue stock certificates endorsed with a statement that the stock is subject to the terms of the buy-sell agreement.

If few shareholders are involved, the cross-purchase agreement is advantageous from a tax standpoint in two respects. First, the sale of stock by a deceased shareholder's estate will always be treated as a sale or exchange. Thus, the estate gets favorable capital-gains tax treatment. This makes the cross-purchase agreement the preferable form of buy-sell agreement for a family corporation where a stock redemption would often result in taxable dividends to the estate. Second, the surviving shareholders are direct purchasers, and each receives an income tax cost basis in his or her stock equal to the amount of the purchase price paid.

If life insurance is used to fund the agreement, each shareholder should purchase adequate life insurance on the life of the other shareholders. Each individual shareholder then becomes owner, premium payer, and beneficiary for the life insurance policies covering the lives of the other shareholders. At a shareholder's death, the surviving shareholders will receive the death benefits from the policies and will transfer the death benefit proceeds to the deceased shareholder's estate in exchange for the appropriate amount of his or her stock. Since individual shareholders must be relied upon to maintain the funding for agreement, there is often the concern that some parties will not live up to the terms of the contract. To ensure that the cross-purchase agreement is carried out, a trustee is often used to hold the policies and oversee the purchase and sale of stock at a shareholder's death.

Sole Proprietorship Continuation Agreement. The sole proprietorship is by far the most common form of business ownership. It is distinct from other forms of business ownership in that there is no legal distinction between the business and personal assets of the owner. Only one individual can be the owner of a sole proprietorship. As such, when the sole proprietor dies or loses legal capacity to transact business, the sole proprietorship must terminate. Planning for this possibility is essential if the sole proprietor's family can expect to get full value for the business interest. The buy-sell agreement will bind the proprietor's estate to sell and the purchaser to buy the proprietorship assets.

Choosing a Purchaser. A critical step for a proprietorship buy-sell agreement is to find the appropriate purchaser. A natural successor to the sole proprietor may not exist. There are no co-owners of the sole proprietorship waiting to take over, and the sole proprietor may have no family successors who are able and/or willing to step in at the sole proprietor's death. Choosing the appropriate buyer requires careful planning.

Often a key employee or group will be selected as purchaser. Such individuals, if available, are logical choices for two reasons:

- First, the key employee or employees of the sole proprietorship are familiar with the business interest. This is particularly important if the business requires unique skills to perform its function.
- Second, the key employees may be willing to enter into a buy-sell agreement to protect their own future employment. Without a buy-sell agreement, the sole proprietorship will often be liquidated or sold to outsiders at the death of the proprietor. This could leave the key employees unemployed and without a future in the proprietorship.

If there are no key employees or natural successors to the sole proprietor, a careful search will have to be made. The sole proprietor can hire and train an employee who has the potential to take over the business. Alternatively, the sole proprietor could seek a buyer from competitors who may desire to take over the proprietor's business. This is particularly appropriate for a professional practitioner who has developed substantial goodwill and a large patient/client list. The death of the sole practitioner will result in the loss of that goodwill unless a purchaser can be found for a buy-sell agreement.

Life Insurance Funding. The life insurance arrangements for a sole proprietorship buy-sell agreement are relatively simple. The purchasing party is obligated to provide the purchase price from the life insurance proceeds to the deceased proprietor's estate. The applicant, owner, and premium payer for such life insurance should be the purchasing party. The purchaser should obtain sufficient coverage on the life of the sole proprietorship to make the required payments to the estate. Insurable interest exists for such a policy, because the purchaser has a financial obligation created by the buy-sell agreement. The insurance funding the agreement should be reviewed periodically, and the purchaser should obtain additional coverage necessitated by an increase in the value of the proprietorship.

Benefits of the Buy-Sell Agreement. Although contemplating death is not pleasant for anyone, proper estate planning employing a buy-sell agreement offers several advantages. The benefits of such an agreement are as follows:

- It guarantees a market for the business interest.
- It provides liquidity for the payment of death taxes and other estate settlement costs.
- It helps establish the estate tax value of the decedent's business interest, making the estate planning process more reliable for the owner.
- It provides that the business will continue in the hands of the surviving owners and/or employees.
- It makes the business a better credit risk, as the probability of its continuation is enhanced.

Chapter Two Review

Key terms and concepts are explained in the glossary. Answers to the review questions and the self-test questions are found in the back of the book in the Answers to Questions section.

Key Terms and Concepts

multiple-of-income approach
human life value approach
present value
present value of $1 per annum
financial needs analysis approach
capital distribution method
capital conservation method
group term life insurance
executive bonus life insurance plan Sec. 162
split-dollar life insurance
endorsement method
collateral assignment method
nonqualified deferred-compensation
qualified retirement plans
key person life insurance
buy-sell agreement
entity plan
cross-purchase agreement

Review Questions

1. Explain the multiple-of-income approach to life insurance planning and its shortcomings as a planning method. [1]
2. Explain the process of providing for the post-death financial survivors' needs using financial-need analysis and capital-needs analysis. [1]
3. Explain the five-step process for estimating a person's economic value for purposes of the human value approach. [2]
4. Explain group life insurance and Sec. 79 rules. [4]
5. Explain the executive bonus life insurance plan (Sec. 162) and its advantages. [4]
6. Explain split-dollar life insurance, its purpose, the main types of arrangements, and how it is taxed. [5]
7. Explain deferred-compensation plans and how life insurance is used in these plans. [6]
8. Explain how life insurance can be used in qualified retirement plans. [6]
9. Explain the need for key person life insurance and how this insurance plan works. [7]
10. Explain the general needs for a buy-sell agreement, and the types of buy-sell plans that can be used for business continuation. [8]

Self-Test Questions

1. The human life value approach is based on

   (A) the capitalized present value of an individual's potential lifetime earnings
   (B) the amount of life insurance an individual owns
   (C) the standard of living an individual wishes to have
   (D) an individual's eligibility for Social Security income

2. Which of the following statements concerning executive bonus life insurance plans (Sec. 162) is correct?

   (A) The plans must comply with the nondiscrimination rules of ERISA.
   (B) The participating employee is the owner of the policy covering his or her life.
   (C) The employer's contributions to the plan are tax free to the participating employee.
   (D) The employer's contributions are nondeductible, because the death proceeds are received tax free.

3. Which of the following statements concerning key employee life insurance is correct?

   (A) The key employee should name the beneficiary.
   (B) The premiums paid by the employer are taxable income to the employee.
   (C) The proceeds of the key employee policy are included in the estate of the key employee.
   (D) The business should be the owner and beneficiary of the key employee life insurance.

4. Three partners have an equal one-third interest in a partnership valued at $900,000. If a cross-purchase type of buy-sell agreement is selected, how much coverage should each partner have on the life of the other partners?

   (A) $100,000
   (B) $150,000
   (C) $300,000
   (D) $450,000

5. The taxable amounts of coverage for group term life insurance are taxed according to:

   (A) PS 58 rates
   (B) Table 2001 rates
   (C) Table 1 rates
   (D) Sec. 162 rates

6. When planning for post-death income needs, the liquidating approach, using both principal and interest from life insurance proceeds, is known as the:

   (A) financial needs analysis approach
   (B) capital needs analysis approach
   (C) human life value approach
   (D) capital conservation approach

7. Which of the following statements regarding the needs analysis approach to insurance planning is (are) correct?

   I. A client's needs must be translated into estimated costs.
   II. A deficit between a client's goals and needs, and his or her current financial resources indicates a need for life insurance.

   (A) I only
   (B) II only
   (C) Both I and II
   (D) Neither I nor II

8. Which of the following statements concerning the capital-needs analysis approach to calculating the insurance needs of a family's income earner is (are) correct?

   I. Divide the income amount by the applicable interest rate representing the after-tax investment return anticipated on the capital sum.
   II. The lower the after-tax investment return rate, the higher the capital fund needed to provide the same amount of income.

   (A) I only
   (B) II only
   (C) Both I and II
   (D) Neither I nor II

READ THE FOLLOWING DIRECTIONS BEFORE CONTINUING

The questions below differ from the preceding questions in that they all contain the word EXCEPT. So you understand fully the basis used in selecting each answer, be sure to read each question carefully.

---

9. All of the following statements are true concerning deferred-compensation plans EXCEPT

   (A) Part of the employee's compensation over the employee's service-providing years is deferred until a later period.
   (B) Discrimination in favor of shareholder-employees and key executives is not permitted in nonqualified arrangements.
   (C) Deferred-compensation plans can be categorized as either qualified or nonqualified.
   (D) Qualified plans include pension plans, IRAs, profit-sharing plans, and Sec. 403(b) plans.

10. All of the following statements concerning qualified retirement plans are true EXCEPT

   (A) A qualified plan must generally purchase life insurance in order to provide any substantial preretirement death benefit.
   (B) An insured preretirement death benefit can be provided in either a defined-benefit or defined-contribution plan.
   (C) An employer contribution may pay life insurance premiums if the amount qualifies under the tests for incidental benefits.
   (D) The IRS considers nonretirement benefits in a qualified plan incidental if the cost of these benefits is less than 50 percent of the cost of providing all the benefits under the plan.

TERM LIFE INSURANCE 3

Learning Objectives

An understanding of the material in this chapter should enable you to

1. Describe the nature and features of term life insurance.
2. Describe why the period for renewability for term insurance is limited.
3. Explain the renewability and conversion provisions.
4. Compare term insurance variations and their usefulness.
5. Discuss methods for marketing to, prospecting for, and approaching life insurance prospects.

This chapter reviews the features of the life insurance policy and contract, focusing on term insurance. It then introduces a few of the main variations of these basic policy designs. The chapter concludes with a discussion of marketing to, prospecting for, and approaching prospects regarding life insurance products.

Who Are Today's Life Insurance Buyers?

Although the "average" individual life insurance buyer may not change much from year to year, there are many factors that affect who buys, what they buy, and how much they buy. These factors include the buyer's stage of life, gender and age, and product introductions, such as return-of-premium term, secondary-guarantee universal life, and life settlements. The following is a brief summary of demographic trends in life insurance purchases.

Americans purchased $3 trillion of new life insurance in 2012, 1 percent less than in 2011. By the end of 2012, total life insurance coverage (individual, group and credit) in the United States was $19.3 trillion, a decrease of 0.5 percent from 2011. Individual life insurance protection totaled $11.2 trillion at the end of 2012, growing at an average annual rate of 2 percent over the last 10 years. The average size of a new individual life policy decreased since its peak in 2008 to $163,000 in 2012. The number of newly issued life policies purchased increased 0.5 percent in 2012 (American Council of Life Insurers 2013 Fact Book).

The good news is that individual life insurance sales increased 2 percent in 2013 with the improving economic recovery. Universal life sales have remained flat since increasing 20 percent in 2010, and whole life increased 4 percent since 2010. Whole life annualized premium now represent 31 percent, its largest share of the market since 1998. Variable universal life sales still lag as confidence in the stock market is still shaky. Term insurance sales were off 3 percent in 2012, resulting from increased rates and some products being taken off the market. Indexed Universal Life sales grew at a faster rate than other types of insurance in 2012. (ACLI's 2013 Life Insurer's Fact Book).

Male/Female Buyers

The following information was taken from a LIMRA International Study released in January of 2007 based on studies of life insurance sales in the United States in 2005. (2007, LIMRA International Inc., Individual Life Buyers in the United States. Sales data updated where available.)

Men purchase the majority of individual life sold in any given year. In 2005, males purchased 54 percent of the life insurance policies sold to adults (this number has not changed significantly since 2003). Men also purchased larger individual life insurance policies than women. Both genders increased their average policy size by approximately 25 percent, but the coverage amount for women is still 40 percent lower than the average coverage for men. Women are catching up, though. With the exception of buyers over age 64, coverage amounts for younger adult women are consistency closer to the amounts purchased by younger men.

On average, both male and female buyers of all ages purchased larger policies in 2005 than buyers did in 2003. This is especially true for the older buyers who tend to have more cash and are more likely to purchase larger universal life (UL) policies with guarantees. The emerging life settlement market may also have an impact.

Senior Buyers

Seniors have generated a lot of marketing interest over the last few years with regard to the life settlement market and guaranteed death benefit UL products that target this age group. While it is too soon to see the impact of life settlements on buyer demographics, changes have been seen in the senior market:

- While seniors purchased only 11 percent of the total individual life insurance policies sold in 2005, more than 20 percent of the policyholders who purchased UL policies were 55 or older (up from 12 percent in 2003). These older buyers accounted for two-thirds of the single premium UL policies sold in 2005. Policyholders likely have additional cash available to them at this age, as they often have higher incomes, less debt, and are generally not raising children.
- Seniors, a group inclined to reduce financial risks, are also more likely to purchase universal products with long-term secondary guarantees—hot products since they were introduced. Death benefit guarantee products represent over half of new UL premium in 2008 and 2009. In fact, over one-third of those who bought guaranteed UL products were over the age of 54, compared to less than 20 percent who bought other types of UL products.
- About one-third of policies bought by consumers aged 65 or over and one-quarter of sales in the 55 to 64 market were whole life (WL) policies. These WL policies tend to be significantly smaller than the UL policies seniors buy. In fact, more than half of older adults who purchased WL policies had an average policy size of $10,000 or less (likely final expense coverage).
- Seniors represent only 7 percent of the total number of recurring premium WL policies sold. When looking at buyers over the age of 17, however, 18 percent of WL policies were purchased at age 55 or older. Still, seniors dominate single premium WL sales, representing half of single premium buyers and 71 percent of premium.

Term Insurance Buyers

Term is most popular among buyers between the ages of 25 and 54. The majority of young adult buyers purchase some form of term coverage, because it is very affordable for the youngest adults who generally have less disposable income. The cost goes up with age and buyers have increasing demands on their cash flow, thus making term insurance more attractive. Term's share of policies purchased increases with age until buyers reach 44. After that, its market share starts to drop as older age groups tend to concentrate more on permanent insurance.

Return-of-premium (ROP) term products have likely played a part in these trends. Of the companies able to provide their ROP sales data, just over 60 percent of ROP sales were sold with a 30-year premium payment period, and more than one-third were sold with either a 15- or 20-year payment period.

Universal Life Insurance Buyers

The recent decrease in policy size reverses a long trend. The average size UL policies purchased by adult males and females in 2012 were significantly larger than in 2009 (32 percent larger), and continued to increase slightly in 2012, not a victim of the economic recession. Increases in recent years may be explained by the influx of UL products designed to provide long-term death-benefit guarantees and high early-cash accumulation.

Sales of death-benefit-guarantee UL products is likely higher because these buyers tend to be older and more affluent, and purchase the policies for estate planning purposes. Those purchasing cash accumulation products may provide lower coverage amounts as policyholders put more money toward excess premium and not toward death benefit.

Large Policies: Fewer Sales and Larger Premiums

Policy size decreased in 2009, but face amounts have generally been on the increase. Although only 6 percent of the policies purchased in 2005 provided the buyer with $1 million or more of coverage, because of their size, these policies accounted for almost half of new premiums.

The majority of buyers in this market purchased term insurance. The low cost of term allows policyholders to purchase larger policies which they might not be able to afford otherwise. One-third of the people who purchased at least $5,000,000 of coverage in 2005 did so by buying UL products. While half of the buyers in this highest face-amount range purchased term insurance, UL represented over 70 percent of new annualized premium corresponding to these jumbo policies.

Because of the higher premiums associated with large policies, buyers in this market tend to be older than buyers in general. Insureds age 45 or older account for more than half of the policies with a face amount of $5 million or more. Also, most people purchase life insurance for income replacement and income usually increases with age, which means older buyers have larger coverage needs. These buyers are also more likely to be male as men still represent a larger proportion of the high-income population, although these gaps are closing.

The Future

Life settlements will continue to impact buyer demographics in the future. Through the efforts of companies and state regulation underway, however, the impact will likely lessen. According to a recent LIMRA survey, three-quarters of participating companies have either discouraged or prohibited their agents from engaging in life settlement transactions.

The gap between the average size policy issued to males and females may continue to close, as it has been doing over the last few decades. The U.S. Department of Labor estimates that women will account for 51 percent of the increase in the labor force between 2004 and 2014. The gap between male and female salaries is also slowly closing; hence, women will need greater coverage amounts for income purposes and will be able to afford them.

Table 3-1 LIMRA Estimates of U.S. Individual Life Annualized New Premium* Market Share by Product

	Universal Life	Variable Life	Variable Universal	Term	Whole Life
1980	–	–	–	18%	82%
1981	2%	1%	–	19	78
1982	9	2	–	18	71
1983	18	2	–	15	65
1984	30	3	–	12	55
1985	38	3	1%	11	47
1986	35	3	3	12	47
1987	27	3	7	12	51
1988	26	1	7	13	53
1989	27	1	6	13	53
1990	26	1	6	13	54
1991	26	1	5	13	55
1992	24	2	7	13	54
1993	22	3	10	13	52
1994	22	3	13	14	48
1995	24	3	12	15	46

	Universal Life	Variable Life	Variable Universal	Term	Whole Life
1996	22	3	17	17	41
1997	21	3	20	18	38
1998	20	3	25	19	33
1999	19	3	28	21	29
2000	18	3	33	23	23
2001	22	2	30	21	25
2002	27	1	23	22	27
2003	34	1	16	24	25
2004	37	1	15	23	24
2005	39	+	14	23	24
2006	41	+	15	22	22
2007	42	+	14	22	22
2008	41	+	12	24	23
2009	39	+	7	27	28
2010	40	+	6	24	30
2011	39	+	8	22	31
2012	41	+	6	21	32

Source: LIMRA estimates. 2013, LIMRA International, Inc. U.S. Individual Life Insurance Sales Trends, 1975–2012, Product Research, Ashley Durham.

– Not applicable; + Less than one-half of a percent

*Annualized premium excludes excess (dump-in) premiums on universal and variable UL plans; includes 10% of single premium and excludes large-case corporate-owned life insurance.

** Preliminary estimates. Data for previous years have been revised.

Term Insurance

There are several basic types of life insurance contracts: term, WL, UL, and endowment. The role of these contracts is to create a principal sum or estate, either through the death of the insured or through the accumulation of funds set aside for investment purposes. The primary purpose of life insurance, regardless of the type, is to protect a family's financial future. Should the insured die, life insurance can help pay off mortgages, fund college educations, take care of final expenses, offset the loss of the insured's income and allow the family to continue its standard of living. In most cases, insurance proceeds pass to beneficiaries free of probate costs, legal fees, state inheritance taxes, and federal income tax. To the extent permitted by state law, insurance benefits are protected from claims of the insured's creditors. Benefits are generally paid promptly to beneficiaries through a convenient, interest bearing, no fee checking account, or through a prearranged settlement option that provides periodic payments until the proceeds are paid in full.

Nature of Term Insurance

The trend in product development has been for companies to offer more substantial premium guarantees. Initially, 5- and 10-year level premium periods were an alternative to the traditional yearly renewable term structures (which are still offered by about a third of companies). The popularity of these plans with producers and consumers has led to longer level premium guarantees. Today, almost all companies offer both 10- and 20-year plans, while more than three-quarters also offer a product with a 30-year level premium guarantee. The 20-year contracts are the most popular.

Return-of-premium (ROP) designs have become popular. A growing number of carriers market a ROP term product that allows for a full refund of premium paid if the policy reaches the end of the level term period without lapse or the payment of a death benefit. Most plans will also return a prorated portion of premium if the policy lapses after year 5. This concept is also seen in permanent products, especially ULs, due to their popularity in the term market.

Term Insurance Characteristics

The two principal characteristics of term insurance are (1) the insured must die for any benefits to be paid; and (2) by definition, the contract expires at the end of the term. A term life insurance policy promises to pay a death benefit to a beneficiary only if the insured dies during the specified term.

Term insurance is the best solution for many situations, but not for others. It is pure death protection with little or no lifetime benefits. As with all insurance products, we must ask the following questions:

1. Will death protection alone meet the need?
2. Will the coverage last as long as the need?
3. Will the policyowner be able to afford the premium?

These questions help us focus our analysis on selecting the appropriate coverage—the product must match the need.

All life insurance policies have at least two costs, costs for mortality and costs for expenses. With term insurance, you pay only mortality and expense charges, nothing else. One-year term insurance is the best example of this concept. The actual life insurance amount a company has to pay for any type of life insurance is the net amount at risk. In this sense, all insurance is term insurance, because all life insurance includes the cost of term insurance by applying the mortality charge to the net amount at risk. The difference between policies is really more a matter of how one will pay for the life insurance over time. With term insurance, the policy itself and the net amount at risk are virtually synonymous.

Initial premium rates per $1,000 of coverage are lower for term insurance than for other life products issued on the same basis, since the period of protection is limited. Premiums for term coverage, however, can escalate rapidly as the duration of the policy lengthens.

Figure 3-1
One-Year Level Term

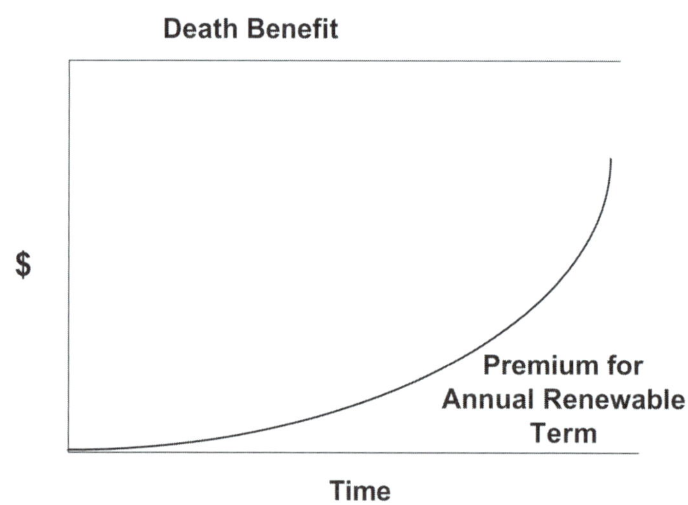

Many insurers and buyers treat term insurance as a commodity, an item that is essentially the same irrespective of the supplier and is therefore sought at the lowest price. As commodity profit levels are ordinarily low, many insurers' attempt product differentiation strategies and innovations. Term insurance buyers are generally a price-sensitive group, and consider term policies easily replaceable, since few penalties usually result from early termination. Consequently, term lapse rates are higher than lapse rates for other types of policies. Most recent experience indicates that term lapse rates have declined from the 15 percent to 20 percent range in the early policy years to a more level pattern of about 10 percent per year, perhaps because of the trend towards longer-term durations.

evidence of insurability

Such policies may insure for the agreed term only, or they may give the insured the option of renewing the protection for successive terms without evidence of insurability. *Evidence of insurability* is the basic purpose of underwriting, or evaluating the insurance risk by the insurer. When underwriting a proposed insured, the insurer asks for documentation and other information regarding the physical condition and other attributes of the insurance applicant. This information is then evaluated to determine the acceptability of the applicant and to what rating class he or she will be assigned. Applications for term insurance are carefully underwritten; restrictions may be imposed on the amount of insurance, the age before which it must be obtained, and the age beyond which it cannot be renewed.

Term insurance is generally regarded as temporary insurance and is more comparable to property and casualty insurance contracts than to cash value life insurance contracts. If a person insures his or her life under a 5-year term contract, no obligation is incurred by the insurance company, unless the death of the insured occurs within the term. The typical pattern of premiums is for the rate to increase for each $1,000 of insurance at each renewal. All premiums paid for the term protection are fully earned by the company by the end of the term, whether or not a loss has occurred, and the policy has no further value. This is similar to auto and homeowners insurance.

adverse selection

The premium for term insurance is initially relatively low, despite the fact that it contains a relatively high expense loading and an allowance for adverse selection. *Adverse selection* is the general tendency in insurance for selection against the company; that is, for the law of large numbers to be inoperative, because those who know they are vulnerable to specific risks are most likely to acquire and retain insurance to cover related losses. Adverse selection produces poorer loss experience among those who are insured than those who are not insured. The insurer must make every effort to prevent adverse selection in its underwriting and pricing by selecting a large, safely diversified, profitable group of applicants. However, adverse selection also occurs in term insurance when premiums increase as members age, prompting healthy members to withdraw from the plan and seek better rates. This produces an abnormal increase in mortality rates for those less healthy and less insurable members who remain in the group. Term insurers must account for this tendency in their renewal pricing as insured groups age.

The reason term premiums can be low is that most term contracts do not cover the period of old age when death is most likely to occur and when the cost of insurance is high. In other words, a term policy, because its term may end prior to the insured's death, insures against a contingency, and not a certainty, as permanent insurance policies do. Term is priced to expire before the majority of insured individuals, so a death claim will probably not occur. If permanent remains in force, it will pay the death claim eventually.

When insurance companies put term insurance in force, they must estimate expenses and the number of people who are going to die (mortality) while covered. Actual results will inevitably differ from these estimates. An insurance company can price aggressively by assuming mortality rates as closely to probability estimates as possible, and charging as little as possible for expenses. To protect themselves, the insurer will specify in the contract that they reserve the right to raise rates in the future if projected premiums are less than the mortality and expense costs actually incurred. Conservative estimates used to be the norm, but today the norm is to charge aggressively and reserve the right to increase rates in the future, if necessary. You will see this in illustrations and policies by the difference between current rates and maximum guaranteed rates that may be charged, and in how long current rates are guaranteed.

Limiting Renewability

If the surviving members of the insured group should continue to renew their insurance year after year, the steadily increasing premiums would cause many to question continuing the insurance. After a point, there would be a tendency for the healthy individuals to give up their protection, while those in poor health would continue to renew their policies, regardless of cost. This is an example of the adverse selection problem as discussed above.

The withdrawal of the healthy members would accelerate the increase in the death rate among the continuing members and, unless ample margins were provided in the insurance company's premium rates, could produce death claims in excess of premium income. In this event, the loss would be sustained by the company, because the rates are guaranteed for the entire period of renewability. For this reason, companies offering term insurance on an individual basis place a limit on the renewal period.

Even without restrictions on the renewal period, term insurance is not usually feasible for long-term protection. Increasing premiums cause many policyowners to discontinue their insurance at a time when, due to physical condition or other circumstances, they cannot obtain other insurance easily or cheaply. They are likely to resent that after years of premium payments at increasing rates, the insurance protection is lost, with no tangible benefits for the sacrifice involved.

Few individuals are able and willing to continue their insurance to advanced ages when death is most likely to occur. Yet the great majority of individuals need insurance that can be continued until death, at whatever age. This need led to the development of level premium insurance. Yet, the renewal premium may increase substantially at the end of the level term period, leaving the policyowner with the difficult option of renewing at a high premium, or dropping the coverage when it may still be needed.

Many term insurance contracts contain an option to renew for a limited number of additional periods, usually of the same length. The simplest policy of this type is the yearly renewable term (YRT) policy, which is a one-year term contract renewable for successive periods of one year each. Longer-term contracts, such as 5- and 10-year term, are also usually renewable.

Renewable Term Characteristics
• Coverage for a stated period • Premium based on age at beginning of each new period • Premiums increase with age • Rate of premium increases accelerates after age 40 • Can be renewed for a new period without evidence of insurability (up to limiting age specified in policy) • Additional charges for adverse selection included in premium at advanced ages • Does not provide living benefits such as cash values, policy loans, and so on

Renewal Privilege. The following is a typical renewal privilege as it might appear in an insurance contract:

> The insured may renew this policy for further periods of 10 years each without medical examination, provided there has been no lapse in the payment of premiums, by written notice to the company

at its home office before the expiration of any period of the insurance hereunder and by the payment in each year, on the dates above specified, of the premium for the age attained by the insured at the beginning of any such renewal period in accordance with the table of rates contained herein.

renewability

The key to *renewability* is the right to renew the contract without a medical examination or other *evidence of insurability*. This means the policyowner can renew the policy without submitting to a medical examination or providing other evidence of good health, but simply by paying the renewal premium. Where the term policy contains no renewal privilege, or where it can be renewed only upon evidence of insurability satisfactory to the company, the insured may find that coverage cannot be continued as long as needed. Because of poor health, a hazardous occupation, a dangerous hobby, or some other reason, the insured might be unable to renew the contract or to obtain any other form of life insurance protection. The renewal feature prevents this situation. Its chief function is to protect the insurability of the insured.

Under a term insurance contract, the premium increases with each renewal, based on the attained age of the insured at the time of the renewal. The term insurance premium for a person aged 50 or above, for example, may be higher than the premium for a WL contract acquired before age 35. Within the contract period, however, the premium is level. Over a long period, with several renewals, the premium will consist of a series of level premiums, each series higher than the previous one. The rate will normally continue to increase with each renewal. The scale of renewal rates is published in the original contract and cannot be changed by the company as long as the contract remains in force. Companies protect themselves by having a guaranteed renewal rate, as well as the scheduled current renewal rate. The guaranteed renewal rate is higher than the scheduled rate in case experience goes against the company and future experience develops differently than anticipated.

Renewability Features

- Can renew without medical evaluation or other review
- Premiums change upon renewal
- Some insurers prohibit renewals beyond a specified age

Insurers have mixed feelings about renewable term insurance. There is no question that if properly used, it fills a real need. However, it presents certain problems for the company that writes it. Whether the policy is a YRT or a longer-term contract, there is likely to be strong selection against the company at time of renewal, and this adverse selection will become greater as the age of the insured, and hence, the renewal premium, increases. Because of this, term policies will place to a maximum age beyond which renewal is not permitted.

Convertibility

convertibility

In addition to the renewable privilege, a term policy may contain a *convertibility* provision that permits the policyowner to exchange the term contract for a permanent insurance plan, without evidence of insurability. A term insurance policy may be both renewable and convertible. These features add to the cost of the policy.

The convertible feature serves the needs of those who want permanent insurance, but are temporarily unable to afford the higher premiums required for whole life and other types of cash value life insurance. Convertibility is also useful when the policyowner desires to postpone the final decision as to the type of permanent insurance to be purchased until a later date when, for whatever reason, it may be possible to make a wiser choice. Thus, convertible term insurance provides a way to obtain temporary insurance and an option on permanent insurance in the same policy.

Insurability is protected by the conversion feature in an even more valuable manner than under the renewable feature, because convertibility guarantees access to permanent insurance—not just continuation of temporary protection. The two features together afford complete protection against loss of insurability.

attained age

Attained Age Conversion. The conversion option may be effective as of the date of the conversion or as of the original date of the term policy. If the term policy is converted as of the current date, it is referred to as the *attained age* method since the current age determines the premium level. This is by far the most common type of term conversion exercised.

retroactive conversion (original age)

Retroactive Conversion. A conversion using the original date of the term policy for the conversion is referred to as the *original age* method or a *retroactive conversion.* Some insurers allow a policy to be converted retroactively within the first few years after issue. When the conversion is effective as of the original date, the premium rate for the permanent contract is that which would have been charged had the new contract been taken out originally, and the policy form is that which would have been issued originally. The advantage of the lower premium is obvious, but in many cases, the contract being issued at the original date contains actuarial assumptions, policy language or other features more favorable than those found in current policies.

Offsetting these advantages, however, is the fact that a financial adjustment—a payment by the policyowner to the company—is required, which may be quite substantial if the term policy has been in force for several years. Most companies specify that the payment will be the larger of

1. the difference in the reserves under the policies being exchanged (some companies specify the cash surrender value), or
2. the difference between the premiums paid on the term policy and those that would have been paid on the permanent plan, with interest on the difference at a stipulated rate.

Under the second type of premium adjustment, an allowance is frequently made for any dividends that would have been payable under the permanent policy. Some companies require a payment equal to the difference in reserves, plus a charge of up to 8 percent to provide the previously forgone investment return. The purpose of the financial adjustment is to place the insurance company in the same financial position it would have been in had the permanent contract been issued in the first place.

The insured will pay a smaller premium, but by making up the deficiency in the term premium, will pay it over a longer period. Actuarially, the two sets of premiums are equivalent. The policyowner pays the company the interest it would have earned had the larger premium been paid from the beginning.

The insured should consider many factors in making a choice between the two types of conversion, one of the most important being the state of his or her health. The insured would not want to convert retroactively—and pay a substantial sum of money to the insurance company—if he or she is in poor health. The sum the insured pays immediately becomes a part of the reserve under the contract and will not increase the amount of death benefits. The payment will simply reduce the effective amount of insurance.

In most cases, if the insured has surplus funds to invest in insurance, he or she should consider purchasing additional insurance or prepaying premiums on existing policies, including a newly converted one. Subject to certain limitations, most companies permit the insured to prepay fixed premiums, either in the form of premium deposits or through discounting of future premiums. The two procedures are very similar. The principal difference is that under the discount method, credit is taken in advance for the interest to be earned on the deposited funds. Under both arrangements, the funds deposited with the company are credited with interest at a guaranteed rate, but they may be credited with the current interest rate, a rate in excess of the guaranteed rate. In the event of the insured's death, the balance of any such deposits is returned to the insured's estate or beneficiaries in addition to the death benefit of the policy. Some companies permit withdrawal of premium deposits at any time, in which case a lower rate of interest may be credited, while others limit withdrawals to anniversary or premium due dates. A few companies permit withdrawals only in case of surrender or death, and some companies credit no interest or penalize the insured if the funds are withdrawn.

Time Limit for Conversion. A conversion must take place within a specified number of years after issue. If the term of the policy is no longer than 10 years, a conversion as of a current date can usually be accomplished throughout the full term. If the term is longer than 10 years, the policy may stipulate that the conversion privilege must be exercised before the expiration of a period shorter than the term of the policy. For example, a 15-year term policy must usually be converted within 12 years from date of issue, a 20-year term policy within 15 years.

The purpose of a time limit is to minimize adverse selection. There is always a substantial degree of adverse selection in the conversion process. As the time limit for conversion approaches, those policyholders in poor health are more likely to convert and pay the higher premiums than those who believe they are in good health. If the decision to convert must be made some years before the expiration of the term policy, a higher percentage of healthy policyowners, uncertain of their health some years hence, will elect to convert. Experience has shown that the death rate among those who convert is higher than normal. This accounts for the fact that premium rates for convertible term insurance are somewhat higher than for those without the conversion privilege. Because policies with renewable and convertible features extend the risk to the insurer, the premiums are higher than policies without those features, or with those features that terminate earlier.

If the policy is renewable, the only time limitation may be that it is converted before age 60 or 65. In other cases, the contract will state that the policy must be converted within a certain period before the expiration of the last renewal period. In all cases, conversion may be permitted beyond the time limit, but within the policy term, by providing evidence of insurability.

Some companies issue term policies that are automatically converted at the expiration of the term to a specified plan of permanent insurance. It is doubtful that this procedure is effective in reducing adverse selection, since healthy individuals may fail to continue the permanent insurance.

Types of Term Insurance

There are a number of different types of term insurance. We will now review the major types.

One-Year Term

YRT is the most efficient way to provide for life insurance needs when maximum protection is desired with the current minimum outlay of cash. Sales of YTR represent about 5 percent of new term policies sold. Because of its simplicity, low cost and lack of long-term commitment, advisors view this product as the easiest life insurance product to sell, by far.

Reentry Term

reentry term insurance

select mortality

The life insurance industry developed a term insurance policy intended to charge higher premiums to those in poorer health when they renew their term insurance, thereby reducing the degree of adverse selection. The product is commonly called *reentry term insurance*. It is a policy subject to two different renewal premium schedules. The lower premium rate is based on *select mortality* (applicable to an insured who has recently given evidence of insurability). The select rates are available as long as the insured is able to provide new evidence of insurability at each renewal date.

ultimate mortality

The higher premium schedule is based on *ultimate mortality* rates (applicable to insureds some period of time after they last provided evidence of insurability). Insureds that cannot provide evidence of insurability acceptable to the insurer when required must pay the higher premium schedule rates to renew their coverage. They are known to be poorer risks and have to pay for the increased risk now and with each subsequent renewal, unless they experience an improvement in insurability.

It is hard to argue with the logic or fairness in this approach. The reentry approach transfers some of the risk traditionally assumed by the insurer to the policyowners. In order to get the lower premiums while healthy, the individual should be willing to pay the higher premium when his or her health deteriorates. However, it is questionable whether the policyowner realizes the full import of a decision to buy reentry term insurance. Young people in good health believe they are immortal and will never have to pay the higher rates. Few of them stop to consider that they may actually end up paying the ultimate rates and that when that happens they may not be able to buy coverage from another insurer. The level premium term insurance they could have bought instead of reentry term might have been a significant bargain. Unfortunately, when that realization sinks in, it is too late to select that option.

Reentry term is economical for those who remain healthy into their retirement years, but it may end up being very costly for anyone whose health deteriorates at about the same rate as that of the general population. On average, people start to experience declining health between the ages of 45 and 55. If they reach their life expectancy (at least 50 percent should), they can live 40 to 50 years in an impaired physical condition—paying the higher term rates for many more years than they enjoyed lower term rates.

EXAMPLE

Mary purchased a reentry term policy 3 years ago. She saved 10 percent based on the premiums that would have been required for a traditional renewable term policy that guarantees future premium rates. Mary suffered a severe heart attack just before she was required to have her health reassessed for the reentry term. Her new premium is more than double what the renewal premium would have been under the traditional renewable term policy. That difference may get even larger in the future.

The decision to purchase reentry term insurance should involve comparison of the high renewal rates of competing insurers for similar coverage. If the insured cannot provide satisfactory evidence of insurability, the lower premium schedule is irrelevant. Helpful in making such comparisons are projected premiums (both high and low rates) for each policy being considered at a range of premium increase dates. Another important point for evaluation is whether the insurer considers the policy a new contract with a new contestable period after the insured fails a reentry test. Some insurers treat the new premium as an adjustment on continuing coverage, but others impose a new contestable period.

Long-Term Level Term

level term

While term contracts used to provide protection for a relatively short period, subject to renewal for successive periods of the same duration, most term contracts today are designed to provide long-period protection. *Level term* is used to describe both a premium and face amount that remain the same during the policy period. These policies often give prospects the option to purchase waiver-of-premium and accidental death benefits, as well as other policy benefits.

Today, you can find many companies offering 5-, 10-, 15-, 20-, and 30-year terms. Term policies with 10- and 20-year level premium periods represented 67 percent of term sales in 2011 (LIMRA 's Individual Life Insurance Survey). In addition, 15- and 30-year level premium plans have also grown in popularity over the last few years (25 percent of new sales combined). These designs attempt to avoid the objection people have to the annual increase in the cost of term insurance. The insurance company adds up the number of annual premiums that will be required on the policy in total, divides by the number of years for which the level premium is guaranteed, discounts for the time value of the money using assumed interest rates, and charges the resulting level premiums. This process is similar to the process used for all level premium plans. The insurance company charges more in the beginning, so they will not have to charge a higher amount as time goes on. This is also riskier for insurers, since aggressive pricing and underwriting are common in a very competitive environment, and reserves and margins may not be sufficient years down the line on the longer guaranteed periods. To offset the increasing adverse selection in longer-term contracts, the policy may change to an annually renewable premium schedule after a certain age or time period.

A level term-to-65 contract, for example, provides a level premium from the age of issue to age 65. It is not to be confused with YRT or other forms of term insurance that can be renewed until the insured reaches age 65. The period covered by this contract is normally shorter than the life expectancy, but its termination date coincides with the age generally regarded as the normal retirement age. Because the term is shorter than that of WL contracts, the premium will be smaller. A conversion privilege may be offered, requiring conversion prior to age 60 or within the first 10 policy years.

Nonlevel Term Insurance

The preceding discussion focused on term insurance for which the amount of insurance is level throughout the term of the policy. This is not necessarily the case, since the amount of insurance may increase or decrease throughout the term.

decreasing term insurance

Decreasing Term. A substantial portion of term insurance provides systematic decreases in the amount of insurance from year to year. This type of term insurance, called *decreasing term insurance,* may be written in the form of a separate contract, a rider to a new or existing contract, or as an integral part of a combination contract. Mortgage redemption insurance is the most familiar form of decreasing term insurance. The premium remains level as the death benefit declines as the insured ages. This type of insurance is useful when the insurance need at the insured's death diminishes over time. In addition to a decreasing loan balance, the need to provide funds for dependent children decreases as they grow. Each year a parent survives and provides a dependent's support is one less year needed should the parent die before the child reaches maturity.

If the decrease in the term insurance is offset by an increase in an investment fund, the total amount of cash available at death remains constant. This is one line of reasoning in the "buy-term-and-invest-the-difference" argument, which we will discuss later.

payor benefit

The *payor benefit*, available as a rider to a policy insuring a juvenile, is an example of a decreasing term rider. This rider provides a death benefit and waiver-of-premium benefit on the life of the premium payor, usually a parent. The decreasing death benefit on the payor's life is sufficient to pay all the premiums that would be due on the juvenile's policy from the payor's death to the insured's age 21 or similar age. The benefit is designed to ensure that the premium due on the juvenile's life insurance policy will be paid if the premium payor dies.

increasing term

Increasing Term. *Increasing term* provides insurance for which the face amount increases monthly or yearly while the premium remains level. It can be written as both a separate policy and as a rider, but is mainly found in combination with cash value policies under special plans, such as cost-of-living protection, return-of-cash value and ROP riders.

The cost-of-living adjustment (COLA) rider to a cash value policy allows for automatic face-amount increases each year in conjunction with the rate of inflation, as measured by an index such as the Consumer Price Index (CPI). The policyowner is billed for the increases with the regular premium notice. No evidence of insurability is required for these increases as long as the rider remains in force and is exercised each year. This requirement minimizes the possibility of adverse selection.

Another type of increasing term insurance is provided by the ROP feature or rider. This feature provides that, if the insured dies within a set number of years from the policy issue date, the death benefit will be increased by an amount equal to all or a portion of the premiums paid to that point. The increasing term benefit is set to equal the sum of premiums paid up to that year. This feature makes the term insurance more attractive to prospects who may not like the fact that no benefit is paid if the insured survives to the end of the term period.

one-year term option

The same concept is used in the "fifth-dividend" or *one-year term option* in participating policies. Some amount of dividend can be applied each year in an amount equal to the year-end cash value. Applying this option can insure the cash value, so that in the case of the death of the insured, the cash value would be paid in addition to the death benefit.

Indeterminate or Adjustable Premium Term

Another approach known as indeterminate or adjustable premium term provides for maximum guaranteed premiums chargeable during the life of the contract. The initial premiums reflect the select rates available through recent underwriting, as well as competitive pricing pressure. Traditionally, insurers have not had the right to change premiums after the policy is sold. Since policies may continue for many years, insurers must use conservative mortality, interest, and expense estimates in the premium calculation. Adjustable premium insurance, however, allows insurers to offer insurance at lower current premiums based on less conservative assumptions, with the right to change these premiums in the future. The initial low premium is guaranteed for the first renewal period, depending on the contract's duration, with subsequent premiums dependent on the insurer's future mortality, investment, and expense experience. In no case will the subsequent premiums exceed the guaranteed maximums in the contract. The guaranteed premiums are considerably higher than the current rates projected.

Return-of-Premium (ROP) Term

ROP term products have become more popular over the last decade. They tend to be middle-market focused and target individuals concerned with protecting mortgage payments, as well as income and savings. ROP policies tend to have smaller average face amounts than non-ROP policies. Return of premium is offered as a rider attached to a level premium term policy, or as part of the base plan. Fifteen, twenty and thirty-year level premium periods are the most common ROP offerings.

The advantage of traditional term life insurance is affordability. The downside is that it is a pure risk policy, and if you outlive the policy, it has no further value and the policy terminates. Nothing is paid to either the policyowner or the beneficiary. The perception is that the premium has been "thrown away," since nothing is returned and no claim payment is made. (This is, of course, an inaccurate perception, since the insurance protection was provided during the term of coverage. Nevertheless, many individuals see it this way.)

return-of-premium term

Under *return-of-premium term*, if you live to the end of the policy period, your premiums are returned, and a few companies offer a partial return of premium if the policy is terminated prior to the end of the full policy period. If the policy is surrendered, there may be no refund, and there may be a surrender charge schedule in the early years. The longer premium payments are made, the higher the percentage of return. Some argue that ROP life insurance is an excellent combination of the best features of both term and WL.

The insurance company benefits from the extra premium it charges, which is approximately 1.5 to 4 times the premium for non-ROP term. This extra premium will earn an investment return—enough to provide the money for insurance companies to return premiums, cover their expenses, and earn a profit. The policyowner does not get the investment return on the extra premium paid over a traditional term policy. That money is kept by the insurance company, which is how they offer this product, taking their expenses from the investment component. It is not "free" insurance, but to many it feels like it is. People do not like to spend money on something they don't think they will use. Statistics vary, but approximately 95 percent of all term policies sold do not result in a death claim.

The main determinant of the extra charge for the ROP feature is the length of the coverage period. The longer the period of coverage, the lower the cost of the policy, because there is more time for the additional funds to grow. This approach makes good financial sense with a 20- or 30-year term, but it is less attractive if the term is less than 20 years. Shorter periods will be considerably higher, since there is less time for the insurer to pay back the premiums plus cover its costs and provide a profit. Holders of term insurance keep their policies an average of only 7 to 9 years before they drop the coverage or switch policies. Over a 20- or 30-year period, a policyowner may drop the more expensive ROP policy and consequently pay more than a regular term product.

Premiums paid that are returned are not taxable, because they are a return of premium. The return of premium is now included in other products, such as UL.

Combination Plans

Combining different types of coverages is nothing new, and appears to be gaining popularity in new product development. Insurers are always seeking ways to package benefits that will appeal to a larger market segment or help overcome objections to buying certain coverages.

For example, one insurer has recently introduced a ROP term product with coverage for major medical, disability, doctors' visits, routine dental care, and prescription drugs. Policyowners can control their exposures and costs by selecting the plan benefits and premiums that best suit their needs and budget. This concept has been used to link together long-term care and other benefits in permanent insurance policies. This trend is expanding.

Riders Available on Term Insurance Policies

There is a wide variety of riders available on term policies, many may be available on policies you sell. Below is a listing of common riders found with term insurance. Some of them may be similar, but reflect the possible names for riders found throughout the industry.

- Waiver-of-premium rider
- Children's level term rider
- Spouse and children's rider
- Accidental death-benefit rider
- Accidental death and dismemberment rider

- Accelerated death-benefit rider
- Additional insured rider
- Other covered insured rider
- ROP rider
- Guaranteed premium rider
- Five-year term rider
- Increasing-premium term rider
- Policy purchase option rider
- Spouse's paid-up insurance purchase option rider
- Guaranteed insurability rider
- Living benefits rider
- Unemployment waiver-of-premium rider
- Long-term care rider
- Long-term care with terminal benefits rider
- Long-term care with terminal benefits and extension-of-benefits rider
- Critical illness rider
- Disability income rider (accident only or accident and sickness)
- Family income rider
- Cost of living rider
- Level term-to-65 rider

As you can see there are many and this list is not exhaustive.

Uses and Limitations of Term Insurance

Term insurance has long been the subject of debate. Many people, not familiar with or perhaps not sympathetic to the principle of level premium cash value insurance, advocate the use of term insurance in all situations, to the exclusion of permanent insurance. There are some insurance "consultants" who, when they find permanent plans in an insurance program, advise that the permanent insurance be surrendered for cash and replaced with term insurance. It will be helpful to point out the areas that can legitimately be served by term insurance and to analyze briefly some of the arguments that have been advanced in favor of term insurance. We will then look at the limitations and shortcomings of term insurance.

Uses of Term Insurance

Term insurance is suitable when

1. the need for protection is purely temporary;
2. the need for protection is permanent, but the insured temporarily cannot afford the premiums for permanent insurance;
3. it is used as a supplement to permanent life insurance.

Temporary Need for Protection

In the first case, term insurance is the complete answer, but it should be renewable in the event that the temporary need should extend over a longer period than was originally anticipated. The policy need not be convertible, but since relatively few people carry an adequate amount of permanent insurance, and since the loss of insurability is a constant threat, it is advisable to obtain a policy with a conversion privilege.

Examples of temporary needs that can, and should, be met through term insurance are situations in which the protection need will expire simultaneously with the term expiration date. One example is the need to hedge a loan. A term policy for the loan amount, payable to the lender, not only protects the lender against possible loss of principal, but also relieves the insured's estate of the burden of repaying the loan if the insured dies. Lenders frequently request, and sometimes require, that borrowers purchase life insurance as a condition for the loan. A mortgage redemption policy serves the same purpose. An individual who has invested heavily in a speculative business venture should protect his or her estate and family by obtaining term insurance in the amount of the investment.

If a business firm is spending a considerable sum in an experimental project, the success of which depends on the talents and abilities of one individual or a few individuals, term insurance on the key person or persons will protect the investment. A parent with young children is likely to need more insurance while the children are dependent than he or she will need when they have grown up and become self-sufficient. The additional insurance during the child-raising period can be—and usually is—provided through term insurance. Frequently, decreasing term insurance is superimposed on a plan of permanent insurance. For example, parents who depend on their current earnings to finance their children's college education find term insurance to be a useful means through which to provide the necessary college education fund in the event of the death of the breadwinners.

In each of the forgoing examples, a financial loss occurs only if the insured dies before a specified date. These examples are just a few of the many situations in which term insurance is especially useful. However, the use of term insurance is not limited to providing protection to individuals whose needs are for a specified period. If budget constraints prohibit purchasing the desired amount of permanent insurance, term insurance is often substituted.

EXAMPLE

Tom and Marsha have two very young children and need more life insurance to protect them. However, Marsha will become the recipient of a large trust in 8 years. At that time, they will have a diminished need for life insurance. Term insurance is appropriate for this temporary need.

A concept that may be useful in selling term insurance is known as laddering. Just as one may ladder bonds or certificates of deposit, an individual can purchase several term policies of varying durations to meet specific needs. For example, a parent may buy a 10-year level-premium term policy to ensure money is available for the children's college costs; a 20-year policy to pay off what remains of the mortgage; and a 30-year policy for income replacement for the spouse. These three policies cost far less than a single 30-year policy covering all the risks. It also helps the policyowner remember the purpose of the policy and the need that it addresses. By looking out for the client's best interest, the client may come to view the advisor as trustworthy, which could lead to further sales and referrals. This term concept is a way for advisors to increase their business and develop long-term relationships with clients.

Lack of Finances for Permanent Insurance

Term insurance is useful for people with low incomes and high insurance needs. Good risk management principles suggest that a family should be protected against catastrophic losses. If current family income cannot afford permanent insurance in adequate amounts, the prospect has no choice but to buy term if adequate financial protection is to be provided.

Term insurance can be useful for those who have placed essentially all of their resources in a new business. Death of the business owner could result in loss of the invested capital. It also means that all resources have been committed and there are none for surviving family members. Term insurance can serve as a hedge, especially in the vulnerable early stages of the business. Additionally, term will have a low premium requirement, as it is newly underwritten and has select rates.

Term insurance is particularly important to young people who expect substantial improvement in their financial situation as the years go by. Young professionals who have made a considerable investment in their education and training, but whose practices must be built up gradually, are likely prospects for term insurance. They may have student loans that need to be repaid. If they should die before the loans are repaid, that obligation could fall on their estate. Young business executives are also good prospects. Term insurance provides a high level of protection at a low premium. In these circumstances, term is used not because the need is temporary, but because the financial condition is temporary. Convertible term is especially useful in these situations, because it assures the later availability of permanent insurance.

To protect the insurability of people in these situations, term insurance purchased should be renewable and convertible. The conversion privilege is the bridge that spans the gap between the need for permanent insurance and the financial ability to meet the need. Since the insured's financial situation might persist longer than anticipated, the policy should be renewable, as well as convertible and ideally should be incorporated in all term policies.

A Supplement to Permanent Life Insurance

In other situations, the life insurance need is not temporary but is still met with term insurance. Many established people need more death benefit than is affordable on a permanent basis. These persons may decide to sacrifice living benefits (cash values) in order to provide their families with adequate premature death protection.

An excellent use of term insurance is as a rider to a permanent insurance plan. The combination provides the desired amount of insurance protection within a budget, provides some permanent protection with cash accumulation, and allows for conversion of the term rider if desired in the future. This may be especially useful in the child-rearing period of a young family, or when children go to college or pursue other post-secondary education. Level, increasing, or decreasing term riders are often packaged with permanent forms of insurance to create a combination of death benefits and living benefits that fit a person's particular needs and resources. For example, an individual requires $200,000 in life insurance coverage, but can not afford the premium for a permanent plan of this amount. An affordable option may be to purchase a $50,000 permanent policy with a $150,000 term rider. That mixture would provide the desired amount of insurance with limited cash value accumulation, at a premium that fits within a given budget.

Limitations of Term Insurance

Every policy has advantages and limitations, and term is no different. There are disadvantages to using term when there is a need for permanent life insurance:

1. You have to die to "win." Although term insurance provides needed and valuable protection, when the term coverage ends, so does the protection. If you stop paying premiums, the coverage ends. No policy values are recovered, unless death of the insured occurs during the term period. Term is often compared to renting a house. As long as you pay the rent, you get full use of the house, but as soon as the lease expires, you must leave and you have no equity or value that belongs to you.

   Suppose an insured is covered with $500,000 of term insurance. The coverage has been in force for 10 years, and the policy expires at midnight on December 31. If he dies at 11:59 on New Year's Eve, his family receives the full $500,000 in death-benefit proceeds. However, if he dies at 12:01 on January 1, the family receives nothing under the policy, since the contract has expired.
2. The need for life insurance may extend beyond the policy period. The insured may become uninsurable and be unable to renew or obtain a new policy. Not all policies have renewal or conversion rights, and even when they do, they expire after a certain age or a certain number of years of coverage.
3. The premium increase at renewal may be beyond the policyowner's ability to pay. Premiums increase until they become prohibitive at later ages. A person may buy term coverage in his or her 20s because it seems more affordable than cash value insurance with the same death benefit. By the time they're in their 40s, the coverage seems a bit pricey, as the rate goes up. In their 50s, the cost has generally outstripped the cost of permanent insurance. Finally, in their 60s, if not sooner, they drop the coverage, not because they no longer need the protection, but because they cannot afford it, or do not want to spend that amount of money on it.
4. Term has no tax-free automatic savings features. Many people benefit from the savings feature of cash value life insurance. Permanent insurance can serve as a vehicle for accumulating

funds for emergencies, retirement, and other savings goals. Many people are unable to save for an extended period unless faced with some compulsion or penalty. Traditional cash value insurance addresses this problem. Even those who save regularly will be less likely to raid their cash value life insurance than other savings vehicles. The cash value growth within the life insurance policy is tax-deferred, giving it an advantage over currently taxable vehicles. Additionally the waiver-of-premium clause will allow the savings plan within permanent insurance to be "self-completing" if the insured become permanently disabled.

5. Although the premiums are initially lower, term insurance may be more expensive than permanent insurance in the long run. Mortality assumptions used in calculating term premiums project higher death rates than those used in WL policies, because of the higher adverse selection associated with term policies. Despite the initial higher premiums under the level premium plan, permanent insurance can actually be less expensive over a lifetime.

Danger of Relying Solely on Group Term Insurance

Many employers offer life insurance as part of their benefits package for employees. It is an effective way to insure a worker, and often the worker's family members, at a cost that is generally lower than purchasing individual coverage. However, relying solely on group insurance may not be the best way to ensure that the family is provided for in the case of the death of the breadwinner.

In these times of fierce competition, unemployment and corporate downsizing, it can be precarious to rely heavily on employer-provided group life insurance to satisfy all or most of a family's death-benefit needs. ACLI's 2013 Fact Book Study found a continuing increase in the proportion of insured households having only group insurance—39 percent in 2012, down from 44 percent in 2002. The main disadvantage of employee life insurance is that it is term insurance and the protection usually ends when the employee terminates employment. If a person leaves their current position for another, there is always the possibility that the new employer will not provide employee life insurance. This could leave the worker without life insurance protection.

Additionally, the group term may not be flexible and adaptable to individual needs. Group life insurance is geared toward meeting the general needs of the group being covered. In most cases, it cannot be customized to meet individual needs. Since there is no individual underwriting on group life, individually underwritten term may be cheaper, since the group term must account for the adverse selection resulting from liberalized underwriting. It is best to think of group term life as a supplement to a personally owned life insurance program.

Individuals should find out how much of the employer group coverage can be converted after an involuntary termination of employment, for example, mandatory early retirement, workforce reduction, plant closing, reorganization after a merger or acquisition, employer bankruptcy, statutory banning of a product (freon, for instance), or chronic health impairment resulting from accident or disease. Individual term insurance may be appropriate to cover the potential reduction in coverage after post-employment conversion of the existing coverage. The safest way for the individual to cover this risk is to purchase an individual policy while he or she is still employed. The cost of such risk avoidance is the amount spent on premiums for coverage in excess of the individual's current needs, between buying a policy and termination of employment.

Arguments in Favor of Term Insurance

Some of the arguments in favor of term insurance can be described as criticisms of cash value life insurance. Most of the arguments can be consolidated into two points of view:

1. Level premium insurance overcharges the policyowner.
2. The accumulation and protection elements should be separated.

The basis for the first claim is the fact that if a policyowner dies in the early years of the contract, premium outlay under the level premium plan is considerably larger than it would have been under a term plan. According to the term advocates, the policyowner paid a larger premium than was necessary. Term advocates question whether it is wise for the insured to pay in advance for something he or she may never need or live to enjoy. They argue that it is better "to pay as you go and get what you pay for."

There is no question that insureds are far better off financially with term insurance if they can be sure they will die within a relatively short time. On the other hand, they are far worse off if they guess wrong and live to a ripe old age. Although no one knows whether he or she will die young or live to an old age, the chances of living to an age where the total term premiums exceed the total premiums paid under a level premium plan are relatively high.

The level premium cash value plan protects the insured against the consequences of living a long time and having to pay prohibitive premiums for insurance protection. It shifts a portion of the premium burden of those who live beyond their life expectancy to those who die young and produce an exceedingly large return on their premium outlay. Since no one can know at the outset which group he or she is in, payment of the level premium by all is a fair and satisfactory arrangement.

Those who argue that level premium insurance overcharges policyowners, sometimes assert that the reserve under permanent forms of insurance is forfeited to the company in the event of the insured's death. To correct this "inequity," they contend the normal death benefit should be increased by the amount of the reserve.

This argument strikes at the very heart of the level premium plan. The essence of the level premium plan is a gradual reduction in the net amount at risk as the reserve increases. If the reserve is to be paid in addition to the face amount of the policy, this reduction in the amount at risk does not occur, and premiums that were calculated on the assumption of a decreasing risk will be inadequate. Companies that offer a contract that promises to return the reserve in addition to the face amount of the policy have premiums that increase according to the additional risk amount, like UL increasing death benefit option.

The second claim—that the savings and protection elements of the contract should be separated—is based on the proposition that an individual can invest his or her surplus funds more wisely and with a greater return than the life insurance company can. Those who believe this recommend that individuals buy term insurance and then place the difference between the term premium and the premium they would have paid for level premium insurance in a separate investment program. This is known as a "buy-term-and-invest-the-difference" strategy. Some suggest investing this difference in premiums in government bonds, others recommend investment trusts or mutual funds, while others advise an investment program in common stocks. This argument needs to be analyzed in terms of the objectives of any investment program, and will be discussed later.

Term Product Selection

The selection of a particular type of life insurance policy or product portfolio is largely a personal decision. Just as some people prefer to lease an automobile or rent an apartment, others prefer to own them. While some individuals may prefer to put down a large sum of money and pay off a loan or mortgage as quickly as possible, others want to make a minimum down payment and stretch payments out for as long as possible. For many clients, there is an emotional comfort in ownership, while for others, ownership ties them down and restricts their freedom of choice and flexibility. Similar comparisons can be made to life insurance policies. Some clients do not want to pay for years and have nothing to show for their investment, while others may have been told for years to buy term and invest the difference. There is really no right answer, unless we know when the insured will die. For most clients, the right course of action usually lies in choosing the option with which they are most comfortable, since peace of mind is one of the most important reasons for purchasing a life insurance plan.

When comparing term policies, consider the following:

- In the case of renewable term, check the schedule of future renewal premiums. A policy with the lowest initial premiums may have higher renewal premiums than other policies. A policy that is priced aggressively may not be able to sustain those premiums when renewal time comes.
- Check the age to which coverage may be continued without evidence of insurability. A policy with a lower premium may discontinue the automatic right to renewal before other higher priced policies.
- Check the age to which a convertible policy may be converted without providing evidence of insurability. It may be worth paying additional premium to guarantee this right for additional years. Check if the conversion clause allows the client to convert the term to permanent with a waiver-of-premium provision without evidence of insurability. Some companies allow conversion when the insured is disabled and on a waiver-of-premium benefit, so that the converted policy is now on waiver. Some companies do not allow a waiver-of-premium rider on the converted policy, unless the insured shows evidence of insurability. Some companies will allow the converted policy to have a waiver-of-premium rider without evidence of insurability, but will restrict the waiver benefit to disabilities that occur after the date of conversion.
- Check the periods of coverage with respect to waiver-of-premium and other riders, and the provisions of those policy features that are important to the client. Many small differences in policy terms and clauses can make big differences in benefits and premiums. In

general, it is worth paying a higher premium to have a policy that has more liberal rules regarding policy benefits.

Marketing, Prospecting, and Approach

The financial advisor's primary concerns are getting in front of the right people (qualified prospects) and knowing what to say and ask once he or she is before them. Based on research by LIMRA, there are several recommendations that may guide your marketing and prospecting efforts. Contact current clients, many of whom are aware that they need more insurance; target young parents and households whom are more likely to underinsured and more likely to buy; and middle market households, many recognizing a need for additional insurance. One key component of your prospecting must include helping consumers prioritize their needs and explore the critical financial risks their families face by delaying insurance purchases. We will now take a brief look at some basic concepts for life insurance marketing and prospecting.

Marketing

marketing

Marketing is the planning and implementation of a process to identify specific consumer needs, isolating groups of people who have those needs, and then producing and customizing the products and services that satisfy those needs. It is the art of planning when, where, why, how, and to whom to sell. Successful marketing focuses on the needs of the consumer and produces a mutually beneficial relationship between a buyer and seller.

Marketing versus Selling

selling

Because marketing involves planning, much of marketing does not involve interaction with a buyer for the purpose of making a sale. Many believe that marketing and selling are the same, but in reality, selling is a part of marketing. *Selling* is the end result of successful marketing. It is the transaction resulting from the encounter between buyer and seller, the exchange of the product or service for the buyer's cash.

Objectives of a Marketing Strategy

The goal of the selling/planning process is to win clients. Any effective marketing strategy you create should accomplish four goals:

1. Create a perpetual qualified prospect machine.
2. Decrease your appointments to sales ratio (increase efficiency in winning clients).
3. Decrease your contacts-made-to-appointments ratio (decrease the amount of time and energy devoted to prospecting).
4. Focus and specialize to create a higher value for your services.

Perpetual Qualified Prospect Machine. A perpetual prospect machine provides you with a continuous flow of new prospects and requires little intervention, and no cold calls. The best way to create such a machine is through referred leads. For example, if each good client gives you two referrals that turn into sales with other good clients, your business would grow exponentially. One client could result in multiple good clients through referrals, and each of them could result in multiple referrals, creating a perpetual stream of prospects in a manner requiring little time and resulting in more sales for your efforts. People tend to associate with others who share similar values, characteristics, and needs, so there is a good chance that the referrals will be good clients.

Lower Appointments-to-Sales Ratio. Your plan or strategy should help you decrease the number of appointments it takes to generate a sale. The fewer appointments it takes to generate a sale, the better you are doing in your sales interview, prospecting, and marketing. If your strategy does not improve your ability to convert prospects into clients, you need to revise it.

Lower Contacts–Made-to-Appointments Ratio. You can also measure a strategy's effectiveness by whether or not it is reducing the number of contacts needed to set up an appointment. A good strategy will allow you to spend less time prospecting and more time helping your clients.

Focus and Specialization. If you had to have heart surgery, who would you like to perform the surgery, a heart surgeon or a general surgeon? Naturally, you would want the specialized heart surgeon. In the same way, a prospect will feel more comfortable with your services if they know you have worked with others *like them,* namely their peers and friends.

A good marketing strategy will help you focus on a market or a few related markets for which you can become the insurance or financial services expert. By establishing a marketing focus, you will be able to create a reputation that will precede you and greatly enhance your referability. You will want to make sure the market you focus on will be profitable. This will have a direct impact on your ability to see more qualified prospects, and thus, create more clients. It will not happen overnight and it certainly will not happen if you do not have a plan.

target marketing

Instead of pursuing opportunities and choosing a market in a random fashion, take a more systematic approach. This approach is called *target marketing*, in which you look for a group of people (a segment) which is large enough, so you will never run out of potential contacts, and small enough that the members are interrelated to the degree that your reputation will precede you. The group should be identifiable and accessible, with members who have common characteristics and needs, and communicate with one another.

Target marketing can occur inside or outside of your natural markets. A natural market is the group of people to whom you have a natural affinity or access because of similar values, lifestyles, experiences, attitudes, and so on. General markets are people in general, undifferentiated, meaning anyone and everyone is a prospect. Because of the advantages of selling in your natural markets, it makes sense to begin your target marketing efforts within them. In this section, you will learn to target market within your natural markets by

- identifying groups with similar characteristics and needs (also known as market segmentation), and
- finding and targeting groups that meet the target market criteria.

The Benefits of Target Marketing

You will find that using the target marketing process will

- increase your efficiency within your natural market
- create a perpetual qualified prospect machine
- increase your visibility and prestige
- provide for systematic expansion of your natural market
- help you identify new opportunities

Using this process, you will be able to set appointments and sell more efficiently, which translates into either more time to see more people or more free time.

Segmenting Your Market

The first step of target marketing is to find possible target markets. Do this by dividing or segmenting your general and natural markets into small groups based on common characteristics. This simply means that you should organize your natural market into groups of potential prospects who have similar characteristics, needs, motivations, and buying behaviors. Segments can be identified and categorized by occupation, lifestyle, attitude, age, and so forth. They should be large enough to warrant your time, but small enough that they have some differentiated characteristics or needs. The process of discovering your target markets involves market segmentation.

Qualifying Prospects for Life Insurance

qualified prospect

The prospect selection process requires qualifying your prospects, moving them from being "suspects" to "prospects." To do this you will have to establish the four characteristics of a *qualified prospect*. Qualified prospects display certain characteristics that make them potential customers for life insurance:

- They need protection from loss of life.
- They can afford to pay the premiums for the protection.
- They can be approached by you.
- They are insurable.

Needs and Values

It would be rare to find a person that had no need for your products or services. However, they may or may not value the service and products you provide. The key, as always, is to ask questions and listen. Explore whether or not there have been any major financial changes in the prospect's life over the past year. You might ask if they have purchased a new home, had a baby, had a death in the family, received a promotion or raise, or made any significant purchases. The answer to these questions and others will indicate if they have needs, and if so, how they want to meet them.

The Ability to Buy

Based on what you know or can observe personally, you may be able to assess whether a prospect can afford your products and services. You might not know the details until you get involved and start gathering information, but your initial observation should start you on the way. Despite someone's needs and values, limit your contacts to people who can afford to pay the premium.

Approachability

It is not always easy to determine the approachability of a prospect. You may discover that people who might be good prospects are simply not approachable. This is why we have stressed the importance of identifying and working in and from your natural markets. It will increase your ability to establish rapport through common attitudes and interests, and perhaps similar lifestyles, incomes, or education. Most advisors work with prospects with whom they share common interests.

Insurability

You might not know whether a prospect is insurable until you begin working with them. Be sure you know your company's guidelines for standard issue. As you talk to people, keep these qualifications in mind. If you know about a prospects' poor health or other reasons they cannot meet underwriting requirements, you will need to make a business decision. While they may not be prospects for life insurance, they may be prospects for annuities, or they may be centers of influence or sources of referrals.

Motivating Prospects: What They Want and Do Not Want

There are many reasons why prospects do not buy the life insurance they say they need. LIMRA International conducted a study of 68 couples, empty nesters, and childless couples to explore why they remained underinsured, entitled, "101 Excuses Not to Buy Life Insurance" (2007, LIMRA International Inc.). The findings are summarized on the next several pages.

Life insurance prospects have many unresolved issues with the process of purchasing products, which helps to explain their inertia and lack of motivation. Understanding how people feel about life insurance and the process of purchasing will help you relate to prospects and find ways to help them take positive action. As the old saying goes, "life insurance is not bought, it is sold."

Table 3-2 Why They Don't Buy the Life Insurance They Say They Need

Reason	Major Reason	Minor Reason
Dread high-pressure tactics	60%	26%
Have other financial priorities	55%	28%
Prefer other financial products	25%	48%
Can't afford	21%	46%
Difficult to decide what type	46%	38%
Difficult to decide how much	44%	39%
Worry about making wrong decision	36%	43%
Don't know who to buy from	31%	34%
Haven't gotten around to it	34%	33%
No one has approached me	21%	26%
Unpleasant to think about dying	6%	39%

Why Are Prospects Unlikely to Buy Now?

Prospects are unlikely to buy now for the following reasons.

The Topic Is Unpleasant and Stressful. Many react to the topic of life insurance with an array of negative emotions. They say it is boring, hard to understand, difficult to do the math, scary to think about, and makes them feel old. These feelings keep them from even starting the process. Life insurance is something they feel they can put off and buy tomorrow.

They Feel Overwhelmed. Individuals feel there are too many decisions to be made when buying life insurance. It is complex and confusing. There are too many choices. They don't know what type or how much to buy.

They Do Not Understand the Basics. Many lack even basic knowledge of life insurance. They don't understand why they need it, the different types, how much is needed, or how the policies work.

They Procrastinate. Some people feel they are too busy and do not have the time to buy life insurance. Some are waiting for someone to approach them. Some will do it tomorrow.

They Mistrust the Distribution System. Some individuals want help, because they know it is a complex topic and they do not understand it. However, they question whether an advisor will take the time to understand their needs or have their best interest in mind. They feel that advisors will not always suggest the best product for them, but the best product for the advisor to sell to them. This may be because they have not had contact with advisors, or because they have had negative experiences with sales representatives in the past. They are afraid advisors will "hammer away for hours" and not leave their home until they close the sale.

They Do Not Have a Trusted Advisor. They do not have a trusted advisor to turn to or who contacts them on a regular basis. Most see an advisor as "a necessary evil."

They Resist Approaches. Many ignore the industry's attempts to reach them. Direct mail advertisements and inserts in their bills leave them cold. They dread advisors calling them, even though they recognize they need more life insurance. If you call, they just say they are busy and hang up.

It Is Not a High Priority. It is difficult to find extra dollars for life insurance when there are so many other pressing financial needs. They want to use the money in other ways that provide more immediate gratification, such as an HD television, a vacation, or a new car. Most will not admit that life insurance competes against consumer comforts, so they say they need to replace household necessities like a furnace; buy other insurance, such as homeowners or health; or save for retirement. They are willing to take the risk for now. They do not understand risk management concepts when it comes to life insurance.

They Have Family Expenses. For those with children, much of their extra money goes towards expenses for the kids, like private school, sports, music lessons, and orthodontics. All these activities and needs are seen as just as important as life insurance. They see the need to spend on purchases that will provide immediate results versus something that they may or may not need. When making trade-offs for their disposable dollars, some are willing to risk financial disaster in the event of death, which might not happen, in order to provide value for the family today.

To update this information, similar findings were reported in the Household Trends in U.S. Life Insurance Sales Trends, 1975–2012 study done by LIMRA in 2012 (2013, LL Global, Inc.). Households delay buying life insurance for four primary reasons: they have other financial priorities right now, they think it is too expensive, they have difficulty making decisions about the purchase, and they just plain procrastinate.

What Has Worked in the Past

Key triggers that have motivated people to buy in the past include the following.

Life Events. Having children is a common motivator; so is purchasing a home. Reaching prospects after key life events, such as the birth of a child or a home purchase, is still a successful strategy. Listed below are life events you may choose to focus on

- having or adopting a child
- getting married
- buying a home
- taking on debt
- changing jobs
- making changes in marital status
- planning for college
- planning for retirement
- death of a loved one
- supporting aging parents

Intervention. Some individuals buy life insurance only because others intervene and initiate the process, such as parents who encourage the purchase, advisors who contact them, or advisors who meet with them socially. Unfortunately, most of the individuals in this underinsured group have not seen or heard from advisors in years.

Trusted Advisor. Trust is vital to the life insurance purchase process, and consumers are more likely to buy if their advisor is recommended to them by someone they trust, or if they already have a relationship with the advisor. However, finding a trusted advisor can sometimes be difficult, risky, and time consuming.

Life Experience. People who experience or observe the consequences of the premature death of a parent, spouse, friend, or relative are more motivated to have adequate life insurance coverage. However, this does not mean they will proactively seek out the additional life insurance coverage they believe they need.

What Is Not Working

Confused messages from the industry over the years have helped create very resistant consumers.

Advertisements. For many, advertisements are not memorable and do not provide useful information. This is especially true for those under 45, who feel life insurance ads are directed towards their parents and grandparents, so they do not pay attention to them. They do not remember or even understand the ads.

Do You Still Sell Life Insurance. With company name changes, the broadening of product lines, and mergers and acquisitions, consumers are confused about who is still in the business of selling life insurance. Does XYZ still sell life insurance?

Lack of Personal Contact. The current face-to-face model is not connecting with the underinsured effectively. Lack of regular contact with an advisor significantly reduces the likelihood an individual will obtain enough life insurance. Few underinsured individuals have a life insurance advisor, and positive experiences with advisors are rare. Lack of agent contact and lack of meaningful company contact exacerbate distrust of the industry and its sales representatives. Policyowners do not understand what they own and are not aware of new product options available. It is difficult for them to seriously consider additional coverage when they do not understand what they already have.

You Don't Listen. Consumers depend on the integrity of the advisor to give them reliable information, options, and suggestions that meet their specific needs. Sometimes we do not listen. Start with what they want and what concerns them. Be patient. Listen to the prospect first.

Rush to Close. Advisors either do not want to spend the time or do not understand the importance of building relationships with their prospects before trying to close sales. Pressing to close a sale in one meeting does not sit well with many consumers. They feel they need more than one contact, with time between meetings to review the options and suggestions. When the prospect is a stranger, the advisor has to spend time building a relationship before rushing to sell. When advisors appear to be too eager to close the sale, prospects believe they are not interested in what is best for them, and are only thinking about the commissions.

Scare and Guilt Tactics. People find it distasteful for advisors to make leading statements that are insulting and demeaning. Telling someone they do not love their family because they will not buy life insurance is not a good relationship-building tactic.

What They Want

Prospects want the buying and selling/planning process to be easy and pain-free. Some critical factors that have an impact on whether they will buy are as follows.

Simple and to the Point. They want plain, blunt talk, and they want the terminology used to be easy to understand. They desire a short meeting with an advisor who will listen to them and talk about what they need, not what you want to sell them. They have busy lives and do not want to spend hours talking with an advisor. An hour is suggested as a reasonable time for the advisor to give them the information they need. Prospects have three basic questions they want answered when buying life insurance:

1. What is it?
2. What do I get?
3. What do I pay?

No High Pressure. They do not want to deal with anyone who uses high-pressure sales tactics. While they prefer to buy face to face, they will consider alternatives to meeting with advisors, such as seminars or buying through the worksite, which they believe offer low-pressure sales environments.

Someone I Can Trust. They want to deal with advisors they can trust and who can help them with the buying process. Face-to-face contacts allow them to ask questions, look the advisor in the eye, and make a personal assessment. You must show them that you are interested in them, understand what they need, want to build a relationship, and are willing to educate them.

Understand MY Situation. They want the advisor to understand not only their life insurance situation, but also their financial situation. They want multiple options, so they can buy what they can afford now, and add on to it later.

Appealing Products. They want products that are simple and straightforward. They are motivated to buy insurance for the traditional purposes of protecting the home, replacing income, paying final expenses, and providing for their children's education.

Prospecting Methods

There are three categories of potential contacts: (1) people who know you favorably, (2) people recommended by those who know you favorably, and (3) people who do not know you at all. Now let's consider the most common prospecting methods used to find people in these three categories.

Referrals

Successful advisors have found referrals to be the most efficient and effective means of generating a perpetual supply of prospective clients. Referrals are people to whom you are introduced in one fashion or another, by someone who knows and values your work. Think of referrals as *borrowed trust.* Obviously, trust must be earned. That is why a relational, client-focused approach to sales is critical in creating a perpetual prospecting machine.

In their highest form, referrals are unsolicited. This is when the client enthusiastically tells people about you and compels them to call you in the same way they tell friends about a must-see movie. While this does happen, and the more it happens the easier selling becomes, until you can build your business, you will need to solicit referrals and not rely on word of mouth.

The effectiveness of referrals is unquestioned, because a referral from your client is a strong endorsement of your work. Compare that to a cold call, where the person does not know you and has no reason to trust you. People do not like to do business with total strangers.

To be referable, your clients must see value in you and what you do. You must communicate the idea to them that you would like to pass along the benefit of your services to people they value. You want to become referable, and selling a product does not make you referable. Taking a person through a valuable and memorable process does. Trust is the basis of any professional relationship. If you have demonstrated your trustworthiness to the client and developed a relationship based on this trust, and the client recognizes it, you will become referable.

When to Ask for the Referral. There are many opportunities during the normal course of a sale to ask for referrals. They include

- after the sales interview is complete, when you have demonstrated your service and value, and established rapport and trust with the client
- at policy delivery, when you have satisfied your client with your professionalism
- when you provide a service to your client
- when you conduct an anniversary review

Some say you should constantly request referrals. If you receive a warm response and good referrals, continue this approach. However, be careful in creating tension for the client. High pressure can lead clients or prospects to suspect you will do the same to the referral, which might have a negative impact upon the relationship with the people they refer. They will not give you referrals if they feel this way.

Look for signs that the client values your work. The most obvious time is when they agree to buy the product. However, look for other moments in the selling/planning process that point to their perception of you as a trusted advisor, regardless of whether or not they purchase a product.

What You Should Say. If you fail to plan, you plan to fail, so think about what you want to say and put it in writing. This will eliminate the fear of not knowing how to ask. Here are some things to keep in mind as you develop your script:

1. Reflect the value the client has received from the process. Probe for this information by asking what he or she has found helpful about this product.
2. Explain that you consider the client's stated value of the process extremely important.
3. Ask if there are people in his life who may need and value the same service. You could say "Do you know three people who may benefit from my services?"
4. If the prospect stumbles, present some alternatives with a simple, "Do you know someone who…" and fill the blank with a description of what you are looking for in a prospective customer. Use a description of a prospect from your target market or natural market.

Centers of Influence

centers of influence

A variation of the referral process is the center of influence. By definition, *centers of influence* (COI) are those influential people you know, who know you favorably, and who agree to introduce or refer you to others. Clients may become effective centers for you, just as COI may become clients, but this is not necessary to the relationship you need to establish.

In general, you will find that COI

- are active in a community or sphere of influence
- are sought out for advice by the community or within their sphere
- seek to communicate with others
- are givers, not takers

COI know you well enough, and have enough confidence in you, to refer you to prospects. An important aspect of a COI is that they have a personal interest in helping you succeed. They may or may not be clients. They may be a friend of the family or someone you have worked with in the past, either in business or in a community activity.

Like any other relationship, COI must be cultivated. You must think of the person's interests and needs, and what you can do for them. You will find your COI willing to promote your cause if you promote his or her interests in return. Think of this process as a two-way street. It is a cooperative effort in which there is something in it for both parties, not just something for you. It is best if there is something of direct benefit for the referrer. Remember that he or she should be pleased with their relationship with you, and that you have earned the right to his or her help. This type of relationship often takes time to develop.

Your key to letting people know who you are and where to find you is your social mobility. Social mobility means being involved in your community and giving people the opportunity to see you working for common interests. If you think about it, you will recognize that the places where you have social mobility are also the places where you have prospects and COI.

Networking

Networking is the process of continuous communication and sharing of ideas and prospect names with others whose work does not compete with yours, but whose clients might also be eligible to become your clients. Conversely, your clients may need their products. It's a two-way street.

Cold Canvassing

Cold canvassing is challenging, time consuming, and rarely as productive as getting referred leads from clients or COI. There are many times, however, when going out and knocking on doors can generate some new and exciting situations that might not otherwise have occurred. Many advisors make successful use of canvassing as part of their prospecting repertoire.

Speaking to Groups

An opportunity that puts the advisor before someone's club meeting, association luncheon, church circle, or neighborhood gathering can be an informal group presentation or a highly structured seminar event. They are both good ways to get started in the mass marketing of your products. Seminar selling provides you with an opportunity to gather a group of people together so you can present ideas that address problems and concerns common to the group members. You will want to arouse interest in your products and services, so individual appointments will follow and lead to sales.

Direct Mail

Direct mail will get your name and your company's name in front of as many people as you wish. Hopefully, it will isolate those who are ready to talk about insurance. You can get your message in front of people who might not be available to answer your phone call or your knock on the door. The most important point to remember about direct mail is that it only works if you use it regularly. Inconsistency will not work. It must have ample chance to succeed and you must follow up on each mailing. When used regularly, you will generate leads and interest in your products and services.

Approaching the Prospect

The next step in the selling/planning process is approaching the prospect. It is the process of obtaining the prospect's consent to see you about the services you provide, as well as setting the date, time, and place of the appointment.

It is a rare life insurance buyer who both recognizes a need and initiates the purchase. It is important to recognize the tendency for procrastination, lack of knowledge, and denial of need with which prospects approach life insurance.

The role of the insurance advisor is to use the client-focused sales approach to help a person recognize and accept a need, and to seriously consider resolving that need.

Effective and successful selling begins with getting in front of quality prospects on a consistent basis. You want to look for individuals that have a high probability of being qualified prospects. You want to find people who will value you and what you can do for them, and who will be a source for repeat business and referrals. A systematic approach will help you find target markets of potential buyers and will enable you to market efficiently and effectively.

The advisor must have a constant flow of prospects. It is an ongoing activity and must be attended to daily to maintain the flow of potential customers. Everyone who is successful at marketing and selling life insurance has a means to gather and organize names. They collect them consistently and systematically, so that they have new people to call every day, people who may be interested in addressing their financial concerns.

Chapter Three Review

Key terms and concepts are explained in the glossary. Answers to the review questions and the self-test questions are found in the back of the book in the Answers to Questions section.

Key Terms and Concepts

evidence of insurability
adverse selection
renewability
convertibility
attained age
retroactive conversion (original age)
reentry term insurance
select mortality
ultimate mortality
level term
decreasing term insurance
payor benefit
increasing term
one-year term option
return-of-premium term
marketing
selling
target marketing
qualified prospect
centers of influence

Review Questions

1. Describe the basic nature of term insurance. [1]
2. Describe the protection provided by renewability provisions in term life insurance contracts. [2]
3. Explain why there are time limitations on conversion rights for term insurance, and describe different forms of such limits. [2]
4. Compare the attained-age method of converting term insurance with the retroactive conversion method. [3]
5. Describe the variations of term insurance. [4]
6. Explain how select and ultimate term (reentry term) differ from traditional forms of term insurance. [4]
7. How do term-to-65 policies differ from shorter duration term life insurance contracts? [4]
8. Describe the most common situations for which term insurance is suitable and useful. [4]
9. Differentiate marketing and selling, and the objectives of target marketing. [5]
10. Briefly discuss methods of prospecting. [5]

Self-Test Questions

1. Term insurance policies always provide

   (A) a benefit only at the end of the term
   (B) only temporary life insurance protection
   (C) a small cash payment at expiration
   (D) convertibility within the term to another plan of insurance

2. Reentry term insurance allows insureds to keep a select premium rate after the initial period if:

   (A) they meet underwriting standards
   (B) they are under the age of 40 at initial application
   (C) mortality tables do not increase more rapidly than 10 percent per annum
   (D) the company still issues insurance in that policy series at subsequent 5-year intervals

3. Which of the following statements concerning YRT is correct?

   (A) The insurance company may experience some adverse selection at renewal time.
   (B) The premiums do not increase from year to year.
   (C) Evidence of insurability must be furnished at the time of each renewal.
   (D) The insured can renew the policy each year by completing a medical exam.

4. The tendency for healthy individuals to give up their insurance as its cost increases, while those in poor health continue to renew regardless of its cost is referred to as

   (A) risk pooling
   (B) risk tolerance
   (C) adverse selection
   (D) YRT

5. Which of the following statements about marketing and selling is true?

   (A) Selling is planning and marketing is exchanging the product for money.
   (B) Marketing and selling are one and the same.
   (C) Marketing is more important than selling.
   (D) Selling is the end result of successful marketing.

6. Which of the following statements are arguments in favor of term insurance and against level premium insurance by those who advocate buying term insurance?

    I. Level premium insurance overcharges the policyowner.
    II. The accumulation and protection elements should be separated.

    (A) I only
    (B) II only
    (C) Both I and II
    (D) Neither I nor II

7. Which of the following statements concerning reentry term insurance is (are) correct?

    I. The initial premium is based on an ultimate mortality table if the insured's health is better than average.
    II. Future premiums will be based on a select mortality table if satisfactory evidence of insurability is periodically provided as required by the insurer.

    (A) I only
    (B) II only
    (C) Both I and II
    (D) Neither I nor II

READ THE FOLLOWING DIRECTIONS BEFORE CONTINUING

The questions below differ from the preceding questions in that they all contain the word EXCEPT. So you understand fully the basis used in selecting each answer, be sure to read each question carefully.

---

8. All of the following statements regarding term insurance are true EXCEPT

    (A) If the term is converted as of a current date, it is called an attained age conversion.
    (B) Renewability allows a renewal without a medical exam, but the premium may increase.
    (C) Reentry term is based on select and ultimate rates.
    (D) Term insurance allows for two types of conversions, original age and retroactive conversion.

9. All of the following statements concerning term insurance are true EXCEPT

(A) Term insurance is comparable to property insurance in that both provide coverage for a limited time.
(B) Term insurance policies always provide protection from a certainty (death).
(C) The chief function of the renewable feature in term insurance is to protect the insurability of the insured.
(D) There is an adverse selection opportunity against the insurer at each renewal.

10. All of the following statements concerning yearly renewable term insurance are true EXCEPT

(A) The premium is determined by the death rate at the insured's attained age.
(B) The right to renew coverage may be limited to a specified age or period of years.
(C) The policyowner must furnish evidence of insurability to renew coverage.
(D) The face amount of the coverage is paid to the beneficiaries at the death of the insured.

WHOLE LIFE INSURANCE 4

Learning Objectives

An understanding of the material in this chapter should enable you to

1. Describe the features of whole life insurance policies.
2. Compare the differences between limited-payment policies and ordinary whole life policies.
3. Explain how joint life policies work and compare them to single life policies.
4. Explain how combination plans offer the coverage and benefits of long-term care and life insurance in one policy.
5. Describe the concept of endowment life insurance and be aware that many endowment policies are still in force.
6. Explain the adjustable life policy design.
7. Describe current assumption variations of whole life insurance.
8. Discuss the arguments for and against buying term or whole life insurance.
9. Explain the investment philosophy for whole life products.
10. Describe the objectives of the initial interview with the prospect.

This chapter will review the characteristics of whole life insurance and some of its variations. It will then discuss the objectives of the initial interview and some guidelines for conducting your initial meeting with the prospect.

Since the introduction of universal life, whole life has held approximately one quarter of new annualized premium market share, with universal life holding around 40 percent in recent years. With the economic recession in 2008–2009, variable universal life sales have declined and much of that decline has been picked up by whole life. In 2012, according to LIMRA, whole life annualized premium increased by 1 percent and sales increased 1 percent, and now represents 32 percent of new annualized premium, its largest since 1998. Whole life is characterized by guarantees, and in this economic climate, that is exactly what many people are seeking.

Whole Life Insurance

whole life

limited-payment whole life

Term insurance pays benefits only if the insured dies during a specified period of years, whereas whole life insurance pays the policy's face amount upon the death of the insured, regardless of when death occurs. It is this characteristic—protection for the whole of life—that gives the insurance its name. If the premiums are to be paid throughout the insured's lifetime, the insurance is known as *whole life;* if premiums are to be paid only during a specified period, the insurance is called *limited-payment whole life.*

Traditional whole life insurance policies have fixed and guaranteed premiums, cash values, and death benefits. Coverage can never be cancelled and premiums can never be increased. It is a feature-rich, customizable policy which can be tailored to suit the client's needs and goals.

In contrast, nontraditional, or interest-sensitive policies, give policyowners greater flexibility, including the ability to change premium amounts and total death benefits. The increase in contractual flexibility of these products comes at the price of reduced guarantees and the shifting of some of the risk inherent in the policy from the insurer to the policyowner.

Table 4-1 Individual Life Insurance Policies in Force, by Product Type

Product Type	Percentage of Policies
Whole Life	49%
Universal Life	14%
Variable Life	Less than 1/2 of 1%
Variable Universal Life	1%
Total Permanent	64%
Term Insurance	36%
Total	100%

Source: Individual Life Insurance Sales Trends, 1975–2012, LIMRA International, Inc. 2013

A key aspect of whole life insurance is that the product is based on guarantees: guaranteed premiums, guaranteed cash values and guaranteed death benefits. These elements seem to have resounded with the public after the economic uncertainty brought about by the recession of the last several years. Consumers have been shaken by the recession, collapsing job security and an unstable investment marketplace. Whole life sales showed significant increases in 2012, because it provides exactly what consumers are seeking—confidence, certainty and predictability.

Ordinary Life Insurance

Ordinary life insurance is a type of whole life insurance with a fixed face amount, where it is assumed that a definite premium will be paid each year in the same amount until the insured's death. The terms whole life and ordinary insurance are interchangeable, but it is desirable to define whole life insurance this way, since in many cases, life insurance is purchased with no intention of the policyowner to pay premiums as long as the insured lives. The insurance is often purchased anticipating the use of dividends to pay the premium sooner than the life expectancy of the insured. In other cases, the plan may be to eventually surrender the insurance for an annuity or for a reduced amount of insurance. Whole life should not be considered a type of insurance on which the policyowner is committed to pay premiums as long as the insured lives or even into the insured's extreme old age. Rather, it should be viewed as a type of policy that provides permanent protection for the lowest total premium outlay and some degree of flexibility, to meet changing needs and circumstances for both long-lived persons and those with average-duration lifetimes.

Whole life is based on the level premium concept, which generates a cash value based on the advanced premium used to create the level premium. The level premium produces an insurance plan that combines protection and savings. Both the need for protection and long-term savings should be present to make this an economical and effective insurance purchase.

In permanent, or cash value, life insurance, policyowners pay additional premium over and above the term premium (net amount at risk) to create a cash value as well as a level premium. Because the inside buildup of the cash value in a life insurance policy is tax-deferred, the pretax earnings on the accounts within the policy are used to pay the term insurance costs that would otherwise be paid with after-tax earnings. The fact that a policyowner can purchase life insurance with these pretax earnings is unique to permanent life insurance.

All types of permanent insurance should be thought of as a solution that can meet many long-term financial goals. It performs very poorly as a short-term savings vehicle. Surrender of the policy within the first 5 to 10 years will result in a considerable loss, since the surrender values reflect the company's recovery of initial policy acquisition expenses. Permanent insurance should be purchased with the intent of keeping the policy for 20 years or more.

Ordinary life insurance is an appropriate foundation for any insurance program and in an adequate amount can well serve as the entire program. Its distinctive features are discussed below.

Permanent Protection

The protection provided by the ordinary life contract is *permanent*—the term does not normally expire, and the policy never has to be renewed or converted. If a policyowner continues to pay premiums or pay up their policy, they have protection for as long as the insured lives, regardless of the insured's health; eventually, the face amount of the policy will be paid.

Figure 4-1
Whole Life

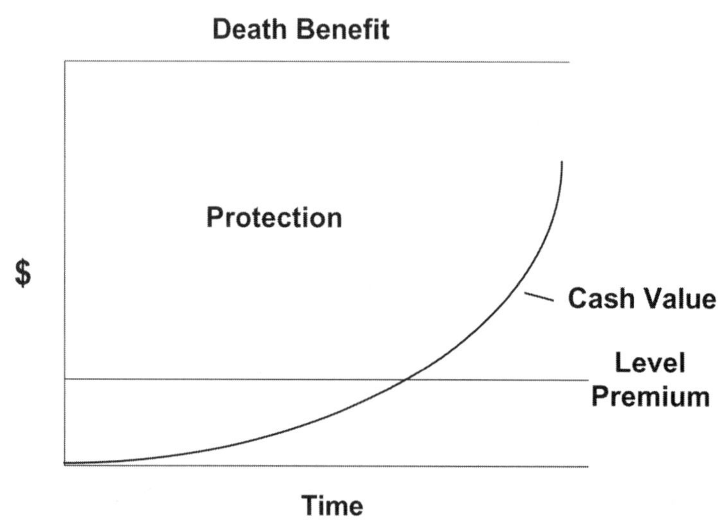

In this sense, the ordinary or whole life policy is an endowment. If the insured lives to the maturity date, the face amount is paid to the policyowner, or can be continued under a settlement agreement or a continuation rider that keeps the policy in force. This is a valuable right, because virtually all people need some insurance for as long as they live, if for nothing more than to pay last illness and funeral expenses. In most cases, the need is much greater than that.

Lowest Premium Outlay

The premium is the price charged by the life insurance company for an insurance contract. To calculate the premium, the first step is to develop a number that equates to the value of benefits promised under the contract. If the premium is paid in one sum, it is called a single premium. Once the single premium is calculated, the modal premiums of annual, semiannual, quarterly and monthly can be derived. These more frequent premiums are actuarially equivalent to the single premium. The calculation of premiums requires three fundamental assumptions: a rate of mortality, a rate of interest, and a rate of expense. The net premium takes into account only the first two factors, a rate of mortality and a rate of interest. The net premium is sufficient to provide all benefits owed under the contract. To this is added an amount to cover expenses, unforeseen contingencies and profit, called loading, and together with the net premium make up the gross premium that is charged to the policyowner.

Whole life insurance premiums are expected to be paid over the lifetime of the insured. Naturally, the longer the period over which the single-sum payment is spread, the lower each periodic payment will be. Limited payment life policy premiums are paid only over a specified period or to a specific age, so the shorter the premium paying period, the higher the premium will be in order to equal the net single premium. The extreme form of the limited payment spectrum is the single-premium whole life policy. Limited-payment insurance contracts provide benefits that justify the higher premium rates. If, however, the insured's objective is to secure the maximum amount of permanent insurance protection per dollar of annual premium outlay, then he or she will be best served by the whole life contract.

Cash Value or Accumulation Element

As a by-product of the level premium, whole life develops cash values. These values result from the reserve the insurer needs to accumulate in the early years of the policy so there will be sufficient money, together with interest earned on the reserve and ongoing premium payments, to pay the promised benefits. Without the reserve, the level premium would be insufficient to pay the increasing mortality costs. The reserve gradually increases and eventually equals the face amount of the policy at maturity. However, the reserve at all durations is lower than other forms of limited payment whole life insurance. In other words, the protection element in whole life is higher than forms of limited pay life, where premiums and reserves are larger. Consequently, many believe that the whole life contract offers the optimal combination of protection and savings. The contract emphasizes protection, but it also accumulates a cash value that can be used to accomplish a variety of purposes. In the early years, the amount of protection is lower relative to the premium than with term insurance. However, later, as term rates increase while the whole life premium remains level, the reverse will be true.

Cash values are not generally available during the first year or two of the insurance, because of the cost to the company of putting the business on the books. Common exceptions are single-premium policies and some limited-payment whole life policies whose first-year premiums are large enough to exceed all first-year expenses incurred to create the policy and maintain policy reserves.

The rate of return on the cash value within whole life has been a point of dispute and criticism. This is particularly true since the arrival of the interest sensitive and variable products in the marketplace, especially when interest rates in the economy are high, and the stock market is in a bull market. Whole life performs particularly well during economic downturns. When safety of principal, conservative risk and investment management, contractually guaranteed liquidity, and the cost of protection are combined, whole life offers a package of benefits that satisfy a broad range of financial objectives.

Living Benefits. The cash value component also translates into what are called the "living benefits" of cash value life insurance. These benefits can be accessed while the insured is alive, when they are needed as supplemental funds for living. The cash value component can serve as an emergency fund during key life events, such as the birth of a child, a second marriage, a child going to college, or a transition to retirement. Cash value life insurance lends itself to a multitude of financial needs, through policy loans and withdrawals of dividends.

Creditor Protection. Depending on state laws, cash value life insurance may not be treated as an asset subject to liability judgments. If someone is sued, life insurance policies, unlike many investments, such as savings accounts, remain untouched, providing the policyowner with financial options, regardless of the outcome of the lawsuit.

The state laws providing protection for life insurance against the claims of creditors are complex and varied. All states and the federal government have enacted legislation providing protection for life insurance against the claims of creditors. States vary according to which benefits are protected and the interest of the debtor in the policy. Whether the debtor is the policyowner, insured or beneficiary will change the protections provided from one state to another. The amounts of death benefits and cash values that are protected vary as well. It is best that you look up the creditor protection laws in the states where you do business, since it is impossible to summarize state protections against creditors.

Investment Objectives. Whole life follows a conservative investment strategy. Its investment goals are safety of principal and a steady flow of income in order to guarantee future benefits. Investments must be safe and predictable. The dollars backing whole life are invested in the insurance company's general portfolio. The general portfolio of the insurance company is composed primarily of high-grade, long-term corporate and government bonds and mortgages. The quality of the company and its investments vary, so it is important to study how a company invests its money.

You can expect investments within the general portfolio to perform in a similar way to a portfolio that is approximately 95 percent long-term bonds and 5 percent stock. The historic return on these investments is between 5 percent and 6 percent. It is because of these investments that whole life returns are what they are. They are not variable investments, stocks, derivatives, options, futures, high-yield bonds and the like. They are investments emphasizing safety and income; yield is sacrificed in this risk-return equation for the more prominent objective of safety.

Whole Life Product Investment. Whole life provides permanent protection at a relatively modest outlay because the mortality costs are spread over the entire policy period through the level premium design. The premium paid for a cash value policy is not a measure of the policy's cost. A policy can have a relatively high premium yet be low in cost by having large dividends, cash values, or excess interest credits. Interest crediting generally has the largest impact on reducing policy costs.

general account method

Insurance companies traditionally use the portfolio or general account method of crediting interest. This blends all of the investment returns over years of investing and pays a general rate based on the combined return on the entire general account. No attempt is made to distinguish rates earned at different periods. The portfolio method homogenizes rates and makes them more stable over time. Portfolio rates lag behind current interest rate changes, something like trying to turn a battleship as opposed to a speedboat. When interest rates are declining, portfolio rates will be higher, and when interest rates climb, portfolio rates will lag behind.

new-money method

Some companies feel it is more competitive and fair to use a current or *new-money method* of crediting interest to policies. With the new-money method, the return earned on money invested in the insurance policy depends on when the investment is made. The rate of return is determined by the rate the company is able to secure at the time the policyowner purchases the policy. Different blocks of policies will receive different interest crediting and dividend amounts under the new-money method. Portfolio rates change slowly, but new-money rates move more quickly in response to market changes.

Universal life products introduced new-money interest rate crediting at a time when interest rates were historically high, which meant that projections of potential future policy values were particularly attractive to prospects. Many purchasers, as well as advisors, were not well informed about the risks inherent in policy illustrations and confused current projections and policy guarantees. As interest rates fell, many discovered that new-money rates could fall as fast as they rose, and that they are more volatile than general account rates. Actual results did not meet expected results and there were many disappointments for all concerned.

participating

Participating and Nonparticipating Policies. If the insurer is profitable, a portion of that profit may be distributed to policyowners through dividends, if the policies are *participating*. Life insurance dividends are considered a return of excess premium paid, based on the actual experience of the company. Dividends, which are not guaranteed, result from saving in mortality or expense charges, or excess interest earned, compared to the original assumptions used to create the premium. Investment results usually account for the largest portion of dividends. Participating policies typically charge a small extra margin in the premium in anticipation of returning part of the premium later as a dividend. This allows the company to maintain a stronger contingency margin, and still adjust the cost to policyowners after results are evaluated. Dividends can be applied to an eligible participating policy as paid-up additions, dividend accumulations, reduced premiums, or cash.

nonparticipating

Nonparticipating policies are not eligible for dividends. They have a premium that is lower than participating policies and do not have the adjustment mechanism that dividends provide. If dividends are paid, the net cost for participating policies may be less than for nonparticipating policies. Most flexible premium policies, such as universal life, are nonparticipating. These policies allow for adjustments due to actual experience, through changes in interest crediting, and mortality and expense charges.

Whole Life Riders

Like term insurance, whole life is a highly customizable product. There are many riders to meet a client's needs. The following are just a sampling.

- Waiver-of-premium rider
- Children's level term rider
- Spouse and children's rider
- Accidental death-benefit rider
- Accidental death and dismemberment rider
- Accelerated death-benefit rider
- Additional insured rider
- Other covered insured rider
- Children's rider
- Return-of-premium rider
- Guaranteed premium rider
- Five-year term rider
- Increasing premium term rider
- Paid-up additions rider
- Policy purchase option rider
- Spouse's paid-up insurance purchase option rider
- Guaranteed insurability rider
- Living benefits rider
- Unemployment rider
- Long-term care rider
- Long-term care with terminal benefits rider
- Long-term care with terminal benefits and extension-of-benefits rider
- Disability income rider
- Family income rider
- Cost of living rider
- Level term-to-65 rider

Policy Loans

policy loan

All cash value policies (for example, whole life, universal life, adjustable life, variable life, variable universal life, and current assumption whole life) have provisions for policy loans, as required by law. *Policy loans* give the policyowner access to the cash value that accumulates inside the policy without having to terminate the policy.

The policyowner requests a loan and the life insurer will lend the funds confidentially. The loan provisions in the policy specify what portion of the cash value is available and how interest will be determined. In most policies, approximately 90 percent of the cash value is available for loans and any portion of the available cash value can be borrowed. Some policies may restrict the amount of loanable funds to 92 percent of the cash value in recognition of an 8 percent policy loan interest rate.

The money is always available without question. Policyowners indicate in their requests the amount desired, and they can take out more than one policy loan as long as the aggregate amount of all outstanding loans and accrued interest applicable to those loans does not exceed the available policy cash value. The insurance company does not ask why the policyowner wants to borrow. There are no credit references, background investigations, or cosigners involved.

Policy loans incur interest charges on the borrowed funds. The policy will stipulate either (1) a fixed rate (commonly 5 to 8 percent) or (2) a variable interest rate tied to some specified index. The variable rate may be set by formula, such as Moody's composite yield on corporate bonds or a formula that uses the interest rate being credited to the cash value, plus a specified spread.

The contractual right to borrow may cause confusion for some people who object to "borrowing their own money." Although a policy loan is termed a "loan," it is different from a commercial loan. It is actually an advancement against the cash value (during the lifetime of the insured) or death benefit (after the death of the insured). An ordinary debtor-creditor relationship is not created. The policyowner does not borrow from a savings fund that has been created through the payment of premiums. No such fund exists. The policyowner is borrowing the company's money, using the cash value and death benefit of the policy as collateral.

Meanwhile, the policy's cash value continues to increase at the same rate as if the loan had not been taken. As a result, the interest credited in the cash value accumulation grows, because the loaned value still earns interest. Clients should be advised to save the use of this right for emergencies. Like other emergency funds, life insurance equity should be conserved. Unless interest payments or repayment of loans are made, the loan amount will steadily grow to the point that the policy cash values and death benefits are depleted.

The policyowner has the option of paying the policy loan interest in cash or having the unpaid interest charge added to the balance of the outstanding loan(s). The latter choice can be costly, because future interest charges will be applied to the unpaid interest amount, as well as the initial policy loan. The policyowner may choose to pay any part of the principal or interest charge at any time, since there is no repayment schedule or requirement.

If the policy loan and accrued interest are not paid in cash, the life insurer can recover the outstanding balance of the loans and accrued interest from the death benefits if the insured dies, or from the cash surrender value if the policy is terminated. In fact, the policy will automatically terminate if the policy loan balance plus unpaid interest exceeds the policy cash value. Loan interest may have to be paid to keep the policy in force if the cash value is heavily borrowed.

Some whole life policies give policyowners an *automatic premium loan option*. When this option is selected, a premium due past the grace period will be paid automatically by a new policy loan. This will keep the policy in force as long as there is adequate cash value to cover each delinquent premium. However, the policy will terminate if the cash value is exhausted.

The automatic premium loan provision does not apply to flexible premium policies, because the insurer deducts mortality charges and other expenses directly from the cash value, not from premium payments. Therefore, no interest charges are incurred for skipped premium payments.

Policy loans result in the life insurer's release of funds it would otherwise invest to earn investment income. If the rate of investment return on the insurer's portfolio is greater than the rate being applied to the policy loan, the insurer experiences a reduction in earnings. For that reason, the insurance company takes steps to offset such loan-induced losses in order to preserve equity between policyowners who leave their cash values invested, and those who prevent the insurer from reaping the higher yield by borrowing from them.

In the past, participating whole life policy dividends were not affected by policy loans. Most participating whole life policies being sold today use a method of dividend crediting called *direct recognition,* which reduces dividends on policies with outstanding loans. This not only adjusts for the differential in earnings, but also discourages policy loans.

For universal life policies and other nonparticipating designs, there are no dividends to adjust; insurers may compensate for lost earnings on policy loans by reducing the earnings rate being credited to the cash value. If there are no policy loans, the insurer credits its normal crediting rate to the full cash value. However, if there are policy loans, the insurer can credit the current rate to the unloaned portion of the cash value and a lower rate (often 2 percent lower) to the portion of the cash value equal to the loan indebtedness. When the loan is repaid, the insurer resumes crediting the higher rate to the full cash value.

The creation of a policy loan does have negative consequences on the policy. The death benefit paid to the beneficiary is reduced by outstanding policy loans and accrued interest. A policy loan is really an advance against the death benefit; the death benefit is adjusted to reflect the prior disbursement.

Outstanding policy loans also reduce the *nonforfeiture benefits*. The net cash value available to provide either extended term insurance or reduced paid-up insurance is decreased by the loan. In the case of extended term insurance, the amount of term insurance is reduced from the original amount of coverage by the amount of loan indebtedness as well.

delay clause

State statutes allow life insurers to delay lending funds for up to 6 months after requested through the *delay clause*. This is a form of emergency protection for the insurance company and is the same as the protection provided for policy surrenders. It provides protection in the event policyowners' demands for loans or surrenders require the insurer to liquidate assets at significant losses to satisfy the loan demands. Insurers are reluctant to invoke this provision. In actuality, delaying access to funds is an indication of financial weakness that insurers wish to avoid, since this will further erode policyowner confidence. Those life insurers that have failed in recent years chose not to invoke their right to delay policy loans. Quick access to cash values was terminated only after the insurance commissioner seized control of the companies.

Policy Loan Features
• Available to policyowner on demand • Interest charges apply • Depending on the specific contract, interest rates are either fixed or variable • Variable interest rates tied to a published index • Unpaid interest charges added to loan balance • Repayment of loans is at discretion of policyowner • Outstanding policy loans plus unpaid interest is recovered from either death benefit or surrender value • Policy terminates if loans plus unpaid interest ever exceed the policy cash value

Whole Life—Term Blends

In the late 1960s, "economatic" life insurance, blending term and whole life together, was developed by mutual companies. By adding term insurance to participating policies, the premium could be lowered to compete with nonparticipating policies. The mix between term and whole was such that anticipated dividends could purchase paid-up additions that would eventually equal and replace the term amount.

When whole life lost market share to new products such as universal life, product design changes reflecting more flexibility were introduced. Combinations of level and decreasing term riders with lower whole life face amounts and paid up additions riders allow traditional policies to be more competitive from a price perspective. As a result of the economic crisis beginning in 2008, there has been a shift towards traditional whole and away from variable and universal life. The public is seeking safety, security and quality in insecure economic times.

Limited-Payment Life Insurance

Limited-payment life insurance is a type of whole life insurance for which premiums are limited by contract to a specified number of years.

The limitation in limited-payment policies can be expressed in terms of the number of annual premiums or the age beyond which premiums will not be required. Policies whose premiums are limited by number usually stipulate 10, 15, 20, 25, or 30 annual payments, such as 20-pay life. The greater the number of premiums payable, the more closely the contract approaches the whole life design. For those who prefer to limit their premium payments to a period measured by a terminal age, companies issue policies that are paid up at a specified age—typically, 60, 65, or 70, and are named Life Paid Up at 65, for example. The objective is to enable the insured to pay for the policy during his or her working lifetime. Many companies issue contracts that are payable to a higher age, such as 85, but for all practical purposes, these contracts are very similar to whole life contracts.

paid-up insurance

When the final premium is paid, the policy is paid up. *Paid-up insurance* means that no more premiums are required contractually, even though the policy's face amount remains in force for life. The policy's reserve value is sufficient, so that with each of the remaining years that interest is earned on the reserve, there will be enough funding to pay the costs of insurance and increase the cash values and reserves to the maturity date without further premium payments.

The net single premium of a limited-payment whole life contract at the date of issue is precisely the same as a whole life contract. Because there will be fewer premium payments under the limited-payment policy, each premium is larger than the comparable premium under a whole life contract. The fewer the guaranteed premiums specified, or the shorter the premium-paying period, the higher each premium will be. However, the higher premiums are offset by greater cash and surrender values.

The limited-payment policy will provide a larger fund for use in an emergency and will accumulate a larger fund for retirement purposes than will a whole life contract issued at the same age. It is suitable when a prospect wants the premium period to end on a specific date, or when a prospect's working lifetime or high-income period is limited (such as a professional athlete). On the other hand, if death takes place within the first several years after issue of the contract, the total premiums paid under the limited-payment policy will exceed those paid for a whole life policy. The comparatively long-lived policyowner, however, will pay considerably less in premiums for the limited-payment plan than the whole life, because a greater portion of the insurance costs will be paid by investment earnings.

There is no financial advantage between policy types in the whole life portfolio of products. They are *actuarially equivalent*. The choice depends on circumstances and personal preference. The limited-payment policy offers the assurance that premium payments will be confined to the insured's productive years, while the whole life contract provides maximum permanent protection for a lower annual outlay. The limited-payment policy contains the same policy features as whole life, such as surrender options, dividend options, settlement options, and other features that make for significant flexibility.

vanishing premium

It is important to differentiate between a limited-payment policy (in which paid-up status is guaranteed at the end of the premium-paying period) and a premiums-paid-by-dividend approach (which uses policyowner dividends to pay all of the premiums after they are adequate to do so). Premiums-paid-by-dividend approaches have been sold using the term *vanishing premium*. The notable difference between the two is that under the "vanishing premium" approach, dividends are not guaranteed and may decline in the future. If dividends turn out to be inadequate to pay the premiums, the policyowner will have to resume premium payments out of pocket, or let the policy lapse. There is no guarantee that so-called vanishing premiums will actually vanish, or that if they do vanish they will never reappear. This concept created many sales in the 1980s, as well as many disappointed consumers and class-action lawsuits when interest rates plummeted in the 1990s and premiums failed to vanish.

Single-Premium Life Insurance

single-premium life (SPL)

The ultimate form of limited-payment contract is the *single-premium life* insurance policy *(SPL)*. Under this plan, the number of premiums is limited to one. The policy is fully paid up with the single premium. No further premiums are needed or permitted. The effective amount of insurance protection (net amount at risk) is substantially less and the investment element is correspondingly greater than in whole life. Such contracts are purchased largely for accumulation and income purposes. They offer a high degree of security, a satisfactory interest yield, and are readily convertible to cash, guaranteed by the insurer for the duration of the contract. Since the single premium represents a substantial amount of money, and since there will be no return of any part of it in the event of the insured's early death, it has only limited appeal for protection purposes. It is of interest to investors who desire estate liquidity, or wish to gift or transfer wealth to specific beneficiaries or charities. The tax-free death benefit instantly increases the value of the estate. Additionally, many *SPL*s have living benefit features, so the client can gain access to their money through policy loans or accelerated benefit riders if they need money for chronic long-term care expenses or in the event of a terminal illness. If a client has a substantial lump-sum distribution, such as when funds become available from the sale of a residence, after tax distributions from qualified plans, annual bonuses, or "lazy money," such as certificates of deposit or inherited funds, and has needs such as described above, SPLs can be a good solution. SLPs offer many advantages over other savings vehicles, such as tax-deferred growth and an immediate, increased, guaranteed tax-free death benefit.

These policies provide a cash value interest rate that is competitive with investments of comparable risk. The initial interest rate is guaranteed for one year, although there are some three-year and five-year guarantees available. These policies also provide a long-term guarantee that the rate credited to the cash value will not fall below a stated minimum. Single-premium policies are by definition modified endowment contracts (MECs) that will be discussed later.

Although SPLs are available to most ages, it is best suited for mature, affluent pre-retirees or retirees. It provides financial security and the potential for long-term capital growth. It may not be well suited for younger clients needing income, since income will be taxable to the extent of gains under MEC rules, and borrowing should be restricted until after age 59½, at which point the premature penalty tax will not apply. Single premium life is commonly combined with long-term care benefits to make each benefit more appealing, and to provide a benefit in case the insured needs long-term care services, with any excess accumulated benefits passing to heirs as a death benefit at the death of the insured.

Modified Premium Whole Life Insurance

modified premium whole life (MPWL)

In *modified premium whole life (MPWL)* policies, the premium for the first few years of the contract is lower than that required for the remainder of the premium-paying period. A variation of this concept is the graded premium policy that has gradually increasing premiums over a period of up to 20 years, which are followed by level premiums thereafter.

The distinctive feature of MPWL is the way the premiums are structured. For the first several years, MPWL premiums are lower than they would be for the same amount of whole life (and higher than for comparable term insurance). After the initial period, the premiums increase to a level higher than the whole life premium at the issue age, and remain at that level for the life of the policy. This premium is less than the premium would be at the attained age at the end of the modified premium period. MPWL premiums are *actuarially equivalent* to whole life. Cash values and other nonforfeiture values accumulate in proportion to the premiums paid. The variations on the structure of the lower premiums in the early years vary greatly in the number of years the "step-rates" last, the number of steps, and the size of the steps in arriving at the ultimate level premium. All other policy features and benefits are the same as whole life.

MPWL policies allow people who want whole life insurance to make the purchase even though their current income cannot support the whole life premium. In later years, when income levels are greater, there should be less difficulty in paying the higher premiums. This type of policy may be well suited to a professional student, such as a medical, dental, or law student for example, who, upon graduating may have significant debt and low income, but as he or she develops a practice will see their income and insurance needs increase.

Joint Life Insurance

joint life

survivorship life

The typical life insurance contract is written on the life of one person and is known as *single life insurance*. A contract can be written on more than one life, and is known as a joint life contract, also called a *first-to-die joint life* policy. A joint life contract is one written on the lives of two or more persons and payable at the death of the first insured to die, at which point the contract ends. If the face amount is payable upon the death of the last of two or more lives insured under a single contract, it is called either *survivorship life* or a *second-to-die* policy. Survivorship policies have become popular as a means of funding federal estate taxes of wealthy couples whose wills make maximum use of the unlimited marital deduction at the first death. Joint life policies are also used for funding business buy-sell agreements.

The joint life policy may cover from 2 to 12 lives, but because of expenses and other practical obstacles, most companies limit the number to 3 or 4 lives. A few insurers will issue policies on more than 12 lives if they all have related business interests. The contract is usually written as a whole life or universal life plan. It is seldom written as term, since separate term policies on each life for the same amount would cost little more than a joint policy and would offer the advantage of continued protection to survivors.

The premium for a joint life policy is somewhat greater than the combined premiums on separate policies providing an equivalent amount of insurance. For example, the premium for a $200,000 joint life policy covering two lives is larger than the sum of the premiums on two separate contracts providing $100,000 each. This is because only $100,000 is payable upon the death of the first of the two insureds to die with separate policies, while $200,000 is payable under a joint life policy. Moreover, since two lives are covered, the cost of insurance is relatively high, and cash values are relatively low. However, a joint life policy costs less than two separate policies providing $200,000 each.

The provisions of the joint life contract closely follow those of the single-life contract. Terms vary by policy. The clause allowing conversion to other policy forms differs in that it allows conversion policies on separate lives as follows:

1. Conversion to single-life policies on the same plan as that of the joint policies upon divorce or dissolution of business
2. Division of the amount of insurance among the insured lives either equally or unequally
3. Dating of the new policies as of the original date of issue of the joint policy

Joint Life Features

- Insure more than one life with one policy
- Pay only one death benefit
- First-to-die policies pay death benefit when the first death of the insureds occurs
- Survivorship or second-to-die policies pay death benefit when the second insured person dies (no benefit at first death)
- Survivorship policies often used to prefund federal estate taxes of husband and wife
- May be converted to single-life policies if insureds divorce or dissolve their business relationships

Business partners sometimes take out a joint policy covering the lives of all partners and written for an amount equal to the largest interest involved. Upon the death of the first partner, the surviving partners receive funds with which to purchase the deceased's partnership interest. Stockholders in a closely held corporation may follow the same practice. Because the insurance usually terminates upon the first death of the partners or stockholders, the remaining members of the firm will not only be without insurance, but may also be uninsurable.

Some life insurers offer a short period of extended coverage for the surviving partners or shareholders and guarantee their insurability under a new joint life policy similar to the previous one. A few insurers have introduced joint life policies that allow allocations of unequal amounts of death proceeds to match actual unequal ownership interests.

A joint life policy may be suitable for a husband and wife when the death of either will create a need for funds, as would be true if estate taxes and administrative expenses were involved. It can be used for pension maximization needs where retirement income is lost when the first spouse dies, for college planning, for retirement planning, and for joint mortgage redemption needs.

There is a growing number of insurance companies that offer first-to-die riders that are attached to survivorship life plans. In this arrangement, a death benefit is paid at both the first and last death. There are also term riders that can be used with the first-to-die plan that will pay additional benefits when the survivor dies.

Survivorship Life Policies

Survivorship life, also referred to as second-to-die or last-to-die, insures two or more lives and pays the death proceeds upon the death of the second or last insured to die. Some survivorship policies are traditional whole life or interest-sensitive permanent designs (universal and variable universal life), while others are term.

This policy is priced and based on the probability of having to pay benefits at the death of the last to die. Since it is a form of joint life insurance, it has premiums that are lower than the cost of separate policies on each of the insureds. Premiums normally continue after the first death, but some products provide that premiums cease at the first death, or offer this feature as a rider.

With some permanent survivorship policies, cash values increase dramatically at the first death. The reason is that the policy is designed to pay benefits following the occurrence of two deaths. The reserves (cash values are a function of reserves) required by the insurance company are minimal when payment of the face amount is contingent upon two deaths rather than one. However, when the first insured dies, the death benefit will become payable upon the occurrence of only one death, so the reserve requirements for this contingency become much greater. As a result, the cash value increases substantially after the first death.

Survivorship life is particularly attractive in estate planning situations in which the unlimited marital deduction is used, but may be applicable in any situation where estate liquidity is needed and life insurance can provide the cash. It can also serve to provide for wealth replacement, estate equalization, charitable gifts, and asset transfer to the next generation.

The unlimited marital deduction allows 100 percent of assets to be passed from one spouse to another at death or by gift without paying estate or gift taxes. Upon the death of the surviving spouse, taxes may be due, since there is no marital deduction. The second death triggers payment of the insurance policy benefit and the proceeds are used to pay estate taxes and administrative costs. It can also be used in many business and family situations. It is particularly attractive in those situations where a business or family could survive financially after one death, but not after a second death.

Underwriting benefits come from covering two insureds in one policy. It is even possible to get coverage for a person who would be considered uninsurable under individual underwriting standards.

Survivorship policy riders include term insurance that will pay a death benefit at the first death or at the second death (may be increasing, level, or decreasing), and a paid-up additions rider. Additionally, many contracts provide an exchange provision for separate policies under specific circumstances, such as changes in the Internal Revenue Code that would eliminate or reduce the unlimited marital deduction, or reduce by a certain amount or eliminate the estate tax. Some companies will allow a split if the insureds become legally divorced while the policy is in existence.

Mass Market/Payroll Deduction Products

Working with personal insurance prospects and business owners can lead to the sale of life insurance through the mass marketing/payroll deduction method. Many insurance companies offer a special mass-marketed individual permanent life product, such as whole life or universal life, for this purpose. These plans typically feature simplified underwriting, level premiums and face amounts, and inexpensive dependent coverage. The employee personally owns them, so upon leaving their employer or retiring, the employee may continue with the plan. Most are sold on a money-purchase basis; that is, the insured employees decide how much to set aside each week from their paychecks for life insurance. The amount of insurance these payroll deductions purchase depends upon the insured's age and underwriting class.

After the initial sale to the employer, mass-marketed policies are made available to the employees through individual or group sessions. Each employee is asked to sign up for the plan, or decline it, using special enrollment cards. The plan is then administered by the employer, who makes the deductions from the participants' pay and forwards the money to the insurance company in one check on a periodic statement bill.

This is a highly effective, cost-efficient way to sell life insurance. It also builds solid relationships with the employer and enables you to do further life insurance planning with the employees on a selective basis.

Combination Products

Long-term care insurance (LTCI) combination plans have been a niche market in the life insurance industry for many years. The Pension Protection Act of 2006 introduced several new tax features that should increase interest dramatically. As of 2010, charges to the cash value of an annuity or life insurance policy to pay for a qualified long-term care rider reduce the investment in the contract and are not included in gross income. Additionally, the act established that a Section 1035 exchange is allowed for long-term care combination products from 2010 on. An existing annuity, endowment, or life insurance policy can be exchanged for qualified stand-alone LTCI or a combination product with a qualified LTCI rider.

In today's marketplace, there are two basic approaches to life insurance with long-term care benefits. In the "integrated or hybrid" design, single-premium whole life or universal life policies are sold with both life insurance and long-term care coverage. The second approach uses an optional rider on a whole life, universal life, or variable universal life policy where premium is paid on an on-going basis.

Under both designs, the death benefit is accelerated to cover qualifying long-term care expenses, typically after a 90-day elimination period. For an additional cost, the policyowner may be able to elect an extension of benefits option that provides for continuation of long-term care coverage to several times the life policy death benefit. Inflation protection is also offered. The long-term benefits are tax-qualified, so benefit triggers and covered expenses are largely uniform across companies and mirror tax-qualified stand-alone LTCI plans. Covered expenses include home health care, assisted living, nursing home care, and adult day care. The policyowner chooses a desired total LTCI available fund and a period of time over which that fund will be paid out (24, 36, or 48 months are common, with a few carriers offering 60 months or lifetime payouts).

Consumers are concerned with needing long-term care at some point in their lives, and recognize the peace of mind an insurance product can provide. Consumers like the idea of a combination product that will allow them to get something for their premium payments, regardless of how life unfolds. If they need long-term care, the LTCI benefits can be used. If not, they or their beneficiaries would receive the life insurance death benefits or cash value living benefits. Be aware that these products provide either a full life insurance death benefit, or a full long-term care benefit, but not both. If the prospect has a need for both, these products may not be the best choice, unless other coverage is in place.

These products appeal to two markets. The first is the older, affluent client who has a primary long-term care need. The individual is typically over 50 with invested assets of $100,000 or more, and wants to plan for retirement and health care needs. The LTCI combination provides a means for leveraging existing assets that may have been set aside for potential long-term care funding. The second market is the younger, upper middle-income client who has a primary life insurance need. This client is between 40 and 60, with $50,000 or more in annual income.

Endowment Policies

endowment life insurance

An *endowment life insurance* contract pays the face amount of the policy, whether the insured dies prior to the endowment maturity date or survives to the end of the period. Endowments provide level death benefits and cash values that increase with time, so a policy's cash value equals its death benefit at maturity. Whole life can be regarded as an endowment at age 100 or 120. If age 100 is considered the end of the endowment period, as well as the policy maturity date, then a whole life policy is equivalent to an endowment contract that pays the face amount as a death claim if the insured dies before age 100, or as a matured endowment if he or she survives to age 100. Endowment contracts make the same benefit payable in whole life at age 100 available at younger ages, such as a 20-year endowment. Endowment policies are available for a set number of years or to a specified age.

The endowment contract was designed to provide a death benefit that is equal to the target amount during an accumulation period. Purchasing an endowment policy with a face amount equal to the desired accumulation amount assures that the funds will be available, regardless of whether the insured survives to the target date.

Sales of endowment contracts were declining in the United States even before the federal income tax law was changed in 1984 (Deficit Reduction Act of 1984—DEFRA) to take away the tax-free buildup of flexible-premium endowment policies' cash value. Congress was concerned that life insurance policies, especially endowments and universal life policies, with high cash values relative to their death benefit amounts, were being used as a tax-advantaged accumulation vehicle by the wealthy. To counteract this trend, Congress enacted a test for flexible-premium life insurance in *IRC Sec. 101(f)* that eliminated the tax preference that flexible premium endowments previously enjoyed, although it retained the preference for policies in force before 1985. Subsequently, *IRC Sec. 7702* extended the test to all life insurance policies, including fixed-premium endowments, entered into after October 22, 1986. IRC Sec. 7702 defines the two tests—the cash value accumulation test and the guideline premium and corridor test—that must be met for the death proceeds of life insurance contracts to be fully excludible from the beneficiaries' income. These tests were introduced to control the amount of premium that may be paid into a life insurance contract and still maintain the tax benefits of the Internal Revenue Code afforded to life insurance contracts.

Outside of the United States, especially in countries with high savings rates, the endowment policy is still quite successful and widely used to accumulate funds for a variety of purposes, such as to fund retirement or children's higher education. Endowment policies purchased in other countries are usually bought for the same reasons permanent life insurance policies are purchased in the United States. Regardless of the society or its tax laws, the primary factor motivating life insurance sales is an individual's concern about financial security for his or her children, spouse, parents, and/or business partners. The individual's particular needs tend to change in predictable ways over a normal life cycle.

Adjustable Life Insurance

adjustable life

Families' changing needs for life insurance over long periods of time prompted some insurers to introduce whole life insurance that can be adjusted when needed to accommodate life-cycle shifts. The *adjustable life* policy, which can be positioned anywhere along the spectrum from short duration term insurance through single-premium whole life insurance, gives the policyowner the right to request and obtain a reconfiguration of the policy at specified intervals.

Adjustable life insurance is a product that contains all of the same guarantees regarding cash values, mortality, and expenses as whole life insurance, but has the flexibility to allow the policyowner to adjust the plan of insurance, the premiums, and/or the face amount after it is in force. This allows changes to be made within the original policy, instead of issuing a new policy each time financial needs change. It appeals to purchasers who want the ability to restructure their coverage without assuming any of the investment or mortality risks.

Adjustable life is a whole life policy with fixed premiums that can be changed. A policy change requires a formal request agreed to in writing by both insurer and policyowner before it can be made. The premium remains fixed and inflexible between formal adjustments. Most changes can be made without evidence of insurability, but the insurer can require such evidence if the proposed change increases the amount at risk. Examples of adjustments may involve lowering the premium level to lessen the cash flow burden, or increasing the premium as the policyowner's discretionary income improves.

Adjustable life was introduced in the mid-1970s and gained modest success before the advent of universal life policies. The introduction of adjustable life marked the first major change in the insurance industry toward the development of flexible products. The sales thrust is to coordinate current life insurance needs and premium-paying ability. Interest in adjustable life waned after the success of universal life, which broadened the concept of flexibility.

Adjustable life can be changed, within limits. The policyowner may

- increase or decrease the premium
- increase or decrease the face amount
- lengthen or shorten the protection period
- lengthen or shorten the premium payment period

Basic Policy Features of Adjustable Life

- Death benefits are flexible at the option of the insured. Increases in the death benefit may be subject to evidence of insurability.
- Premiums may be flexible but are designed to be level and fixed for a chosen period between policy changes. The policyowner may change the premium amount as desired within policy limits.
- Cash values depend on premium and face amount.
- Policy loans are available as with whole life insurance.
- Dividends reflect current experience and can be paid in cash, used to reduce premiums, accumulate at interest, or added to the policy values, either increasing the death benefit or lengthening the protection period. Once applied under this last option, dividends become a part of the guaranteed value and may not be surrendered separately.
- Like many other products on the market today, adjustable life uses a new-money pricing method, and generally uses current mortality.

Adjustable life has significant sales appeal in that it can be marketed as the last or only policy a client will ever need to purchase. As insurance needs or premium-paying ability change, adjustments can be made within the framework of the single policy. An unscheduled premium privilege allows policyowners to make lump-sum payments, which will lengthen the protection period or shorten the premium-paying period. For example, a large enough payment might change a plan from term to age 43 to term to age 56, or from life paid-up at 75 to life paid-up at 68. In selling this feature, advisors should be aware of, and remind prospects about, the MEC rules.

The premium for adjustable life is usually somewhat higher than that for a comparable whole life policy. However, the policyowner may end up paying less in the long run, since they will avoid having to buy new policies or exchange existing ones every time changes are needed. To help policyowners keep track of what they have, a report showing current benefits is sent every year from the company.

Current Assumption Whole Life Insurance

current assumption whole life

Current assumption whole life (CAWL) is a variation of traditional whole life that lies between adjustable life and universal life. As the name implies, the policy values (cash value, interest earnings, mortality, and expense charges) are based on current experience and are capable of changing in the short run based on actual results, rather than the long-term and preset values found in the traditional whole life policy.

redetermination

The cash value development of CAWL is more like that of universal life than any other policy. It has a *redetermination* feature that resets the premium amount, and in some instances the death benefit, in reaction to the most recent interval of experience. This interval varies by company, but is frequently five years, although it can be as short as two years or as long as seven years. The main feature that differentiates CAWL from universal life is the absence of total premium flexibility in the renewal years (see figure 4-2).

CAWL is sometimes described as universal life with fixed premiums. This is an oversimplification, because premiums can and will be restructured at specified policy anniversary dates, but, the analogy is useful in developing an understanding of this policy, and how it differs from whole life, adjustable life, and universal life. It is another example of refinements in policy design that fill in some of the missing points along a continuum of possibilities between both extremes—all fixed components and guarantees at one end and all flexible and non-guaranteed components at the other.

Figure 4-2
Adjustable Life Policy Recast at Policyowner's Request at A, B, and C

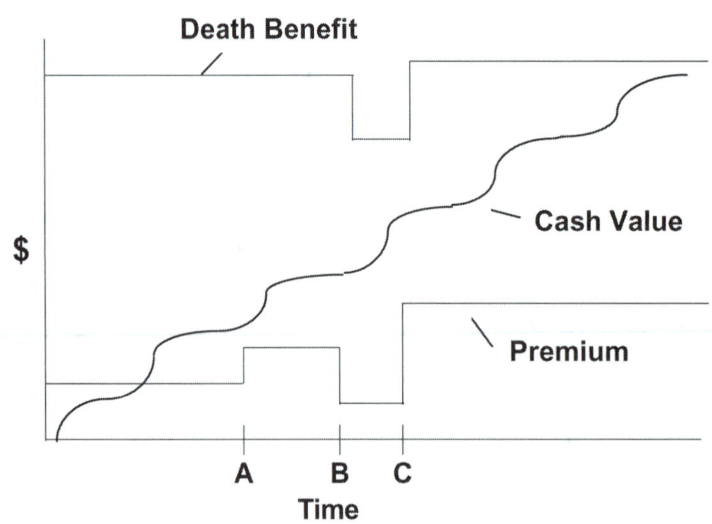

interest-sensitive whole life

There are a few guaranteed elements in CAWL policies: a guaranteed death benefit and a minimum guaranteed interest rate credited to policy cash values. Some companies guarantee the mortality charge and the expense charges. When mortality and expense charges are guaranteed, the policy is often referred to as an *interest-sensitive whole life* policy, because excess interest (current interest minus guaranteed interest) credited to the cash value becomes the only non-guaranteed element in the contract. However, the bulk of CAWL policies have some degree of flexibility in the expense elements.

indeterminate premium whole life

Because many of these designs periodically reset the premium amount based on recent experience, some of these policies are referred to as *indeterminate premium whole life* policies. The actual mortality, interest, and expenses can give rise to lower premium charges, because of favorable experience under the policy. An indeterminate premium whole life policy is similar to ordinary whole life except that it provides for adjustable premiums. The company will charge a "current" premium based on its current estimate of investment earnings, mortality, and expense costs. If these estimates change in later years, the company will adjust the premium accordingly, but never above the maximum guaranteed premium stated in the policy.

CAWL policies are nonparticipating policies that have some after-the-fact adjustment mechanisms without creating dividends. These adjustment mechanisms, charges, and credits, based on actual company experience underlying the particular blocks of policies, allow the insurer to fine-tune its policy and keep it competitive in the marketplace. For competitive purposes, CAWL gives the insurance company a product with a mechanism for sharing favorable investment returns with policyowners. These policies take away the advantage that participating whole life policies had over nonparticipating whole life policies.

CAWL Illustrations

Generally, CAWL policies are illustrated in a manner similar to universal life. The typical CAWL illustration has a guaranteed cash value column and a separate column for excess accumulations (non-guaranteed values). The total cash value for the policy is the sum of the guaranteed cash value and the accumulation supplements. The most complete representation tends to have three different columns for cash values—one for the guaranteed amount, one for the excess accumulations, and one representing the total of the two components.

This approach makes the policy look like the cash value accumulation account reported under most universal life policies: premiums are shown as an incoming item that is reduced by expense charges before being added to the cash value account. Interest on the account balance is usually credited before any mortality charges are deducted. After mortality charges are deducted, the end-of-year fund balance is derived. The significant difference between the accumulation accounts in CAWL and universal life is that universal life policies tend to charge off both expenses and mortality before crediting investment earnings. CAWL policies tend to deduct expenses from premiums, but then credit that amount to the cash value and reflect a credit for investment earnings before deducting a mortality charge.

This approach has led many people to describe CAWL as a hybrid of universal life and traditional whole life, because it has cash value accumulations of excess interest crediting, but still maintains a rigid level premium structure that can be changed on redetermination anniversaries.

Low-Premium/High-Premium Designs

The proportion of excess accumulations is highly dependent on the premium level in the base design. Some insurance companies use a relatively low-premium CAWL design. Adjustments on redetermination dates are more likely to involve an adjustment of the death benefit to make the policy compatible with the premium level being paid. However, sometimes adjustments are made to the premium (up or down), which may or may not change the death benefit.

At the other end of the spectrum, some insurers utilize a high-premium design, where the premium paid is usually more than adequate and normally does not require an upward adjustment on a redetermination date. The high-premium design is more likely to involve projections of how long premiums may be needed until the policy is expected to be self-supporting without further premiums from the policyowner. It is a form of the "vanishing-premium" design. The premium is paid through policy values, either by dividends in a whole life type policy, or by excess interest in a universal life type policy. This concept is different from paid-up status, where the premium no longer needs to be paid.

The caution, however, is that excess accumulations are not guaranteed, nor is the projected period of premium payments guaranteed to make the premium vanish at the end of that period. The policy will be paid up only if the future experience under the policy from that date forward is such that the interest credited and the accumulation account generates enough funds to cover all mortality charges and expenses over the remainder of the contract. The accumulation account might have to be supplemented at some point if mortality charges and expenses cost more than the accumulation account can provide.

On the optimistic side, the policy could continue to exceed expectations even after it reaches paid-up status. If the investment returns on the accumulated fund keep the balance in that account more than adequate to pay all mortality charges and expenses, the policy could continue to enhance the benefits on each redetermination date. This would most likely involve an increase in death benefits since there are no further premiums to reduce at that point.

Redetermination

The level of premiums influences the frequency of *redetermination.* The lower the premium design, the more frequent the policy's redetermination dates. In some of the more recent policy designs, redetermination can be every year; more often the redetermination frequency is every 2 years or every 5 years. On policy anniversaries when it is applicable, the insurance company looks at its actual experience for the block of policies since the previous redetermination date and decides what adjustments, if any, are necessary, based on the assumption of what to expect in the period before the next redetermination.

Policyowner Options. The policyowner generally selects the method to adjust the policy he or she prefers from an available group of options when redetermination occurs. For example, if the redetermination results in a potentially lower premium, the policyowner usually has the following options:

- continue the past level of premiums and have the favorable results applied to enhance the policy's cash value
- increase the death benefit (assuming the insured can provide satisfactory evidence of insurability)
- pay the lower policy premium amount

When experience is less favorable than expectations, the policyowner again has a range of options, including lowering the death benefit, increasing the premium amount, or maintaining the status quo and allowing the policy accumulation account to decrease as the mortality and expense charges exceed the investment earnings on the accumulated fund. This last choice, if available, may have restrictions on its use, since this option may eventually lapse the policy.

Figure 4-3
Current Assumption Whole Life Premiums Changed at Policy Redetermination Anniversary Date

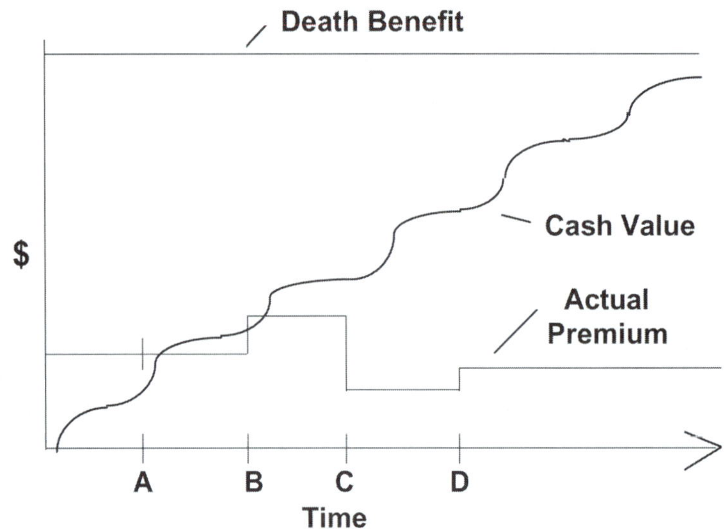

Uses of Current Assumption Whole Life. In a CAWL policy, current interest rates are used to enhance the accumulation account, but the policy does not provide the premium flexibility of a universal life policy. CAWL whole life is an appropriate policy choice for individuals who need the discipline imposed by its fixed-premium design, but want to participate at least in part in the positive investment returns beyond the guaranteed interest rate in the policy. Under this type of policy, the policyowner assumes some of the investment risk and a limited portion of the mortality risk. If actual experience turns out to be poor, the policy may be periodically downgraded on each redetermination date. If actual experience is positive, the policyowner participates in the upside as the result of assuming those risks. Costs in the long run may turn out to be much less than the original projections if experience is favorable enough over the duration of the contract. The real challenge with this and many other life insurance products in which policyowners assume some of the risk is to make sure policyowners understand the nature and extent of the risk being assumed.

Term Versus Permanent: The Age-Old Argument

Whether term or permanent is the better product can only be answered if we know when the insured will die. If you knew the answer to that question, you could design a policy that exactly meets that period. Since we do not know when the insured will die, we need the type of insurance that best meets our ability to pay premiums and meet our financial goals and needs, over our lifetimes, so that the policy will be in force when death occurs or the need for insurance protection ends.

Only about 4 percent or 5 percent of term policies result in death claims, because the great majority of term policies are not in force when death occurs. One reason for this is that term insurance coverage has often ended before people reach life expectancy. In many cases, this is intentional. While initially people intend to keep term policies in force, they often change their minds when situations change. This occurs especially after retirement. Term insurance premiums become increasingly higher, no cash reserves are accumulating, and an expiration day is approaching. The insured's only option is to convert if a need still exists, perhaps at a premium beyond what the insured can afford or wants to pay. Another reason that term policies do not mature as death claims is that they have been converted to permanent policies.

Term or permanent—which is better? Many clients will seek your opinion. You and your clients need to take into consideration all of the factors that could influence their situation, make realistic projections, and monitor the performance of their plan, being aware of changes in their life and how these affect their insurance needs.

Buy Term and Invest the Difference

Some financial advisors argue that people can do better with their money by buying term and investing the amount they will save by not paying the higher permanent premiums. The side investment would eventually be large enough to offset the steadily increasing term premium and, in the end, the insured would be many dollars ahead.

Proponents of the buy-term-and-invest-the-difference strategy present several compelling arguments against purchasing whole life and other permanent products:

- Both the term face amount and side fund are available to meet financial goals. If the term and side fund are used, the increasing investment fund is a possible source of hedging for inflation. If a level amount is required to meet financial goals, the increasing investment fund offsets the reduction in the face amount if decreasing term insurance is used.
- Life insurance needs are not as great during old age. Although assets are necessary to take care of permanent and temporary needs of later years, the savings (investment) fund should be sufficient to meet the requirements.
- Earnings in the side fund may be significantly greater than the amounts credited to the cash value accumulations, particularly in traditional products like whole life.
- There is no protection from inflation with a traditional whole life policy, due to the fixed nature of the face amount.

These are reasonable ideas, in theory, but the buy-term-invest-the-difference plan can run into trouble in practice. Here is why.

First, many people do not have the discipline to make regular deposits to an investment account. Fewer still have the skill or time needed to manage a crucial investment program continuously. We use "crucial" deliberately, because the funds involved are neither discretionary nor speculative investment monies. They represent the foundation of a family's financial security. Any mistakes or mismanagement could be disastrous. Additionally, many who may be successful in saving regularly in investment programs may be tempted to use those funds for opportunities or other reasons, spending their "nest egg" prematurely. The save-and-spend scenario is a common one. Permanent insurance offers a method of "forced savings" which is more likely to be successful.

Further, even though the investments may do well enough, the difference between the term and permanent premiums that is left to invest is going to become ever smaller with passing time. The term premium will continue to increase, and commissions and fees will have to be paid to investment advisors.

Permanent policy cash values grow income tax deferred, which is not the case with earnings in most noninsurance investments, such as stocks or savings accounts. They are taxed annually on the growth or distributions. The investment side fund will have to show consistently good performance to offset the effect of taxes and fees. In addition, by investing in side fund investments, the individual also gives up the credit protection offered life insurance.

Conversely, life insurance cash values have guarantees. Any investment fund that will yield the returns needed to make this plan succeed will also bring with it an additional amount of risk. Depending on the risk profile of the investor, this risk may or may not be worth taking or be suitable.

The debate also includes whether the prospect needs to have insurance at older ages, and whether he or she wants to have life insurance at death. If this need exists, there is a strong argument in favor of permanent insurance. Individuals may have problems affording term insurance at an advanced age, or may become uninsurable due to unanticipated medical problems. Life insurance needs may continue beyond the ages at which term insurance is available or affordable. Needs during later years may not be determinable at the time of purchase.

For some, "buy term and invest the difference" may be a legitimate option, while for others, permanent insurance is a more feasible planning method. The decision is a personal one, and either strategy has merit, because both, if followed faithfully, can have successful results. The "pay-yourself-first" strategy (save before you spend) is a good one, but good intentions do not always translate into positive actions. For most people, it becomes "buy term and spend the rest." Some people are so overwhelmed by the financial burdens of everyday life that they neglect to put money aside for their future. If this happens, the entire "buy-term-and-invest-the-difference" strategy collapses. With permanent insurance, the client has the peace of mind provided by the death benefit, the assurance that the product will survive any economic downturn, and a source of contingency funds in the form of guaranteed cash values.

A unique characteristic of the investment return inside a cash value policy is that it can be used to pay the mortality and expense charges within the policy without the return being taxed. Since the cash value growth is tax-deferred, the policyowner is effectively paying mortality and expense charges (term insurance) with pre-tax dollars. The annual increases in cash values are not subject to federal income taxes as they accrue, while the earnings from a separate investment program would be taxed as ordinary income.

When a prospect tells you that he or she wants to "buy term and invest the difference," ask them how they are doing so far. Everyone wants to do it, but few actually do. You may also ask them on what date they plan to die. If the client has long-term or permanent needs, then the solution needs to be permanent.

In the final analysis, the best program and solution lies in a combination of whole life and term products. They each have their place and purpose.

Insurance Company Investment Objectives

One of the building blocks of a life insurance policy, interest, has a profound effect on the performance of the policy. The premium paid into a permanent policy in excess of the mortality and expense charges constitutes the investment component. Most of the differences in life insurance policies sold today can be attributed to how insurance companies handle the interest component of their policies.

The principal objectives for an insurance company's general investment portfolio, and the whole life insurance product specifically, are safety of principal, yield, and liquidity, based on a portfolio of conservative and diversified investments. The general account of the insurance company is the reserve that stands behind all of the promises made by the company. State insurance regulators establish rules and procedures about how companies must manage their general accounts. Whole life cash values never go down unless withdrawn. Regarding safety of principal, the life insurance industry has compiled a solvency record over the years that is unmatched by any other type of business organization. It has survived wars, depressions, and inflation; composite losses to policyowners have been relatively rare. Even the few companies seized by the regulators in recent years have been able to rescue most of their policyowners' contracts.

This excellent record has been achieved through quality investments and concentration on government bonds (federal, state, and local), high-grade corporate bonds, and real estate mortgages, as well as through emphasis on diversification. Investments are diversified by industry, geographical distribution, maturity, and size. Many of the larger companies have from 100,000 to 200,000 different units of investment.

An individual policyowner's cash value (investment component) is combined with all other policyowners' cash values. The insurance company has invested in assets to offset these liabilities (reserves). In effect, each policyowner owns a pro rata share of each investment unit in the company's portfolio. Such diversification—which is the keystone of safety—is obviously beyond the reach of the individual investor. Only by investing exclusively in federal and state government bonds, with the consequent interest rate risk and sacrifice of yield, could the individual investor hope to match the safety of principal that his or her funds would enjoy with a reputable life insurance company. In addition, higher rates of return will require additional risks and volatility than required by insurance company general accounts. There is always a trade off.

Life insurance companies obtain the highest possible yield corresponding with the standard of safety that they have set for themselves. Many individuals are able to obtain a higher yield than that provided by a life insurance company by investing in common stocks or other equity investments, and some exceptional investors will be able to do it under virtually any circumstances. It is highly questionable, however, whether the typical life insurance policyowner can, over a long period, earn a consistently higher yield than a life insurance company, regardless of the type of investment program he or she pursues.

With respect to the third objective of an investment program, the liquidity of a life insurance contract is excellent. The policyowner's investment can be withdrawn at any time with no loss of principal. This can be accomplished through surrender for cash or through policy loans. The insured never faces the possibility of liquidating his or her assets in an unfavorable market; nor can the insured's policy loans be called because of inadequate collateral. Certain types of investments approach the liquidity of life insurance cash values, but no investment whose value depends on the market can match the liquidity represented by the life insurance contract.

Principal Investment Program Objectives
• Safety of principal • Yield • Liquidity

More important, perhaps, than any of the preceding factors is the question of whether savings under a separate investment program will be accomplished in the first place. Life insurance that develops cash values is a form of "forced" saving. Not only do its periodic premiums provide a simple and systematic mechanism for saving, but when the savings feature is combined with the protection feature, there is also far more incentive for the insured to save than there would otherwise be. An individual who is voluntarily purchasing a bond a month or setting aside a certain amount per month in some other type of savings account may skip a month or two if some other use for the money is more appealing. If, however, failure to set aside the predetermined contribution to a savings account would result in loss of highly prized insurance protection that might be irreplaceable, he or she will be far more likely to make the savings effort. The insured saves because it is the only way of preserving his or her protection. Level premium life insurance, therefore, should be the foundation of any lifelong financial program.

Term: Least Expensive or Most Expensive?

Term insurance offers maximum protection with minimum outlay. It is the best source of temporary protection to solve temporary needs. When term is used as a permanent solution to permanent needs, it may no longer be either efficient or effective. In fact, if the insured dies one day after the term insurance expires, it is probably the most expensive and inefficient protection that could have been purchased. Otherwise, for short- and medium-range needs, term is a perfectly good solution.

Term insurance is appealing to people who may not be able to afford permanent insurance premiums, but who realize that their needs are clearly long term. Term insurance can be helpful to these people in providing the protection they need right away. If they continue to rely on term protection, however, serious consequences may result if their need is permanent. First, unless the term is converted to permanent protection, the insurance will be discontinued by the company at the end of the contract term, which may be short of life expectancy age. However, well before then, the term premiums that were once so attractively low will have risen to prohibitively high levels. Additionally, if the insured's insurability changes negatively during the term of coverage, it may be difficult or impossible to buy insurance at the end of the term contract. When the term coverage terminates, so does the protection.

Check your company's rates. Compare the premium for $100,000 of permanent insurance at age 30 to the same amount of term protection to age 60 (purchased at age 30). Then consider the fact that the term premiums all went to buy "pure insurance." They were "pure" cost, just like a rented apartment. See how that compares to the cash value that has accumulated in the permanent policy by the time the insured is 60. Which would you rather have been paying for all that time?

Term is, however, a valuable addition to your product portfolio. If properly sold, it can be a flexible, important part of your clients' life insurance programs. The real argument centers around what needs are long term, or if long-term needs are best addressed with life insurance.

Some Guidelines in Buying Term or Whole Life (Permanent)

- Buy term if the client has a high-risk tendency. This could be associated with keeping options open in case the right opportunity arises, and not being committed to a strategy or solution. It could also work with a buy-term-invest-the-difference strategy, especially in a variable product or investment portfolio.
- Buy term if the client has a "lease-rather-than-own" mentality.
- Buy term if there is no other way to satisfy the need without it.
- Buy term insurance if the insurance need is for 10 years or less.
- Buy whole life (or some other permanent product) if the client has an "own-rather-than-loan" type personality.
- Buy whole life (permanent) if the need is to fund a buy-sell agreement.
- Buy whole life (permanent) if the client wants something to show for his money.
- Buy a mix of term and whole life if the client is like most people and is not on one end of the spectrum or the other.
- Buy a combination of whole life and term when the client can cover the entire death need and is able and willing to allocate additional dollars to appropriate permanent coverage.
- Buy whole life if the client thinks he or she will live longer than average.
- Buy a combination of term and whole life if the need will last between 10 and 20 years.
- Buy whole life if the need is expected to last 15–20 years or longer.
- Buy permanent coverage if the need is expected to last to, or beyond, age 55, or if the prospect wants life insurance when he or she dies.
- Buy permanent insurance if the policy is designed to pay death taxes and estate administration expenses, provide estate liquidity, transfer wealth to the next generation, or fund charitable giving goals.

Meet the Prospect

> Harvard Business School professor emeritus Theodore Levitt once said, "People don't want a quarter-inch drill, they want a quarter-inch hole."
>
> Similarly, your prospect doesn't want a product; she wants a solution. You need to listen to uncover your prospect's hidden needs, and then sell your product as a solution. It's not about what you're selling—it's about how what you're selling can help the customer. Be valuable. And remember—a good salesperson walks away if he cannot truly help his prospect.

The Objective of the Initial Interview

initial interview

The objective of the *initial interview* for the advisor is to establish rapport and get the client's agreement to do fact-finding and continue the selling/planning process. In the sales process, the advisor must help the prospect with a life insurance need to understand the nature and extent of the problems that may develop as a result of not having adequate life insurance. The potential problems must be clearly identified and understood by the buyer before he or she will be motivated to take action. The buyer must have a strong desire to solve these problems and the advisor must present compelling reasons why the buyer should act now, rather than later, if the sale is to be made and the problems resolved.

This process takes form in the initial interview. Whether you use a sales track supplied by your company or create your own compliance-approved presentation, the purposes are essentially the same. There are four basic objectives for the initial interview:

1. Create a sense of rapport and credibility, and build trust.
2. Uncover insurance and other financial needs and determine priorities.
3. Establish your ability to help.
4. Obtain the prospect's permission to proceed, and establish his or her commitment to work with you.

Let's look at each one of these objectives separately.

Create a Sense of Rapport and Credibility

Begin building a strong sense of rapport and credibility with your prospect. If you fail to establish your credibility in the initial interview, you may not have another chance. People want to do business with people they feel understand them, with whom they share something in common, who are competent, and whom they can believe and trust. It is important to establish this as quickly and as early as possible in the relationship. Having something in common increases the prospect's level of comfort about doing business with you and allows the relationship to develop.

When you meet the prospect, introduce yourself and chat for a few moments. As you do this, you can begin with things you know you have in common. You want to expand on this as much as possible, since people feel comfortable with those whom they share something in common. You may notice something in the room you are familiar with, or want to remark on a common interest. If this prospect is a referral, you want to refer to the person who gave you the prospect's name in a genuine and sincere manner. The referrer might be able to give you some of the prospect's interests to help you find common ground. You want to engage the client in conversation that builds warm, positive feelings of trust and rapport.

Your manners, appearance, and confidence will create an immediate impression. They will say much about your attitude about yourself, your business, and the prospect. Do you look like you know what you are doing? Are you dressed appropriately? You need to communicate your intention to be helpful and your competence. Your words must be backed up with consistent body language and tone of voice.

Make sure you know your presentation and are comfortable using it. The only way to prepare for the interview is to practice what you plan to say. It helps to practice with other people who can respond to your questions and make comments at the appropriate places.

Empathy. Trust equals empathy plus credibility. Credibility is only part of building trust. The other part is empathy, the ability to see things from the prospect's point of view. You understand how the other person feels, although you may not necessarily feel the same way.

As an advisor, empathy refers to the way you demonstrate a focus on solving the prospect's problems. Empathy involves allowing the prospect to see that you see things from his or her point of view, that you understand their problems and feel their pain, by expressing accurately those things that bother them and need to be fixed. It involves the capacity to lay aside your own set of experiences in favor of those of your clients—as seen through their eyes, not yours. It involves skillful listening, so you can hear not only the obvious, but also the subtleties of which even the client may be unaware.

Communicate your understanding by sharing your thoughts with the prospect. Confirm that your perceptions are accurate before proceeding.

Image, rapport, and trust are the foundation of the relationship you are trying to build with your prospects. They are part of the developing relationship that makes everything you do important, including mannerisms, listening skills, dress, speaking style, and nonverbal expression. Keep in mind that the objectives are to build credibility through establishing needs and demonstrating how you can help satisfy those needs.

At the initial meeting, trust is a serious issue for the prospect if they do not know you. Many people behave defensively in new situations because they feel threatened and insecure. Some of this may be seen in nonverbal behavior such as tone of voice, folded arms, quietness, and so on. You want to be aware of this and work to reduce this tension. Small talk and finding topics of common interest are a starting point. Asking questions that encourage them to think about what is important to them helps build trust, as you show that you are concerned about their future.

Uncover Insurance Needs and Establish Priorities

Your second objective is to identify needs using open-ended questions designed to elicit the prospect's goals, attitudes, and feelings. As you ask a question and get a response, pay attention to which topics seem more important to the prospect. Comment on how those issues of particular interest are expertly handled by you, your agency, and your company, for many people who have faced the same or similar problems, if this is the case. Discuss problems common to people in the prospect's situation, such as survivor income, saving for college, and retirement, to see how the prospect feels about these issues. These issues may be more formally addressed in the data-gathering session that may follow this initial interview, or at another time in the future.

Establish Your Ability to Help

Let the prospect know how you can help them find solutions for their needs. Explain what you do, how you do it, and the scope of your business. This establishes in your prospect's mind that you can help, and most importantly, that you are the one who should help. Explain that you are in the business of helping people achieve their financial goals. You are a problem solver.

The key to becoming a successful advisor is to make yourself appealing by setting yourself apart from your competition. You should ask yourself why a client should want to work with you rather than hundreds of other professionals in the marketplace. If you can't answer that question yourself, how can you expect your prospect to know the difference and choose you? You must understand what you offer, how it is different and better than what your competition offers, and why people should want to work with you. Determine your strengths and match them to the needs of your potential clients. Look at your background, past work experience, education, personal philosophies, values, and attitudes to find strong points. Talk to your manager and other advisors about ways you can promote yourself professionally. This is not about you; it is about how you can help the client. To be a success, you must develop a client-centered, engaging message that differentiates you from your competition.

Obtain Prospect's Permission to Proceed

Finally, you must get the prospect's permission to proceed. You cannot ask sensitive questions of someone who is not prepared to answer them. Explain why gathering personal information is important. You have to understand his or her full financial and personal situation to make intelligent recommendations. You must obtain agreement on what you and your prospect will do together. This is the first commitment you make to each other. This must be a mutual commitment; the prospect must be serious about participating in the process, and be in a position to seriously consider acting on any need that is uncovered. He or she must also be willing to make the time commitment necessary to complete the process. By taking this step, you begin to build an advisor-client relationship that should continue long after the sale is completed. It will also go a long way toward preventing the possibility of future lapse or cancellation of the policy.

Conducting the Initial Interview

Your Purpose

Begin the meeting by stating your purpose. Let the prospect know why you are calling and how much time you need. Get confirmation that the time you need is available now. If you sense that interruptions may occur, ask that they not be allowed to intrude on your conversation. In your opening comments, introduce yourself and your services and products. Explain briefly how they might be beneficial to your prospect and why the time you spend together will be profitable for all concerned.

Explain that, as a financial advisor, the service you offer is the review and analysis of financial goals and needs in relationship to a client's family's current income and budget. Add that your objective is to determine the appropriate types and amounts of protection suggested by his or her personal and financial situation. Describe the process you will be using (both the format and subject matter). Explain that this process is essential in order to discover his or her current financial and personal situation and future goals and needs, and that everything discussed will be held in the strictest of confidence.

You should explain how they will benefit from these services. You want to give some predictions of outcomes the prospect might reasonably expect. You will be dealing with many important concerns, such as the immediate and long-term financial consequences of an income earner's death, the adequacy of the family's life insurance planning, the need to budget for financial security protection, and the importance of having up-to-date wills, topics to which most people have not given enough consideration. There is no obligation for these services, of course, yet the information and analysis you will provide will be valuable whether there is a need for additional insurance or not, and whether or not the prospect acts on your recommendations.

As you describe your services and products, ask the prospect what he or she thinks about each one and if they might be interested in it. The answers will help the prospects to participate in the interview. If the answers are positive, it will mean that you have agreement to continue. Ask this type of question frequently throughout the meeting.

Throughout the selling/planning process, you should continually be doing the following:

- Creating a positive atmosphere
- Asking questions
- Listening actively
- Qualifying the prospect and opportunities for both parties
- Discovering hot buttons (what's in it for them)
- Building rapport
- Establishing trust
- Developing credibility
- Developing a valuable relationship
- Addressing objections
- Planning next action steps

- Confirming understanding
- Asking for referrals
- Seeking additional opportunities to serve and sell
- Evaluating responses and results (positive and negative)
- Affirming decisions (minimizing buyer's remorse)

Opening the Interview

In the initial planning session, you might propose the agenda by following this guideline:

Purpose	What You Say
Communicate what you intend to accomplish during the meeting.	During this meeting, we will discuss some life planning issues that may be of concern to you.
Explain how you will work with the prospect.	First, Let me tell you a little about who I am and the company I represent.
	Then we will talk about your concerns, goals, and desires regarding your financial planning.
	Next, we will look at how your financial status currently stands in regard to your net worth, cash flow, and budget.
	Finally, we will identify any problems or gaps in your current long-term plan.
State the benefit for the prospect.	That way you can determine whether it will be valuable for us to move ahead and develop a planning strategy tailored for you.
Check for acceptance.	How does that sound?

By proposing the agenda in this way, stating the benefit to the prospect, and checking for acceptance, you are sharing control of the interview with your prospect, which helps you to establish rapport. It may be advisable to reassure the prospect of your continuing commitment to the process by adding the following:

> "If in the course of our work together we should discover that you have a need for a product I offer, I will assist you in devising a

customized plan that addresses your individual concerns. I will then help you to implement that plan and promise to monitor and service that plan in the future."

When planning your agenda for your client meeting, get their agenda items prior to the meeting. First, this will make sure you have time to review what they perceive as most pressing. Second, if they come with one or more items you did not expect, it could destroy your agenda.

After you present your agenda, ask if there are any other concerns that your prospect wishes to discuss. Write them down and be sure to cover these concerns in your discussion. Do so even if the concerns fall under categories you had on your agenda. Your prospect's input is an important first step in the open exchange of data and feelings.

Summary of the Initial Interview

- Make a statement of your intentions—the purpose of your meeting with the prospect.
- Include what will happen and why. What is the benefit of this meeting to the prospect?
- Ask permission to ask questions.
- Ask open-ended questions designed to obtain information and feelings about the prospect's financial situation and goals.
- Ask more specific questions about needs and desired solutions.
- Address how your products and services may apply to the prospect's situation.
- Make a summary statement of how the prospect sees the situation. Ask checking questions (solicit feedback) to be certain that what you understand is accurate.

Chapter Four Review

Key terms and concepts are explained in the glossary. Answers to the review questions and the self-test questions are found in the back of the book in the Answers to Questions section.

Key Terms and Concepts

- whole life
- limited-payment whole life
- general account method
- new-money method
- participating
- nonparticipating
- policy loan
- delay clause
- paid-up insurance
- vanishing premium
- single-premium life (SPL)
- modified premium whole life (MPWL)
- joint life
- survivorship life
- endowment life insurance
- adjustable life
- current assumption whole life
- redetermination
- interest-sensitive whole life
- indeterminate premium whole life
- initial interview

Review Questions

1. Describe the general features of whole life insurance policies. [1]
2. Explain how combination plans offer the coverage and benefits of long-term care and life insurance in one policy. [1]
3. Describe how limited-payment life insurance differs from ordinary life insurance. [2]
4. Describe the two types of joint life insurance policies and indicate their common uses. [3]
5. Explain how combination plans offer the coverage and benefits of long-term care and life insurance in one policy. [4]
6. Explain how endowment life insurance differs from whole life insurance and why endowment policies have nearly disappeared from new policy sales. [5]
7. Explain the adjustable life policy design. [6]
8. Describe the current assumption (interest-sensitive) variations of life insurance. [7]
9. Discuss the arguments for and against buying term or whole life (permanent) insurance. [8]
10. Explain the investment philosophy for whole life products. [9]

11. Explain what should take place in the initial interview and the objectives of the initial interview. [10]

Self-Test Questions

1. Policy loans require the policyowner to

   (A) have collateral
   (B) be charged interest on the loan
   (C) agree to a repayment schedule
   (D) complete a form disclosing the reason for the loan

2. An unpaid loan against the cash value of an ordinary life policy will

   (A) cancel the death benefit
   (B) increase the death benefit
   (C) decrease the death benefit
   (D) not change the death benefit

3. At maturity, the face amount of an whole life insurance policy will

   (A) be paid to the policyowner
   (B) be paid to the beneficiary
   (C) pay the cash value plus mortality adjustments
   (D) remain in trust until death occurs, but premiums will stop

4. The type of life insurance policy that provides insurance on two lives, with nothing payable upon the first death, is often called

   (A) estate insurance
   (B) first-to-die insurance
   (C) joint survivor insurance
   (D) survivorship life insurance

5. Which of the following statements concerning adjustable life insurance is (are) correct?

   I. The adjustable life policy gives the policyowner the right to request (in writing) and obtain a reconfiguration of the policy at specified intervals.
   II. The adjustable life policy offers all of the same guarantees regarding cash values, mortality, and expenses as traditional whole life policies.

   (A) I only
   (B) II only
   (C) Both I and II
   (D) Neither I nor II

6. Which of the following statements concerning limited-pay whole life insurance is (are) correct?

   I. The limitation on the number of premiums to be paid may be expressed as either a number of years or an age beyond which premiums are not payable.
   II. If the insured dies during the premium-paying period, the total premiums paid will exceed those paid for an ordinary life policy of the same face amount issued at the same age.

   (A) I only
   (B) II only
   (C) Both I and II
   (D) Neither I nor II

READ THE FOLLOWING DIRECTIONS BEFORE CONTINUING

The questions below differ from the preceding questions in that they all contain the word EXCEPT. So you understand fully the basis used in selecting each answer, be sure to read each question carefully.

---

7. All the following statements concerning whole life insurance are correct EXCEPT

   (A) Policy dividends are considered a refund of overpaid premiums.
   (B) Cash values are the by-product of the level-premium method.
   (C) MPWL has reduced premiums for an initial period and higher premiums later.
   (D) Single-premium policies typically provide protection for only a limited period.

8. In the initial interview, you should try to achieve all of the following EXCEPT

   (A) Establish yourself as a person who can help.
   (B) Uncover insurance needs and establish priorities.
   (C) Develop rapport and credibility.
   (D) Analyze the prospect's situation and propose solutions.

9. In the initial interview, your objectives include all of the follow EXCEPT
   (A) Use empathy to communicate your understanding of the prospect's views.
   (B) Present solutions for the prospect's needs and ways to achieve their goals.
   (C) Uncover insurance and other financial needs and priorities.
   (D) Obtain the prospect's permission to proceed and commitment to work with you.

10. All of the following statements are correct concerning whole life insurance EXCEPT
   (A) Vanishing premium policy designs are really limited-payment life policies.
   (B) Limited-payment life insurance policies will have higher cash values than ordinary life policies for the same face amount issued at the same age in the same year.
   (C) Investments of whole life reserves are invested in the insurer's general portfolio account.
   (D) A whole life policy can be regarded as an endowment at age 100 (or age 120).

VARIABLE AND UNIVERSAL LIFE INSURANCE 5

Learning Objectives

An understanding of the material in this chapter should enable you to

1. Describe the features of variable life and understand its dual regulation status.
2. Explain the income tax definition of life insurance and the tests life insurance must meet for income tax benefits.
3. Describe the universal life policy and explain how its features differ from whole life policies.
4. Describe variable universal life insurance policies.
5. Discuss the information-gathering interview and its objectives.
6. Discuss analyzing the prospect's situation based on information gathering to prepare solutions for goals and needs.

Over the past decade we have experienced the full range of financial and economic cycles. Individual life insurance weathered most of the storms, experiencing setbacks in 2009 and 2010. Like the rest of our economy, individual life insurance thrived in the economic boom years after 2001, reaching a peak in 2002, but remained fairly steady until 2007. At the highest sales levels , flexible premium products, universal life (UL) , and variable universal life (VUL) products accounted for approximately 56 percent of new annualized premium.

Variable products tend to follow securities market performance. After the market crash in 2008, the lasting effects of market turbulence and uncertainty have had a negative effect on variable product sales. Even when equity markets rebounded in 2010, VUL sales remained relatively flat, falling from 7 percent of the market in 2000 to 1 percent in 2012. Fixed premium variable products (VLI) represent less than one percent of individual life insurance annualized premium. The impact of the financial crisis in 2008 was felt throughout the industry, with variable products particularly hard hit. Gaining market share over the past two years, indexed universal life products have become an alternative to variable products.

Although sales were diminished in 2008 and 2009, UL products continue to hold the largest portion of individual life insurance sales. Even though variable universal life sales never recovered, the market share of flexible premium products continued to increase because of the popularity of death benefit guarantee universal life products. By the end of 2012, death benefit guarantee UL represented about one-half of new UL premium. Death benefit guarantee UL products tend to target higher income levels at older issue ages, focusing more on estate planning needs. Other UL products aim for preretiree issue ages to focus more on protection and retirement planning needs (U.S. Individual Life Insurance Sales Survey, 2013 & LIMRA Estimates).

Variable Life Insurance

variable life insurance

Variable life insurance (VLI) was the first life insurance policy designed to shift the investment risk to policyowners. A *variable life insurance* policy provides no guarantees of either interest rate or minimum cash value. Theoretically, the cash value can go down to zero. In order for policyowners to gain the additional benefit of better-than-expected investment returns, they also assume all of the downside investment risk.

FINRA

Consequently, the Securities and Exchange Commission (SEC) requires VLI policies to be registered with the SEC and all sales to be subject to the requirements applicable to other registered securities. Policy sales can be made only after the prospective purchaser has received the policy prospectus. The SEC also requires that the insurance company be registered as an investment company and that agents become *FINRA* registered representatives by passing the Series 6 or 7 licensing exam. Agents who sell VLI policies must be licensed as both life insurance agents and securities agents. Companies that offer variable contracts are subject to dual supervision by the SEC and the various state insurance departments.

Investment Choices

The first generation of VLI was a fixed-premium product (see Figure 5-1). The product was a whole life design and the only real innovation was the variable investment aspect. VLI cash values are funded by a separate (segregated) account of the insurance company. The separate account is segregated from the general investment portfolio of the insurance company and is not subject to the claims of the creditors of the insurance company.

Figure 5-1
Variable Life Fixed Premium

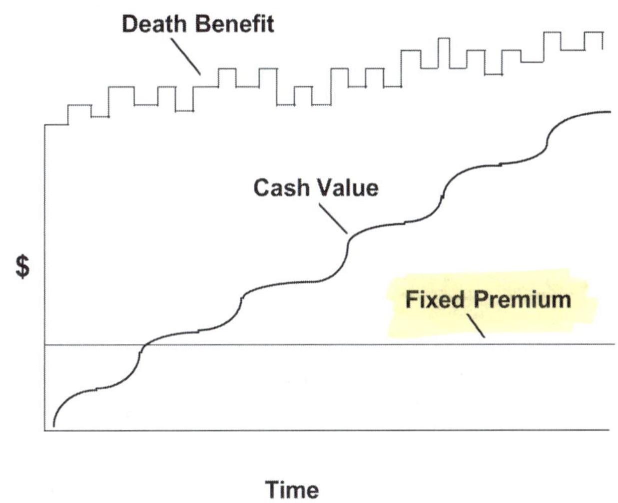

separate account The *separate account* contains subaccounts that are similar to mutual funds. The policyowner is permitted to select among a number of investment subaccount choices, and to change these choices within limits and rules established in the policy. Although the policyowner chooses among the offered funds, he or she has no control over the assets purchased and sold by the individual funds. That portion of the investment decision process is still within the hands of the insurance company's portfolio management team, or within the management of external portfolio managers from investment companies. The results of the investment performance, positive or negative, are reflected directly to the policy cash values.

Death benefits and cash values vary to reflect the investment experience of the separate account subaccounts. The policy must provide a guaranteed premium and death benefit set at policy issue, and mortality and expense risks must be borne by the insurance company. The basic policy structure is similar to whole life insurance in that the stated face amount at the issue age requires a specific, level, fixed premium. Once the policy is issued, the cash value increases or decreases daily based on the investment experience of the underlying subaccounts. VLIs guarantee that the face amount will not fall below the originally issued face amount, and that the guaranteed premium will keep the policy in force, regardless of investment experience. If investment experience is positive during a policy year, on the policy anniversary the face amount will be adjusted upward to reflect that investment experience. If investment experience is negative, the face amount will be adjusted downward, but never below the face amount originally issued.

Ability to Tolerate Risk

Individuals who are already experienced in equity investments may be comfortable with the VLI policy. However, this policy is subject to daily portfolio fluctuations and can provoke great anxiety in individuals who are not used to or comfortable with such market value fluctuations. Therefore, only those who can tolerate these investment risks, and have a suitable risk tolerance, should be candidates for a variable policy.

A VLI policy is a market-driven phenomenon, and its popularity is influenced by general investment market conditions. The policy becomes more acceptable to consumers after a long period of market increases and falls out of favor when the market experiences a general decline in prices. This was clearly seen in VLI sales when the stock market plunged in 2001 and 2008. In 2000 and 2001, variable life products (VLI and VUL) had the largest market share of individual life products; however, for the last decade, sales have tumbled, as both clients and advisors have reservations about VLI. Over the last several years, VLI represents less than one percent of all life insurance sales. As the stock market rebounds, interest in these products tends to return.

Increased Number of Investment Fund Options

VLI designs have not been static since their introduction in the mid-1970s. Originally providing only three investment options, life insurance companies now offer a large number of investment subaccounts. There are usually a variety of stock, bond, and managed funds available as portfolio choices. The policyowner can put all of the policy funds in a managed portfolio fund and have the investment allocation decisions made by a professional money manager. With a managed portfolio policyowners can reap all of the long-term advantages of a VLI contract without having to perform the investment allocation function themselves. Additionally, there are usually minimal or no fees or income taxes when transferring assets between subaccounts, as there would be within taxable mutual fund accounts.

Most insurance companies have formed alliances with large mutual fund groups that make their entire range of mutual funds available. Such alliances make it possible for these life insurance companies to gain access to the administrative services already in place in these large mutual fund family groups. Insurers may also hire external portfolio managers to manage specific subaccounts.

Insurance Charges

VLI contracts are not exclusively investments. They also sustain mortality charges for the death benefits they provide. Consequently, the pretax return on the invested funds within a VLI contract will never equal that of a separate investment fund that does not provide death benefits but invests in assets of a similar type and quality.

VLI should not be purchased as a short-term investment vehicle. Although investment performance in equities tends to equal or exceed inflation in the economy over the long term, the correlation is not perfect in the short term. It is possible for inflation to exceed increases in the investment performance for short durations of time. In addition, the combination of sales load, mortality charges, and surrender charges will significantly reduce any potential gains in the policy's early years.

Policy premiums paid under VLI contracts are often subject to an administrative charge; the balance of the premium payment goes into the cash value account. The actual value of the cash component is determined by the net asset value of the separate account funds that make up the policy portfolio. The cash value fluctuates daily. Each day's net asset value is based on the closing price for the issues in the portfolio on that trading day. Cash value accounts are further diminished by mortality charges that support the death benefits.

Policy Loans

Like traditional life insurance contracts, the VLI policyowner has access to the cash value through policy loans. The earnings on the cash value are affected by any outstanding policy loans. When a loan is taken, the insurance company moves an amount equal to the loan into a fixed-rate, guaranteed account not subject to market risk, where it will typically earn 2 percent less than the loan interest rate. The policyowner accrues indebtedness at the applicable policy loan interest rate. The loan fund will remain in that account, securing the loan, until the loan is paid off. If the policyowner borrows at a time when the subaccounts are decreasing in value, he or she avoids those potential loses. However, if borrowing occurs when those subaccounts are appreciating, the cost of the loan includes the loan interest charges and the lost appreciation in the subaccounts.

Policy loans can be repaid at any time in part or in full, but there is no requirement that policy loans be repaid at any time during the existence of the life insurance contract. For any portion of the loan not repaid, interest accrues on a compound basis. Outstanding policy loans reduce the death benefit payable. The policy loan is always fully secured by the remaining cash value in the policy. Whenever the outstanding loans plus accrued interest equal the remaining cash value, the net cash value becomes zero and the policy lapses.

The net cash value in the contract is also closely related to the nonforfeiture options available under the policy. VLI contracts provide the same range of nonforfeiture options as do traditional whole life policies.

VLI policies contain the usual form of reinstatement provisions, including a prohibition on reinstatements if the policy has been surrendered for its cash value. Contracts also have the standard waiver-of-premium option, since premiums are fixed and the policy will lapse if they are not paid.

The Prospectus

VLI cannot be sold without an accompanying *prospectus*, which must be presented to the prospect before any discussions regarding VLI take place. The VLI prospectus mandated by the SEC is similar to the prospectus required of new stock issues. The prospectus provides thorough and accurate information to the prospective purchaser concerning the company issuing the life insurance contract. It also provides a full disclosure of all the provisions of the contract, including expenses, investment options, benefit provisions, past performance of the investment options, and policyowner rights under that contract. It is a lengthy and detailed document.

Expense Information

The prospectus explains all of the expenses charged by the insurance company within VLI contracts. This includes commissions paid to advisors, state premium taxes, and administrative charges. The prospectus also indicates whether there is any maximum guarantee on administrative fees over the duration of the contract.

Primary Focus of Prospectus Disclosure	
• Operating expenses	• Surrender charges
• Marketing expenses	• Investment charges
• Taxes and fees	• Investment performance
• Cost-of-insurance charge	

In addition, the prospectus sets forth the manner in which charges are made against the separate account to cover the cost of insurance. The prospectus specifies what rate will be used to determine *cost-of-insurance* charges and the maximum insurance rates. It also explains the manner in which investment management fees associated with the various types of investment accounts are made against the separate account itself.

Surrender Charges

The charges applicable to policy surrenders are usually set forth in a table, giving the policy year and the applicable percentage for the surrender charge in that year. Surrender charges are commonly levied during the first 10 to 15 years of the contract to recover policy acquisition costs. The actual number of years and specific rates are always set forth in the prospectus.

Investment Portfolio Information

The prospectus sets forth the investment objectives of each of the investment funds and a record of their historical performance. It includes detailed information on the current holdings of each of the portfolios, usually supplemented by information about purchases and sales of individual equities or debt instruments by the fund over the previous 12 months. Further information is given about earnings during that same period of time, and usually for longer intervals of prior performance if those funds have been in existence long enough to give investment results over 5 or 10 years. Any investment restrictions applicable to these portfolios are fully disclosed.

There are also projections of future performance under the contract if the separate accounts generate a fixed level of investment earnings over the projected interval. Under SEC regulations, the permissible rates of return that can be projected are the gross annual rates after tax charges, but before any other deductions at 0, 4, 6, 8, 10, or 12 percent. The insurance company or advisor can decide which of those permissible rates it chooses to project.

A problem regarding investment returns reported with variable products is that they focus on illustrating average returns, rather than actual, fluctuating returns as they actually occur. We will discuss this topic in more detail when we cover variable universal life.

Risks the Policyowner Assumes

Fixed-premium VLI contracts are very similar to whole life insurance contracts, except that the policyowner assumes the investment risk. The fixed-premium provision does not allow the policyowner to increase or decrease the death benefit as in universal life. Favorable results automatically translate into increased death benefit amounts.

One unique benefit of a VLI policy is that it does guarantee a minimum death benefit equal to the original face amount of the contract, regardless of how badly the investment performance turns out to be. If all of the required premiums are paid, the insurance company guarantees that the death benefit equal to the original face amount will be paid, even if the investment funds are otherwise inadequate to support the policy. Therefore, the variable feature of this contract can provide additional coverage if investment experience warrants, but the policyowner will never be required to pay more or be permitted to pay less than the guaranteed premium.

A fixed-premium VLI policy provides more guarantees to the policyowner than universal life and variable universal life. Due to the introductions of universal and variable universal life, and the market's performance over the last decade, the market share of VLI is only minimal—less than one percent of all premiums paid annually.

The Income Tax Definition of Life Insurance

Income taxation is an important aspect of the operation and value of life insurance products. Life insurance policies receive favorable tax treatment under the law. Sec. 101 of the Internal Revenue Code provides that the proceeds of a life insurance policy maturing as a death claim, subject to the exceptions stated in the law, are not subject to income tax when paid. This and other tax benefits are extremely important reasons for the growth of the life insurance industry and the value of life insurance products. In order for life insurance to qualify for these benefits, the policy must meet the income tax definition of life insurance.

With the passage of the Tax Equity and Fiscal Responsibility Act of 1982 (TEFRA), Congress provided a mechanism to allow Universal Life–type policies to be treated as life insurance for tax purposes. TEFRA addressed only "flexible premium" life insurance and left a need for a legislative definition of life insurance as a whole. Subsequent to TEFRA, the Deficit Reduction Act of 1984 (DEFRA) was passed. Basically, DEFRA took the TEFRA rules and modified them, providing a general set of qualifications for any life insurance contract to qualify for income tax benefits. DEFRA introduced the language that limited the amount of premium that could be paid into a policy, and required a minimum amount of pure risk coverage in order to qualify. Since DEFRA, compliance is a matter of ongoing mathematical calculations and testing to assure policies meet the statutory definition both at issue and while they remain in force.

Prior to TEFRA and DEFRA, there was no specific federal tax law that defined life insurance. By providing a statutory definition of life insurance, DEFRA provided a way for life insurance policies to qualify for the favorable tax rules provided by the Internal Revenue Code. We will now look more closely at DEFRA and the tests used to qualify a life insurance policy for favorable tax treatment.

Sec. 7702 of DEFRA

Sec. 7702 of the Deficit Reduction Act of 1984 (DEFRA)

Sec. 7702 of the Deficit Reduction Act of 1984 (DEFRA) defines life insurance for income tax purposes, for the first time in history, requiring a certain amount of the death benefit to be at risk, depending on the insured's age. For life insurance to qualify for the income tax benefits afforded by the U.S. tax code, there must be a statutory amount of death benefit in excess of the cash value. These rules were created to limit how much money can be put into a life insurance policy, to prevent its use as a tax-shelter. DEFRA was designed to prevent the abuse of the true purpose of granting tax benefits to life insurance, which is to encourage citizens to purchase it for the protection of family and business interests. The definition in the law is expressed in terms of the net amount at risk: "...only the excess of the amount paid by reason of the insured's death over the contract's net surrender value should be deemed to be life insurance."

The inside buildup in life insurance policies has been a contentious issue in Congress for a long time. The inside buildup is the cash value that accumulates and compounds inside the policy without taxation, allowing for potentially tax-free earnings. Since the death benefits of life insurance are income tax free, the earnings and amount at risk in the policy can escape taxation entirely at death. There are additional life insurance policy features that escape taxation. For example, the policyowner can move money within a variable policy from one separate account to another without triggering capital-gains taxes. Investment strategies, such as dollar-cost averaging, asset allocation, and rebalancing can be used without creating taxes. Money in the policy can be accessed through loans or withdrawals without creating a taxable event. The purpose of Sec. 7702 of DEFRA was to limit how much someone can put into such a tax-advantaged contract, by requiring that there be a certain amount at risk in relation to the cash surrender value.

Sec. 7702 of the Internal Revenue Code lays out the requirements for the "net amount at risk" to be considered life insurance for tax purposes. Sec. 7702 establishes two alternative tests, the cash value accumulation test and the guideline premium/cash value corridor test, and the policy must pass at least one of these for it to be considered life insurance. The test method is chosen at policy issue, and once a test is chosen, it cannot be changed. It is not sufficient for the policy to meet the test once; it must be met throughout the life of the contract. If the policy fails to meet the tax test, it will be separated into its pure insurance (amount at risk) and savings portions, and the income earned on the savings portion will be taxable as ordinary income to the owner each year. These tests are described below.

Cash Value Accumulation Test (CVAT)

cash value accumulation test (CVAT)

The *cash value accumulation test (CVAT)* requires that the cash value (net surrender value) not exceed at any time the net single premium required to fund the future benefits of the policy. The net single premium is calculated assuming an interest rate which is the greater of the guaranteed interest rate or 4 percent, the guaranteed mortality charges of the contract, and any other expense charges specified in the contract.

The CVAT test maintains a net single premium relationship between the cash value and the death benefit. In other words, for every dollar of cash value, the death benefit must be at least the amount that could be purchased on a guaranteed basis at the insured's attained age, using the cash value as a single premium. This is similar to what happens with the paid-up additions dividend option on a traditional participating whole life policy. The PUA purchase is a net single premium using the annual dividend to buy paid-up

Good prospects for VL - young, risk averse, life insurance need

insurance based on the insured's attained age. If the cash value increases to a point where it is greater than the net single premium required to fund future contract benefits, the company will typically return any premium to the policyowner that causes this test to fail.

Guideline Premium /Cash Value Corridor Test

guideline premium (GPT)/cash value corridor test

The *guideline premium (GPT)/cash value corridor test* is really two tests combined into one, both halves of which must be satisfied. The guideline premium half requires that the sum of the premiums paid under the contract do not exceed, at any time, the greater of the guideline single premium or the sum of the level guideline premiums. Payment of premiums in excess of these amounts is not permitted. The guideline single premium (GSP) is the one time premium which would fund the future benefits of the contract. It is calculated for the policy to endow based on the greater of a 6 percent interest rate or the rate guaranteed in the policy, and the guaranteed mortality and expense charges. The guideline level premium (GLP) is the level annual premium necessary to fund future policy benefits until age 95 under the guaranteed assumptions as before, but using a 4 percent interest rate. Since companies make different assumptions and guarantees regarding mortality and expense charges, these premium amounts will vary by company and contract.

The GPT test defines limits on premiums paid relative to the death benefit. If the guideline single premium is reached, no further premium can be paid until the sum of the guideline level premiums is greater than the guideline single premium. The policyowner may then continue premium payments as long as they do not exceed the guideline level premium each year. Companies will normally return any premiums that exceed these limits.

The GPT also defines the relationship between the cash value and the death benefit. Unlike CVAT, where the cash value determines the minimum death benefit, with GPT the death benefit limits the permissible cash value based on the corridor percentage test. With GPT, the death benefit limits the premiums that can be paid, or the cash value that can exist at any attained age. The policy must meet the death benefit or "corridor" requirement at all times. The corridor refers to the minimum percentage relationship of the policy's death benefit to the policy's cash value, which varies based on the insured's attained age. For example, at any age below 40, the death benefit of a GPT policy must be equal to at least 250 percent of the cash value.

Table 5-1 Corridor Test for Cash Value Life Insurance		
Age	Death Benefit Must Exceed Cash Value by This Multiple	Cash Value May Not Exceed This % of Death Benefit
0 to 40	2.50	0.40
41	2.43	0.41
42	2.36	0.42
43	2.29	0.44
44	2.22	0.45
45	2.15	0.47
46	2.09	0.48
47	2.03	0.49
48	1.97	0.51
49	1.91	0.52
50	1.85	0.54
51	1.78	0.56
52	1.71	0.58
53	1.64	0.61
54	1.57	0.64
55	1.50	0.67
56	1.46	0.68
57	1.42	0.70
58	1.38	0.72
59	1.34	0.75
60	1.30	0.77
61	1.28	0.78
62	1.26	0.79
63	1.24	0.81
64	1.22	0.82
65	1.20	0.83
66	1.19	0.84
67	1.18	0.85
68	1.17	0.85
69	1.16	0.86
70	1.15	0.87
71	1.13	0.88
72	1.11	0.90

Age	Death Benefit Must Exceed Cash Value by This Multiple	Cash Value May Not Exceed This % of Death Benefit
73	1.09	0.92
74	1.07	0.93
75 to 90	1.05	0.95
91	1.04	0.96
92	1.03	0.97
93	1.02	0.98
94	1.01	0.99
95	1.00	1.00
Source: IRC Sec. 7702(d)(2)		

Universal Life Insurance

universal life insurance

Universal life insurance (UL) was introduced in 1979 as a revolutionary new product. It was the first variation of whole life insurance to offer truly flexible premiums. It is very much influenced and shaped by Sec. 7702, because of its flexible nature. UL introduced several innovative features that changed the life insurance industry:

- transparency (unbundling of policy elements)
- flexible premiums
- flexible Death Benefit
- death Benefit Options
- withdrawal feature

We will now review these innovative features.

Transparency

unbundling

UL brought total disclosure to the life insurance industry. The specific cost-of-insurance charges, expense charges, cash values, death benefits and interest crediting are itemized and available to the policyowner through annual reports. This disclosure is known as *unbundling*. These costs and credits are in all other insurance policies, but are not quantified or disclosed to the policyowner. Other types of policies are in a sense black boxes, and all we can see is the exterior, not the inner workings of the policy. The transparency of a UL policy allows the policyowner to take advantage of the flexibility of the product. To facilitate this transparency, the policyowner receives an annual statement that includes the following information for the prior policy year: premium payment activity, current cash value, monthly interest crediting, monthly mortality costs and administrative fees, and loan or withdrawal activity.

Flexible Premiums

The true innovation of UL insurance was the introduction of completely flexible premiums after the first policy year, the only time a minimum level of premium payments for a UL policy is rigidly required. The insurance company requires only that a minimum specified level of first-year premium payments be paid. After the first policy year, it is completely up to the policyowner as to how much premium to pay and even whether or not to pay premiums. Due to Sec. 7702, maximum premiums are determined by tax law. Because UL is a flexible premium product, the policyowner gives up the certainty of a guaranteed premium, as in whole life, in exchange for the ability to pay flexible premiums and a potentially lower outlay.

Because of lower premiums and premium flexibility, the insurer transfers the premium sufficiency risk to the policyowner. The policyowner can manage the policy to meet his or her needs. With UL, there is not a premium in the conventional sense, as in fixed-premium products such as whole life. The premium is based on assumptions regarding rates of return and costs of insurance and expenses, which are all changeable based on actual experience over time.

The aggregate premiums paid, regardless of their timing, must be adequate to cover the costs of maintaining the policy. The policy charges are deducted from the balance of the policy's cash values, and the life insurance coverage will remain in effect as long as the cash surrender value is sufficient to cover these charges. If the policy cash value is allowed to drop too low (for example, the cash value is inadequate to cover the next 60 days of expense and mortality charges), the policy will lapse. In this way, UL is similar to term insurance in that it has a pay-as-you-go expense structure. When UL was introduced, interest-crediting rates were relatively high, and many policies were funded on a minimum premium basis. When interest rates fell, many policies were distressed and lapsed, which led to the current emphasis on secondary guarantees that are popular today, and discussed later.

If an additional premium payment is made soon enough, the policy may be continued without a formal reinstatement process. However, if an injection of additional funds comes after the end of the grace period, the insurance company may force the policyowner to request a formal reinstatement before accepting any further premium payments.

Consider the analogy of an automobile's gas tank, where premium payments are synonymous with filling the tank. Premium payments (tank refills) can be made frequently to keep the tank nearly full at all times. With that approach, the automobile is never likely to run out of gas. The same automobile, however, can operate on a just-in-time philosophy, where premium payments of minimal amounts are made only as frequently as necessary to keep the car from running out of gas. The driver has full discretion in deciding how to maintain an adequate amount of gasoline in the car. He can fill it up and drive for hundreds of miles until the next fill-up, or stop at every gas station and buy one gallon. If the operator fails to keep enough gas in the tank, the vehicle may run out of gas and be inoperable until the tank is refilled. Likewise, under a UL insurance policy, if the policy cash value is allowed to drop too low (inadequate to cover expense and mortality charges), the policy will lapse.

Additional Premium Payments

The flexible features of UL premiums allow policyowners to make additional premium payments at any time the policyowner desires without negotiation or agreement with the insurance company. The only limitation on paying excess premiums is associated with the income tax definition of life insurance (IRC Sec. 7702). The insurance company will refuse additional premium payments if the policy's cash value is large enough to encroach upon the upper limit for cash values relative to the level of death benefit granted in the policy.

Prefunding/Overfunding

Prefunding a UL policy means putting more money into the policy than is currently needed to cover the costs of keeping the policy in force. The higher the amount of prefunding, the more investment earnings will be available to cover policy expenses. This demonstrates the adage that there are two sources of money: people at work and money at work. By putting money into the policy early, the money starts earning interest and therefore reduces the amount of premium payments needed from people at work at later policy durations. The ultimate extreme of prefunding is the single-premium approach, where an adequate fund is created at the inception of the policy to cover all future costs. The more common approach is a level-premium structure in which partial prefunding creates an ever-increasing cash value that in turn generates increasing investment returns to offset mortality and administrative costs.

All premium suggestions—that is, target premiums—are based on some assumed level of investment earnings. The policyowner bears the risk that actual investment earnings will be greater than those necessary to support the suggested premium. Even though investment earnings cannot go below the guaranteed rate, a long-term shortfall may require either an increase in premiums or a reduction in coverage at some future point.

At the other end of the spectrum is the minimum-premium approach, which is virtually synonymous with annual renewal term insurance. There is minimal, if any, prefunding, and premium payments barely cover the current mortality and expense charges. Under this approach, the premiums must increase as the insured ages, since mortality rates increase with the age of the insured. Premiums increase rapidly at advanced ages because there is still a maximum amount at risk (the cash value is very low, and the mortality rate must be applied to nearly the full death benefit amount). Under the partial prefunding approach, however, cash value increases make the amount at risk decrease as the insured ages, and the increasing mortality rate is applied to a smaller at-risk amount.

Under traditional whole life insurance policies, insurance companies designed a wide range of level-premium contracts, each with a different level of fixed premiums. Contracts with a higher level of premium develop cash values more rapidly. Once the policy cash value is adequate to prefund the policy totally, the policy can be converted to a guaranteed paid-up status. Under participating designs, dividend can exceed the premiums after the policy has developed a large enough cash value to prefund all future policy elements. Under the traditional whole life policies, the only mechanism for returning any policy overfunding is dividends.

With UL policies, however, the accumulations from prefunding are credited to the policy's cash value and are quite visible to the policyowner. The earnings rates applied to those accumulations are also clearly visible as they fluctuate with current economic conditions. Universal life, because of its flexible premium, can be designed to mimic any of the variations found in traditional whole life insurance, and accomplish the same objectives.

Target Premium

target premium

Most UL policies are issued with a target-premium amount. The *target-premium* is the premium used to calculate the full first year commission for the selling agent. The target premium is generally about 75 percent of the amount of the whole life premium for the same insured and face amount. For companies licensed in New York, an advisor will receive full first year commission (50 percent) on premiums paid up to the target premium and 3.5 percent (or some similar amount) on premiums paid above the target premium. The commission rate may be up to 100 percent of the target premium for companies not licensed in New York.

The term target premium is also used as the suggested premium to be paid on a level basis throughout the contract's duration. The target premium is the premium the company considers adequate to maintain the policy on a long-term basis and carries no liability if it is inadequate to maintain the contract. In some insurance companies, the target premium is sufficient to keep the policy in force (under relatively conservative investment return assumptions) through age 95 or 100 and to pay the cash value equivalent to the death-benefit amount if the insured survives to either age 95 or 100. On the other hand, some companies with a more aggressive marketing stance have chosen lower target premiums, which are not adequate to carry the policy in force to advanced ages, even under more generous assumptions of higher investment returns over future policy years.

Probably the best indication of whether or not the target premium is adequate to keep the policy in force up through age 95 or 100 is to compare it with premiums for a whole life policy of a similar face amount and issue age. UL target premiums less than premiums for a comparable whole life policy should be suspect. The only people who will ever really find out whether or not their policy target premiums are adequate are those who pay the premiums throughout the duration of the contract and live to an age old enough to test the target premium. This is another reason why secondary guarantees were introduced and are a popular UL feature today.

EXAMPLE
Bert is now 70 years old. He has paid the target premium on his UL policy for the last 15 years. He was not told, and he did not realize, that the target premium was only intended to keep coverage in force to age 65. Bert wants to keep his coverage, but the target premium he is paying is not adequate to support it. He will have to increase premium payments by more than 20 percent to keep the same amount of coverage, or he will have to reduce the amount of coverage to a level where the target premium is adequate to support the reduced coverage.

Internal Funds Flow

Although UL policies are still relatively young in the history of life insurance products, some policies are already in their fifth or sixth generation of policy series development. As with all products, the individual policy designs constantly evolve in response to the economy, competitive pressures, tax code changes, and creative marketing.

Expenses. Most of the first generation of UL policies were heavily front-end-loaded. They took a significant proportion of each premium dollar as administrative expenses and the remaining portion was then credited to the policy cash value. Competitive pressures caused insurance companies to minimize front-end loading to allow nearly all premium dollars to go directly into the cash value account.

UL policies quickly evolved to a back-end loading design. They lowered or eliminated most of the up-front charge levied against incoming premium amounts and instead imposed new or increased surrender charges applicable to the cash value of a policy surrendered during the contract's first 7 to 15 years. Back-end loaded surrender charges compensate the company for acquisition costs if the policy lapses or is surrendered in the early years. Surrender charges are highest during the first policy year and decrease on a straight-line basis over the remaining years until the year in which the insurance company expects to have amortized all excess first-year acquisition expenses. At that point, the surrender charge ends. Surrender charges are based either on the cash value amount or on the target-premium level. Some insurers have developed a hybrid that depends on both approaches to generate the full surrender charge. The surrender charge usually decreases by the same percentage on each policy anniversary until the charge reaches zero. The net amount payable for a surrendered policy is determined by deducting any applicable surrender charge from the policy cash value, minus any unpaid policy loans and interest.

Companies with the highest surrender charges tend to have little or no front-end expenses charged against premiums. Some companies have policies that combine moderate front-end loading and moderate surrender charges. There is a preference for higher surrender charges and little or no front-end loading in most UL policies being marketed today.

The actual component of the front-end loading can be a flat annual charge per policy, plus a small percentage of premium dollars actually received, and a charge of a few cents per each $1,000 of coverage in force under the policy. The charges applicable to the premiums and the amount of coverage are deducted monthly from the policy cash value. Similarly, the current interest rate is usually applied monthly. These are the deposits and withdrawals from our gas tank.

Some companies have eliminated charges based on the amount of coverage in force. Expenses are still being charged internally, but the manner in which they are handled is not easily seen by the consumer. For example, expenses can be embedded in the spread between actual mortality costs and actual mortality charges, or in the spread between investment earnings and the interest rate credited to the cash value accounts.

No insurance company can operate without generating legitimate costs of operations above the amount needed to pay death benefits. These expenses must be covered, and the method of allocating them is nothing more or less than a cost-accounting approach. The exact allocation formula is always arbitrary and to some extent guided by the philosophy of the insurance company management team. It must address such issues as equity among short-term and long-term policyowners, the appropriate duration for amortizing excess first-year expenses, and how much investment and operations gains to retain for company growth and safety margins, and how much to distribute to policyowners.

Mortality (COI). In all UL policies, after the funds reach the policy cash value, they are subject to charges for current death benefits in the form of a mortality charge or *cost of insurance*, based on the amount at risk. In most insurance companies, the mortality rate actually charged is often in the neighborhood of 50 percent of the guaranteed maximum mortality rate set forth in the policy contract for each attained age of the insured. The difference in the mortality rate actually charged and the maximum permitted mortality rate published in the policy represents the safety margin the insurer is holding in reserve. If future mortality costs for the block of policies turn out to be more expensive than initially assumed, the insurer can increase the mortality rate, not to exceed guaranteed maximum rates specified in the contract.

The waiver-of-premium benefit in UL is somewhat different than those in whole life and term products. There are actually two options, a waiver of premium and a monthly deduction waiver option. The waiver of premium is based on a formula for premium actually paid by the policyowner, as defined in the policy. This option continues the policy as though the premium is paid as it has been, adding to cash value increases. The monthly deduction waiver waives the monthly cost-of-insurance and expense charges if the insured becomes disabled as defined in the policy. This second option does not contribute to the cash value, but does continue the policy while the waiver is in effect.

Interest. After deductions for expenses and mortality, the cash value account is increased at the current crediting rate to reflect investment earnings on the cash value. These are the dollars at work for the policyowner that help reduce his or her current and future out-of-pocket premium expenses. The actual rate credited is a discretionary decision on the part of the insurance company, within contractual guarantees, and it fluctuates, reflecting current economic and competitive conditions.

Interest-crediting rates have been the focal point of most of the competition among companies selling UL policies. There has been very little emphasis on the mortality rates charged or the expense charges levied against incoming premiums. In reality, the interaction of all three factors creates the cost of the policy. Interest rates can be (and have been) intentionally elevated to a level above what an investment portfolio actually supports, but they work for the insurer by compensating with higher levels of mortality charges and expense deductions. When consumers focus on only one of the three elements (interest crediting), it is not surprising that marketing efforts zero in on that element. The assessment of overall policy efficiency requires that all factors be considered together. Policies with lower interest rates can have higher cash values than those with higher interest-crediting rates, because they have lower expense and/or mortality charges.

Flexible Death Benefit

If a policyowner wants the insurer to increase the amount at risk (life insurance amount) the insured must provide evidence of insurability and pay the increased cost of insurance (COI). A decrease in the amount of life insurance, or amount at risk, merely required a written request for a policy change, and the COI will decrease with the decrease in coverage.

Death-Benefit Options

death benefit options

UL insurance gives policyowners a choice of *death benefit options,* level death benefits and increasing death benefits.

Level Option (Option 1)

The level death-benefit design is much like the traditional whole life design. When the death benefit stays constant and the cash value increases over the duration of the contract, the amount at risk or the protection element decreases. Both death benefit options may also be available on term riders on the base plan.

Figure 5-2
Universal Life Option I—Level Death Benefit
(If Target Premium Is Always Paid)

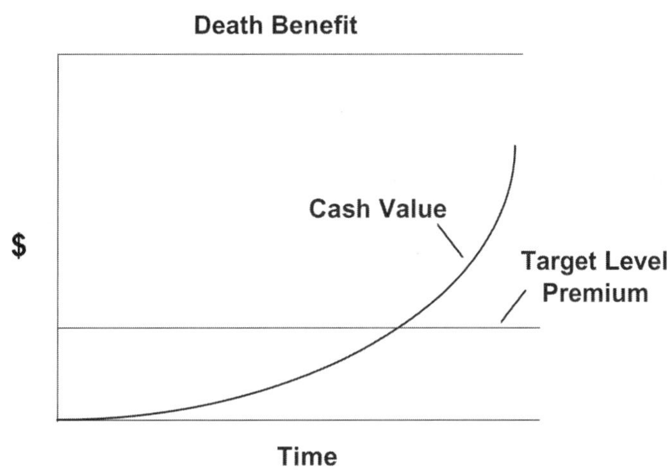

The level death benefit designed under UL policies is a function of a tax law definition of life insurance (IRC Sec. 7702) that was added to the Code shortly after the introduction of UL insurance policies, requiring that a specified proportion of the death benefit be derived from the amount at risk. Whenever the cash value in the contract gets high enough that this proportion is no longer satisfied, the UL policy starts increasing the death benefit (corridor test) even though the contract is called a level death benefit contract. This phenomenon typically does not occur until ages beyond normal retirement, and it is not a significant aspect of this design.

Death Benefit Type Mortality Charges
• Level death benefit type mortality charges apply to a decreasing amount at risk. • Increasing death benefit type mortality charges apply to a constant amount at risk.

There is a significant difference over time between the level and increasing death benefit options regarding the amount of insurance in each option, based on the amount at risk concept. The cost of insurance (COI) that results (mortality rate x amount at risk = COI) can become substantial over time because the level death benefit option has a decreasing amount at risk as the cash value increases. In the level option, the mortality charges are stabilized, or at least do not increase as rapidly as they do in the increasing option. Because the rate per 1,000 of insurance increases with attained age, the COI on the increasing option (constant amount at risk) increases substantially over time as the insured's age increases, and proper funding should be made to compensate for these increasing mortality charges.

Increasing Option (Option 2)

The increasing death benefit design is a modification that was introduced with UL policies. Under this approach, there is always a constant amount at risk in addition to the policy's cash value. As the cash value increases, so does the total death benefit. As a result, the amount at risk is always the face amount.

Figure 5-3
Variable Universal Life Option II—Death Benefit = Level Amount at Risk + Cash Value (Uneven Premium Paid)

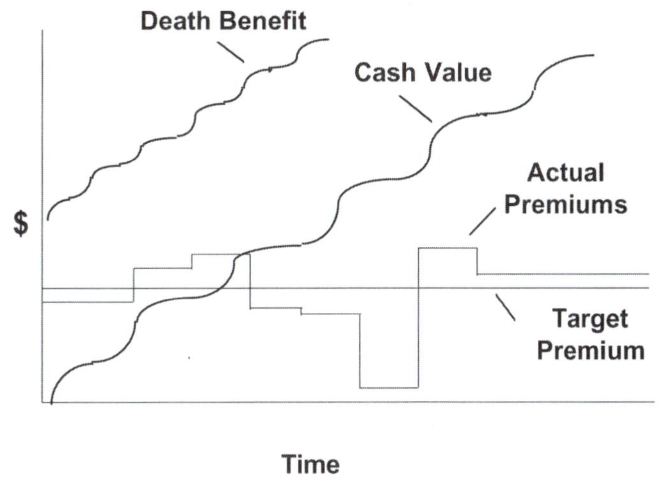

A reduction in the cash value will reduce the death benefit. This design pays both the policy's stated face amount and its cash value as death benefits. Policies with an increasing death benefit design overcome the criticism of whole life policies—that the death benefit is partially made up of the contract's cash value, and as a result the insurance amount is decreasing since the cash value is not paid in addition to the face amount. By selecting the increasing death benefit option under a UL policy, the policyowner is ensuring that the death benefit will be composed of the cash value and an at-risk portion equal to the original face value of the contract.

There is nothing magical about this larger death benefit amount. As is often said, there is no free lunch. The larger amount at risk under this design requires more premium to cover the COI. The COI is determined by multiplying the rate per 1,000 of insurance at the insured's attained age by the amount at risk. These factors offset each other in the Option I model, as the rate of insurance increases and the amount at risk decreases. With Option II, the COI increases with age and must be properly funded to maintain the policy as the insured ages.

There are similarities between the increasing death benefit design for UL and the paid-up additions option under a participating whole life policy. Under a whole life policy, dividends are used to purchase single-premium additions to the base policy. In both types of policies, the excess investment earnings are used to increase the cash value and the death benefit.

Return-of-Premium Option (Option 3)

A variation on the increasing option provides a variable death benefit equal to the policy face amount, plus the total premiums paid (less any partial withdrawals and any surrender charges assessed due to face amount decreases). The option 3 death benefit will fluctuate with the cumulative premium paid into the policy. In all other respects, it is the same as option 2, the increasing death-benefit option.

Withdrawal Feature

Another feature introduced with UL is the policyowner's ability to make partial withdrawals from the policy's cash value without having the withdrawal treated as a policy loan. Money can be taken out of the UL cash value just like a withdrawal from a savings account, and there is no obligation to repay those funds; nor is there any incurring interest on the amount withdrawn. Withdrawals affect the policy's future earnings, because the policy's cash value, which is the source of future earnings, is reduced by the amount of the withdrawal. Its effect on the death benefit depends on the type of death benefit in force.

Because the structure of the two death benefit designs of the UL policies are slightly different, the effect of partial withdrawals on the death-benefit amount differs. Partial withdrawals reduce the death benefit amount under the level death benefit design by the amount of the withdrawal. They decrease the amount of the policy's cash value and correspondingly increase the amount at risk. As a result, the mortality charge will increase after the partial withdrawal to pay the mortality risk applicable to the greater amount at risk.

Partial withdrawals under the increasing death benefit design will reduce the death benefit payable because the withdrawal decreases the cash value that makes up part of the death benefit. However, such withdrawals will not reduce the mortality charges for the amount at risk, because that at-risk amount remains constant. Reducing the cash value by the amount of the partial withdrawal does have a negative impact on the amount of investment earnings credited to the cash value.

Flexibility to Last a Lifetime

The astonishing flexibility of premiums under UL policies and the ability to adjust death benefits upward and downward have created life insurance policies that can keep pace with the policyowner's needs. The policy can be aggressively funded when the premium dollars are available, and premium payments can be intentionally suspended during tight budget periods, such as starting a new business or while children are attending college. The policy's death benefit can be increased (sometimes requiring evidence of insurability) if the need exists, and after any temporary needs have expired, the policy can be adjusted downward to provide lower death benefits if that is what the policyowner wants. The ability of a UL contract to fit constantly changing policyowner needs and conditions has led some to see it as the only policy one should ever need, because its versatility allows it to be adapted to almost any situation.

Secondary (No-Lapse) Guarantees

Universal Life was a hot product in the early years after its introduction. Agents and companies were dazzling consumers with illustrations showing returns of 10 percent and 12 percent with rapidly vanishing premiums or very impressive accumulations in a period of high interest rates. As interest rates fell, many of those who bought these policies discovered that the lower interest rates were insufficient to maintain them or achieve the projected high cash values, leaving these customers surprised and dismayed (and in many cases, very angry).

secondary guarantee

Over the last 15 years, insurance companies have introduced a *secondary guarantee* associated with their UL products to restore interest and confidence in the product, referred to as secondary guarantee UL (SGUL) or no-lapse premium guarantee (NLPG). The purpose of a no-lapse guaranteed product is to provide the greatest amount of permanent insurance coverage for the least cost. Although this product will eventually have no cash or surrender value, the death benefit is guaranteed to stay in force for life, assuming the policyowner has paid the planned premiums as required by the contract.

Secondary or no-lapse guarantees promise to keep the policy in force for a set number of years or to a certain age. They guarantee to pay the full death benefit as long as the premium is paid in an amount equal to or greater than the premium amount required at each premium-payment interval. These plans function like a term-to-age-100-and-beyond, with minimal cash value build-up (the cash value is used to pay the premium), and an emphasis on death-benefit protection. These plans keep the death benefit in force even when the policy cash values are depleted. Accumulation under these riders is a secondary objective, trading off the cash accumulation for the death benefit guarantee. By comparison, whole life and accumulation UL policies focus on higher premium funding and have cash values at older ages, resulting in a small net amount at risk.

Interest rate crediting may be lower, and the charges for mortality and expenses may be higher than a policy without the no-lapse guarantee. The lower crediting and higher mortality and expense charges are an indirect, but additional cost of the guarantee that allows the company to lower the premium.

Under the first generation of no-lapse products, premiums were generally payable to age 100 and were available via a rider that guaranteed the face amount would not reduce, nor the premium increase, so long as the client paid the premium as specified in the rider. These policies had a strict requirement that premiums must be paid on or before the due date. Late or skipped payments had a significant negative impact on the guarantee. A late premium, policy loan, cash withdrawal, or payment of a smaller than required premium would void the lifetime guarantee, or drop the guarantee to an earlier age.

With the new 2001 mortality tables, companies have introduced a current generation of products that integrate no-lapse provisions. They are generally designed to have the lowest possible cash values and lowest possible premiums for the death-benefit guarantees. These products are currently very popular for situations in which cash value accumulation is not a major goal and are ideal for estate planning and other long-term life insurance needs.

As with all policy features, be sure to explain the secondary guarantee to your clients; they can lose these no-lapse guarantees by not paying enough attention to payment requirements or misunderstanding their grace period and catch-up provisions. Some policyowners have already jeopardized these guarantees and do not even know it. If you have clients who purchased these types of UL plans from another agent, it is worth visiting with them to be certain these guarantees are still intact, and that they understand how they work. If the guarantees are not intact, it is likely they cannot be reinstated. This could be a sales opportunity if the client is still insurable.

Single-Premium UL

The single-premium concept can facilitate a number of goals and solve a number of problems, particularly for older clients who have accumulated a sum of money that can be applied as a single premium. Generally, this product is designed to protect a client's assets and serve other needs that life insurance can satisfy, funded by a single premium.

One variation of this product is a blended or combination product, which offers an option to access the death benefit on a tax-free basis during the insured's lifetime to cover the cost of long-term health care. Many individuals feel that long-term care insurance is too expensive or that they may pay large sums of money into a policy and never use it. A blended life insurance policy with long-term care benefits solves this problem. The policyowner selects the amount of monthly benefit that can be accessed to pay for home health care, assisted living, adult day care, or nursing home confinement. The remaining death benefit not used for long-term care can pass at the death of the insured to beneficiaries as tax-fee life insurance proceeds.

Many of the other UL-type features are provided. Access to a policy's tax-deferred cash value is available through partial cash surrenders and/or policy loans. The death benefit, minus any loans, withdrawals, or long-term care benefits paid, is guaranteed. Current interest rates are declared monthly, not to fall below a minimum guaranteed interest rate. Premium charges and surrender charges apply.

Survivorship Universal Life

Survivorship Universal Life offers the flexibility of UL on two (or more) insureds in one plan. It is essentially the same as the survivorship concept in a whole life policy, using a UL design. As with single-life UL, the premium frequency and amount may be varied according to the policyowners circumstances and goals. The increasing or level death benefit options may be selected and changed as needed, and the face amount may be increased (subject to evidence of insurability requirements) and decreased. The policy will lapse if at any time the cash surrender value is insufficient to pay the monthly deductions. This can happen due to insufficient premium payments, if loans or withdrawals are made, or if the current interest rate decreases or morality rates or expenses increase. For these reasons, it is important to monitor the status of the policy frequently and to fund it properly

Indexed Universal Life

indexed universal life insurance (IUL)

Indexed universal life insurance (IUL), or equity indexed universal life (EIUL), is permanent life insurance that offers all the benefits of UL with accumulation values tied to a stock market index. IUL has characteristics of both fixed and variable UL. Their returns vary more than a fixed UL, but less than a VUL, so there is more risk than a fixed UL, but less than with a VUL.

An IUL policy has a fixed minimum guaranteed interest rate component, as well as an indexed account option. Whereas traditional ULs may credit 4 percent to 6 percent, an IUL has the ability to receive index-linked gains as high as 18 percent or more today. In years in which the index does well, interest-crediting rates will rise, and in years in which the index performs poorly, interest crediting will fall. The policyowner can reap the rewards of stock market-type gains, but is protected with minimum guaranteed interest rates in case the stock market loses. Otherwise, IUL has all of the typical features of traditional UL and operates under the same policy mechanisms.

The major difference with IUL is the option to participate indirectly in the upward movement of a stock index without accepting the normal risk associated with investing in the stock market. The actual interest credited to a policy's cash value is determined by the changes in an equities index. Most insurance companies use the S&P 500 Index® as the underlying index for their IUL product. The potential to realize higher upside returns without the downside risk makes the IUL policy a unique and attractive cash accumulation vehicle.

This product has seen increased sales and an increased number of companies offer it. While many VUL policies recorded big losses in the stock market drop in 2000 and after, IUL owners recorded no losses and some even reported small gains. While the low interest rate environment hurt returns on fixed ULs, IULs were crediting higher returns due to their links to stock market indexes.

Policyowners can direct premium into the fixed account at the current interest rate, or all or a portion of the premium into the indexed account. When premium is transferred into the index account, an indexed account segment or index period is created. Each indexed segment has a segment date on which the beginning value of the underlying equity index is recorded and the percentage change in the index value is calculated. Segment index periods vary by company.

Minimum IUL guarantees are not always credited annually; some companies credit over a five-year period or even the lifetime of the policy. There are several methods of excess interest crediting based on rate changes over daily, monthly, and annual periods. These methods include annual point-to-point, monthly averaging, daily averaging, and variations on these methods. The index crediting method is the process of calculating the index growth rate at the end of the index period. Nearly every company offering IUL today uses the *annual point-to-point method*. With this method, the beginning equity index value is recorded and compared to the index value at the end of the period.

The selected stock index is the IUL's benchmark upon which the crediting of excess interest is based. Most policies use a *participation rate*, which is the percentage of positive movement credited to the IUL policy. For example, if the S&P 500 increased 10 percent, and the IUL had an annual participation rate of 60 percent, the policy would receive an interest credit of 6 percent at the policy anniversary. Participation rates today range from 60 percent to 135 percent. There is a maximum interest rate that will be credited to IUL for the year (or period), called the *cap rate*, which is the maximum index growth rate upon which interest will be calculated. The actual growth cap rate varies by company, but is currently around 10 percent to 14 percent annually, with guaranteed minimum cap rates at 3 percent to 4 percent annually. Participation and growth cap rates may be changed at the company's discretion.

In years where the underlying equity index is flat or loses value, the cash value is subject to the growth floor. The floor is generally guaranteed to be 0 percent if the return is negative. Additionally, most companies offer a cumulative guarantee that assures a minimum effective interest rate over a given time period. For example, one company guarantees that over a 5-year period, if the segment growth rate does not reflect at least a 2 percent minimum effective annual interest rate, the segment value will be increased to that 2 percent level.

How does the insurance company offer a policy that can offer the upside potential for stock market type gains without passing the risk to the policyowner? The truth is that the insurer is not actually investing in an equity index. Instead, the insurance company is investing premiums in fixed-interest investments, and using the earnings from those investments to purchase *call options*.

Call options provide the right, but not the obligation, to purchase a specific amount of a given index at a specified price within a specified period. If the equity index increases, the insurance company can exercise the option at a previously agreed upon price and then credit the interest to the policyowner. If the equity index decreases, the company will not exercise the option, and will lose only the cost of the option. Consequently, the insurer does not need to credit a negative interest rate to the policy's account. The price for call options varies by economic conditions and the interest rate environment. In order to have the flexibility to match options costs with potential benefits to policyowners, the insurance company must have the ability to limit the upside interest credited, through participation rates and growth caps, in times when market conditions dictate.

Innovative new products are being developed rapidly in this line. A few companies offer an extended no-lapse product similar to no-lapse UL. Among cash value permanent products, these provide the most insurance for the lowest premium. Several carriers offer "rainbow" crediting methods. This involves the use of more than one index, such as the S&P 500 Index, the Dow Jones Industrial Average, the NASDAQ 100, or an international index. Insurers then credit the greatest percentage from the best performing index and correspondingly lower proportions of the others. One carrier, for example, credits 75 percent of the return from the best performing index, 25 percent from the next best, and 0 percent from the third index. Another company has introduced a return-of-premium product. Several companies have a single-premium product, and there are indexed survivorship UL products on the market.

The real value of the IUL policy is its ability to earn a credited interest rate higher than a traditional UL or whole life insurance policy, with some guarantees, without accepting the risk of loss associated with the VUL policy. The IUL policy is designed to capture the best elements of both the fixed whole life and the VLI policies, enabling it to earn an acceptable middle-of-the-road interest rate without taking on unnecessary risk.

Variable Universal Life

variable universal life (VUL)

Variable universal life (VUL) combines the protection and tax efficiencies of life insurance with the investment potential of a comprehensive selection of variable investment options. It incorporates the premium flexibility and policy adjustment features of the UL policy with the policyowner-directed investment aspects of VLI. This design discards the fixed-premium features of the VLI (Variable Life Insurance or Variable Whole Life) in favor of the UL chassis.

Between 1999 and 2001, variable life products (VLI and UL) had the largest market share among individual life products (U.S. Individual Life Insurance Sales Trends 1975–2012, LIMRA, 2013). With the precipitous fall in the stock market, both advisors and clients have shied away from variable products. New sales dropped to minimal levels, but as the markets have rebounded, so have variable products. Like the secondary guarantees in UL that have been very popular over the last few years, VUL has been introducing additional guarantees to alleviate prospects' fears about the product and reverse sales declines.

Several companies have introduced policy features and riders that allow policyowners to lock in cash value gains annually, provide secondary no-lapse guarantees, loan-lapse protection, and minimum distribution and earnings guarantees. These features are being developed due to their popularity in the annuity and fixed UL markets. These riders require specific initial or subsequent premium levels and allocations, or reallocations to investment accounts.

VUL adopts the death-benefit designs applicable to UL policies, the level or increasing death-benefit design. Under the level option, the death benefit does not change, regardless of the investment performance within the contract. If the policyowner wants the death benefit to vary with the investment performance within the policy, he or she must choose the increasing death-benefit design.

VUL policies offer the policyowner a choice among a specified group of separate accounts, similar, but not identical to mutual funds, which are created and maintained by the insurance company or by selected investment management firms. Many VUL purchasers are looking for a policy that builds a cash value benefit, in addition to the death-benefit protection, that they can use later on to supplement their income in retirement.

Like VLI, VUL policies are securities and are subject to the same license and registration regulations, including a prospectus requirement, by the SEC and by the state insurance departments. While the VUL policy has the potential for greater returns, it is important to emphasize to clients that earnings within the investment divisions will vary with market conditions, and the accumulated cash value may be at risk. The decrease in cash value can decrease the amount of insurance coverage, and can place the policy in jeopardy of lapsing. Determining a client's risk tolerance and suitability are essential for selling VUL.

Ultimate Flexibility

VUL is a UL policy with the added feature that the policyowner can choose the investment accounts, as under fixed-premium VLI contracts. VUL offers the ultimate in both the flexibility afforded to the policyowner and the amount of risk shifted to the policyowner. There are no interest rate or cash value guarantees and very limited guarantees on the maximum mortality rates applicable. Policyowners have wide open premium flexibility under this contract. They can choose to fund it at whatever level they desire, as long as it is at least high enough to create coverage similar to yearly renewal term and not in excess of the amount that would drive the cash accumulation account above the maximum threshold set forth in IRC Sec. 7702. Policyowners do not need to negotiate with the insurance company or inform the insurer in advance of any premium modification or cessation.

There are a number of expense charges associated with this product. VUL premium payments are subject to a premium expense charge. Monthly deductions are made from the separate accounts to cover mortality (COI) charges, monthly administrative charges, and any rider costs. Daily deductions are made for investment management and administrative costs associated with the separate accounts and for the mortality and expense charge. VUL insurers undertake certain risks, such as guaranteeing death benefits when markets fall, and guaranteeing future expense charges regardless of inflation. The mortality and expense charge is one way they charge for providing these guarantees, and it also serves as a source of insurer profits.

These contracts permit partial withdrawals that work just like those under UL policies. Early partial withdrawals may be subject to surrender charges, and surrender charges are applicable to total surrenders in the policy's early years when the insurance company is still recovering excess first-year acquisition costs. The surrender charges vanish at a specified policy duration, typically 10–15 years.

VUL can be aggressively prefunded so that the policy can completely support itself from its cash value. If adequate premiums are contributed to the contract, this can be accomplished in a relatively short number of years. As with UL, VUL policies make no guarantee that once the cash value is large enough to carry the policy it will always be able to do so. The policyowner assumes the risk of investment return and, to a limited extent, some of the risk of mortality rate charges. Consequently, the policyowner has to make adjustments and either pay more premiums or reduce the death benefit at some future time if in fact the cash value subsequently dips below the level needed to totally prefund the remaining contract years.

By choosing the increasing death benefit option under this contract, policyowners are afforded an automatic hedge against inflation. This inflation protection is general in nature and subject to the risk that investment experience may not keep pace with inflation. Over the long haul, however, the investment-induced increases in coverage should equal, if not exceed, general increases in price levels.

Like UL, three death benefit options are common:

1. level and the death benefit is equal to the face amount
2. increasing and the death benefit is equal to the face amount plus cash value
3. increasing and the death benefit is equal to the face amount plus premiums paid

The policyowner is able to switch investment funds from one of the available choices to any other available fund choice whenever desired. Some insurance companies put a limit on how many fund changes can be made without incurring costs for those changes. Some companies allow one change of funds per year at no cost. Others allow one change per open fund per year with no additional charges, and still others specify in the prospectus a set number of fund changes that can be made during any given time interval without incurring additional charges. Switching investment funds does not incur any taxation of gains in the funds. The internal buildup of the cash value is tax deferred as long as the policy stays in force and will be tax free if the policy matures as a death claim.

Like mutual funds, several features automatically manage the investment accounts within the policy. These include:

- an *expense allocation feature*, which allows the policyowner to specify to which investment accounts and in what amounts the policy expenses will be allocated
- *automatic asset reallocation (rebalancing),* which can be scheduled at quarterly, semiannual or annual intervals to reallocate the investment accounts to certain predetermined percentages

- *dollar-cost averaging* which allows premium to purchase units of subaccounts at regular intervals in predetermined dollar amounts, so the costs of the units is averaged over time and over various market cycles
- *interest sweep*, which instructs the insurer to periodically transfer interest earned in the fixed account to the subaccounts at times, frequencies, and in percentages as specified by the policyowner

VUL policies are primarily life insurance contracts that generate cash value as part of the prefunding level premium mechanism. They are not strictly investment contracts and should not be viewed as such. Philosophically for many there is a conflict when policyowners manage VLI or VUL policies for maximum growth when in fact the reason for the contracts is to provide a financial safety net for beneficiaries. If the primary coverage is for its death benefits, it seems more appropriate that the investment allocations not pursue the most aggressive growth objectives, but a more conservative growth approach. On the other hand, if the primary objective for acquiring the contract is for its cash value and the policyowner intends to use the policy's cash values prior to the insured's death, perhaps the more aggressive growth stance is acceptable. This assumes there is an insurance need in the first place.

Variable products are generally designed to generate maximum accumulation value through investments in numerous separate accounts reflecting the risk level and investment objectives of the policyholder. However, investment return and risk are only part of the story. Not all products are designed the same way and each should be evaluated at the contract level to gauge its ultimate design objectives beyond simply accumulating cash. The real product differentiation is at the policy level in the feature, limitations, and current and guaranteed cost structure of each. While it is tempting to try to compare products using sub-account performance, the real test of a product's ability to create policyholder value lies with the contract, or the "wrapper" around the investment components.

Income Tax Traps for Early Depletion

VUL policies should not be used as short-term investment vehicles. There are two potential traps for policyowners who withdraw a policy's cash values during the first 15 policy years. These income tax burdens are in addition to any surrender charges that may be applied within the policy itself.

One potential trap is the modified endowment contract (MEC) provisions of the Tax Code, which treat all cash value distributions as taxable income until all investment gains have been taxed, and before the remainder of the distribution is treated as a recovery of capital. Such treatment is possible whenever material policy changes are made and the policy fails the seven-pay test (reaching the cash value amount for a policy paid up after seven years). If the policy fails the seven-pay test, not only will the distributed amounts be subject to income tax (up to the extent of the gain); there may also be a 10 percent penalty tax applicable to those taxable gains if the policyowner is younger than 591/2 years of age. High cash value/high premium configuration VUL policies are the most likely candidates for this tax trap. Making sure that the cash value before and after any material change is lower than what it would be if the policy were fully paid up after 7 years will avoid this potential problem.

The other potential trap again deals with high levels of cash value approaching the upper limits permitted under Sec. 7702. If a reduction in the death-benefit level forces a distribution of the cash value in order to retain life insurance status under the Code, those distributions may be taxable income to the extent that they represent gain in the policy. The most severe constraints apply to such "forced out" withdrawals during the first 5 years of the policy. Slightly less severe constraints are applicable for policy years 6 through 15. Any policyowner considering a switch from the increasing death benefit design to the level benefit design during the policy's first 15 years should consider these rules before making the switch. As long as there is no forced distribution or concurrent request by the policyowner for a distribution of cash value funds, there will be no problem. Conversely, if the increasing death-benefit form of the contract is already prefunded near the maximum limitations, there is the possibility that some cash value will be forced out to maintain compliance with the Sec. 7702 limitations on life insurance policies.

Neither of these tax traps has any consequence if there are no gains in the contract (premiums paid exceed cash value) when distributions are made. Under MEC provisions, the taxation will apply only if there are distributions of the cash value. If the funds are left in the contract and allowed to remain part of the cash value, there will be no taxation even though the potential still exists for any distribution once the policy has become classified as an MEC.

VUL contracts are not desirable for policyowners who do not wish to assume the investment risk under the contract. Potential policyowners who say they want to assume the investment risk but become extremely anxious over any short-term fall in the value of the selected investment portfolio funds should also be cautioned.

Identifying VUL Candidates

Excellent VUL Candidates

- Those who want control of how their policy premiums are invested versus giving the insurer control
- Individuals with a high risk tolerance who do not want a ceiling on the growth potential of their policy's cash value
- Corporations that wish to use their policy as an executive benefit for key employees

Poor VUL Candidates

- Individuals who want to keep life insurance separate from their investments
- Risk-averse individuals
- Seniors and the elderly who do not have the time these policies require to weather good and bad markets
- Those who do not fully understand the policy

Survivorship Variable Universal Life

The same concepts apply to survivorship variable universal life (SVUL) as to survivorship whole life and survivorship UL This product, as with VUL, allows the policyowner to meet insurance and investment needs. In addition to providing a death benefit and the flexibility of UL in premium and benefit amounts, SVUL allows the policyowner to invest premiums in a variety of investment subaccounts. All other aspects of survivorship policies and VUL policy designs described earlier pertain to this product.

The Information-Gathering Interview

The primary objective of the information-gathering process is to uncover meaningful information about the prospect by asking questions. This will enable the advisor to have a discussion with the prospect about the prospect's goals, attitudes, priorities, current situation, and any changes anticipated for the future. As a result, recommendations can be made from an informed exchange of ideas.

Objectives of the Information-Gathering Interview

The following are the objectives of the information-gathering interview for the advisor:

1. Gather relevant, factual, and objective information about the client's current situation, including important personal and employment information, assets and liabilities, financial information, and other related data.
2. Gather subjective data, including important values, feelings, and attitudes towards financial issues. Most importantly, determine the client's goals, and needs. This includes prioritizing goals in terms of importance and completion target date(s). One important piece of information is risk tolerance, the client's attitude towards risk. Another is the expectations the client has for the process.
3. Gain a dollar commitment for the amount the client is willing and able to spend to accomplish the identified goals.

Outline of the Information-Gathering Interview

The following is a brief outline of the actions the advisor wants to take in the information-gathering interview.

1. ***Communicate the process to the prospect.*** This includes explaining the purpose, the process, and the potential benefits derived from the information-gathering interview. A time commitment to the process should be agreed upon. The role of the advisor should be defined and the expectations of the advisor and prospect discussed and established.
2. ***Completion of fact-finding and feeling-finding information gathering.*** This involves gathering and recording information, normally through a structured fact-finder form. The advisor should understand the subjective rationale (attitudes, values, feelings) behind the objective facts.
3. ***Identify and prioritize goals, needs, and objectives.*** Goal setting is fundamental to the planning process. Goals should be quantifiable, measurable, and have time horizons. For example, if a prospect states a goal of wanting to live comfortably in retirement, you should work to define the goal more precisely. An ideal goal statement might be that the client and his wife want to retire in 20 years with an after-tax income of $60,000 a year in current dollars, and continue that income for as long as they live, with increases of 3 percent per year for inflation, without depleting their principle.

The more precisely the goal is defined, the more accurately we can establish programs to accomplish the goal.

Prioritizing the prospect's goals involves ranking them by order of importance and completion date. These two dimensions can be managed as necessary, depending on client resources and other factors. Through the information-gathering process, we need to determine where the prospect is now and where he or she wants to be. Our solutions will help the client close the gap between the two. In this way, the recommendations that ultimately emerge will be in line with the client's goals, their importance, when we need to achieve them, and the resources committed to attain them. Finally, summarize your findings and get confirmation from the prospect that your understanding of their problems and goals is accurate. This is known as a discovery agreement.

4. ***Get a dollar commitment.*** Determining the dollar amount that the client can afford and is committed to spending is an important step in the process to accomplishing satisfactory results for both the client and you. It is essential that this commitment be realistic and genuine. The client must be able to maintain the plan for it to be successful, and the advisor must know what he or she has to work with to accomplish the client's objectives and/or solve his or her problems.

Using the Fact-Finder

The following is an overview and summary of fact-finding skills.

- ***Questioning***—Ask open-ended questions to probe for feelings and goals. Ask confirming questions to ensure understanding.
- ***Listening***—Actively listen. Restate or rephrase to confirm your understanding.
- ***Motivating***—Ask open-ended questions designed to help the prospect see the reality of the situation and the necessity of taking action to accomplish their goals.
- ***Note-taking***—Write down important numbers, facts, goals, needs, priorities, and feelings.
- ***Summarizing***—Ensure understanding before proposing next steps.
- ***Proposing***—Propose next steps based on a consensus (discovery agreement) between the prospect and yourself.

Fact-finding and Feeling-finding

fact finding

feeling-finding

The information-gathering, or *fact-finding* process involves asking questions of a factual and objective nature about topics such as income, savings and investment amounts, and similar pieces of information. Of equal importance are questions of a subjective, emotional, and more personal nature. These are the reasons why people have made certain decisions and the factors that affect their decision-making process. *Feeling-finding* involves identifying the goals, attitudes, and values that are the rationale and background for the factual data. It is critical that you, as the advisor understand the subjective aspect of the prospect's life as well as possible.

For example, the prospect owns a whole life policy for $25,000 purchased 10 years ago. This is an objective fact. The subjective or feeling aspect associated with this fact includes the reason it was bought, what this purchase was intended to accomplish, and how the prospect feels about it now. To the extent practical, this subjective information should be gathered about most, if not all, of the objective information you gather.

Analyzing the Information

This section discusses analyzing the information gathered in the fact-finding interview to determine the client's current financial situation and to develop appropriate solutions to achieve the prospect's desired goals.

Determining the Prospect's Situation

To this point in the selling/planning process, you have gathered the facts, figures, goals, priorities, attitudes, and values that constitute a profile of your prospect. Now that you have a reasonably complete picture of the prospect, what do you do with it? You examine the situation to pinpoint real problems and needs that you can solve with your products and services.

You will need to ask yourself several questions as you analyze a case after a data-gathering interview.

1. What are the desires, concerns, objectives, and needs to be considered?
2. Where is the prospect now in relation to established goals?
3. How is the prospect's situation likely to change in the future?

4. How far will existing life insurance and other benefit sources go toward meeting these needs? What outcomes may be expected if the prospect does nothing?
5. What additional life insurance or other recommendations are needed to make up the shortfall or complete the plan?
6. What are the goal priorities of the prospect?
7. What product solutions fit this situation?
8. How much can and will the prospect pay for the protection?
9. What objections can I anticipate?
10. Who are the decision makers in this sale?

Review the Facts

Compile and categorize the answers to the key questions listed above. This process determines the facts of the prospect's current financial situation—where the prospect is now. Next, review the prospect's goals to define where they want to be. You will then be in a position to calculate the amount of any additional insurance or investments needed to close the gap between their present situation and their desired situation. Finally, design a solution, with alternatives, to present to your prospective client to achieve this task. Let us briefly examine each of the main areas you will consider in your analysis.

The analysis of the prospect's situation involves taking the relevant information gathered from the fact-finder and designing a plan that reflects the prospect's needs, goals, and premium commitment. Creating a solution to meet the prospect's needs depends heavily upon the quality of the information gathered during the fact-finding process. The solution must be based on the prospect's circumstances and preferences. Thus, the importance of a thorough fact finder cannot be overemphasized.

Your objective is to help the prospect get the best value for his or her money through an effective plan design. Plan design is a balancing act between the prioritized coverage needs of the prospect and his or her premium commitment. One way to approach this task is to begin with the basic coverage design, creating an "ideal plan." Then, using the premium commitment and the prospect's priorities, begin adjusting the plan to create an optimal solution that will best meet his or her priorities within the specific premium commitment.

Decisions can be made about each aspect of the coverage by referring to the information gathered in the fact-finding process. The fact-finder will provide information about the existing and projected resources, preferences for types of coverage, coordination with other assets, and so forth. Unfortunately, there may be many variables to account for, and objectives may conflict. Furthermore, there may be a long period between the purchase of the coverage and the eventual occurrence of a claim. As a result, the advisor and prospect must make some assumptions about future events.

You should prepare a few alternatives to give the prospect choices based on the features and benefits of each option. Having choices is something that most buyers appreciate. The advisor is seen as an expert, a counselor and consultant, who educates the buyer on the key advantages and differences between product choices. The buyer is then free to control the decision to buy.

While a policy with all the features that everyone would like to have is desirable, if its premium is beyond what a prospect can or will pay, then presenting this solution may be a formula for losing the sale. Instead, develop some alternative policy designs that reflect the prospect's priorities and fall within his or her premium commitment. Limit your choices to just a few, so that you do not confuse the prospect. You can always customize further by using a few basic designs and illustrations as a starting point and introducing modifications by adding or subtracting certain features.

In preparing your recommendations, review the prospect's key issues discovered in the fact-finding.

- How long will they need the coverage?
- What level of premium will they be paying?
- Is premium flexibility important?
- What are the prospect's financial priorities, goals, and budget constraints?

Review Needs

The list of your prospect's needs, concerns, and desires identified in the information-gathering interview represents your sales opportunities. You should be able to attach both a monetary value and a priority to each of them. List any foreseeable changes that are likely to occur in the prospect's personal or business life, such as marriage, birth, inheritance, or promotion. These should be incorporated into any current insurance planning.

Most people do not buy what they need—they buy what they want. Listen carefully to what the prospect is telling you he or she wants and what he or she needs. Do not transfer your own standards and values in determining the prospect's motives.

Existing Program

Some people are already well protected, while others need extensive additional planning and protection. You should know or be able to determine the eligibility, amount, and duration of any employer- or government-provided benefits, as well as present life, disability, and health insurance coverage. You should also know the present beneficiary, ownership, and payout arrangements for each of your prospect's existing policies. You want to evaluate and take into account the strengths and weaknesses of the current plan in designing the proposed plan.

Additional Protection Needs

There are several techniques used to measure the need for additional protection and personal life insurance planning. Simpler techniques can calculate needs manually or with a simple calculator. The more sophisticated and complex techniques will require a computer and printouts. They are covered in an earlier discussion of life insurance planning methods.

Product Solutions

At this point, you are considering possible product solutions that may apply to this prospect's situation. A final decision of a product or products should not take place until the completion of your analysis. However, you can make some initial "ballpark" generalizations to assist you in considering what may help the prospect.

The number and variety of life insurance products available to meet consumer needs are enormous. An in-depth knowledge of the products you sell is essential in analyzing your prospect's needs and designing appropriate solutions. A general treatment cannot take the place of a thorough study of your company's product line. Know the features and benefits of your products and how to present them to prospects. Know what your products can and cannot do, whom they are designed for, and what the requirements are for selling them. As any experienced salesperson will tell you, there is no substitute for product knowledge. Just because you should not tell each prospect everything you know, does not mean you should not know it.

The Choice of Product

After needs and amounts are determined and agreed upon in the fact finding interview, you should then consider the types of policies that best fit the prospect's needs. With numerous policies, options, and riders available, the possibilities are almost unlimited. The process of elimination should be guided by the fact finding and analysis steps of the selling/planning process.

When analyzing the information collected from fact finding, consider the following questions to determine what products may provide the best solutions for the client:

- Prospect's premium commitment—What is his/her ability to pay ongoing premiums?
- Face amount—What are possible choices for the base policy plus any combination of riders?
- Length of coverage period—How long does the prospect need the coverage?
- Length of the premium-paying period—Is there any reason for a particular premium schedule?
- Pattern of death benefit—Is there a need for level, increasing, or decreasing coverage? Is there any period(s) that the need is larger or smaller?
- Risk Tolerance—What is the client's view of risk? What is their time horizon? What is their objective for life insurance protection? What is their overall financial situation and other financial assets?
- Traditional (whole life or term) versus nontraditional (UL, VUL, IUL) Products
    - Product choice reflects the funding backing the product (general versus separate accounts). For the general account in traditional products—the company makes investments and assumes the investment risks. The general account is subject to the claims of company creditors. For separate accounts in variable products—the policyowner selects investment options and assumes investment risk. Only separate account assets back insurance products and are not subject to the claims of company creditors.
    - Traditional products have fixed schedule of death benefits, premiums and cash values. Nontraditional products have flexible premiums and death benefits, and performance based account and surrender values.

- Would a participating or nonparticipating product be best?
- Would a single life or multi-life product be best?
- Would individual or group product be best?

The Appropriate Type of Life Insurance

No valid generalizations can be made with regard to the best life insurance policy. The best policy is the policy that most effectively meets your prospect's needs. Thus, emphasis in planning must be placed on your individual prospect's needs, and not on the relative merits of a particular kind of policy.

This decision requires a high degree of familiarity with the products you offer. You must know what their inherent risks are, and what trade-offs are involved in selecting one product versus another. This also requires broad knowledge of your client's situation and an awareness of existing client resources and objectives, so they can be matched with the proper product. You must have sensitivity to client risk-taking tendency and a feel for client views regarding such things as guarantees, premium levels, and policy flexibility. Only then should you evaluate alternatives and make recommendations.

Will It Be There When Needed?

The most important question to ask about any insurance is, will it be there when it is needed. The best life insurance policy is the one that is in force when the insured dies, if there is a need for it then. All of the arguments, pros and cons and strengths and weaknesses of a product are meaningless if needed insurance is not in force at death.

A chief difference between life insurance and other forms of insurance is the degree of certainty about whether the peril will occur. Many perils never happen; death always does. The only question is when. As years pass, the likelihood of death increases. Logically then, if a life insurance policy is to do its job, it must be in force at death, at whatever age, and in the right amount, based on the prospect's needs.

Analyzing Needs

Based on your analysis of the prospect's current situation, determine which life insurance needs are temporary or short-term, and which are permanent or long-term. Break down needs into those that could be of a shorter duration, lasting less than approximately 20 years, and those that could be longer term, such as lifetime, beyond age 65, and those lasting more than 20 years. A major consideration in this area is whether the prospect wants life insurance into older ages approaching and beyond life expectancy.

Some additional considerations that can be matched with policy characteristics include the following:

- ***Variations of planned premium-paying period.*** Premium payments may include a limited-payment schedule, paid-up additions riders, paying premiums using dividends, lump-sum dump-ins, and other premium variations to alter a fixed payment schedule.
- ***Emphasis on saving versus protection.*** Permanent cash value policies promote savings. Term will provide pure protection.
- ***Desire for inflation protection.*** Variable products with stock investments generally will offer the best hedge against inflation, and UL offers an increasing death benefit. Whole life with paid-up additions can also offer additional insurance. The use of a guaranteed insurability option is another possibility to purchase life insurance in the future.
- ***Importance of yield versus safety in the savings component.*** If the prospect's risk tolerance permits, VLI, UL, or VUL may be appropriate as a way to achieve a higher yield than with traditional whole life policies.
- ***Unbundling of cost components.*** If a prospect wants to know where his premium dollars go and receive an itemized disclosure of mortality and expenses costs and interest investment crediting, he should consider VLI, UL, or VUL.
- ***Premium-paying flexibility.*** UL or VUL can be appropriate if premium flexibility is important to the prospect.

How Will the Prospect Pay for It?

An inescapable companion question is how to pay for life insurance in old age when it is most needed, because death is nearer and insurance is most expensive for the same reason. While some forms of permanent insurance have higher premiums in early years, such policies may have lower or no premium payments in old age. Term policies have lower early-year premiums that increase over time. A person's inability to pay increasingly steeper premiums in older ages may jeopardize their ability to maintain coverage.

The fact-gathering interview should have provided a budget commitment and financial and personal information about your prospect. Use this to determine the type and amounts of coverage to recommend. You will know how much the prospect can afford to pay, or have a good idea of the prospect's general financial situation. You have an agreed upon amount of coverage desired, or information that can be used to determine that amount. You also should have information about the prospect's goals, needs, and wants that can be used to design a plan.

Risk Tolerance and Suitability

Many of today's policies have transferred some of the risks from the insurance company to the policyowner. No discussion of policy selection would be complete without a consideration of risk tolerance.

risk tolerance

suitability

Risk tolerance is the degree to which a client is willing or reluctant to accept the risk that his investment may decline in value and that the premium may increase over time. Ask questions concerning your prospect's past investment decisions, investment experience, total assets, asset allocation, diversification, time horizon, liquidity needs, and investment objectives to determine the suitability of a product. Your company should have a questionnaire and guidelines for this process, especially when selecting variable products. A product recommendation must always be suitable and in the client's best interest, regardless of type. *Suitability* deals with the appropriateness of the product for the client based on their overall need, financial situation, ability to pay the premium, and risk tolerance, as discussed above.

Calculations and Projections

After you have itemized and reviewed the prospect's personal and financial information, you are ready to begin the number-crunching part of your analysis. Your objective is to arrive at the specific amount of coverage your prospect needs now to be fully protected. There is more than one way to do these calculations. Although your company or agency may endorse one method or another, you should be aware of the various alternatives.

Anticipating Client Concerns

Your recommendations should provide a comparison of the results anticipated from the current plan and those anticipated from the proposed plan, and its alternatives. Each plan will contain certain strengths and weaknesses that should be explained and discussed with the prospect. In the final analysis, the plan must be the client's plan, not the advisor's plan.

Chapter Five Review

Key terms and concepts are explained in the glossary. Answers to the review questions and the self-test questions are found in the back of the book in the Answers to Questions section.

Key Terms and Concepts

variable life insurance
FINRA
separate account
Sec. 7702 of the Deficit Reduction Act of 1984 (DEFRA)
cash value accumulation test (CVAT)
guideline premium (GPT)/cash value corridor test
universal life insurance
unbundling
target premium
death benefit options
secondary guarantee
indexed universal life insurance (IUL)
variable universal life (VUL)
fact finding
feeling-finding
risk tolerance
suitability

Review Questions

1. Explain why VLI policies are subject to SEC regulations, and describe the requirements that regulations impose on the insurers, agents, and policies. [1]
2. Explain how investment options have changed under many VLI policies over the past two decades. [1]
3. Explain how the cash value of a VLI policy differs from that of a whole life policy. [1]
4. Describe the type of information in a VLI prospectus. [1]
5. Describe the risks the policyowner assumes under a VLI policy. [1]
6. Describe the link between investment performance and death benefits under VLI policies. [2]
7. Explain the income tax definition of life insurance under Sec. 7702 of the Internal Revenue Code. [2]
8. Describe UL and explain why it was so successful in the 1980s. [3]
9. Describe UL's flexible premium feature. [3]
10. Explain how partial withdrawals of cash value from a UL policy differ from a policy loan from that policy. [3]
11. Explain the target-premium concept applicable to UL. [3]

12. Describe both of the death-benefit options commonly available to UL purchasers. [3]
13. Explain how policy loans affect UL's cash value and death benefits. [3]
14. Describe the explicit loading charges and surrender charges in UL policies. [3]
15. Explain the investment component of IUL. [3]
16. Explain secondary (no-lapse) guarantees in UL. [3]
17. Describe VUL and explain how it differs from UL and VLI. [4]
18. Explain the objectives of the information-gathering interview. [5]
19. Discuss important elements of analyzing the information from the information-gathering step of the selling/planning process. [6]

Self-Test Questions

1. Which of the following is an objective of the fact-finding process?

   (A) obtain referrals
   (B) make tentative recommendations
   (C) collect objective and subjective information about the prospect
   (D) get agreement on a solution to a need

2. Which of the following statements is correct concerning VLI?

   (A) VLI has mortality charges for the death benefits they provide.
   (B) VLI can be used effectively as a short-term investment vehicle.
   (C) Surrender charges will not significantly reduce potential gains in the early years.
   (D) The policyowner has control over the assets purchased and sold by the individual funds.

3. Which of the following statements concerning UL is correct?

   (A) The level death-benefit option pays the constant amount at risk plus the cash value as a death benefit.
   (B) If the UL policy is underfunded, the policyowner has the choice to either (a) increase the premium or (b) reduce the face amount to continue coverage.
   (C) UL policies require premium payments after the first policy year even if the policy's cash value is adequate to cover the next 60 days of expenses and mortality charges.
   (D) Money can be withdrawn for a UL policy, but it must be paid back with interest.

4. The target premium in a UL policy is

   (A) the suggested premium to be paid on a level basis throughout the contract's duration and upon which the advisor's commission is based
   (B) the amount that must be paid on a UL policy or it will lapse
   (C) the maximum amount that is allowed to paid on a UL policy under Sec. 7702 guidelines
   (D) the amount of premium that will guarantee that the policy will stay in force until age 95

5. The income tax definition of life insurance is provided in which of the following?

   (A) Sec. 101 of the Internal Revenue Code
   (B) Determined by statute in the state in which the policy is sold
   (C) Sec. 303 of the Internal Revenue Code
   (D) Sec. 7702 of the Deficit Reduction Act of 1984 (DEFRA)

6. Which of the following statements concerning UL premium payment is (are) correct?

   I. At no time is there a required minimum level of premium payment.
   II. Nearly every policy is issued with a target-premium amount.

   (A) I only
   (B) II only
   (C) Both I and II
   (D) Neither I nor II

READ THE FOLLOWING DIRECTIONS BEFORE CONTINUING

The questions below differ from the preceding questions in that they all contain the word EXCEPT. So you understand fully the basis used in selecting each answer, be sure to read each question carefully.

---

7. All the following types of life insurance contain a contractually guaranteed minimum interest rate and thus, minimum guaranteed cash values EXCEPT

    (A) limited-payment whole life insurance
    (B) VLI
    (C) current-assumption whole life insurance
    (D) UL

8. All of the following statements concerning UL policies are correct EXCEPT

    (A) Under the increasing death-benefit option the total death benefit equals the stated face amount plus the amount at risk.
    (B) Most policies credit current interest rates on the cash value as long as there are no outstanding policy loans.
    (C) Withdrawals affect future earnings, because the fund still intact to earn interest is reduced by the amount of the withdrawal.
    (D) The target-premium amount is merely a suggestion and carries no liability if it is inadequate to maintain the contract to any duration.

9. All of the following statements regarding VUL are correct EXCEPT

    (A) The policies do not permit the policyowner to direct the investment portfolio.
    (B) The policies shift some of the investment risk to the policyowner.
    (C) The policies treat all cash value withdrawals as policy loans.
    (D) The policies have either a level death benefit or an increasing death benefit.

10. All of the following statements concerning VLI are correct EXCEPT

    (A) Advisors who sell VLI products must be licensed with both life insurance and securities licenses.
    (B) VLI policies can be sold only after a prospectus has been given to the prospective buyer.
    (C) VLI policies become more acceptable to consumers after a long period of market increases.
    (D) VLI policies provide guarantees of both the interest rate and a minimum cash value.

COMPARING COSTS AND POLICY ILLUSTRATIONS 6

Learning Objectives

An understanding of the material in this chapter should enable you to

1. List and explain the methods of comparing life insurance policies, and some strengths and weaknesses of each.
2. Describe the importance of interest adjustments in analyzing policy illustrations and determining the cost of a life insurance policy.
3. Explain the guidelines and regulations that effect the life insurance policy illustration.
4. Identify the issues that led to regulation of policy illustration content and organization.
5. Discuss the factors that affect the illustrated performance of a life insurance policy.
6. Discuss the important elements of developing and presenting the life insurance plan.

This chapter investigates the meaning and methods of evaluating the costs of life insurance policies, especially based on comparing one against another. Tables showing examples of these methods are provided at the end of the chapter. The chapter also looks at policy illustrations, the most common technique for explaining an abstract and intangible financial product such as life insurance to a prospect. The chapter will examine illustrations in depth for the following important reasons:

- They are widely used by financial advisors in working with prospects.
- Misrepresentations and other problems have been associated with their use over the last few decades.
- Advisors need to understand the fine technical points of constructing illustrations in order to avoid the associated problems.

Life Insurance Market Trends

We have experienced the full gamut of financial and economic conditions over the past decade. Individual life insurance has weathered the storms fairly well, except after the economic recession in 2008 and 2009. Like the rest of the economy, individual life products thrived in the economic boom that followed the 2001 recession, reaching a sales peak in 2007. At the sales peak, flexible premium products (universal life and variable universal life) accounted for approximately 56 percent of new annualized premium.

Market Share by Product (in percentages)														
Year	1999	2000	2001	2002	2003	2004	2005	2006	2007	2008	2009	2010	2011	2012
WL	29	23	25	27	25	24	24	22	22	24	28	30	31	32
Term	21	23	21	22	24	23	23	22	22	23	27	24	22	21
VUL	31	36	32	24	17	16	14	15	14	12	7	6	8	6
UL	19	18	22	27	34	37	39	41	42	41	38	40	39	41
Source: LIMRA International Inc., Individual Life Sales Survey (2013)														

Sales and performance of variable universal life strongly reflects the movements of the stock market. VUL sales grew to around one-third of the market until the market collapse in 2000 and 2001, and have continued to drop, particularly in light of the market and financial crisis in 2008 and 2009. Historically, strong performance in the equities markets have helped boost VUL sales, but this no longer appears to be the case. For example, when equity markets recovered in 2003, VUL sales remained relatively flat. Variable product sales have not recovered from the market declines and volatility seen in the securities markets.

The market share of flexible premium products continued to rebound, in spite of the decline of VUL sales, because of the popularity of death benefit guarantee universal life products. By the end of 2007, death benefit guarantee UL products represented just under half of new UL premium.

The market share trend for nonvariable permanent life products has been pronounced. Consumer fears resulting from the financial meltdown and securities market volatility have shifted sales away from flexible premium and variable products to whole life products.

Also showing increased market share and moderate to strong growth are indexed universal life (IUL) products. With VUL products falling to a low point, the reemergence of IUL products has capitalized on the benefits of up potential and reduced downside risks with both producers and consum IUL products have become an alternative to variable products. They provide the security of not losing most or all of the policy value, particularly considering what has happened to VUL in the past decade. With interest rates at historically low levels and the equity markets slowly rebounding, IUL presents an attractive option when compared with the current crediting rates on UL products.

Methods of Comparing Life Insurance Policy Costs

Many studies of the American public have indicated that life insurance consumers do not have a good understanding of life insurance products. They do not understand pricing and the features of life insurance policies. They have a hard time understanding and explaining the differences between whole life and term insurance. Many have not heard of variable life, universal life, or variable universal life, let alone know how they differ. The process of buying life insurance intimidates consumers.

Consumers are interested in the rate of return of cash value life insurance and what return is accruing for their benefit and their family's. They want to know what the capital in their life insurance is doing and to what costs it is exposed.

Over the years, a number of systems have been developed to help consumers with the financial analysis of life insurance policies. These systems can be divided into two types: those that are predictive and use numbers from life insurance illustrations, and those that analyze policies using current policy data. As we will see in the discussion of life insurance illustrations, a predictive analysis based on life insurance illustrations is doomed to fail, because illustrations are based on assumptions that are not known to the public and are not comparable from company to company. If a consumer is trying to select a policy based on an illustration, the process will be flawed and more and more unreliable as they project farther into the future. Using historical data may be productive because it uses actual results, but it may not be helpful in selecting policies.

Life insurance products are complex and extremely difficult to evaluate and compare. Several methods exist for this purpose. While cost comparison methods yield precise figures, this precision can lead to an unwarranted feeling of authenticity and credibility. No single method can take into account all of the factors that should be considered when making a life insurance purchasing decision. All methods have limitations and must make some arbitrary assumptions to derive costs. The most important limitation is that no cost comparison method can take into account the quality and integrity of the advisor and the insurer. Many of the existing comparison methods were developed in simpler times, when policies were based more on guaranteed values, general portfolio interest rates, fixed-premium policies, and less complex policy designs. What had been illustrations of past performance have increasingly become projections of future results based on assumptions. The following is a brief summary of these methods.

Net Cost Method

net cost method

Historically, the traditional *net cost method* has been widely used. Its procedure is quite simple, easy to calculate, understand, and explain. The starting point is to specify the duration of coverage to be evaluated. Typically this is either 10 or 20 years, or to a specified age, such as 65. The steps of the evaluation simply involve totaling all of the premiums paid under the policy, then subtracting the cash surrender value and all dividends paid over that interval. One reason this method is so easy to understand is that it does not take into account the time value of money. In other words, it ignores interest, which can be a significant factor in the cost of an investment over time. The time-value-of-money concept focuses on the timing of money paid or received and the role of interest in determining comparable financial costs and value. Without considering the time value of money, the results of this method are misleading.

The total cash value available to the policyowner on the date chosen is subtracted from the sum of premiums paid to that date to determine the policyowners' net cost. The final cost obtained under the net cost method is considered the cost of the insurance to the client. The main criticism of this analysis is that after 20 years the net cost is usually negative. This means the cash value and dividends paid over the interval exceed the aggregate premiums paid. The implication is that the policyowner has received insurance free of charge, and in fact made a profit on the premiums. In this sense, the policyowner is being paid to keep the insurance. One shortcoming of this method is that it gives equal weight to payment amounts that may be separated by 10 or 20 years. Another is that it does not consider opportunity cost, the simple fact that the money spent on the life insurance could have been spent or invested elsewhere (see Tables 6-4 and 6–5 at the end of this chapter for examples using this method).

The net cost method is not appropriate for comparing policies, whether they are of the same type or different. It is unacceptable under state statutes and regulations for purposes of making replacement evaluations. In fact, under some state statutes, insurance advisors are prohibited from using the net cost method. Policy illustrations and comparisons that do not take into account the effects of interest are by default assuming that the interest rate is zero and inflation is zero. Dollar amounts from different periods are comparable only if money can be borrowed without cost (no interest charged) and if prices remain unchanged over time (no inflation). This is obviously unrealistic and distorts the cost of a financial product. Illustrations that include interest-adjusted figures are preferable, due to their increased accuracy and adjustments for the real world.

Interest Rate Methods

interest-adjusted indices

National Association of Insurance Commissioners (NAIC)

The *interest-adjusted indices* are similar to the traditional net cost approach except that the interest-adjusted indices take into account the time value of money. The *National Association of Insurance Commissioners (NAIC)* developed the interest-adjusted cost indices and model laws regarding their use. The NAIC is a voluntary association of state insurance regulatory officials that issues model insurance laws and regulations for state adoption to promote uniformity in the separate states.

The interest-adjusted index statutes were drafted and adopted during the 1970s, prior to the high interest and inflation rates experienced in the late 1970s and early 1980s. The NAIC developed a model regulation to give consumers a way to compare the relative costs of different policies and to improve the quality of the cost information given to consumers. Under the model regulation, the policy summary on illustrations is required to contain two cost indices of the issued policy. These indices reflect the time value of money (interest) by recognizing that money is paid and received at different times and that policy costs can be better compared by using a specified interest assumption.

Almost every state mandates that a 5 percent annual interest rate be used. The concern of these state regulations is not the accuracy of the interest rate in representing the actual future interest earned, but rather a need for the comparability of indices for different policies and different companies. Indices based on different interest rates are not easily comparable. By prescribing one interest rate, results in comparison indices can be used without further adjustments.

Premiums alone do not always reflect the true cost of a life insurance policy. This is particularly true in permanent insurance, especially the flexible premium universal designs. Naturally, the public perception is that the premium is the price of the contract, so the higher the premium, the higher the perceived cost of the insurance within the policy. However, this is not always true. Additionally, the cost indices are based on illustrations that are themselves suspect, as we will see. Actual results will vary from the nonguaranteed projections in those illustrations.

Actually, several factors (policy premiums, cash values, expenses, and possible dividends) determine the ultimate cost of a policy. We say "ultimate" because until we know how long a policy will stay in force, we cannot know with certainty what the final, true cost will be. The actual cost cannot be determined until the policy ends, through a death claim, lapse, or surrender, and we can look at what actually occurred. Although you cannot tell prospects the exact cost of a policy they will buy today, you can estimate what a policy will cost in different situations. The purpose of cost disclosure is to show the annual cost per $1,000 of insurance if the insured died or surrendered the policy after 10 or 20 years.

Surrender Cost Index

surrender cost index

The *surrender cost index* represents the annual cost per $1,000 of life insurance if a policy is surrendered for its cash value. Unlike the net payment index, this index includes the policy cash value. It is most useful in comparing costs when cash accumulation is a primary concern.

The surrender cost method takes all premium payments, when actually paid, and treats them as if they were put into an interest-bearing account to accumulate interest until the end of the interval for evaluation (10 or 20 years). In a similar manner, all dividend payments are carried as if they are deposited in an interest-bearing account when they are projected to be paid, and that account balance is calculated for the end of the interval under evaluation. After all premium and dividend payments have been adjusted to the end of the comparison interval, the policy cash value and accumulation dividends are subtracted from the accumulated value of all the premiums paid.

The next step is to take that future net cost and divide it by the future value of an annuity due, based on the specified interest rate (5 percent) and the period of time being evaluated, either 10 or 20 years. An annuity due is a series of payments of equal amounts made at the beginning of each of a number of consecutive periods, like premiums. This step adjusts for premiums, dividends, and cash value being paid annually and having an interest adjustment based on the year that they are paid. At 5 percent interest, the annuity due factor for a 10-year period is 13.2068, and for a 20-year period is 34.7193. The result represents the level annual cost for the policy. This is an aggregate policy amount that must be converted to a per-thousand amount, by dividing the level annual cost amount by the number of thousands of dollars in the policy death benefit. For example, the aggregate level annual cost for a $50,000 policy is 50 times greater than it would be for a $1,000 policy. We would therefore divide the level annual policy cost by 50 to determine the level annual cost per thousand dollars of coverage.

These future values appear on sales presentation materials so there is usually no need to calculate them independently. Calculations can be done by hand using compound interest tables, but they are easier and quicker when done on a computer or financial calculator (see Tables 6-6 and 6–7 at the end of this chapter for examples of a surrender cost index calculation).

Net Payment Index

net payment index

The *net payment index* represents the annual cost per $1,000 of insurance if the policy remains in force over a given period. It considers the amount of premiums paid, minus dividends received, if any, but it disregards the cash value. This is to take into account the fact that if an insured with a permanent insurance policy dies, the cash value will be included in the face amount. This index is useful in comparing costs when the cost of the death benefit is emphasized.

Determining the net payment index is similar to calculating the surrender cost index, except that there is no recognition of the end-of-period cash value. Under this calculation, dividends payable over the interval and terminal dividends at the end of period are the only items subtracted from the accumulated premium amounts. This gives a future value of net premiums that is then divided by the annuity due factor for the appropriate period and interest rate. Future values contained in advisors' sales materials are based on a 10- and 20-year interval and a 5 percent annual interest rate (see Tables 6-8 and 6–9 at the end of this chapter for examples).

Net Payment Index Computation

1. Accumulate the premiums at the desired interest rate (5 percent).
2. Accumulate the dividends (if applicable) at the desired interest rate (5 percent).
3. Subtract step 2 from step 1.
4. Divide step 3 by the amount to which $1 paid each year will accumulate for the period selected (20 years) at the desired interest rate (5 percent). This amount is the future value of an annuity due factor for 20 years at 5 percent (the factor is 34.7193). The result represents the estimated level annual cost of the policy.
5. Reduce the result of step 4 to a cost per $1,000 of coverage by dividing it by the number of thousands of dollars in the policy's death benefit. The result is the estimated level annual cost per $1,000 of coverage.

Sample Comparison. A simple example of a fictitious policy is presented in Tables 6-10 and 6–11 at the end of this chapter. In the example there is a premium of $15 per year over a 10-year interval and a dividend of $0.00 the first year and $1.00 the second year, increasing by $1.00 each year until it reaches $9.00 in the 10th policy year. The accumulation at 5 percent of all premiums paid is $198.10; the accumulation of all dividends is $54.14. Subtracting the accumulated value of dividends from the accumulated value of premiums yields a future value of net premiums equal to $143.96. Subtracting the cash value at the end of 10 years ($120) from that amount yields a future value of net cost equal to $23.96. This future net cost is then divided by the future value of an annuity due for 10 years, or 13.2068, which yields a surrender cost index of $1.81. In the same table we can see that by ignoring the cash value, the payment cost index is $10.90 per thousand.

These cost indices are a way of comparing similar policies. The policy with the smaller numerical values for surrender cost and payment cost indices is preferable to policies with higher index values. The method is not acceptable, however, for comparing dissimilar policies—for example, a term policy with a whole life policy. It is also not well suited for evaluating policy replacements. As pointed out earlier, the indices are derived from illustration data and are suspect because they are based on nonguaranteed future values and the assumptions made in the illustration are not generally disclosed to the public.

Surrender Cost Index Computation
1. Accumulate the premiums at the desired interest rate (5 percent).   2. Accumulate the dividends (if applicable) at the desired interest rate (5 percent).   3. Subtract step 2 from step 1.   4. Subtract the cash value at the end of the period from step 3 and divide by the amount to which $1 paid each year will accumulate for the period (20 years) selected at the desired interest rate (5 percent). This amount is the future value of an annuity due factor for 20 years at 5 percent (the factor is 34.7193). The result represents the estimated level annual cost of the policy.   5. Reduce the result of step 4 to a cost per $1,000 of coverage by dividing it by the number of thousands of dollars in the policy's death benefit. The result is the estimated level annual cost per $1,000 of coverage.
Notice that the steps are the same for the net payment and the surrender cost indices, except that there is no subtraction of the 20th year cash value in the net payment cost index.

Calculation Example. In most cases, you can easily find a policy's interest-adjusted indices on its policy summary or in commercial publications. However, the calculation procedure is illustrated here to help you understand how it is derived. You should understand how the cost indices are calculated, so that you can explain it to clients and help them understand what the indices mean. Following are the calculations and, for this example, the assumptions used.

EXAMPLE	
Calculation Assumptions:	
Accumulated value of $1 per year for 20 years at 5 percent (future value of an annuity due) per $1,000 values	$34.72
Annual premium	$21.00
20th year accumulation of cash values	$370.00
20th year accumulation of dividends at 5 percent	$211.00

Calculation:

1. Accumulation of premiums $21.00 x $34.72 — $729.12
2. Accumulation of dividends* — –$211.00

   $518.12

3. Net payment index:

   $518.12/34.72 = $14.92

4. Surrender cost index:

   ($518.12 – $370)/$34.72 = $4.27

   *Omit this step for policies that do not pay dividends.

A simple way to explain these indices to your prospect or client is to treat the policy's premium as being split into three parts: the dividend, the cash value, and the company's share. Even though the premium remains level throughout the life of the policy, the size of these three parts varies through the years. In the early years, dividends and cash value accumulations are small and the company's share large, but as time passes, dividends and cash values increase and the company's share decreases.

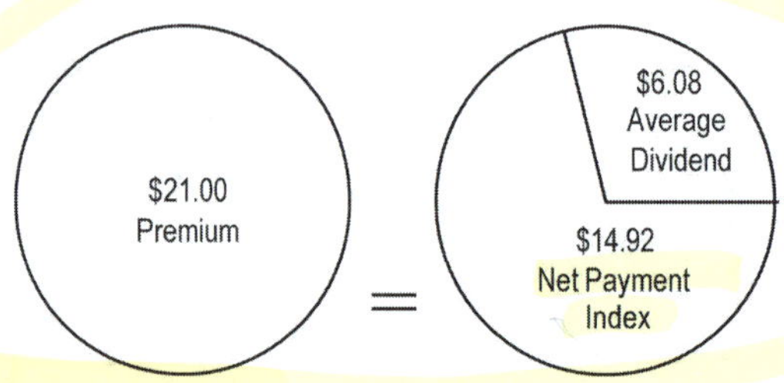

Assume that the annual premium in out example of $21 per thousand can be broken down into the average dividend of $6.08, the average cash value increment of $10.64 (coming directly from the premium, not from earned interest), and the average company share of $4.27. These averages take into consideration the time value of money.

Subtracting the average dividend from the premium leaves the net payment index of $14.92. This is the policyholder's average yearly cost, assuming the policy is still in force 20 years from date of issue.

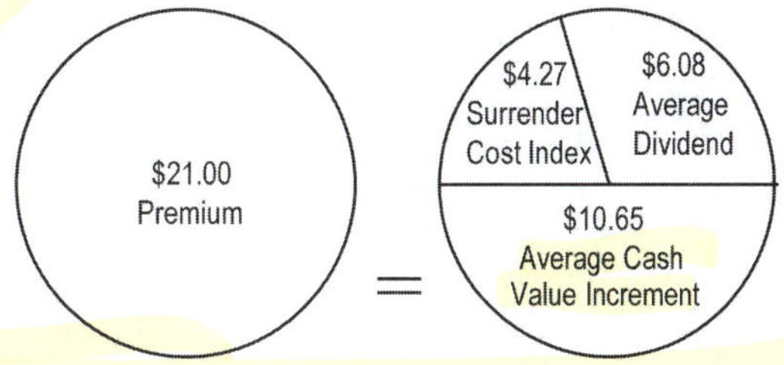

Subtracting the average dividend and the average cash value increase from the premium leaves the surrender cost index of $4.27. This is the yearly cost of $1,000 of life insurance—that portion of the premium the policyowner does not get back—assuming that the policy is surrendered for its cash value in the 20th year.

Equivalent Level Annual Dividend

A third index that might appear on the policy summary is the equivalent level annual dividend. This measures the role that dividends play in the cost of a participating policy. This index, which is labeled the average dividend in the diagram we just illustrated, is an average of the total dividends with interest over the 20 years. It is found by dividing the 20th year accumulation of dividends by the appropriate accumulation of $1 per year factor (future value of an annuity due). Referring to our previous calculation, this index would be $6.08, found by dividing $211 by $34.72.

Cash-Accumulation Comparison Method

cash-accumulation comparison method

The *cash-accumulation comparison method* is much more complex than either the net cost method or the interest-adjusted methods and requires a computer to make the calculations. One of the strengths of this method is that it can be used to compare permanent insurance policies with term policies and for evaluation of replacement proposals.

The technique is simply to accumulate the premium differences between the policies being compared, while holding the death benefits of both policies constant and equal. For example, to compare a whole life contract with a term contract, set the death benefits equal at the beginning of the period, and use the yearly premium differences between the whole life policy and the term policy as the amount to deposit into a side fund to accumulate at interest. The calculation is essentially a buy-term-and-invest-the-difference approach to comparing the policies.

At the end of the interval being evaluated, the side fund accumulation can be compared to the cash value in the whole life or other form of cash value insurance policy. All other things being equal, the policy with the greater accumulation at the end of the comparison interval is the preferable one.

Caution must be taken with the validity and accuracy of any illustration, based on the assumptions made in the illustration. Additionally, any side fund would not have the same tax advantages as a life insurance policy in terms of tax deferred accumulations, and income tax-free death benefits. The side fund may also be subject to death taxes and probate fees, from which life insurance proceeds are normally exempt (see Tables 6-12 and 6-13).

Equal-Outlay Method

equal-outlay method

The *equal-outlay method* is similar to the cash-accumulation method. The same amount of premium dollars is expended for a cash value contract and a term policy. The amount by which the cash value policy premiums exceed the term premiums is deposited into a side fund, and the difference in premium amounts is accumulated at specified interest rates. Then the death benefit of the term insurance, plus the accumulated side fund amounts is compared with the death benefit under the cash value contract. Any dividends are used to purchase paid-up additions and the value of the paid-up additions is included in the death-benefit cash value policy. Under this type of comparison, the policy producing the greater death benefit is considered the preferable contract (see Tables 6-14 and 6-15).

Both this method and the cash-accumulation method are very sensitive to the interest rate chosen to use for the side fund accumulation. Manipulating the interest rate can skew the comparison results. The higher the interest rate used, the more the equal-outlay method will favor the term policy with the side fund. This method can be used to compare two flexible or fixed-premium policies, a flexible and fixed-premium policy, and is popular for comparing a cash value and term/side-fund plan, testing the results of a buy-term-invest-the-difference scenario.

Life Insurance Illustrations

Life insurance illustrations are typically used in the sales/planning process to show the prospective client how a life insurance policy works and how it might perform under various conditions. They display key policy values:

the premium, guaranteed cash values, and guaranteed death benefits. Illustrations normally also show nonguaranteed values based on certain performance assumptions such as interest rates, mortality charges, or dividend scales. Explaining an illustration can be complicated when the cash value accumulation is based on variable investments, or when alternative premium payment arrangements are being proposed. An illustration is not part of the policy and is not a contract between the insurance company and the policyowner.

Prospects do not always understand the differences between guaranteed, illustrative, and current (nonguaranteed) values typically found in life insurance illustrations. If the differences are not clearly explained, a prospect can easily be misled into believing that the policy promises significantly greater values than those that are guaranteed. Allowing this misconception to exist, or actually fostering it, is a serious form of misrepresentation. The illustration shown or given to the prospect should have no highlighting, underlining, or any other marks on it, so as not to emphasize, or detract attention from, certain illustrated values.

Insurance regulators and insurers have placed emphasis on proper formats of illustrations and clearly explaining what is and is not guaranteed in the contract. Because of the NAIC Life Insurance Illustrations Model Regulations (discussed later), insurers and state insurance departments require a full illustration, including all footnotes and explanation pages, of a product purchased be signed by the client. The signature indicates that the client has read and understands the guaranteed and nonguaranteed elements in the illustration. The full explanation of the illustration is especially important when focusing on the projected cash values, dividends, or interest accumulations. Lower credited interest rates or dividends, and increases in administrative expense or mortality charges can all negatively affect the nonguaranteed illustrated cash values.

illustration selling

The life insurance illustration is a tool designed to assist the advisor in explaining an intangible, abstract, and highly complex financial product. In the past few decades, with the advent of the personal computer and financial software, many advisors have turned to *"illustration selling"*. This involves selling the alluring numerical values on the illustration, rather than conducting a fundamental financial planning process, uncovering the client's needs based on sound fact-finding, and designing real solutions to real financial problems and concerns. Illustration selling emphasizes the product "looking for a need," rather than a need looking for a solution. Illustration selling focuses on the numerical values of the illustration, rather than conducting a fundamental financial planning process, uncovering the client's needs based on fact-finding, and designing solutions to financial problems and concerns. **Avoid the trap of illustration selling** and sell life insurance following the selling/planning process. You need to stay focused on the prospect's needs, and how to satisfy them.

Policy illustrations are based on a variety of assumptions about the future. They are an estimate of what may happen in the future, based on projections of past performance and/or assumptions about the future. Although some projections may be accurate some of the time, the chance that all of these factors will occur as proposed is virtually impossible. In fact, the only assumption we can make about a policy illustration regarding the nonguaranteed elements is that what is projected will not happen.

It is easy to believe that there is some connection between these illustrations and reality. However, it is more likely that neither the advisor nor the prospect know the underlying assumptions in the illustration. Companies do not disclose pricing assumptions. The assumptions used in illustrations vary from company to company, which makes illustrations incomparable. Focusing on policy values 10, 20 or more years into the future leads to a compounding of errors, and any resemblance between these numbers and reality is purely coincidental. The bottom line is you cannot depend on illustrations to compare policies.

Types of Policy Illustrations

There is almost an unlimited number of types and variations of policy illustrations. The simplest types show how much will have to be paid out-of-pocket to keep the policy in force. These illustrations show premiums due, dividends projected, guaranteed cash value, and death-benefit values. Illustrations may show increasing death benefits using policy dividends to purchase paid-up additional insurance. Applying dividends to purchase one-year term insurance is another type of illustration an advisor can use that increases the policy death benefit without altering the policy or increasing the premium. These simple illustrations can increase in sophistication to include complex combinations of term and permanent coverage using policy cash values or dividends as funding.

Policy comparisons, especially of term and whole life insurance, using the techniques discussed earlier in this chapter, such as the cash-accumulation method, compare a large amount of information regarding the costs of different policies. The cash-accumulation method compares illustrated cash values and death benefits of whole life insurance with term insurance with a side fund, investing the difference of premium at some assumed interest rate. Universal and variable life illustrations show performance under several different assumptions concerning mortality and expense charges, investment or interest earnings, and guaranteed and nonguaranteed values, which creates many columns and variations to consider.

Illustrations have become an important part of the life insurance sales process, yet many policyowners have been dissatisfied with products that have not performed as projected by policy illustrations. Over the past two decades, there has been an especially large gap between actual and projected performance, as interest rates and investment performance declined from high points, due to falling interest rates and collapsing equity markets. As a result, state regulators and company compliance departments instituted numerous requirements for illustrations that have expanded the policy illustration into a lengthy document. Explanations, caveats, definitions and page after page of numeric tables are now required on illustrations. The policyowner must also sign to indicate receipt of the illustration. These issues will be discussed later in this chapter.

Sample Illustrations

Several types of common illustrations with a discussion regarding them follow. Complete examples of additional illustrations appear at the end of this chapter.

The Participating (Dividend-Paying) Policy

The following is an example of a simple illustration showing only the policy year, gross annual premium, dividends, and net premium after dividends. This illustration uses dividends to reduce premiums. Policy Illustration 1 shows an illustration for a $50,000 graded-premium-paid-up-at-age-95 policy. A graded premium policy is much like modified premium whole life, except that rather than a few changes in premium, graded premium will typically have a series of smaller increasing premium levels over a longer period. This illustration does not present the cash values for the policy. Today these types of illustrations are known as supplemental illustrations, and must be shown with a complete illustration following the NAIC Model Illustration regulations adopted by state laws and company requirements.

Table 6-1 Policy Illustration 1 — Graded Premium Paid-Up at Age 95

Year	Gross Annual Premium	Dividend Used to Reduce Premiums	Premium Due
1	$ 170	$ 0	$ 170
2	170	50	120
3	175	52	123
4	180	53	127
5	185	53	132
	880	208	672
6	190	54	136
7	195	55	140
8	200	56	144
9	205	57	148
10	215	58	157
	1,885	488	1,397
11	230	59	171
12	245	60	185
13	260	61	199
14	275	65	210
15	295	70	225
	3,190	803	2,387
16	315	75	240
17	340	80	260
18	360	90	270
19	390	100	290
20	420	110	310
	$5,015	$1,258	$3,757

NOTE: $50,000 graded premium paid-up-at-age-95 policy for a female, aged 32, with an initial annual premium of $170. Dividends shown are not guaranteed. They are merely based on the current level of dividends, which may change in the future.

Combination Coverage—Whole Life and Term

"Economatic whole life," shown in the next table, uses policy dividends to purchase additional coverage. Economatic whole life provides a basic amount of participating whole life with additional supplemental coverage provided through a combination of decreasing term insurance and paid-up dividend additions. Eventually, the dividend additions should provide all of the supplemental coverage. However, because dividends may not be sufficient to purchase enough paid-up additions at a future date, it is possible that there could be a substantial decrease in the amount of supplemental insurance coverage.

The basic policy is for $18,000 of whole life insurance, supplemented with additional term insurance and coverage purchased with paid-up additions. The term insurance decreases each year as the paid-up insurance increases. The amount of term insurance equals the net amount at risk between the target face amount of $25,000 and the base whole life policy. Eventually the term insurance is totally replaced by paid-up additions. There are no figures in the illustration to indicate the policy dividends. A footnote indicates that the dividend levels assumed for the calculation are not guaranteed.

The first column lists the policy year. The second column shows the gross annual level premium. The third column is labeled "total paid-up value." Study of the illustration reveals that a paid-up value occurs in the second policy year before there is any cash value associated with the coverage purchased with dividends. Thus, it can be deduced that the total paid-up value is the amount of fully paid-up coverage if the total cash value is applied to the purchase. This illustration is based on the assumption that the policyowner will not exercise any policy loans during the 20 years displayed.

The next column, titled "guaranteed cash value end of year," indicates the scheduled cash value for the base whole life policy. Values for the supplemental coverage are not guaranteed.

The "enhancement reserve fund" column shows the cash value for the paid-up supplemental insurance purchased with policy dividends. The "total cash value end of year" column lists the sum of the guaranteed cash value and the enhancement reserve fund.

The last two columns in the table below show the relationship between the premium paid and the annual increase in the policy cash value. During the first eight policy years, the policy premium exceeds the annual increase in cash value. The cash value increases exceed the policy premium in the ninth and subsequent policy years.

Table 6-2 Economatic Whole Life

Year	Gross Annual Premium	Total Paid-up Value	Guaranteed Cash Value End of Year	Enhancement Reserve Fund	Total Cash Value End of Year	Total Cash Value Increase End of Year	CV Increase Less Net Payment
1	$ 320	$ 0	$ 0	$ 0	$ 0	$ 0	$ –320
2	320	285	101	0	101	10`	–219
3	320	1,098	402	0	402	301	–19
4	320	1,863	704	0	704	302	–18
5	320	2,577	1,005	0	1,005	301	–19
6	320	3,291	1,324	0	1,324	319	–1
7	320	3,958	1,642	0	1,642	318	–2
8	320	4,583	1,960	0	1,960	318	–2
9	320	5,226	2,296	7	2,303	343	23
10	320	5,926	2,647	44	2,691	388	68
11	320	6,579	2,983	90	3,.073	382	62
12	320	7,228	3,334	146	3,480	407	87
13	320	7,907	3,703	215	3,918	438	118
14	320	8,569	4,072	296	4,368	450	130
15	320	9,214	4,440	391	4,831	463	143
16	320	9,846	4,809	498	5,307	476	156
17	320	10,494	5,194	619	5,813	506	186
18	320	11,131	5,580	755	6,335	522	202
19	320	11,755	5,965	905	6,870	535	215
20	320	12,398	6,367	1,072	7,439	569	249
	$6,400					$7,439	$1,039

NOTE: Combination of Whole Life and Additional Coverage Purchased with Policy Dividends for female age 40; $18,000 whole life, $7,000 additional coverage, $25,000 death benefit. Annual premium $320. The current dividend scale is expected to continue, and it is now adequate to provide the needed $7,000 of benefits as term insurance for the first eight policy years, then as whole life additions. The dividends are not guaranteed.

The important concept to be understood from this illustration is that the premium is sufficient to create an internal buildup of funds (cash value) in the policy, which are essential for the level-premium policy mechanism to work.

Advanced Underwriting Illustrations

Policy illustrations can become extremely complicated and require expertise and experience to understand. For example, when illustrating split-dollar plans, it is important to use a marginal tax rate in the policy illustration that is the same as the marginal tax rate for the prospective policyowner. Split-dollar, executive bonus, and other applications used primarily for business purposes incorporate the effects of marginal tax rates between the business and the business executives to show the after-tax cost of policies. Knowledge of the federal income tax system, as well as the concept behind the illustration, is necessary to interpret and present these illustrations.

Minor variations in the tax rate can result in significant changes in the after-tax costs to the policyowner and other participants. Illustrations based on tax rates that are significantly different from those of the prospect are misleading and could be considered deceptive sales practices. It is essential to show both the corporate information and the individual insured information for this type of illustration.

Illustrations can include premium-paying techniques using policy loans, such as minimum-deposit, or withdrawing money from the policy for a variety of other purposes. Minimum-deposit illustrations show how policy cash values can be used to pay policy premiums. Policy loans, dividend surrenders, and cash value withdrawals used for premium financing and funding of other financial objectives may be forecast. Additional premiums can be shown to serve a number of purposes, such as paying for additional benefits, potentially shortening the premium-paying period, or accumulating additional funds for future needs. These illustrations will typically include additional columns, showing loan amounts, loan interest, net cash values, and death benefits.

Universal Life

The final illustration—Universal Life—presented in the next table shows an early version of a universal life policy (notice the interest rates paid when UL was new on the scene). This particular policy provides a death benefit of $100,000 until the policy cash value exceeds $95,000. Thereafter, a death benefit will be $5,000 higher than the policy cash value, due to the Sec. 7702 corridor. The annual premium of $1,300 is paid for 25 years. Illustrations for universal life policies may include a column for partial withdrawals (as this one does). Cash value withdrawals are not policy loans, so they do not accrue interest, nor are they expected to be returned to the policy. Because universal life policies can have both policy loans and partial withdrawals, it is likely that some illustrations will have columns for both. If the total of all partial withdrawals ever exceeds the total premiums paid for the policy, the excess will be subject to federal income tax.

Table 6-3 Universal Life

				End of Year			
Policy Year	Annual Premium	Partial Withdrawal	Premiums Less Withdrawals	Guaranteed Cash Value	Assumed Cash Value*	Current Cash Value**	Current Death Benefit
1	$ 1,300	$ 0	$1,300	$ 114	$ 153	166	$100,000
2	1,300	0	2,600	943	1,175	1,212	100,000
3	1,300	0	3,900	1,773	2,275	2,357	100,000
4	1,300	0	5,200	2,604	3,473	3,627	100,000
5	1,300	0	6,500	3,438	4,769	5,025	100,000
6	1,300	0	7,800	4,262	6,161	6,555	100,000
7	1,300	0	9,100	5,077	7,659	8,233	100,000
8	1,300	0	10,400	5,873	9,287	10,091	100,000
9	1,300	0	11,700	6,649	11,048	12,140	100,000
10	1,300	0	13,000	7,393	12,956	14,405	100,000
11	1,300	0	14,300	8,107	15,040	16,924	100,000
12	1,300	0	15,600	8,777	17,308	19,719	100,000
13	1,300	0	16,900	9,392	19,781	22,288	100,000
14	1,300	0	18,200	9,551	22,482	26,288	100,000
15	1,300	0	19,500	10,439	25,427	30,138	100,000
16	1,300	0	20,800	10,845	28,645	34,431	100,000
17	1,300	0	22,100	11,164	32,159	39,218	100,000
18	1,300	0	23,400	11,371	36,006	44,566	100,000
19	1,300	0	24,700	11,449	40,218	50,546	100,000
20	1,300	0	26,000	11,380	44,847	57,252	100,000
21	1,300	0	27,300	11,133	49,933	64,777	100,000
22	1,300	0	28,600	10,685	55,533	73,238	100,000
23	1,300	0	29,900	10,011	61,704	82,766	100,000
24	1,300	0	31,200	9,058	68,524	93,521	100,000
25	1,300	0	32,500	7,702	76,075	105,617	100,000
26	1,300	6,500	26,000	0	75,659	110,198	115,198
27	1,300	6,500	19,500	0	75,284	115,288	120,288
28	1,300	6,500	13,000	0	74,973	120,945	125,945
29	1,300	6,500	6,500	0	74,704	127,229	132,229
30	1,300	6,500	0	0	74,400	134,213	139,213

NOTE: Universal Life for a female nonsmoker, age 40 years; $100,000 death benefit, $1,300 planned annual premium. The guaranteed cash value is based on a 4 percent interest rate.

*Interest rate used for assumed cash value is 9%

**Interest rate used for current cash value is 11%.

This illustration is quite different from a traditional policy illustration in that it has three separate cash value columns, each calculated for a different assumed rate of interest earnings for the cash value. The "guaranteed cash value" column is comparable to the traditional policy examples, because it is based on the interest rate guaranteed in the policy. However, even the "guaranteed cash value" column has its own properties because the premium level is usually inadequate if the current interest rate does not exceed the guaranteed rate. At the guaranteed rate, the cash value peaks at $11,449 in the 19th policy year and declines to zero by the 26th policy year.

The column showing the assumed cash value is calculated assuming the cash value will earn 9 percent interest every year. At that level of interest, the $1,300 premium for 25 years is adequate to keep the policy in force. This scenario indicates increasing cash values until the 25th year, at which point the cash values begin to decrease. There are no guarantees or suggestions that the investment earnings will always equal or exceed 9 percent. This is an example of how the cash value would grow if the actual earnings turn out to be exactly 9 percent each policy year. If premiums do not continue, or additional withdrawals are taken from the policy, that cash value will decline precipitously as mortality charges increase rapidly at the insured's attained ages over age 70.

The "current cash value" column shows how the cash value will increase at an even higher interest rate, 11 percent, if that rate is applied every policy year. These columns demonstrate what compound interest can do at sustained high levels. During the periods of high interest rates during the 1980s, there were companies using rates as high as 14 percent in their illustrations. There were many arbitrary predictions during that time, one being that interest rates would never again drop below 12 percent. Looking back, it was unrealistic to expect interest rates to stay at historically high levels over any protracted period. There was actually a very low probability that the cash value of the policy would reach $134,000 in the 30th policy year. Even a 9 percent rate of return was achievable over such an extended period. Results like these have led insurers to introduce the secondary guarantees to UL and sell policies with higher premium levels. This policy follows the earlier design, and is no longer offered with such a narrow final amount of at-risk death protection.

Variable and Variable Universal Life

When discussing life insurance illustrations for variable products, some serious concerns need to be addressed. One difficulty with variable universal life is that there is no "premium" in the conventional, fixed-premium sense, since the amount of money paid into the policy is flexible and can vary according to the policyowner's needs and goals. Typically, VUL is illustrated using a constant interest rate, based on assumed performance of the separate accounts, that in the real world experience a great deal of volatility. Although a variable investment portfolio may have an arithmetic average return over a period of years, an actual internal rate of return, or compounded average based on year-to-year performance may be quite different. For example, consider an investor who starts with $100 and doubles his money to $200 in one year (a 100 percent return), but then loses 50 percent the following year, and is back to his original $100. The arithmetic average is 25% [100% + (–50%) divided by 2], yet the investor has made nothing.

As we know, stock market volatility is common. For example, a fund may have an average return of 10 percent, but with returns actually posting a 30 percent return one year, followed by a –10 percent return, and so on, the value of the portfolio may actually be earning 9 percent. In addition, while whole life has constantly increasing cash values, variable policies will periodically have declining cash values in declining markets, leaving increasing net amount at risk, which will increase the insurance costs charged against the cash value. A policyowner's return can also be affected by the timing of cash flows into and out of the policy.

This fact is important to younger policyowners, but it is critical at older ages when increasing amount at risk, exposed to increasingly higher costs of insurance, can create a fast-acting negative domino effect. The insurer will need to withdraw more money for the extra insurance charges, further reducing the account value and accelerating the negative spiral. When illustration systems are used to calculate constant returns far into the future, the projection of average returns disguises the reality of fluctuating accounts and changing net amounts at risk.

This can be especially true if the illustration projects withdrawals for college expenses or retirement income. If the policy lapses with outstanding loans, there may be a large tax bill and no cash from the policy to pay for it, a worst-case financial scenario.

Monte Carlo analysis

We cannot realistically forecast the future based on a linear repetition of the past. One method to overcome this problem is called the *Monte Carlo analysis*. The Monte Carlo technique randomizes actual monthly investment returns over the past, to project the probability of an illustration achieving targeted outcomes based on certain premium levels. For example, we might run an illustration through a Monte Carlo analysis using randomized historical returns 1,000 times or

10,000 times, and find that at a given premium level, the success ratio of the policy lasting to age 100 is 52 percent. Is this success ratio acceptable to the client? If the answer is no, then we need to discover what success ratio is acceptable, and what level of premium is necessary to achieve that probability level. Projecting outcomes based on the current financial environment is simply not sufficient. We need to identify the chances of success. The basis for determining premium funding levels should be the risk tolerance of the client and the probability of meeting the client's objectives, not who has the lowest illustrated premium.

Presenting Illustrations

Life insurance illustrations are used in the sales presentation to show the prospect how life insurance works, but they can be misleading when used to decide which of several policies is the best buy. In your presentation, be sure that prospects understand the difference between guaranteed values and the current values shown in the illustration. Describe the assumptions and variables that affect policy performance, both positively and negatively. A complete illustration clearly explains which values are guaranteed and which are not. The actual values will most certainly be different than the numbers shown on the illustration. The full explanation of the illustration is especially important when focusing on the projected cash values, dividends, or interest accumulations. If an abbreviated premium schedule is proposed, you must show the client that the premium will still be required if the illustrated values are not achieved. Lower credited interest rates or dividends, and increases in administrative expense or mortality charges can all negatively affect the illustrated cash values.

Guidelines and Regulations for Policy Illustrations

The arrival of computer illustrations in the early 1980s prompted calls for guidelines to standardize illustrations. Computerized illustrations and software evolved rapidly, yet there were no regulations to monitor and control them.

Competitive pressures pushed companies to become more aggressive in producing the most favorable illustrations for their policies. This led to companies creating assumptions for their illustrations that were regarded by some as misleading, irresponsible, and unrealistic—claims that continue to this day. Projecting values for interest earnings, mortality improvements, and expense reductions that might not be possible or sustainable became a part of the cat-and-mouse game of "out-illustrating" the competition.

Policy illustrations work well to educate clients about how policies work, but they are not an adequate tool for comparing costs of policies from different insurance companies. Illustrations do not create accurate, comparable projections of future performance, due to the differences in assumptions made by insurance companies and the actual future performance of the company and the economy. Actuarial and pricing assumptions are not disclosed, and state regulations permit a wide range of practices.

To understand a life insurance illustration, it is necessary to know the assumptions and factual elements used in the policy, such as mortality charges, cost of insurance, interest crediting rates, expenses, and persistency. Advisors must be able to explain to their clients how these changes will affect the future performance of a life insurance policy and the policy illustration. Understanding how the figures are derived and what they represent will help advisors communicate the risks and benefits associated with a life insurance contract to their clients. Illustrations may vary greatly based on how a company treats these factors. These assumptions are generally unavailable to advisors and the public, and are closely guarded by insurers.

Many life insurance products sold today are adjustable, variable, or interest sensitive. While life insurance products incorporate guarantees, sales illustrations are designed to convey to the prospect the benefits and costs under a set of current non-guaranteed assumptions. Since the insurance company generally limits its responsibility to contractual guarantees, risks associated with the development of a higher benefit or lower cost than that generated by the guarantees are borne by the policyowner.

Factors to Consider in Evaluating a Life Insurance Illustration

Assumptions made in creating illustrations have a considerable impact on them. To understand the illustration properly, an advisor and his or her client must understand how the various assumptions affect the illustration being presented. For example, in looking at mortality assumptions, a company may use recent actual mortality experience, or they may assume mortality improvements in the future. The illustration may assume that investment experience will improve, or use rates from an index not actually tied to company results. Some companies assume that lapse rates will improve, or make other assumptions that may be unrealistic, yet affect the illustration in favorable ways.

Mortality. The mortality charge used in an illustration may reflect the company's actual current or recent mortality experience, current mortality experience modified at an assumed rate of increase or decrease, or a combination of mortality and other expenses. Some insurers include projected mortality improvements in their illustrations, passing the mortality price risks on to the customer. This makes the illustration more attractive than it should realistically be, and makes a comparison from a cost standpoint with other insurers unfair, yet very competitive.

Interest Rate. The interest assumption used may be based upon interest rates earned by the company on all investments now held (portfolio rate), new investments (new money rate), other combinations of actual investments, an independent index such as Treasury bills or Moody's long-term bond index. It may be based on the gross interest rate or the gross interest rate reduced by investment and other expenses. It may be projected as a fixed amount or percentage, assumed to be constant or to change over future years. This adds to the difficulties associated with comparing illustrations between companies.

Expenses. Policy expenses are another factor in designing policies and illustrations. Companies handle these differently. For example, the expense factors used in the illustration may reflect actual recent company experience, or they may assume improvements in experience. Expense factors may differ for new and existing policies, or by product type, underwriting class, policy size, or duration.

Persistency. Some companies will factor an assumption regarding policy lapses into their policy cost calculations and illustrations. If the actual persistency is better than assumed, it may negatively affect illustrated values, since eventually more claims may result. The illustration may involve a persistency bonus to policyholders who pay premiums for a specified number of years. Other factors to consider include:

- How does the company determine non-guaranteed pricing elements?
- Do illustration assumptions differ from the company's current experience?

- Do experience factors underlying the dividend scale or other non-guaranteed elements used in the illustration differ from recent historical experience?
- Will the current illustrative values change if recent experience continues unchanged?
- Does the company treat new and existing policyholders of the same class the same with respect to the underlying factors in pricing?

As you can see, there are many assumptions behind the numbers presented in a policy illustration. Without knowing what the underlying assumptions are, the value of the illustration is diminished. The assumptions must be known and other factors must be understood if the illustration is to have any real value. Unfortunately, in most cases only the actuaries and company officials know these assumptions.

NAIC Life Insurance Illustrations Model Regulation

Life Insurance Illustrations Model Regulation

In 1996 the National Association of Insurance Commissioners (NAIC) adopted the *Life Insurance Illustrations Model Regulation* pertaining to life insurance illustrations. This was the NAIC's first attempt to set standards for policy illustrations. The stated purpose was to provide rules for life insurance policy illustrations that would protect consumers and foster consumer education. Its goals were to ensure that policy illustrations do not mislead purchasers of life insurance and to make illustrations more understandable. A key strategy in the regulation was to clearly define and distinguish for the consumer what is guaranteed in the contract and what is not. The regulation provides illustration formats, prescribes standards to be followed when illustrations are used, and specifies the disclosures that are required in connection with illustrations.

While there were some basic similarities among policy illustrations, such as listings of annual premium and a policy's cash value for each policy year, until 1997 and the introduction of the NAIC Illustrations Model Regulation, there were no uniform policy illustration standards. The organization of illustrative information within a single report varied drastically from one insurance company to another, even if the same information was contained in the report. Rogue insurance companies could publish illustrations with any assumptions they wished, without regulatory consequence.

The model regulation has had a tremendous impact on illustrations, because life insurance companies in every state have moved toward using the same illustration model. By making all their illustrations conform to the most stringent state's requirements, insurers can meet the regulatory requirements in states that adopted the NAIC Illustrations Model Regulation.

According to the regulation, an illustration is one of three types of presentations or depictions that include nonguaranteed elements of a policy of life insurance over a period of years:

1. **Basic illustration** is a ledger or proposal used in the sale of a life insurance policy that shows both guaranteed and nonguaranteed elements.
2. **Supplemental illustration** is an illustration furnished in addition to a basic illustration that meets the applicable requirements of the regulation, and that may be presented in a format differing from the basic illustration, but may only depict a scale of nonguaranteed elements that is permitted in a basic illustration.
3. **In force illustration** is an illustration furnished at any time after the policy has been in force for one year or more.

The life insurance illustrations model regulation applies to all nonvariable group and individual life insurance policies and certificates of $10,000 or more of death benefit. It does not apply to variable life, credit life, or life insurance with a face amount of less than $10,000, nor to individual or group annuity contracts.

The regulation requires the insurance company to declare to the state insurance department, for each policy form, whether or not it intends to use illustrations to market that form of coverage. A copy of each illustration the insurer intends to use must be forwarded to the state insurance department. The regulation contains significant minimum standards dealing with the format and content of any information provided in the illustration. Both the producer and the client must sign the initial illustration, with a copy provided to the insurance company and the client. If the issued policy differs in any way from the originally issued illustration, a revised illustration must be submitted, following the same procedures as above.

Each illustration used in the sale of a life insurance policy covered by the regulation must be clearly labeled "life insurance illustration", and must include the following:

1. name of the insurance company
2. name and business address of the insurer's agent
3. name, age, and sex of the proposed insured

4. underwriting or rating classification upon which the illustration is based
5. generic name of the policy (e.g., whole, universal life, etc.)
6. initial death benefit amount
7. dividend option election or application of nonguaranteed elements if applicable

The NAIC Illustrations Model Regulation prohibit insurers and their advisors from the following:

1. Representing the policy as anything other than a life insurance policy.
2. Using or describing nonguaranteed elements in a manner that is misleading or has the capacity or tendency to mislead. The non-guaranteed elements must be labeled as nonguaranteed.
3. Stating or implying that the payment or amount of nonguaranteed elements is guaranteed. It must clearly be stated that these elements are subject to change and that the actual results may be more or less favorable.
4. Using an illustration that does not comply with the illustration regulations.
5. Using an illustration that is more favorable to the policyowner than the illustration, based on the illustrated scale of the insurer.
6. Providing an applicant with an incomplete illustration.
7. Representing in any way that premium payments will not be required for each year of the policy in order to maintain the illustrated death benefits, unless that is the fact.
8. Using the term “vanish,” “vanishing premium,” or a similar term that implies the policy becomes paid up, to describe a plan for using nonguaranteed elements to pay a portion of future premiums.
9. Using a policy that is “lapse-supported.” This means a policy is not self-supporting, and that the policy is supported by a higher assumption than warranted for the number of policies that lapse.
10. Using an illustration that is not “self-supporting.” The illustration must include actuarial assumptions of self-sustaining profitability.

The NAIC Illustrations Model Regulation specifies that all illustrations must be dated as of the date prepared. All pages must be marked to indicate both the individual page number and the total number of pages in the illustration (for example, page 3 of 7). The illustration must clearly indicate which elements are guaranteed and which are nonguaranteed. Any amount available upon surrender shall be the amount after deduction of surrender charges.

Each illustration must be accompanied by a narrative summary that describes the policy, premiums, and features, and defines column headings used in the illustration. The summary should also state that actual results might be more or less favorable than those shown in the illustration.

Universal Life Policies

The NAIC regulation states that illustrations for universal life policies must comply with the regulation requirements and that the insurance company must issue annual reports to policyowners after the policy is issued. These annual reports must specify the beginning and ending dates for the reporting period. The content of annual reports is specified in the NAIC Illustrations Model Regulation to include:

- All transactions affecting the policy during the reporting period (debits and credits) and a description of each (for example, premiums paid, interest credited, loan interest debited, mortality charges, expenses debited, rider transactions).
- Cash values at the beginning and end of the period.
- Death benefit at the end of the reporting period (for each life covered).
- Cash surrender value at the end of the period after deduction of surrender charge (if any).
- Amount of outstanding policy loans, if any, at the end of the reporting period.
- a special Notice to Policyowners if the policy will not maintain insurance in force until the end of the next reporting period, unless further premium payments are made.

The regulation further stipulates that policyowners have the right to request an in-force illustration annually, without charge. The insurer must provide information regarding where and how to direct such requests and must supply a current illustration within 30 days of the request. Such illustrations are to be based on the insurer's present illustrated scale.

Annual Certifications

Each insurer's board of directors must appoint at least one illustration actuary, who will certify that the illustrations comply with the illustration regulation. The illustration actuary must annually certify the method used to allocate overhead and expenses for all illustrations and file such certification with the insurance commissioner and with the insurer's board of directors. The illustration actuary is required to report any mistakes found in previous certifications to both the commissioner and the board of directors. The insurance commissioner must be notified of any change in the illustration actuary and the reasons for the change.

The model regulation sets forth limits on the methods used for calculating illustrations. These limits are intended to curb some of the overly optimistic projections that some insurers were utilizing in past years in the absence of any standards or constraints. Most of the new constraints are contained in the definitions of currently payable scale, disciplined current scale, and illustrated scale:

- *currently payable scale:* a scale of nonguaranteed elements in effect for a policy as of the preparation date of the illustration.
- *disciplined current scale:* a scale of non-guaranteed elements constituting a limit on illustrations currently being used by an insurer that is reasonably based on recent historical experience, as certified annually by an illustration actuary.
- *illustrated scale:* a scale of nonguaranteed elements currently being illustrated that is not more favorable to the policyowner than the lesser of the disciplined current scale or the currently payable scale.

Illustrations cannot provide a completely accurate prediction of future policy performance, since the future will be influenced by unpredictable changes in the world economy and the performance of any specific insurance company's investment portfolio.

Illustrations are useful tools for showing how a policy works, and its sensitivity to changes in factors such as interest, mortality, and expenses. Policy illustrations do not show what a client will get, but rather what he or she would get if all the company's assumptions about the future actually happen, which is nearly impossible. How will mortality, interest, and expense factors change over the next 20, 30, or 40 years? Obviously, none of these factors can be predicted with certainty.

A second use is to compare the cost or performance of different policies, to a considerable extent based on the erroneous perception that the sales illustration is a likely or best estimate of future performance. Actually, illustrations are ineffective tools for finding the "best" product, unless all the values are guaranteed or all the assumptions that serve as the basis for the projections are provided. Since a sales illustration is simply an extension of the current scale of non-guaranteed elements into the future assuming current assumptions hold to that point, actual non-guaranteed elements will almost certainly vary from those illustrated. Different companies will experience different variances from illustrated values.

Some companies make conservative assumptions to minimize the chances that they will not meet expectations. Other companies are more aggressive to make their product look more attractive. The company with the "best" illustration may simply be the one that has the most optimistic assumptions about the future, not necessarily the one that will actually meet these expectations or deliver the most value to the client.

Therefore, **do not fall into the illustration trap.** Policy illustrations may be policy "illusions." Scrutinize, if possible, the assumptions of the policy and how they impact illustrated values. Investigate the history of the company and their record of meeting policy projections in the past. What is the financial strength of the company? The illustration regulation eliminates some of the past abuses where the assumptions used in illustrations were based on "pie-in-the-sky" optimism. However, the regulations do not constrain illustrations to such an extent that we can compare two different types of policies or policies from different companies.

Developing and Presenting the Plan

After analyzing the client's current situation, it is time to develop a plan and your recommended solutions. You must consider the advantages and disadvantages of different types of term and permanent insurance, and how well they would fit the prospect's circumstances.

Preparing for the Presentation

The key to an effective presentation is preparation. Take the time to prepare and put together a standardized format for your sales presentation. You may organize it in a binder or portfolio if this is your style. As in cooking, presentation is vital. The appearance and organization of your materials will go a long way toward the acceptance of your presentation.

The amount of time needed to prepare will decrease as you gain more experience, but initially you will want to create a detailed presentation outline for each closing interview. Here are some examples of ways you may prepare for this interview:

- ***Analyze your prospect.*** What are his or her attitudes toward life insurance? Does he or she appear to recognize and accept the risk of death? What are the prospect's probable motives for buying? What are the barriers?
- ***Create a summary of the fact-finding interview.*** Use this summary as an outline when you reestablish the need. Use the discovery agreement or a simple outline of the main points established from fact-finding.
- ***Summarize and write down the key points for your presentation.*** Determine the best order for discussing each. Focus on what the prospect cares about. Begin with the most important points and continue in descending order of importance. Outline the presentation. Write down the key points (benefits) and words that will reinforce these points. Avoid industry jargon.
- ***Check your suggested plan alternatives.*** How do they reflect the prospect's needs, priorities, and budget? What are the pros and cons to each alternative? Which do you feel is the best alternative and why?
- ***Collect any company-approved sales material you will use in the presentation.*** If you have a series of such items, put them in order in your sales presentation binder.
- ***Create policy illustrations.*** Develop illustrations for all of your recommendations ahead of time. Check the prospect's information (name, age, and so forth) for accuracy.
- ***Organize written proposals.*** Put together any written proposals you will use with your presentation.
- ***Anticipate any objections or concerns.*** Prepare responses to them.
- ***Rehearse your presentation.*** Concentrate on delivering your key points, but avoid memorizing your presentation. Learn the key points by outlining them. Practice gives you a chance to iron out glitches, formulate and deal with possible objections and concerns, and increase overall professionalism of your presentation. Practice with a fellow advisor—you can help and learn from each other.
- ***Confirm the appointment.*** Call or e-mail the prospect to confirm the time and location of your appointment.

Elements of the Presentation

Although the specifics of an effective presentation will vary from advisor to advisor, there are two main components to every presentation. The first component is to reestablish the prospect's need for life insurance; the second is to present possible solutions.

Reestablish the Need

In a one-interview sale, you simply have to review points regarding the prospect's needs and goals that were established from the fact-finding portion of the interview. In a two-interview sale, some time will elapse between the first and second interviews. Therefore, it is important to reestablish the prospect's interest in and need for life insurance by summarizing the relevant points from the first interview. The best way to rekindle the prospect's interest is to review the gap between his or her desired outcome and the projected outcome without life insurance.

Fundamentally, this should involve nothing more than reviewing the key points of the fact-finding interview, including how the prospect felt about them. You want the prospect not only to recognize the financial gap again, but also to feel it. Here is one method for accomplishing this goal:

Review the Facts and Planning Assumptions. What assumptions were incorporated into planning? Has anything changed since the fact-finding interview? Would the prospect like to change any of the assumptions?

List the Prospect's Objectives. Review and confirm the prospect's objectives, concerns, and priorities. You should summarize the prospect's answers to the following questions:

- What does the prospect want to provide for the family?
- What does the prospect want to leave to his or her heirs or charity?
- What priorities does the prospect have for the family's lifestyle?
- What is the prospect's premium commitment?

It is important to match policy benefits with a prospect's objectives and priorities. These will vary for each prospect depending on his or her age and circumstances. In many cases the sales presentation will be built around the prospect's hot-button issue or primary concern.

Outline the Expected Need for Life Insurance. While reestablishing the prospect's need for life insurance, you should also refresh his or her understanding of just how expensive it will be for the family to live without his or her income. This process can take three steps:

1. Engage the prospect in a discussion of his or her personal need for life insurance. If the prospect does not recognize the need, he or she has no reason to own your product.
2. The prospect must fully understand the financial and emotional consequences of dying without the needed life insurance in place.
3. The prospect needs to clearly understand what it is he or she is considering buying. He or she must understand how he or she and his or her family will benefit from your product.

Summarize the Prospect's Current Plan. This is a review of what may happen if the prospect does not buy life insurance. Recap the information from the fact-finding interview. Give the prospect your professional assessment of the current plan's ability to achieve his or her stated objectives considering his or her current situation.

Focus on Relevant Features and Benefits

One mistake advisors make is to think that the purpose of the presentation is to educate the prospect about the technical, legal, tax, and product aspects of insurance. While an advisor should discuss these aspects, they should be discussed in light of the features and corresponding benefits that are relevant to the prospect and are the basis for your recommendations.

features

benefit

It is important to stress the difference between product features and benefits. *Features* are characteristics of the product itself—what it is. A feature is a fact about the product. Features are descriptive, and are not given values. A *benefit* is what the prospect gets because of the feature. It is what the product does for the prospect and why he or she wants it. Benefits are value-laden and subjective. They are features that are wanted by that individual.

A feature may not have a benefit for one prospect, while it will for another. If you are selling group insurance to a group of young single males, maternity and dependent coverage may not have a benefit, whereas to a group of young married men with families, these features may be of enormous benefit.

When presenting a recommendation, you want to explain what it is, how it solves the problem, and what it does for the prospect. Is it worth the price? Is it the best option? Will it save money? How well will it work for the prospect? These and other similar questions must be addressed and answered if the prospect is to buy your solution. To present and distinguish features and benefits, follow this procedure:

- state the feature
- follow it with the words: "what this means to you is..."
- state the benefit as it relates to a need, value, or objective the client has stated

For example, in presenting the waiver-of-premium rider, you might explain that this policy contains the waiver-of-premium rider and that should he or she become disabled, the company will pay the premium for them. This will give them the peace of mind of knowing that if they cannot work because of a disability, their premium will be paid and their life insurance coverage will remain in effect, protecting their family in the event of their death.

Summarize Your Observations. Summarize your observations about the current plan's inability to accomplish the prospect's objectives. These observations should outline gaps you found in the current plan, demonstrating how important it is that the prospect implement the recommendations you are about to make if he or she wants to achieve his or her stated objectives. Ask confirming questions to get agreement on what is important to the prospect.

Make Your Recommendations. Outline your recommendations, including both insurance and noninsurance solutions. Present your recommendations beginning with the noninsurance solutions that are the easiest to implement. For example, if you notice the prospect does not have a living will, you can recommend that he or she see an attorney and have one drafted. Starting with an insurance recommendation might raise the prospect's fears that you are only interested in making a sale. Use trial closes and checking questions to confirm understanding and the prospect's approval of your recommendations. Then ask the prospect to buy.

Outline the Implementation Plan. The implementation plan provides you with a way to review your recommendations while providing the prospect with the action steps necessary to complete them. It should identify who is responsible for implementing each step and establish deadlines for the implementation.

Keep the Prospect Involved

It is important to have the prospect's participation and involvement in the sales process for several reasons:

- It helps the prospect feel responsible for solving his or her own problems.
- It helps you know whether you are on target with your presentation.
- It builds agreement one step at a time.
- It helps clarify any misunderstanding by either party.
- It helps lead to a logical and successful close—a conclusion to buy.
- It provides opportunities to deal with objections before asking prospects to buy.
- It helps make policy delivery much easier when the prospect understands the why without needing to be sold again when the policy comes back.

For many, the impediment to discussing life insurance is that it involves death, and death is ignored or denied, because it is difficult to contemplate or discuss. Yet, death is the ultimate reality of each individual life. Providing protection against the financial devastation resulting from premature or inopportune death is an expression of love to be recognized, acknowledged, and celebrated. This is even more true when the additional, living benefits provided by life insurance help manage longevity risks for the same expenditure.

An emphasis on the caring and emotions behind the numbers is imperative to help people understand why having life insurance demonstrates love and responsibility. People make financial decisions for more than rational reasons. The widespread refusal to consider death or to come to grips with its financial impact provides compelling reasons why life insurance must be presented both analytically and emotionally. Financial advisors are in a unique position and are qualified to deliver the message and motivate its fulfillment. They have the subject matter knowledge, as well as the experience and empathy to communicate the human dimension of financial risks to motivate prospects to take the necessary and appropriate actions.

Preaching the Gospel of Life insurance. As we as advisors have become more sophisticated and financial planning has introduced a broader perspective of our job, it is important to remember the fundamental reason people buy life insurance. They buy it because they want to protect their loved ones, families and businesses. They buy it because they love someone and care about them. They buy it because they want peace of mind. They buy it because they want to preserve a way of life and standard of living they have worked so hard to provide. These basic reasons for buying life insurance are not shown on fancy policy illustrations or financial planning proposals, or even in the policies that we deliver. People buy life insurance not for what it is, bur for what it does. Communicating that value is like peaching the gospel of life insurance, and it is essential to your success.

Tips for an Effective Sales Presentation. What makes an effective sales presentation? Here are some ideas that should help you with yours.

- Know your product.
- Make it simple. Do not confuse your prospect. Don't use buzzwords, acronyms or any word or phrase that may be in any way confusing to your prospect.
- Make it interesting. This will be good for you as well as the prospect. Don't try to memorize it. Learn the key points and speak conversationally.
- Make it sales oriented—the information you provide points towards an eventual sale. The focus should be on providing a solution to the prospect's need or problem. If the prospect wants it, it should be easy to buy.
- Your presentation should be absolutely on target and address the issues, needs or problems your prospect has to have solved. There should be no gap between your product and the solution the prospect is trying to achieve.
- Your presentation should be a dialogue rather than a monologue. Seek feedback, reaction, comments and an acceptance level from your prospect. Listen to the prospect.
- Your prospect should be psychologically and physically with your presentation and how it applies to them.
- Consistently stress benefits and positive results from the solutions your prospect will receive if they buy your product. Create value for your product. Become a valuable asset to the customer by adding value at every opportunity.
- Be sure you are making your presentation to a qualified prospect.
- Confirm your appointment to make sure you will have a ready and receptive welcome. Confirm who will be attending. Confirm directions, address, and driving time. Arrive early.
- Prepare all necessary sales aids—applications, illustrations, supporting materials, prospectuses, handouts, etc. Be sure the materials are current and appropriate to your prospect. Organize materials so they are in the proper order and you know where everything is. Check one more time before you leave your office.

- Practice your presentation. Anticipate and prepare for objections.
- Visualize your success. See yourself achieving the result you are seeking.

Tables

Table 6-4 Traditional Net Cost

Policy Year	Age	Premium	Cash Value	Dividend	Accum. Dividend	Accum. Premium
1	48	$2,187	$ 0	$ 0	$ 0	$2,296
2	49	2,187	1,456	76	76	4,708
3	50	2,187	2,963	120	200	7,239
4	51	2,187	4,516	170	380	9,898
5	52	2,187	6,119	185	584	12,689
6	53	2,187	7,775	217	830	15,620
7	54	2,187	9,470	280	1,151	18,697
8	55	2,187	11,210	325	1,534	21,928
9	56	2,187	12,992	390	2,001	25,321
10	57	2,187	14,820	415	2,516	28,883
11	58	2,187	16,698	455	3,097	32,624
12	59	2,187	18,625	550	3,801	36,551
13	60	2,187	20,605	615	4,606	40,675
14	61	2,187	22,638	707	5,544	45,005
15	62	2,187	24,720	775	6,596	49,552
16	63	2,187	26,857	845	7,771	54,326
17	64	2,187	29,042	952	9,111	59,339
18	65	2,187	31,276	1,020	10,587	64,602
19	66	2,187	33,559	1,140	12,256	70,128
20	67	2,187	35,900	1,250	14,119	75,931

Table 6-5 Traditional Net Cost

NOTE: $100,000 participating whole life policy for a male, issues age 48.

10-Year Traditional Net Cost		20-Year Traditional Net Cost	
Dividends	$ 2,178	Dividends	$10,487
Cash value	14,820	Cash value	35,900
Total	16,998	Total	46,387
Less		Less	
Premiums paid	21,870	Premiums paid	43,740
Cost	4,872	Cost	–2,647
Divide by $1,000's face	48.72	Per $1,000	–26.47
Divide by number of years	4.872	Per $1,000 per year	–1.3235

Table 6-6 Interest-Adjusted Net Surrender Cost Index

Policy Year	Age	Premium	Cash Value	Dividend	Accum. Dividend	Accum. Premium
1	48	$2,187	$ 0	$ 0	$ 0	$2,296
2	49	2,187	1,456	76	76	4,708
3	50	2,187	2,963	120	200	7,239
4	51	2,187	4,516	170	380	9,898
5	52	2,187	6,119	185	584	12,689
6	53	2,187	7,775	217	830	15,620
7	54	2,187	9,470	280	1,151	18,697
8	55	2,187	11,210	325	1,534	21,928
9	56	2,187	12,992	390	2,001	25,321
10	57	2,187	14,820	415	2,516	28,883
11	58	2,187	16,698	455	3,097	32,624
12	59	2,187	18,625	550	3,801	36,551
13	60	2,187	20,605	615	4,606	40,675
14	61	2,187	22,638	707	5,544	45,005
15	62	2,187	24,720	775	6,596	49,552
16	63	2,187	26,857	845	7,771	54,326
17	64	2,187	29,042	952	9,111	59,339
18	65	2,187	31,276	1,020	10,587	64,602
19	66	2,187	33,559	1,140	12,256	70,128
20	67	2,187	35,900	1,250	14,119	75,931

Table 6-7 Surrender Cost Index

NOTE: $100,000 participating whole life policy for a male, issue age 48.

10-Year Surrender Cost Index		20-Year Surrender Cost Index	
Dividends	$2,515.779	Dividends	$14,119.04
Cash value	14,820	Cash value	35,900
Total	17,335.78	Total	50,019.04
Less		Less	
Premiums paid	28,883.24	Premiums paid	75,931.00
Cost	11,547.46	Cost	25,911.97
Divide by $1,000's face	115.4746	Per $1,000	259.1197
Divide by number of years (13.2068)	8.743575	Per $1,000 per year (34.7193)	7.463274

Table 6-8 Interest-Adjusted Net Payment Cost Index

Policy Year	Age	Premium	Cash Value	Dividend	Accum. Dividend	Accum. Premium
1	48	$2,187	$ 0	$ 0	$ 0	$2,296
2	49	2,187	1,456	76	76	4,708
3	50	2,187	2,963	120	200	7,239
4	51	2,187	4,516	170	380	9,898
5	52	2,187	6,119	185	584	12,689
6	53	2,187	7,775	217	830	15,620
7	54	2,187	9,470	280	1,151	18,697
8	55	2,187	11,210	325	1,534	21,928
9	56	2,187	12,992	390	2,001	25,321
10	57	2,187	14,820	415	2,516	28,883
11	58	2,187	16,698	455	3,097	32,624
12	59	2,187	18,625	550	3,801	36,551
13	60	2,187	20,605	615	4,606	40,675
14	61	2,187	22,638	707	5,544	45,005
15	62	2,187	24,720	775	6,596	49,552
16	63	2,187	26,857	845	7,771	54,326
17	64	2,187	29,042	952	9,111	59,339
18	65	2,187	31,276	1,020	10,587	64,602
19	66	2,187	33,559	1,140	12,256	70,128
20	67	2,187	35,900	1,250	14,119	75,931

Table 6-9 Net Payment Index

NOTE: $100,000 participating whole life policy for a male, issue age 48.

10-Year Surrender Cost Index		20-Year Surrender Cost Index	
Accum. dividends	$2,515.779	Accum. dividends	$14,119.04
Accum. premiums	28,883.24	Accum. premiums	75,931.00
Future value of net premiums	26,367.46	Future value of net premiums	61,811.96
Convert to per $1,000	263.6746	Per $1,000	618.1196
Divide by factor 13.2068	19.96507	Per $1,000 per year (34.7193)	17.80334
Payment index	19.96507	Payment index	17.80334

Table 6-10 Interest Adjusted Cost Method

	Premiums			Dividends	
Year	**Per Year**	**Accum. @ 5%**	**Per Year**	**Accum. @ 5%**	**Cash Value**
1	$ 15	$ 15.75	0	$ 0	$ 0
2	15	32.29	1	1.05	0
3	15	49.65	2	3.20	23
4	15	67.89	3	6.51	34
5	15	87.03	4	11.04	43
6	15	107.13	5	16.84	56
7	15	128.24	6	23.99	75
8	15	150.40	7	32.54	100
9	15	173.67	8	42.56	115
10	15	198.10	9	54.14	120
TOTALS	150	198.10	45	54.14	120

Table 6-11 Surrender Cost Index and Payment Cost Index

Surrender Cost Index		Payment Cost Index	
Future value of premiums	$198.1018	Accum. premiums	$198.1018
		Less accum. dividends	–54.13574
Minus FV of dividends	54.13574	FV of net premiums	$143.9661
FV of net premiums	$143.9661		
Less net cash value	– 120		
FV of net cost	$23.96606		
Divide by annuity factor	13.2068	Divide by annuity factor	13.2068
Surrender Cost Index	1.814676	Payment Cost Index	10.9009

Table 6-12 Cash Accumulation Comparison Method—3 Percent

Policy Year	WL Premium	ART Premium	Prem Diff.	Accum. Diff. @ 3%	WL Cash Values	Term Plus Side Fund	WL + Paid-up Adds.	ART Face Amount
1	$2,187	$365	$1,822	$1,877	$ 0	$100,000	$100,000	$ 98,123
2	2,187	386	1,801	3,788	1,456	100,075	100,075	96,287
3	2,187	409	1,778	5,733	2,963	100,203	100,203	94,470
4	2,187	434	1,753	7,710	4,516	100,527	100,527	92,817
5	2,187	460	1,727	9,720	6,119	100,972	100,972	91,252
6	2,187	491	1,696	11,759	7,775	102,321	102,321	90,562
7	2,187	528	1,659	13,820	9,470	104,408	104,408	90,588
8	2,187	574	1,613	15,896	11,210	107,549	107,549	91,653
9	2,187	628	1,559	17,979	12,992	111,463	111,463	93,484
10	2,187	685	1,502	20,066	14,820	114,876	114,876	94,810
11	2,187	753	1,434	22,145	16,698	119,071	119,071	96,926
12	2,187	838	1,349	24,199	18,625	124,156	124,156	99,957
13	2,187	946	1,241	26,203	20,605	130,507	130,507	104,304
14	2,187	1,071	1,116	28,138	22,638	136,789	136,789	108,651
15	2,187	1,226	961	29,972	24,720	143,896	143,896	113,924
16	2,187	1,427	760	31,654	26,857	152,719	152,719	121,065
17	2,187	1,679	508	33,127	29,042	162,745	162,745	129,618
18	2,187	1,942	245	34,374	31,276	170,345	170,345	135,971
19	2,187	2,483	–296	35,100	33,559	183,682	183,682	148,582
20	2,187	3,127	–940	35,185	35,900	196,132	196,132	160,947

NOTE: $100,000 whole life for a male age 48; dividends buy paid-up additions.

Annual renewable term (ART) decreased to equalize death benefits; interest rate 3% (on accumulations).

Table 6-13 Cash Accumulation Comparison Method—10 Percent

Policy Year	WL Premium	ART Premium	Prem Diff.	Accum. Diff. @ 10%	WL Cash Values	Term Plus Side Fund	WL + Paid-up Adds.	ART Face Amount
1	$2,187	$365	$1,822	$2,005	$ 0	$100,000	$100,000	$97,995
2	2,187	385	1,802	4,188	1,456	100,075	100,075	95,887
3	2,187	405	1,782	6,566	2,963	100,203	100,203	93,637
4	2,187	428	1,759	9,158	4,516	100,527	100,527	91,369
5	2,187	448	1,739	11,987	6,119	100,972	100,972	88,985
6	2,187	473	1,714	15,071	7,775	102,321	102,321	87,250
7	2,187	501	1,686	18,432	9,470	104,408	104,408	85,976
8	2,187	535	1,652	22,093	11,210	107,549	107,549	85,456
9	2,187	574	1,613	26,076	12,992	111,463	111,463	85,387
10	2,187	610	1,577	30,149	14,820	114,876	114,876	84,457
11	2,187	652	1,535	35,149	16,698	119,071	119,071	83,922
12	2,187	703	1,484	40,297	18,625	124,156	124,156	83,859
13	2,187	767	1,420	45,888	20,605	130,507	130,507	84,619
14	2,187	836	1,351	51,963	22,638	136,789	136,789	84,826
15	2,187	918	1,269	58,554	24,720	143,896	143,896	85,342
16	2,187	1,026	1,161	65,687	26,857	152,719	152,719	87,032
17	2,187	1,157	1,030	73,388	29,042	162,745	162,745	89,357
18	2,187	1,265	922	81,741	31,276	170,345	170,345	88,604
19	2,187	1,555	632	90,610	33,559	183,682	183,682	93,072
20	2,187	1,867	320	100,023	35,900	196,132	196,132	96,109

NOTES: $100,000 whole life for a male, age 48; dividends buy paid-up additions.

Annual renewable term (ART) decreased to equalize death benefits; interest rate 10 percent (on accumulations).

Table 6-14 Equal Outlay Comparison Method—3 Percent

Policy Year	WL Premium	ART Premium	Prem Diff.	Accum. Diff. @ 3%	WL Cash Values	Term Plus Side Fund	WL + Paid-up Adds.
1	$ 2,187	$ 372	$ 1,815	$ 1,869	$ 0	$101,869	$ 100,000
2	2,187	401	1,786	3,765	1,456	103,765	100,075
3	2,187	433	1,754	5,685	2,963	105,685	100,203
4	2,187	468	1,719	7,626	4,516	107,626	100,527
5	2,187	504	1,683	9,588	6,119	109,588	100,972
6	2,187	542	1,645	11,570	7,775	111,570	102,321
7	2,187	583	1,604	13,569	9,470	113,569	104,408
8	2,187	626	1,561	15,584	11,210	115,584	107,549
9	2,187	672	1,515	17,612	12,992	117,612	111,463
10	2,187	722	1,465	19,649	14,820	119,649	114,876
11	2,187	777	1,410	21,691	16,698	121,691	119,071
12	2,187	838	1,349	23,731	18,625	123,731	124,156
13	2,187	907	1,280	25,762	20,605	125,762	130,507
14	2,187	986	1,201	27,772	22,638	127,772	136,789
15	2,187	1,076	1,111	29,749	24,720	129,749	143,896
16	2,187	1,179	1,008	31,680	26,857	131,680	152,719
17	2,187	1,295	892	33,549	29,042	133,549	162,745
18	2,187	1,428	759	35,337	31,276	135,337	170,345
19	2,187	1,671	516	36,929	33,559	136,929	183,682
20	2,187	1,943	244	38,288	35,900	138,288	196,132

NOTES $100,000 whole life for a male, age 48; dividends purchase paid-up additions. Interest rate 3 percent

Table 6-15 Equal Outlay Comparison Method—10 Percent

Policy Year	WL Premium	ART Premium	Prem Diff.	Accum. Diff. @ 10%	WL Cash Values	Term Plus Side Fund	WL + Paid-up Adds.
1	$ 2,187	372	$ 1,815	$ 1,997	$ 0	$101,997	$ 100,000
2	2,187	401	1,786	4,161	1,456	104,161	100,075
3	2,187	433	1,754	6,506	2,963	106,506	100,203
4	2,187	468	1,719	9,048	4,516	109,048	100,527
5	2,187	504	1,683	11,804	6,119	111,804	100,972
6	2,187	542	1,645	14,794	7,775	114,794	102,321
7	2,187	583	1,604	18,037	9,470	118,037	104,408
8	2,187	626	1,561	21,558	11,210	121,558	107,549
9	2,187	672	1,515	25,381	12,992	125,381	111,463
10	2,187	722	1,465	29,530	14,820	129,530	114,876
11	2,187	777	1,410	34,034	16,698	134,034	119,071
12	2,187	838	1,349	38,922	18,625	138,922	124,156
13	2,187	907	1,280	44,222	20,605	144,222	130,507
14	2,187	986	1,201	49,965	22,638	149,965	136,789
15	2,187	1,076	1,111	56,184	24,720	156,184	143,896
16	2,187	1,179	1,008	62,911	26,857	162,911	152,719
17	2,187	1,295	892	70,183	29,042	170,183	162,745
18	2,187	1,428	759	78,036	31,276	178,036	170,345
19	2,187	1,671	516	86,407	33,559	186,407	183,682
20	2,187	1,943	244	95,317	35,900	195,317	196,132

NOTES: $100,000 whole life for a male, age 48; dividends purchase paid-up additions. Interest rate 10 percent

Chapter Six Review

Key terms and concepts are explained in the glossary. Answers to the review questions and the self-test questions are found in the back of the book in the Answers to Questions section.

Key Terms and Concepts

- net cost method
- interest-adjusted indices
- National Association of Insurance Commissioners (NAIC)
- surrender cost index
- net payment index
- cash-accumulation comparison method
- equal-outlay method
- illustration selling
- Monte Carlo analysis
- Life Insurance Illustrations Model Regulation
- features
- benefit

Review Questions

1. Discuss the net cost method of comparing life insurance policy costs, how the net cost is calculated, and the method's principle flaw. [1]
2. Describe the cash-accumulation method of policy comparison, and explain its strengths and weaknesses. [1]
3. Explain the equal-outlay method of policy comparison. [1]
4. Describe the interest-adjusted indices, and explain how this method of comparing life insurance policies differs from the traditional net cost method. [2]
5. Describe the relationship between interest rates and accumulated values in policy illustrations. [2]
6. What is the implicit assumption underlying policy illustrations that do not include interest adjustments? [2]
7. Describe the major elements of the NAIC Life Insurance Illustrations Model Regulation. [3]
8. Describe the duties of an illustration actuary under the NAIC Illustrations Model Regulation. [3]
9. Discuss important aspects of developing and presenting the insurance plan to the prospect. [6]

Self-Test Questions

1. A serious shortcoming of the net cost method of comparing life insurance policies is that
   (A) it gives equal weight to payment amounts that may be separated by 10 or 20 years
   (B) it uses time value of money as the basis for its analysis of policy cost.
   (C) it looks for the interest rate that makes the buy-term-and-invest-the-difference comparison exactly equivalent
   (D) it requires a computer in order to be efficient

2. The interest-adjusted indices method of comparing policies is
   (A) very well suited for evaluating policy replacements
   (B) well suited for comparing dissimilar policies, such as term and whole life
   (C) indicates that a policy with smaller numerical values (indices) is preferable to a policy with higher indices
   (D) basically a buy-term-and-invest-the-difference approach

3. Which of the following policy comparison methods appears on most sales presentation materials used by insurance advisors?
   (A) cash-accumulation comparison method
   (B) comparative-interest-rate method
   (C) interest-adjusted indices (surrender cost index and payment cost index)
   (D) Linton yield method

4. Almost every state mandates that the interest rate to be used in comparing policies with the interest-adjusted cost indices is:
   (A) 3 percent
   (B) 5 percent
   (C) 6 percent
   (D) a variable rate

5. It is generally held that policy illustrations are effective in serving which of the following purposes?

   I. They work well to educate clients in the mechanics of how policies work.
   II. They are an adequate tool for comparing costs of policies from different insurance companies.

   (A) I only
   (B) II only
   (C) Both I and II
   (D) Neither I nor II

6. Which of the following statements concerning policy illustrations is (are) correct?

   I. They usually cover at least 10 years of data and often cover 15 or 20 years or more.
   II. The NAIC Life Insurance Illustrations Model Regulation set standards applicable to policy illustration.

   (A) I only
   (B) II only
   (C) Both I and II
   (D) Neither I nor II

7. Which of the following statements concerning policy illustrations is (are) correct?

   I. The NAIC model regulation does not apply to variable life, credit life, or life policies with a face amount of less than $10,000.
   II. The NAIC Model Regulation applies to non-variable life and individual life policies for face amounts over $10,000.

   (A) I only
   (B) II only
   (C) Both I and II
   (D) Neither I nor II

READ THE FOLLOWING DIRECTIONS BEFORE CONTINUING

The questions below differ from the preceding questions in that they all contain the word EXCEPT. So you understand fully the basis used in selecting each answer, be sure to read each question carefully.

---

8. All of the following statements concerning the interest-adjusted indices are true EXCEPT

   (A) The NAIC developed these methods and model regulations requiring their use.
   (B) These methods treat premium payments as if they were put into an interest-bearing account to accumulate to the end of the interval.
   (C) The payment cost index is similar to the surrender cost index, except it does not consider cash value at the end of the interval.
   (D) The surrender cost index is useful in comparing costs when death benefit protection is emphasized.

9. All of the following are criticisms of the traditional net cost method of comparing life insurance policy costs EXCEPT

   (A) It gives equal weight to payment amounts that may be separated by 10 or 20 years.
   (B) It uses time value of money as the basis for its analysis of policy costs.
   (C) It implies that the insurance was free and in fact a profit was made on the premiums.
   (D) It is simple, easy to understand, calculate, and explain.

10. Suitability of a product selection for a prospect involves all of the following concepts EXCEPT

   (A) appropriateness of the product for the client.
   (B) ability of the prospect to tolerate fluctuations in cash value.
   (C) the prospect's ability to pay the premium.
   (D) the product recommendation must be in the advisor's best interest.

POLICY PROVISIONS 7

Learning Objectives

An understanding of the material in this chapter should enable you to

1. Explain the standard policy provisions in a life insurance contract.
2. Identify the provisions that are required by law in life insurance policies.
3. List and describe the required surrender options in a cash value policy.
4. Explain how a policy loan affects surrender options, especially extended term insurance.
5. Identify and explain the types of provisions which insurers are prohibited from including in life insurance policies.
6. Briefly describe the provisions: accidental death, guaranteed purchase option, automatic premium loan, and waiver of premium.
7. Describe the basic settlement option available to policyowners and beneficiaries in a life insurance policy.
8. Discuss the important aspects of implementing the life insurance plan.

Policy provisions make up the insurance contract and dictate how the policy will operate. A complete and accurate understanding of these provisions is essential for the life insurance advisor to effectively perform his or her professional duties of advising and providing services to clients.

Life insurance settlement options and the concepts and rules that govern them, the options available, and the rights and privileges of policyowners and beneficiaries are also reviewed. This chapter ends with a discussion of the implementation of the plan in the selling/planning process.

Policy Provisions

The life insurance policy represents a valid agreement between a life insurance company and the policyowner, and is a contract subject to the general rules of contract law. However, in adapting these rules to the life insurance contract, the courts have introduced substantial modifications because of the peculiar characteristics of the life insurance contract. These characteristics will be briefly described in the following section.

Contract of Adhesion

contract of adhesion

A life insurance contract is a contract of adhesion. A *contract of adhesion* is one that is not negotiated. It is drafted entirely by one party. The other party to the contract is not permitted to alter the terms of the contract and may only accept or reject it. The policyowner and the insurer do not negotiate the terms of the contract. Because the drafting party, the insurer, has the freedom to choose the words of the contract, the law requires the insurer to abide by the words it has chosen, and any ambiguities are generally interpreted in favor of the policyowner. The prospective policyowner performs only these two functions in the creation of a life insurance contract:

- He or she applies for the policy (the contract) by filling out the application and supplying any medical information required by the insurer. This is not a negotiation. The applicant is merely specifying what type of contract he or she would like to be offered. Based on this information, the insurer will make an offer by issuing a policy.
- He or she accepts or rejects the contract as offered by the insurer.

The applicant accepts the offer by paying the initial premium. The applicant rejects the offered contract by refusing delivery of the policy. Even after the applicant accepts the insurer's offer of coverage and a contract is binding on the insurer, the policyowner may reject the contract and get a full refund based on the *10-day free look provision.* Additionally, the policyowner is under no legal obligation to pay the premium and can end the contract by stopping premium payments.

State law generally requires that the contract avoid complex legal terminology. The goal is to make the contract easy to read and understand. A number of required, prohibited, and optional provisions are controlled by state law. Before a policy may be sold in a particular jurisdiction, its provisions must be filed with that state's insurance department for approval.

Policy Face Page

policy face pages

free-look provision

Although the placement of the provisions may vary from company to company, the *policy face pages* of most life insurance contracts are quite similar. The face page of a contract usually contains the following information:

- **the name of the insurance company**
- **specific details for that policy**— the name of the insured and the name of the policyowner, the face amount of the policy, the policy number, and the policy date or issue date (some include both dates)
- **a general description of the type of insurance** provided by that policy contract. For example, the face page of a traditional participating whole life policy might read as follows:

  Whole Life—Level Face Amount Plan. Insurance payable upon death. Premiums payable for life. Policy participates in dividends. Dividends, dividend credits, and policy loans may be used to help pay premiums.
- **a statement about the policy's *free look provision***. This provision gives the policyowner a period, usually 10 days, in which to return the policy after acceptance. The contract will be canceled from the start, and a full premium refund will be promptly made.
- **insurer's promise to pay**. This is the heart of the insurance contract and is called the insuring clause.
- **signatures of the officers of the company** (usually the president and the secretary), which bind the company to the terms of the contract

Standard Policy Provisions

The state insurance codes generally impose a requirement that unless specifically exempted from the law, all life insurance policies delivered or issued for delivery in the state must contain language substantially the same as certain specified provisions. Insurers are also generally given the option to insert provisions different than those specified in the statute if the language in the insurer's provisions is more favorable to policyowners. A company's insurance department determines whether an alternative provision is more favorable to consumers.

Required Provisions

Grace Period

grace period

The *grace period clause* grants the policyowner an additional period to pay any premium after it becomes due. As a result of this provision, a policy that would have lapsed for nonpayment of premiums continues in force during the grace period. The premium remains due, however, and if the insured dies during the grace period, the insurer may deduct one month's premium from the death benefit. The standard length of the grace period is 31 days. If the last day of the grace period falls on a nonbusiness day, the period is normally extended to the next business day.

Although insurers could charge interest on the unpaid premium for the late period, they do not normally do so. If the insured survives the grace period but the premium remains unpaid, the policy lapses (unless a nonforfeiture option comes into play). As with all renewal premiums, the policyowner is under no obligation to pay the premium for the insurance coverage provided under the grace period provision.

Policy Loans

The law requires that the insurance contract permit policy loans if the policy generates a cash value. To understand this requirement it is necessary to make a distinction between loans, policy loans, and advancements.

Loan—A transfer of money (or other property) with an obligation to repay the money, plus interest, at a certain time (or to return the asset transferred)

Policy loan—An advance of money to the policyowner from a policy's cash values. Interest is accrued on the amount borrowed from the policy. Although there is no fixed time for repayment of the money to the insurer, the amount of the loan, plus any unpaid interest, will be deducted from any policy values payable under the policy.

Advancement—Money or other property transferred to someone prior to the anticipated time of payment or delivery

policy loan The term *policy loan* is a misnomer. A policy loan is actually not a loan, but an advancement against the policy's cash surrender value or death benefit. It is not technically a loan because the policyowner assumes no obligation to repay the money taken from the policy. Thus, it is not technically correct to say that the policyowner borrows from the insurer and the loan is secured by the policy cash values. It is more accurate to say that the policyowner makes an advance withdrawal of cash values otherwise available when the policy is surrendered or when the insured dies. However, the distinction is only of academic interest, since the universal practice is to call it a loan.

EXAMPLE

Ms. Policyowner obtains a policy loan of $8,000; it is subject to an 8 percent interest rate. Her repayment options are to:

- repay none of it
- repay interest only
- repay some of balance due
- repay all $8,000 plus interest due

(*Note:* the timing and amount of any repayments are totally at the discretion of Ms. Policyowner unless either the insured dies or the policy is terminated.)

After 2 years at an 8-percent interest rate, the loan balance will be $9,331.20 if no repayments have been made.

$$\$8,000 + \$640 + \$691.20 = \$9,331.20$$

If Ms. Policyowner pays the $640 interest charge each year, the loan balance will remain level at $8,000. Death benefits will be reduced by the loan balance, plus any unpaid interest, such as the $9,331.20.

One might ask why, if it is not a loan, is the insurer permitted to assess an interest rate against the amount borrowed? The policyowner is expected to pay interest on the "loan" because he or she has withdrawn assets from the insurer that are intended to support the level-premium concept. If the policyowner withdraws those assets, it is fair to expect him or her to pay an interest rate that will approximate what the insurer will earn if the money is left with the insurer to invest.

Automatic premium loans are another type of policy loan. These loans are advances the insurer makes from policy cash values to pay any unpaid premiums. They are discussed later in this chapter with optional provisions.

Incontestable Clause

incontestable clause

An *incontestable clause* makes the life insurance policy incontestable by the insurer after it has been in force for a certain length of time. However, the insurance company can still refuse payment of a claim, usually due to a material misrepresentation or fraud on an insured's application. The laws of the states differ as to the form of the clause prescribed, but no state permits a clause that would make the policy contestable for more than 2 years.

After a policy has been in effect for the period prescribed by the incontestable clause, the insurance company cannot have the policy declared invalid. The courts have generally recognized three exceptions to this rule:

1. There was no insurable interest at the inception of the policy,
2. The policy was purchased with the intent to murder the insured
3. There was a fraudulent impersonation of the insured by another person (for example, for purposes of taking the medical exam)

Under these circumstances the incontestable clause does not to apply, since the contract, which includes the incontestable clause, was void from its inception. There is a good deal of variability from state to state as to how these exceptions are treated in court if there is a lawsuit to pay the proceeds at the death of the insured after the contestable period has expired, and the insurer attempts to use one of these exceptions as a defense against paying the proceeds.

EXAMPLE

Abigail and Diane were identical twins, but they had different states of health. Diane had a heart murmur for the decade prior to her death. Four years prior to her death, she purchased a life insurance policy by concealing her heart problem and having healthy Abigail take the physical examination the insurance company requested.

The insurance company discovered the impersonation when they investigated for the death claim, but the policy had been in force for 4 years.

Will the insurer be liable for the death claim?

No. The contract was void from its inception as a result of the fraudulent impersonation at the physical examination. If there had not been any fraudulent impersonation and merely concealment, then the policy would have been voidable until the end of the contestable period. After 4 years, the policy would have been incontestable in the absence of fraudulent impersonation. This result will vary by state.

Divisible Surplus

divisible surplus provision

The *divisible surplus provision* applies only to participating policies. It requires the insurer to determine and apportion any divisible surplus among the insurer's participating policies, typically at annual intervals on the anniversary date. Dividends are not likely to be paid before the second anniversary of the policy. Dividends result from earnings resulting from excess interest earned, and mortality and expense savings over what was assumed in creating the premium for a series of policies. The insurer's board of directors determines what proportion of company earnings will be distributed to participating policies each year.

Entire Contract

Ordinarily, we expect a contract of any type to include all the provisions that are binding on all of the parties. However, this is not always the case in general contract law. Sometimes, a contract will include the terms of another document without actually including that second document in the contract. This is accomplished by referring to the other document and incorporating it into the contract through what is known as *incorporation by reference.* The *entire contract provision* grew out of an attempt to prohibit insurers from using incorporation by reference and to make life insurance contracts easier to understand. This provision ensures policyowners are given a copy of all documents that constitute the contract, and that changes to the contract cannot be made after it has been issued. Because of this, a copy of the application is attached to the policy and becomes a part of the contract.

Reinstatement

reinstatement provision

The *reinstatement provision* allows a policyowner to reacquire coverage under a policy that has lapsed. This right is valuable to both the policyowner and the insurer. Various state laws and insurance contracts impose certain requirements that the policyowner must meet to reinstate the policy. A typical reinstatement provision might provide that the policy can be reinstated within 3 years after the due date of the first unpaid premium, unless the policy has been surrendered for its cash value. The conditions for reinstatement are that the policyowner must (1) provide evidence of insurability satisfactory to the insurer; (2) pay all overdue premiums, plus interest; and (3) repay or reinstate any policy loan outstanding when the policy lapsed, plus interest.

Normally, insurers do not permit reinstatement of a policy that has been surrendered for its cash value, and this prohibition is often included in the contractual definition of the requirements for reinstatement.

Misstatement of Age or Sex

The age and sex of the insured are fundamentally important factors in the evaluation of the risk assumed by a life insurance company. Inaccurate statements about the insured's age or sex are material misrepresentations. Rather than voiding the contract based on such misrepresentations, the practice is to adjust the policy's premium or benefits to reflect the truth after the inaccuracy has been discovered. Adjustments in the policy's premiums or benefits based on misstatements of age or sex are not prohibited by the incontestability clause because incontestability clauses prevent contests of the *validity* of the policy, not the terms of the contract. If a *misstatement of age or sex* clause appears in the contract, an adjustment based on that clause would be an attempt to enforce the terms of the contract, not invalidate it.

EXAMPLE

Janet understated her age when she purchased a life insurance policy. The premium she paid was $900 annually, but should have been $1000 annually for her correct age. The policy face amount will be adjusted down to the amount of coverage she could have purchased with a $900 annual premium based on her true age.

If the insured is still alive when it is discovered that the insured's age or sex has been misrepresented, the parties may elect to adjust the premium to the correct amount rather than to adjust the benefits.

The New York insurance code requires insurance contracts to contain a provision stipulating that if the age of the insured has been misstated, any amount payable or benefit accruing under the policy will be what the premium would have been if purchased at the correct age. A majority of states have similar provisions. A minority of states have a provision requiring a reference to misstatement of sex.

Nonforfeiture Provisions

When insurers developed the concept of level premium insurance policies, the goal was to make life insurance more affordable to older policyowners. This was accomplished by charging a lifetime level premium. In the earlier years of a policy, this level premium is higher than necessary to cover the mortality costs. The excess portion of the premium paid in the policy's early years, and the interest it earns, builds up a cash reserve that is used to pay the mortality costs at older ages, which at that point exceed the level premium being charged. Who was entitled to these reserves when a policy lapses? Originally, these reserves were forfeited by the policyowner and kept by the insurer. This was clearly unfair, and the practice was modified. Today, the states require that insurers provide policyowners who voluntarily terminate their contracts with a fair return of any value built up inside their policies. These laws are known as the nonforfeiture laws.

nonforfeiture options

These laws state that after a cash value policy has been in effect for a minimum number of years—usually 3—the insurer must use part of the reserved excess premium to create a guaranteed minimum cash value. The insurer must make that value available to the policyowner in cash as a surrender value and must give the policyowner a choice of two other *nonforfeiture options*: (1) extended term insurance for the net face amount of the policy or (2) paid-up insurance at a reduced death benefit amount. If the policyowner has not elected between them, the policy must provide that one of these two options will be effective automatically if the policy lapses. This is typically extended term, for then, assuming the lapse is unintentional and the premium may be paid or the policy reinstated, the beneficiary will be protected for the full face amount.

EXAMPLE

Marshall Artiste purchased a $100,000 whole life policy.

$10,000 : cash value

$ 6,000 : outstanding policy loan

The company has given Marshall his choice of the following:

- *Cash surrender value*—$4,000 of cash surrender value will be paid, after subtracting the $6,000 outstanding policy loan from the $10,000 cash value.
- *Extended term insurance*—$94,000 of coverage will be extended for as long as the $4,000 net cash value will purchase that amount as a single premium.

- *Paid-up insurance*—a paid-up whole life policy will be provided for whatever face amount can be purchased with the $4,000 net cash value (based on the attained age of the insured). The face amount will be significantly less than $94,000.

surrender options

The policyowner has the option of choosing the form under which the surrender value is to be paid, so the benefits are called *surrender benefits* or *surrender options.* The nature and significance of the standard surrender benefits are discussed in the following sections.

cash surrender value

Cash. The simplest form in which the surrender value may be taken is cash. After the policy has been in force long enough to have no surrender charges, there is an exact equivalence between the surrender value and the cash that can be obtained upon its surrender, leading many to refer to the surrender value as the *cash surrender value.* The law requires that the surrender value of a policy be made available in the form of cash, but in the case of whole life insurance, it does not require a company to grant cash values until the end of the third year. This limitation on cash values was provided in order to relieve the companies of the expense of drawing checks for the relatively small values that develop during the first and second policy years. It does not relieve the company of the obligation to make available in some non-cash benefit form any surrender value that might accumulate during the first 2 years. Most companies provide a cash value as soon as any value develops under the policy. Provision is made for deduction of any policy indebtedness (policy loans, plus accrued interest) from the cash value that would otherwise be available.

delay clause

The law permits a company to postpone payment of the cash surrender value for a period of 6 months after surrender of the policy. This *delay clause* protects companies against any losses that might arise from excessive demands for cash during an extreme financial emergency. The law has made the inclusion of a delay clause mandatory and has made the delay period of 6 months uniform. This clause would be invoked only under the most unusual circumstances.

Impact of Electing Surrender Benefits. The impact of the election of each surrender benefit on the structure of the underlying insurance contract is illustrated in the following figures. In each case, the underlying contract is a whole life policy, but the principle involved is generally applicable to any type of cash value policy, with some modification.

Figure 7-1
Effect of Cash Surrender on the Structure of Several Types of Life Insurance Contracts

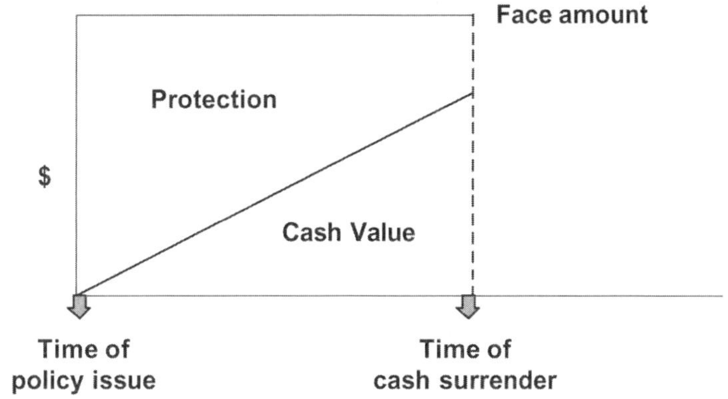

Effect on level death benefit cash-value life insurance contracts

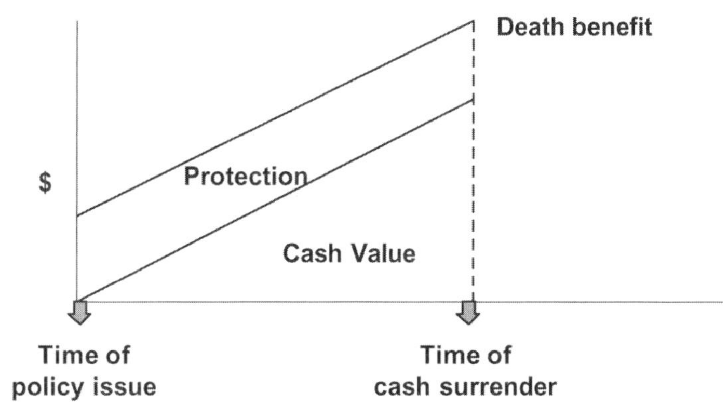

Effect on increasing death benefit type of universal life or variable universal life policies

The previous figure shows the change produced in cash value life insurance contracts by the exercise of the cash surrender option. The figure indicates that up to the point of surrender, the contract is a combination of protection and cash value. By surrendering the policy for cash, the policyowner takes the cash value element of the contract and terminates the protection element. Upon cash surrender, the company has no further obligations under the contract. Reinstatement rights are available only to policies that have terminated for reasons other than a cash surrender.

reduced paid-up insurance

Reduced Paid-Up Insurance. Under the *reduced paid-up insurance* option, the withdrawing policyowner receives a reduced amount of paid-up cash value insurance, payable upon the same conditions as the original policy. If the original policy was either a whole life or a limited-payment life policy, the insurance under this option will be paid-up whole life insurance.

net single premium

The amount of paid-up insurance provided under this option is the amount that can be purchased at the insured's attained age by the net surrender value (cash value, less any policy indebtedness, plus the cash value of any dividend additions or deposits). The net surrender value is applied as a *net single premium* computed on the mortality and interest bases specified in the policy for the calculation of the surrender value. The net single premium is the present value of all expected benefits based only on mortality and interest, and ignoring expenses. The amount of paid-up insurance available at various durations under a whole life and under a 20-payment life policy, issued at age 35, is shown in the following table. A table similar to this one will appear in any cash value policy as a part of the nonforfeiture provision.

Table 7-1 Example of Surrender Benefits at Selected Durations for Ordinary Life and 20-Payment Life

	Whole life				20-Payment Whole Life			
Policy Year	Cash Value	Reduced Paid-up Insurance	Extended Term Insurance		Cash Value	Reduced Paid-up Insurance	Extended Term Insurance	
			Yrs.	Days			Yrs.	Days
3	6	28	1	297	7	29	2	42
5	28	122	6	261	40	157	9	216
10	92	331	13	211	142	468	20	318
15	168	498	16	15	266	743	25	145
20	250	630	16	170	420	1000	7	242
25	336	721	15	186	487	1000	22	175
30	429	794	14	9	558	1000	18	88
35	523	850	12	119	629	1000	14	300

NOTE: Issue Age 35, Male, 1980 CSO Mortality, 4.5 Percent Interest. All values are per $1,000 of insurance.

The effect of the reduced paid-up insurance option on the cash surrender value of the whole life policy is illustrated in Figure 7-2. The greatest impact is on the protection element of the contract. In the example, the cash value before surrender had accumulated to a sum half the face of the policy, which at age 60, for instance, would purchase a paid-up whole life policy in an amount approximately 75 percent of the original face. The entire shrinkage comes from the protection element, however, since the investment element continues to increase until it equals the reduced face at the maturity date of the policy.

Figure 7-2
Effect of Reduced Paid-up Insurance on Structure of Several Types of Life Insurance Contracts

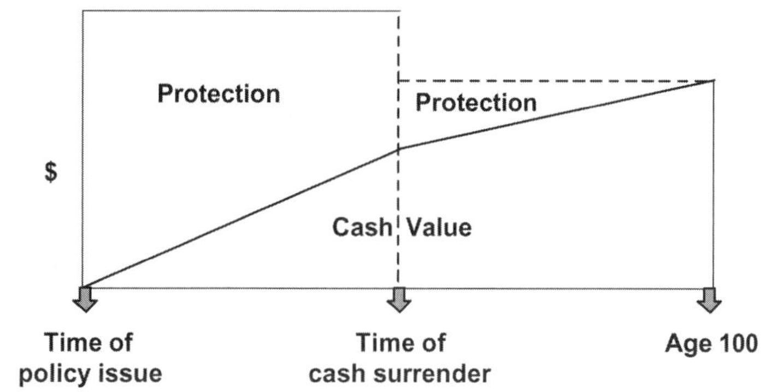

Effect on whole life contracts

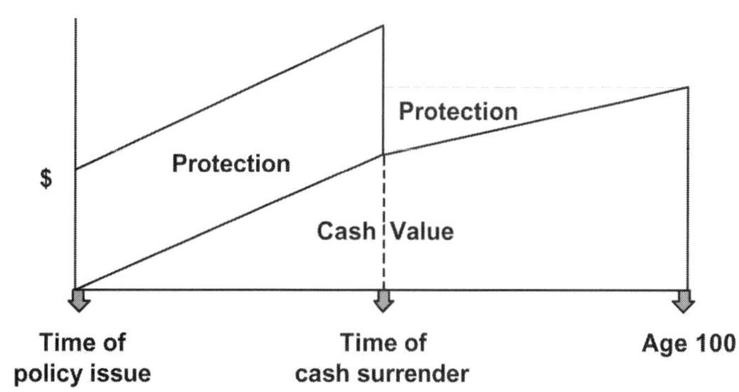

Effect on increasing death benefit universal and variable universal life insurance contracts

Universal life insurance and variable universal life policies provide a non-guaranteed form of the reduced paid-up option. The policyowner can reduce the death benefit so that the existing cash value is sufficient to cover all future charges, helped by the future earnings credited to the cash value. The nonguaranteed element refers to the fact that the variable universal policyowner bears the investment risk, and if the earnings on the cash value drop below the level anticipated when the policy benefit was reduced, further adjustment(s) may be needed.

The investment element of a paid-up term insurance policy can be obtained by surrendering the insurance for cash, subject to the same conditions governing the surrender of reduced paid-up insurance. The policyowner has to request a death-benefit reduction to create the equivalent of a reduced paid-up surrender option for a universal or variable universal life policy.

extended term insurance

Extended Term Insurance. The extended term insurance option provides paid-up term insurance in an amount equal to the original face of the policy, increased by any dividend additions or deposits and decreased by any policy loans. The length of the term is that which can be purchased at the insured's attained age, applying the net surrender value as a net single premium. The period for which term insurance is provided under a whole life policy, and under a 20-payment life policy, issued at age 35, is shown in Table 7-1.

Universal and variable universal life insurance policies do not have a *guaranteed* extended term surrender option. However, they are designed to work in a similar way to extended term insurance. These policies have no fixed or required premiums, and the performance of the policy depends on the account balance of the policy's cash value. The policy will remain in force as long as the cash value is sufficient to cover the next 60 days of charges for mortality (term charges for the net amount at risk) and administration, and until these charges consume the cash value.

Extended Term Insurance Surrender Option
• Amount of coverage is reduced by the amount of policy loans • Surrender value available to purchase extended coverage is reduced by policy loans

If the policy indebtedness is not deducted from the face of an extended policy, the company will be exposed to a dangerous form of adverse selection.

EXAMPLE

Consider the case of a person suffering from an incurable illness who has a $200,000 life insurance policy with a $100,000 cash value. If, to meet the cost of medical treatment or for any other reason, he or she borrows the maximum amount against the cash value, say $95,000, and then dies shortly thereafter, the company will be obligated to pay only $105,000, since the policy loan is deducted from both the cash value and the death proceeds. The total return will thus equal the face of the policy, or $200,000. The deduction of policy loans is based on the principle that a policy loan represents a prepayment of a portion of the face amount.

The effect of deducting the policy loan from *both* the surrender value and the amount of extended insurance is to produce a shorter period of term insurance than would be available if no loan existed. This is because the deduction is a much greater proportion of the cash value than it is of the face amount of the policy.

The change produced in a whole life insurance policy by its surrender for extended term insurance is plotted in Figure 7-3. This diagram reveals that, in direct contrast to the situation under reduced paid-up insurance, the protection element grows progressively larger, and the investment element progressively smaller, until the policy finally expires. The investment element is at a peak at the time of surrender, but is gradually used up in the payment of term insurance premiums.

Figure 7-3
Effect of Extended Term Insurance Option on Several Types of Life Insurance Contracts

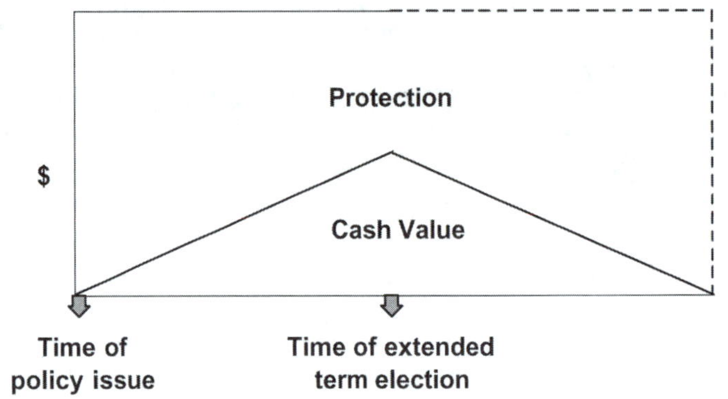

Effect on level benefit cash value life insurance contracts

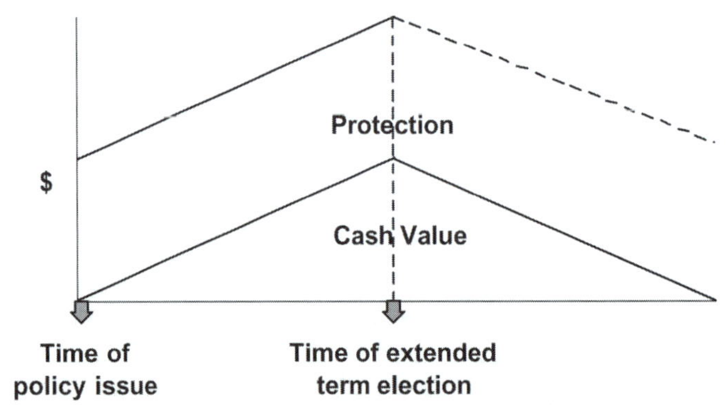

Effect on increasing death-benefit designs of universal and variable universal policies

Prohibited Provisions

backdating

Although the state laws are not uniform, most states prohibit insurers from including certain provisions in their policies. For various reasons, courts and state legislatures have determined that these prohibited contract provisions violate public policy. There are five generally prohibited provisions:

- **The insurance producer, who is the agent of the insurance company, cannot be made the agent of the insured for purposes of filling out the application for insurance.** If the producer could be made the insured's agent rather than the company's agent, then the insurance company could not be charged with knowing facts presented to the agent but not communicated to the insurance company by the agent.
- **Nonpayment of a loan cannot cause a forfeiture (loss of benefits).** The state laws generally provide that as long as the cash value of the policy exceeds the total indebtedness on the policy, the policyowner's failure to repay the loan or to pay interest on the loan cannot cause a policy to lapse.
- ***Less-value statutes* prevent an insurer from promising something on the face of the policy and taking it away in the fine print.** These laws are called less-value statutes because the insurer is prohibited from providing a settlement of less value than the death benefit of the policy.
- **There are limitations on the time for filing lawsuits against the insurer.** All states have *statutes of limitation* that control how long a person may wait before bringing a lawsuit of any type against another party. These statutes are designed to force people to sue in a timely fashion rather than waiting in the hope that evidence favorable to the other side will be lost. After the period specified in the statute has expired, the courts will not hear the lawsuit.
- **No *lengthy* backdating to save age is allowed**. *Backdating* a policy means issuing the policy as if it had been purchased at a date earlier than the effective date of coverage. The advantage of backdating is that the insured will pay lower annual premiums for the policy because the premium will be based on the younger age. The disadvantage is that the insured must pay the premium applicable to the length of the backdating. The policyowner will have paid for insurance protection during a period of time before the policy was issued when no coverage was provided. The statutes generally limit backdating to no more than 6 months.

Optional Provisions

In addition to the required and prohibited provisions, there are other provisions that are optional:

ownership provision

assignment

accelerated benefits

- ***Suicide provision***—Most life insurance contracts do not provide coverage for a death by suicide within the first one or 2 years after the policy is issued. If the policy does not contain a suicide exclusion provision, then a death by suicide is covered by the policy and the death benefit is payable to the beneficiary regardless of when the suicide occurs.

- ***Ownership provision***—Ordinarily the insured is the applicant and owner of the policy. The *ownership provision* describes some of the rights of the owner. The typical ownership provision stipulates that the owner of the policy is the insured, unless the application states otherwise. The provision also usually states that the policyowner may change the beneficiary, assign the policy to another party, and exercise other ownership rights.

- ***Assignment provision***—As with most contracts and most interests in property, the policyowner has the right to transfer some or all of his or her rights to another person. In contract law, this is known as assignment. The right to assign an ownership interest in an insurance policy exists even without an assignment provision in the contract. However, most contracts include an assignment clause because it sets out clearly the conditions upon which an assignment can be made. If the policy contains a provision prohibiting an assignment, any attempted assignment by the policyowner will not be binding on the insurer. If the policy sets conditions for an assignment, the policyowner must comply with these restrictions.

  There are two types of assignments, absolute and collateral. An absolute assignment is a transfer to another (the assignee) by sale or gift all the assignor's (policyowner's) rights. A collateral assignment is a transfer of some of the policyowner's interests to provide security for a loan.

- ***Plan change***—This provision gives the policyowner an important power to change the plan of insurance and provides that the parties may agree to make other changes in the terms of the contract.

- ***Accelerated benefits***—As a result of the AIDS epidemic and public concern about other terminal illnesses, most insurers have added a provision that permits the insured to withdraw policy death benefits under certain circumstances. The accelerated benefits provision states that if the insured develops a medical condition that drastically reduces an insured's life expectancy (to two years or less), then he or she may withdraw a portion of the policy's death benefit.

Additional Common Provisions

Accidental Death Benefits

accidental death benefit

This *accidental death benefit* provision is added to some insurance contracts in the form of a rider, or amendment to the policy. It is also known as the double indemnity provision because it normally doubles the standard death benefit if the insured dies accidentally.

Because this benefit is payable only in the event of the insured's *accidental* death, this term requires definition. In the absence of a specific definition in the rider, the word *accident* means an unintentional event that is sudden and unexpected. An *accidental death* is one that is caused by an accident. This seems quite clear, but it is not always easy to apply. There have been cases in which an insured has been mortally injured in an accident, but the actual cause of death is a disease. In this case, is the accidental death benefit payable? The answer is yes only if the accident was the cause of death. If the insured is in an automobile accident but dies from a heart attack, the accidental death benefit is payable only if the accident can be proven to have triggered the heart attack.

EXAMPLE

The insured died when driving an automobile. The car was severely damaged in the accident associated with the death. The cause of death was determined to be a heart attack.

The policy has a face amount of $50,000 and includes an accidental death benefit rider.

The insurance company claims the heart attack occurred first and caused both the death and the accident.

The beneficiary spouse with minor children thinks the auto accident occurred first and was the cause of the heart attack. The burden of proving this in order to collect the accidental death benefit is almost impossible to satisfy. The most likely outcome is that the insurer will only pay a $50,000 death benefit.

The problems caused by cases in which there is potentially more than one cause of death are eased somewhat by the practice of putting a time limit in the accidental death-benefit provision. Commonly, the death must occur within 90 days of the accident that caused the injury.

These basic definitions exclude coverage for any death that is the natural and probable result of a voluntary act. People are expected to be able to foresee the probable consequences of their actions. If one plays Russian roulette, jumps off buildings, or runs with the bulls in Pamplona, Spain, his or her death as a result of one of those activities cannot be described as accidental.

There are two types of accidental death clauses: (1) the *accidental result* clause, and (2) the *accidental means* clause.

EXAMPLE 1
We will pay this benefit to the beneficiary when we have proof that the insured's death was the result, directly and apart from any other cause, of accidental bodily injury, and that death occurred within one year after that injury and while this rider was in effect.
EXAMPLE 2
We will pay this benefit to the beneficiary when we have proof that the Insured's death was caused directly, and apart from any other cause, by accidental means, and that death occurred within one year after that injury and while this rider was in effect.

The most common type of provision that insurers use is the accidental result clause, because it is more favorable to the consumer. It is also because most courts have recognized that the difference between the two clauses is too difficult for many consumers to understand and have therefore ceased to recognize a distinction between the two types of clauses.

The distinction can be explained as follows: under an accidental means clause both the cause (means) of the death and the result must be unintentional. Under an accidental result clause, only the result must be unintentional. For example, assume that an insured is participating in an obstacle course race at a family reunion, and the race requires the racers to dive over a barrel, do a somersault, and run to the next event. The insured breaks her neck and dies doing the somersault. Because she was doing exactly what she intended to do, the means was not accidental although the result was certainly an accident. The accidental means clause would not pay the accidental benefit, but the accidental result clause would.

Another factor that has made accidental means clauses less attractive to insureds and less frequently used by insurers is the provision requiring that, in addition to being accidental, the means (cause) of death must also be violent and caused by an external agency. Courts have been liberal in their interpretation of these limitations in favor of the public.

Most accidental death-benefit clauses do not provide coverage in the event of the insured's death by suicide. If suicide of the insured (whether sane or insane) is excluded, then an examination of the insured's mental state at the time of the suicide is avoided. If the insured is sane at the time of the suicide, then it is an intentional act and it would not qualify as an accident. If the insured is insane, the suicide might be classified as unintentional because the insured may be presumed not to have been able to intend the consequences of his or her act.

Waiver of Premium

waiver of premium provisions

According to a typical *waiver of premium provision*, if the insured becomes totally disabled as defined in the life insurance contract, the insurance company will waive payment of premiums on the policy during the continuance of the insured's disability.

The disability waiver of premium has some limitations. For example, the waiver is excluded if the insured's disability begins after a specified age, typically age 60 or 65. The provision will typically not waive premiums if the disability is self-inflicted, the result of an act of war, or occurs before the insured’s fifth birthday. As with all contracts, it is important to pay close attention to the language used. Small differences in the language of the provision can make large differences in the obligations the insurer incurs.

It is important to distinguish the waiver of premium rider found in traditional whole life and term policies from the monthly deduction waiver rider found in flexible premium contracts like universal life and variable universal life. *Monthly deduction waiver* waives the monthly deductions (cost of insurance and monthly administrative fees if the primary insured becomes totally disabled. While this rider does not waive the scheduled premium, it waives the costs of insurance and administrative fee to ensure that the policy will not lapse during a period of total disability.

The following is a sample of a typical disability waiver-of-premium rider:

Definition of Total Disability. "Total disability" means that, because of disease or bodily injury, the insured cannot do any of the essential acts and duties of his or her job, or of any other job for which he or she is suited based on schooling, training, or experience. If the insured can do some but not all of these acts and duties, disability is not total and premiums will not be waived. If the insured is a minor and is required by law to go to school, "total disability" means that, because of disease or bodily injury, he or she is not able to go school.

"Total disability" also means the insured's total loss, starting while this rider is in effect, of the sight of both eyes or the use of both hands, both feet, or one hand and one foot.

Proof of Total Disability. Written notice and proof of this condition must be given to us, while the insured is living and totally disabled, or as soon as it can reasonably be done. As long as we waive premiums, we may require proof from time to time. After we have waived premiums for 2 years in a row, we will not need to have this proof more than once each year. As part of the proof, we may have the insured examined by doctors we approve.

Payment of Premiums. Premiums must be paid when due, until we approve a claim under this rider. If a total disability starts during a grace period, the overdue premium must be paid before we will approve any claim.

Refunds of Premiums. If a total disability starts after a premium has been paid, and if it goes on for at least 6 months in a row, we will refund the part of that premium paid for the period after the policy month when the disability started. Any other premium paid and then waived will be refunded in full.

When Rider Ends. You can cancel this rider as of the due date of a premium. To do this, you must send the policy and your signed notice to us within 31 days of that date. If this rider is still in effect on the anniversary on which the insured is age 65, it will end on that date.

This rider ends if the policy ends or is surrendered. It will not be in effect if the policy lapses or is in force as extended or paid-up insurance.

Guaranteed Insurability Option

guaranteed insurability option

The *guaranteed insurability option*, also called the *guaranteed purchase option*, helps protect policyowners in the event they become uninsurable. Under the standard provision, the policyowner receives the right to acquire additional insurance in specified amounts at specified times or ages. Typically, this provision allows additional purchases every 3 years and after the birth of a child, provided the events occur before the insured reaches a specified maximum age (often 45). The right to purchase additional insurance does not require *evidence of insurability* to exercise the option and the new coverage is normally not subject to a new suicide provision or a new incontestability clause.

The additional insurance need not be on the same plan as the basic policy to which the option is attached; the option is exercisable for any standard whole life or other cash value insurance policies offered by the company. Premiums for the new insurance are payable at standard rates at the insured's attained age on the option date. If the original policy contains a waiver-of-premium provision and accidental death benefits, the new policies will contain the same features, at the policyowner's option. For some, but not all companies, if premiums are being waived on the original policy at the time an option for additional insurance is exercised, premiums on the new policy will be waived and will continue to be waived if the insured is totally disabled, until the insured recovers.

EXAMPLE

Larry purchased a policy with a guaranteed purchase option when he was age 7. He exercised his right to purchase more coverage every 3 years until his 39th birthday. Because his children had entered college and the costs of tuition were squeezing his budget severely, he did not purchase more coverage when he was 42. Unfortunately, he was diagnosed with cancer at age 44. Consequently, he wants to exercise his guaranteed purchase option at age 45. The insurance company informed Larry that the option lapsed when he did not use it at age 42.

The options vary, but typically the policyowner is permitted to purchase up to $10,000 of additional insurance at 3-year intervals beginning with the policy anniversary nearest the insured's 25th birthday and ending with the anniversary nearest the insured's 40th birthday. The amount of insurance that can be purchased on each specified policy anniversary is usually limited to some percentage of the original face amount up to a specified maximum dollar amount, such as $60,000. Some policies also specify an aggregate limit (for example, two times the original face amount) on the amount of coverage that can be purchased under this option without evidence of insurability. Option amounts vary from company to company but may be as high as $100,000 per exercise option with some insurers. When the insured passes an age or event that triggers the right to purchase additional insurance but he or she does not exercise that option, the option lapses.

Some contracts also permit the purchase of additional insurance upon the insured's marriage or following the birth or adoption of the insured's children.

Some contracts even provide coverage automatically for 60 to 90 days after each option date.

The option is available for an extra premium that varies with the age of issue. These premiums reflect the company's estimate of the average amount of extra mortality that it will experience on policies issued without evidence of insurability. From the insured's standpoint, the premiums are the cost of ensuring his or her insurability. Premiums for the option are payable to the last anniversary at which it can be exercised—usually age 40—or to the end of the premium-paying period of the basic policy, whichever is earlier.

Automatic Premium Loan

The automatic premium loan feature states that at the request of the policyowner any premium may be paid by means of a loan against the surrender value provided a surrender value is available and large enough to cover the loan. Such a loan bears interest at the rate applicable to policy loans.

automatic premium loan provision

The *automatic premium loan provision* provides that any premium unpaid at the end of the grace period will be automatically paid and charged against the cash value without request from the policyowner. This automatic option must be requested previously by the policyowner, normally at the time of application.

The effect of the premium loan clause is to allow the policy to remain in force, decreased by the amount of premiums loaned with interest. Such extension will continue as long as the cash value at each premium due date is sufficient to cover another premium. Each premium loan increases the cash value by paying the premium until the next anniversary and cash value increase, lengthening the period during which the process can be continued. At the same time, however, the indebtedness against the cash value is growing by each loan and the accrual of interest. Eventually, a premium due date will be reached when the remaining cash value is not large enough to cover another full premium.

The principal advantage to the policyowner of an automatic premium loan provision is that in the event of inadvertent nonpayment of the premium or temporary inability to pay the premium, the policy is kept in force. Several additional advantages flow from this basic fact. First, premium payments can be resumed at any time (as long as the equity in the policy remains sufficient to pay premiums as they become due) without furnishing evidence of insurability. Second, special benefits—such as waiver of premium, disability income, and accidental death or double indemnity—remain in full force, contrary to the situation under the paid-up insurance options. Finally, if the policy is participating, the policyowner continues to receive dividends, which is usually not true of paid-up term insurance (nonforfeiture option).

Unless the provision is used only as a temporary convenience, it may be disadvantageous to the policyowner. If premium payments are not resumed, the *period* during which the policy is kept in force and the amount payable will usually be less than under extended insurance, and the disparity will become greater with each passing year.

In the event of the insured's death during the period covered, the insurer is better off financially under the automatic premium loan arrangement than under extended term insurance because the insurer receives additional premiums by way of deduction from the policy proceeds.

The effect of the automatic premium loan feature on the structure of a whole life policy is shown in Figure 7-4. Upon default of the first premium the effective amount of protection is reduced by the amount of the premium. Each year thereafter that the feature is exercised, the amount of protection is reduced by the premium due that year, plus interest on that premium and all unpaid premiums of previous years. Hence, the protection element will decline at a constantly increasing rate. The surrender value will be exhausted, however, before the protection element is reduced to zero.

Figure 7-4
Effect of Automatic Premium Loans on Whole Life Insurance Contracts

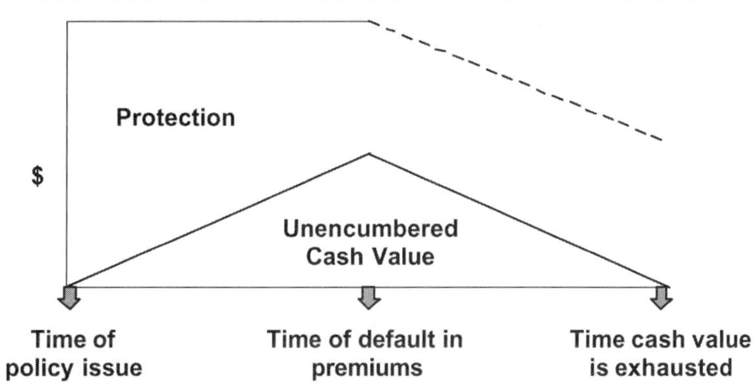

Protection From Creditors

The statutory protection provided for life insurance against creditors' claims is a complex subject. A life insurance policy is a valuable property right and thus creditors may attempt to acquire an interest in the policy's values. All states and the federal government have enacted legislation providing protection for life insurance against the claims of creditors.

Complicating the understanding of these protection statutes is the interest that a debtor may have in a policy. For example, the debtor may be the owner, the insured, the owner and insured, a collateral assignee, a beneficiary, or an owner that names his or her estate as the beneficiary. The main intent of these statutes is to protect the debtor's dependents, rather than the owner's interest, from financial destitution in the event of the debtor's death. The relationship of the debtor to the policy is the key to determining whether and to what extent protections from creditors may be available.

Creditors may seek to satisfy their claims out of the cash value of an in-force policy, or out of the proceeds of a matured policy. In practice, creditors have been unsuccessful in collecting cash values because insurance companies are under no obligation to pay money to anyone unless the policyowner gives permission to do so. Courts have been reluctant to force a policyowner to surrender a policy.

Once policy proceeds are paid to the owner or owner's estate, however, they are available to estate creditors on the same basis as any other unrestricted estate assets. If the proceeds are payable to a third-party beneficiary, they become the beneficiaries' property at the insured's death, and are free from the creditors of the policyowner or insured. The proceeds may then become attachable by the beneficiary's creditors.

Special rules exist when the federal government is the creditor. A federal government's tax lien overrides state exemption statutes, and may require an insurer to withdraw policy loan values up to the amount of the federal tax due. The federal government may also attach policy proceeds if the lien was attached prior to the insured's death.

The state exemption statutes are diverse in nature. The minimum objective is to protect against the claims of the insured's creditors for all or a portion of the proceeds payable to the insured's spouse and children. The most common goal is to protect the benefits of the insurance policy payable to anyone other than the insured's estate, during the insured's lifetime or at death, from the creditors of the insured.

Spendthrift laws, found in most states, are concerned only with the protection of proceeds held under a settlement agreement against the claims of the creditors of the beneficiary. These laws protect the proceeds only while in the hands of the insurer, and not after they have been received by the beneficiary, to "protect the beneficiary from themselves." The policyowner would insert this provision to prevent an irresponsible beneficiary from squandering a lump-sum distribution.

Look up the exemption statutes in states where you do business, since it is not possible to summarize state protections against creditors.

Common Disaster and Simultaneous Death

The rights of the policyowner or insured and the beneficiary are vitally affected in the case that the insured and beneficiary die in a common disaster, such as family members in a car accident, plane crash, an explosion or other tragic event. In some cases it may be impossible to determine who survived the other. Most all states have adopted the Uniform Simultaneous Death Act, which states that in the absence of evidence to the contrary, each person is presumed to be the survivor of his or her own property. In the case of life insurance, when the insured and the beneficiary have died and there is no sufficient evidence that they died other than simultaneously, the policy proceeds will be distributed as if the insured had survived the beneficiary. This result can be achieved by inserting a common disaster clause into the policy, which expresses the same interpretation as the Simultaneous Death Act.

An additional problem can occur if the beneficiary survives the insured, even by a moment. In this case the proceeds would be paid to the beneficiary's estate, delaying payment of the proceeds and adding administrative expenses to the process of passing the money on to the next in line. In an effort to avoid the undesirable consequences of a beneficiary's short-term survivorship of the insured, some states and some companies use a provision that states that the proceeds will be payable to a designated beneficiary only if the beneficiary survives the insured by a specified period of time, such as 10, 15, or 30 days or longer. This clause, requiring the beneficiary's survivorship of the insured for a certain period is known as a delayed-payment clause.

Policy Filing and Approval

If a policy is sold in a state but does not include a required provision or has not been filed with the state for approval, the courts will treat the policy as if it did include all the required provisions under the law of that jurisdiction.

The policyowner or beneficiary will be permitted to enforce the policy against the insurer as if it complied in all respects with the applicable state law. The state insurance commissioners are responsible for seeing that the insurance companies doing business in their state comply with their state's law regarding the permitted and prohibited policy provisions. A policy may not be issued or delivered in a state until it has been approved by the department.

If an insurer issues a policy that has not been approved by the insurance department, the policyowner may seek a refund of premiums paid or seek to enforce the policy. If a lawsuit is filed, the courts will enforce the unapproved contract against the insurer on behalf of the policyowner or the beneficiary. If a required provision is more favorable to the policyowner than the one actually included in the contract, the courts will treat the contract as if it included the more favorable provision. The insurer that violates the laws requiring filing of the policy and approval of its provisions by the state will also be subject to fines or other penalties (such as revocation of the insurer's right to do business in that state).

Settlement Agreements

Most life insurance policies provide that at the death of the insured, the proceeds are payable to the designated beneficiary in one sum, generally referred to as a *lump sum.* Many life insurers make the lump-sum death benefit payable through an interest-bearing account against which the beneficiary can draw checks. These accounts work much like a money market fund. The beneficiary can withdraw the total proceeds in one transaction or make partial withdrawals as funds are needed by writing checks. The balance in the account continues to earn interest until withdrawn. Even though the beneficiary can leave the benefits in the account and earn more investment income, over 90 percent of beneficiaries choose a single lump-sum withdrawal and take possession of all the proceeds.

settlement options

As an alternative to a lump sum payment, life insurance companies have a wide range of periodic income options available to beneficiaries and policyowners. Collectively, these contractual choices are known as *settlement options.*

General Concepts and Rules

When the proceeds of a life insurance policy are payable in a lump sum, the company's liability under the policy is fully discharged. If, however, the company retains the proceeds under one of the optional methods of settlement, its liability continues beyond the maturity of the policy and must be evidenced in a legal document, known as the *settlement agreement.*

The typical *settlement agreement* is one entered into between the insurance company and the policyowner to control the distribution of the policy proceeds to third-party beneficiaries after the insured's death. The agreement may be a part of the insurance policy, or it may be separate and distinct from the policy. It may be drawn up at the time the policy goes into effect or at any time prior to the insured's death. Although the policyowner can revoke the agreement at any time and substitute a new agreement, he or she can revoke the beneficiary designation only if such right has been specifically reserved. The policyowner may or may not give the primary beneficiary the right to dismiss the prior agreement after the insured dies. Upon the insured's death, the insurance company's obligation under the original contract terminates, and it assumes a new obligation defined by the terms of the settlement agreement. The insured may also enter into a settlement agreement with the insurer to provide payments to himself or herself from a surrendered policy's cash value.

If the insured did not elect a deferred settlement, or did elect one but gave the primary beneficiary the right to reject it, under the rules of most companies, the beneficiary may elect a settlement option and enter into an agreement with the company to govern the distribution of the proceeds. The beneficiary is usually given 6 months after the insured's death to elect a settlement option, provided the check offered by the insurer in full settlement of the death claim has not been cashed. Insurers pay interest on the portion of proceeds they hold after the insured dies, accruing from the date of death and continues accruing until the underlying proceeds are distributed to the beneficiary.

spendthrift clause

When a beneficiary elects the settlement option, or when the policyowner elects a settlement for his or her own benefit, a spendthrift clause cannot be included in the settlement agreement. A *spendthrift clause* states that the proceeds will be free from attachment by the beneficiary's creditors. This clause may be included in a life insurance policy or settlement agreement obtained by one person for the benefit of another, but it cannot be incorporated into an agreement by the person for whose benefit the agreement is being drawn up. Because of this, the policyowner may want to elect the settlement option on behalf of the beneficiary, especially if the beneficiary has credit problems, or could have them in the future.

Under the rules of many companies, a settlement agreement entered into between the company and the beneficiary must provide that any proceeds unpaid at the time of the beneficiary's death will be paid either to his or her estate in a lump sum or installments to designated contingent beneficiaries.

Contract Rates versus Current Rates

contract rates

The proceeds of a life insurance policy are in most cases taken by the beneficiary as a lump-sum payment. In making other modes of settlement available, the company promises to pay a series of installment benefits, based on various patterns of distribution, that have a present value precisely equal to the lump-sum payment. The policy contains tables that show the amount of periodic income that will be payable under the different options for each $1,000 of proceeds left with the company. These are referred to as *contract rates.* Under each option, a specified rate of income per $1,000 of proceeds is guaranteed in the policy. Insurers can, and often do, pay interest earnings in excess of the guaranteed rate to settlement options.

Interest Rates in Settlement Options

- Contract interest rates (such as 3.5 percent) are guaranteed as a lower limit on current rates when interest rates in the economy drop below the guaranteed rate.
- Contract interest rates remain fixed for the entire contract duration.
- Current rates are rates actually being paid under the settlement agreements.
- Current rates usually exceed contract rates.
- Current rates fluctuate with economic conditions.

current rates

From time to time, a company will modify the actuarial assumptions underlying the benefits provided under the optional modes of settlement, which means that the amount of periodic income per $1,000 of proceeds will change. Due to declining interest yields and growing longevity, these modifications will produce lower benefits per $1,000 of principal. Such benefit modifications can be made only for those policies and settlement agreements issued after the change. The benefits under existing agreements cannot be modified without the consent of the policyowner. Consequently, insurers rarely take steps to modify existing settlement agreements. Rates that are applicable to contracts currently being issued are referred to as *current rates.* There is no difference between the contract and current rates for policies and agreements issued since the latest rate changes. For all others, however, the difference can be significant.

Restrictions on contract rates are intended to protect the insurance company from adverse mortality and financial selection. For example, if a beneficiary could elect a life income option at any time, his or her attitude toward that right would be influenced by the condition of his or her health. If, after the insured's death, the beneficiary's health deteriorates, he or she will not consider a life income option appropriate, unless it is the cash-refund type. On the other hand, if the beneficiary's health over the years has been excellent, he or she might elect a life income option. Since beneficiaries as a group can be expected to behave this way, without a time limit or option selection the company would find itself with an undue proportion of healthy annuitants.

Right of Withdrawal

The beneficiary may be given the right to withdraw all or a portion of the proceeds held by the insurer under a deferred-settlement arrangement. If the beneficiary can withdraw all of the proceeds at any one time, subject only to a delay clause, he or she has an *unlimited right of withdrawal.* If the privilege is subject to restrictions, it is generally referred to as a *limited right of withdrawal.*

The right of withdrawal may be limited as to the frequency with which it can be requested, the minimum and maximum amounts that can be withdrawn at any one time or in any one year, or both. Limitations are imposed by insurers to control the cost of administration, and to prevent too rapid depletion of the proceeds by the beneficiary.

To hold down the cost of administering proceeds under deferred-settlement arrangements, life insurance companies will not hold small amounts (such as $10,000) under a settlement option. Most companies will not make monthly payments of less than $5 per $1,000 under this option. This rule is designed to assure liquidation of all proceeds and interest within a reasonable period.

Most policies reserve the right to delay cash withdrawals under settlement options for a period of up to 6 months. This is a counterpart to the delay clause required by law in connection with loan and surrender requests.

A right of withdrawal is included in a settlement agreement in order to provide flexibility. It can be used to obtain funds for emergencies or to meet the problem of inflation. It is especially desirable during the period when the beneficiary is caring for dependent children. In most cases, however, the right should be limited with reasonable restrictions to prevent premature exhaustion of the proceeds.

Right of Commutation

The right of *commutation* is related to the right of withdrawal. To commute means to withdraw the present value of remaining installment payments in a lump sum. The term is applied to proceeds distributed under a settlement option. It does not apply to proceeds held under the interest option. For all practical purposes, the right of commutation is identical to an unlimited right of withdrawal. The right of commutation is not automatically included in an installment arrangement. It must be specifically authorized in the settlement agreement.

Types of Settlement Options

Life insurance settlement options include

- the interest option
- the fixed-period option
- the fixed-amount option
- the life income option

The Interest Option

The simplest and most flexible of all settlement options is the *interest option*. The company pays interest to the beneficiary, but the proceeds are held until the expiration of a specified period or until the occurrence of some specific event. The interest option postpones the ultimate disposition of the proceeds. It must be followed by a liquidating option or a lump-sum distribution.

Interest-Only Option

- The interest-only option is frequently used for the primary beneficiary (keeping the proceeds intact for liquidation for a contingent beneficiary).
- Most often the interest-only option is payable to a surviving spouse. Frequently, the contingent beneficiaries are the children.

The company guarantees a minimum rate of interest on the proceeds, which is payable at periodic intervals, usually monthly. If the policy was participating, the proceeds are credited with the actual rate of interest earned by the company or, more likely, a rate approximately equal to the interest factor in the dividend formula. Excess interest is usually paid once a year on one of the regular interest-payment dates.

The primary beneficiary can be given varying degrees of control over proceeds held by the company under the interest option. If the policyowner wants the proceeds to go intact eventually to the contingent beneficiaries, he or she will give the primary beneficiary no rights in the proceeds, other than the right to receive the interest for a lifetime or for some other specified period. If the policyowner wants to provide flexibility to meet unforeseen needs, he or she may grant the primary beneficiary a limited right of withdrawal.

The beneficiary may be given complete control over the proceeds by receiving an unlimited right of withdrawal during his or her lifetime, as well as the right to dispose of the proceeds after his or her own death. If the primary beneficiary is given an unlimited right of withdrawal, the guaranteed rate of interest may be lower. Most companies will retain proceeds under the interest option for the remaining lifetime of the primary beneficiary, or for 30 years, whichever is longer. Thus, the interest option may be available to contingent beneficiaries. From the company's standpoint, some limit is necessary to control the cost of administration and to avoid an indefinite projection of contract rates. Generally, a company will not accumulate the interest; it requires payment of interest at least annually.

Fixed Options-No Life Contingencies

fixed-period option

fixed-amount option

The *fixed-period option* provides payments over a stipulated period, while the *fixed-amount option* provides payments of a stipulated amount. The two options are based on the same mathematical principles. They differ only as to whether emphasis is attached to the duration or to the amount of the payments. If the insured or the beneficiary wants the assurance of some income, however small, over a specified period, he or she should select the fixed-period option. If, however, the need is for temporary adequacy of income, irrespective of its duration, the insured or the beneficiary should choose the fixed-amount option.

The Fixed-Period Option. The essence of the fixed-period option is the certainty of the period over which the proceeds will be distributed. Any developments that increase or decrease the amount of proceeds available are reflected in the size of the monthly payments and not in the duration of the payments. Additional proceeds payable because of the insured's accidental death, prepaid premiums, dividend accumulations, or paid-up additions increase the amount of the monthly payments. Policy loans, if still outstanding at the policy's maturity, reduce the proceeds available and the size of the monthly benefits.

The Fixed-Amount Option. This option distributes a specified sum each month, or at some other periodic interval, until the proceeds are exhausted. Mathematically, it is based on the same compound-discount function that underlies the fixed-period option.

The principle can be explained in terms of $1,000 to be distributed in equal annual payments of $100, the first payment being due immediately. The liquidation will extend over a minimum period of 10 years, because the principal alone will provide payments for that period. The problem is to determine how much longer the payments will continue as a result of crediting compound interest to the remaining portion of the principal.

Because the amount of each payment is fixed under this option, any increase in the proceeds or interest lengthens the period over which payments will be made, and any decrease shortens the period. Thus, dividend accumulations, paid-up additions, accidental death benefits, and excess interest extend the period of liquidation, whereas loans outstanding at the insured's death and withdrawals of principal by the beneficiary shorten the period.

life income option

Life Income Options. Any settlement option based on a life contingency is called a *life income option.* The proceeds of a life insurance policy may be paid at a fixed rate over the lifetime of one or more beneficiaries. This type of arrangement, unique to life insurance companies, protects a beneficiary against the economic hazard of excessive longevity—outliving his or her income.

The principle underlying a life income option is identical to an immediate annuity. A life income option is simply the annuity principle applied to the liquidation of insurance proceeds (each payment is composed partly of principal and partly of interest on the unliquidated principal). Hence, the life income options are the same as the types of immediate annuities. The single-life annuities include

- pure or straight life annuity
- life annuity with guaranteed installments
- installment refund annuity
- cash refund annuity.

There are other types of annuities based on two or more lives, and combinations of the above annuities. While there is a counterpart among the life income options for every type of *immediate annuity*, it is not customary for a company to include the whole range of annuity options in its life insurance policies. The typical policy provides for a life income with payments guaranteed for 10, 15, and 20 years and the installment-refund option. Some companies include the joint-and-last-survivor annuity, and a few offer the straight life annuity.

Mathematically, the *straight life income* option is equivalent to a pure immediate annuity. It is a life annuity due (annuity payment made at the beginning of the period), because the first payment is due immediately upon maturity of the policy or upon election of the option, whichever is later. The monthly income provided per $1,000 of proceeds depends on the age and gender of the beneficiary and the insurer's assumptions of mortality and interest. Although the schedules of income guaranteed under various insurers' policies are similar, there is little uniformity among companies as to the combination of mortality and interest assumptions used to calculate the income payments. Benefits are provided at *net rates* (no expense charge), and there is no charge for the use of the life income settlement.

The *life income option with a specified period of guaranteed payments* is mathematically a combination of a fixed-period installment option of a specified number of years and a deferred life annuity. For example, a life income option that promises to provide payments of a specified amount to a beneficiary aged 45 throughout his or her remaining lifetime, guaranteed for 20 years, is a combination of a fixed-period installment option running for 20 years and a life annuity deferred to the beneficiary's age 65. If the beneficiary does not survive to age 65, the portion of the proceeds allocated to the deferred life annuity is retained by the insurance company.

Because the life income settlement options are essentially annuity contracts available without any applicable sales commissions or other expense loadings, they often provide more benefits for the same contribution than do separate annuity contracts. The only way to be certain that the settlement option is less costly is to make price and benefit comparisons with the annuity contracts available from other insurers. If an annuity contract is found to be more advantageous than the settlement option, that life insurer should be carefully scrutinized to determine its long-term financial strength.

The *installment refund option* is a combination of a immediate life annuity and decreasing term insurance in an amount sufficient to continue payments until the proceeds, without interest, have been paid out in full. This option promises to continue the monthly payments beyond the annuitant's death until the proceeds of the life insurance policy have been returned. At inception, the term insurance is in an amount equal to the proceeds, less the first payment (due immediately), but it decreases with each periodic payment and expires when the cumulative payments equal the life insurance proceeds committed to the installment-refund option.

The *cash refund option* is also a combination of a immediate life annuity and decreasing term insurance. Since the refund is payable in cash, rather than payable in installments, a slightly larger amount of term insurance is required.

The life income option is extremely inflexible. Benefits are calculated based on the age and sex of the primary beneficiary, and once the payments have begun, no other person can be substituted for the designated beneficiary. No right of withdrawal is available and no commutation privilege exists. Otherwise, persons in poor health would be inclined to withdraw the proceeds.

Implementing the Plan

The term *closing* means to make complete, to come together, to end, to conclude, finish, or culminate. Although closing comes at the end of the selling/planning process, it signals the beginning of a new account and a new relationship, as the prospect becomes a client. Ideally, closing should not be hard and should not be a negative experience for you or the prospect. It should be viewed simply as the culmination of the process, as securing commitment to your proposed recommendations, and receiving approval from the prospect to take action.

Preparing for the Closing Interview

In preparing for the closing interview, you should review the information gathered previously and highlight key areas. Refresh your memory on the details discussed, so you are very familiar with the client's information when you meet again. Review the client's needs, goals, and priorities, making note of factual and subjective information. Review any issues and concerns the client has raised in your conversations. You are now ready to prepare your closing presentation.

Review your recommendations and the reasoning behind the decisions you have made regarding the solutions you have designed. Analyze the alternative plans you have prepared, and be ready to discuss the benefits and drawbacks of each option. This will give your client the information he or she needs to decide what is best for them.

Mentally walk through the presentation, anticipating objections, concerns, and points of resistance that the client may raise. This will sharpen your focus on the important points of each option and the pros and cons to be considered. Be sure to organize any presentation materials you wish to show. Review these materials, so everything you plan to discuss is fresh in your mind. Check your briefcase to be sure all application materials are in adequate supply. You are ready to go!

Asking for the Sale

Closing requires carrying the interview to its natural conclusion, which is asking for the sale. The advisor must develop the skill of knowing when and how to ask the question that leads the prospect to make the decision to buy. It is a matter of commitment for the client to accept the product recommendation, the company, and the advisor. For the advisor, it means being skilled at asking the question in a way that demonstrates sincerity and integrity, avoiding any perception that you are a stereotypical life insurance salesperson just "turning a sale."

At this point, you can ask an open-ended question:

- Where do we go from here?
- How would you like to proceed?
- What's our next step?

Or, you can be more direct with a closed-ended question:

- Would you like to start this plan today?
- Is there any reason why you would not want to get this started?

Closing is simply seeking agreement from the prospect that the solution proposed is a proper and acceptable plan to address the need or needs uncovered in the process.

Watch your client's interest level and buying signals. If the client is acting and speaking in ways that indicate he or she is ready to buy, stop talking and confirm the sale. Observe nonverbal cues, such as leaning forward, listening carefully, open arms, and relaxed posture. These all indicate interest. If the nonverbal communication is negative, such as crossed arms, negative expression, tense posture, or gazing off into space, ask if they have a question about something you have presented or if there is something on their mind.

Checking Questions

You may stop occasionally during your presentation to draw out questions from your prospect, or to ask a few questions yourself. In this way, you can continually check what your prospect is thinking and feeling, and manage your sales approach to take into consideration your prospect's understanding. This is empathy in action.

Explain to your prospect that while you are presenting your recommendations, you would like them to please interrupt if anything is unclear. Encourage your prospect not to leave a question until later, unless they know it will be answered in the course of the presentation.

Here are a few examples of checking-type questions, or trial closes, that will keep you in tune with your prospect during the closing interview. Some of your questions should require more than a "yes" or "no" answer. Hearing yes too often will lull you into complacency.

- Is this making sense so far?
- Do you see where we are headed with this line of reasoning?
- What do you think so far?
- Wouldn't you agree?
- Isn't that right?
- Is that the way you see it?
- Does that coincide with your thinking?
- Do you agree?

If you notice your prospect frowning or making a facial expression that demonstrates a reaction other than understanding or agreement, stop and ask about it.

- Did the point I just made raise an issue?
- Suppose this was not a concern. Would there be any other reason why we could not put this program in force today?

This final checking question is designed to reveal the true objection. Once known, it can be addressed.

Dealing with Objections

Although the list of reasons not to buy life insurance seems almost unlimited, most objections can be grouped into four main categories:

- No need
- No trust
- No hurry
- No money

Even though each objection must be dealt with individually, it is reassuring to know that most can be identified and treated in ways that will soon become second nature to you. Further, by categorizing objections this way, you are able to organize your thoughts, see objections as less threatening than they may seem otherwise, and respond to them with more confidence and from a position of strength.

Addressing Objections and Managing Resistance

The first step in answering an objection is to listen to the prospect. No one likes to be interrupted or feel they are not being heard. Listening to what the prospect has to say will help you understand the objection. Encourage the prospect to explain his or her feelings about the issue.

Give yourself and the prospect the opportunity to confirm your understanding of the objection by restating, or rephrasing it. This gives you an opportunity to learn more about the exact nature of the objection. This also puts you in a better position to address it.

As you talk with your prospect, use trial closes, such as, "Other than affordability, is this the product you think will best suit your needs?" or "Is this a feature you would definitely like in your plan?" Because answering objections takes practice and experience, it is important not to become discouraged if at first you are not successful.

Five Steps for Handling Objections and Concerns

The process for handling objections involves five steps:

1. **Listen** to the prospect.
2. **Summarize** or rephrase what the prospect tells you
3. **Wait** for the prospect to respond.
4. **Clarify** and categorize the response.

5. **Deal** with it directly, honestly, and completely; then resume your presentation.

Let's examine each step in this process to see how it can help you become more comfortable and proficient in dealing with your prospects' questions, comments, and concerns.

Listen. In order to be able to respond to an objection, you must be sure you understand it. When your presentation is interrupted, listen carefully to what the prospect has to say. Do not take a glib, "yes-but" approach to every objection the prospect offers. Listening carefully will reassure your prospect about their concerns. It tacitly acknowledges that they may be uncertain and prone to skepticism, while it treats as legitimate their genuine concerns and objections. This process deals with prospects' questions and concerns the way you would want yours treated if you were the prospect.

Validate the prospect's thoughts and feelings on the topic. If you do not acknowledge a concern, but instead try to wrestle it down, all you succeed in doing is putting more distance between you and your prospect. Responses such as "I understand how you feel," or "I can appreciate that," show your prospect that you are listening to him or her and that you care about what he or she has to say.

Rephrase What You Heard. The next step is to repeat what the prospect told you to make sure you heard it correctly. Restate what the prospect said using key phrases as a summary. Communication is a tricky process. The message sent by one person is not necessarily the one received by the other. By repeating what the prospect said, you are making sure that you received the message correctly. You are also communicating that you are interested in the prospect and concerned about correctly understanding what they think and how they feel.

Part of your goal in repeating the prospect's comment or question is breaking it down into its main parts. For instance, a prospect might tell you he and his wife are planning a very expensive vacation this summer and it will tie up their cash for several months. He likes what you've told him, but it isn't something he and his wife can handle financially until after they get back and pay their bills.

Does this mean that your prospects will be ready to start the plan soon after they return from their trip, or does it mean that it may be several months before they will be able to afford it? That would certainly be a major consideration in how you approach their situation. A 3-week delay is one thing; a 6-month postponement is quite another.

By repeating the comment back to your prospect, you make sure you get the right message. In this case, you might respond by indicating you would like to make sure you understood what he just said. Reiterate that he mentioned that he liked the recommendations, but that he and his wife have planned a rather expensive trip this summer and would not be able to begin this plan until after they return and pay their vacation bills. After you repeat your understanding, let the prospect confirm that the message was correctly, or incorrectly, received. This shows the prospect that you are an attentive listener interested in understanding their situation and perspective.

Another technique is to rephrase the objection in the form of a question. Rephrase what the prospect just told you, and then ask the prospect to give you more information or clarify their concern. Encourage your prospect to expand and tell you more. When the objection has been precisely defined, you will be in a better position to respond to it.

Wait For a Response. By asking for confirmation or correction, you keep the prospect talking. Giving your prospect the chance to respond to your version of their objection will bring amplification of the part that is of greatest concern. For example, what the prospect might really be saying above is that it is not so much the vacation that is preventing the implementation of the plan as it is a cash flow problem. In fact, the situation may not be corrected even after the travel expenses are paid. This information is critical and needs to be discussed further. This is why the next step is so important.

Clarify and Categorize the Response. Rephrase the question or comment to clarify it. Explore the meaning of the response. For example, you might be able to clear up the matter of when the plan can be implemented by asking if he means he and his wife will be able to begin the plan within a week or two after they return, or if he feels it will take longer than that for their finances to get back in shape. If the prospect says that the situation is temporary and will be resolved within a week or two after the vacation, you can treat the matter lightly. Reassure the prospect and go on with your closing attempts. If, on the other hand, the prospect tells you that it will be a matter of several months before the plan can begin, you may be facing an objection that will stop the sale unless it is satisfactorily resolved.

The Shopper
"(Prospect), if you feel you want to 'shop,' that's fine. You might find a bargain policy and the 'best' company if you have the time, the inclination, and the perseverance.
May I make a suggestion? Rather than shop for a bargain policy and the 'best' company, find the best advisor—one in whom you can have complete faith and confidence.
I would like to be considered for that job as your insurance advisor. May I show you the kind of work I do so that you will be in a position to judge?"

If, when you attempt to close, the prospect tells you that it is too expensive, ask how much too expensive it is. Is it $50 a month too expensive? Is it $100 a month too expensive? If we were to make it less expensive by $50 a month, would you be able to commit to it? If the prospect says yes, you have a sale; if the prospect says no, you have identified an objection that you may or may not be able to overcome. If you got a dollar commitment earlier, this should not happen. If it does, it may indicate that the prospect is not serious about or ready to make a commitment to a plan.

By rephrasing the comments and waiting for a response, you isolate a yes or no answer. Get your prospect to talk out whatever it is that is really bothering them. Enable your prospect to withdraw the comment gracefully, or pinpoint specific information you need about the question or comment to deal with it effectively.

Remember the value of silence. After you have paraphrased the prospect's remarks, do not say anything until the prospect has responded. If you break the silence first, you will probably lose the intended result.

Reassure and Resume. You can reassure the prospect in one of several ways. You may be able to use a motivating story or anecdote. You may use a sales visual appropriate to the situation or go back to one of the supporting materials you used in the presentation. You are deliberately treating the comment or question directly, honestly, and completely.

Feel, Felt, Found

An excellent technique to use to respond to a prospect's concern is called "feel, felt, found."

> "I understand exactly how you feel."

"Many of my clients felt the same way..."

"...until they found that this plan was a good solution for their situation."

Notice that this technique begins by using the acknowledgement step. You then put the prospect at ease by reassuring him or her that this is a common feeling. You finally point out that once others were introduced to this new idea, they often accepted it. This neutralizes the situation and gives you an opportunity to address their concern. People like to do what other people do. It gives reassurance to know that others have already done this, and have gone through a similar process or faced a similar problem. The herd instinct is very powerful for many people in unfamiliar situations. Once they decide, reassure them that they made a good decision.

Chapter Seven Review

Key terms and concepts are explained in the glossary. Answers to the review questions and the self-test questions are found in the back of the book in the Answers to Questions section.

Key Terms and Concepts

contract of adhesion
policy face pages
free-look provision
grace period
policy loan
incontestable clause
divisible surplus provision
reinstatement provision
nonforfeiture options
surrender options
cash surrender value
delay clause
reduced paid-up insurance
net single premium
extended term insurance
backdating
ownership provision
assignment
accelerated benefits
accidental death benefit
waiver of premium provisions
guaranteed insurability option
automatic premium loan provision
settlement options
spendthrift clause
contract rates
current rates
fixed-period option
fixed-amount option
life income option

Review Questions

1. List the types of information generally found on the face page of a life insurance policy. [1]
2. Explain why standard policy provisions might be more accurately called required provisions. [1]
3. List the goals of entire contract statutes. [1]
4. What benefit does the grace period provide for the policyowner? [2]
5. List the typical requirements that must be met for a policyowner to reinstate a life insurance policy. [2]
6. Explain how the backdating of a life insurance policy provides both an advantage and disadvantage for the policyowner. [3]
7. Explain how the automatic premium loan feature works on fixed-premium policies. [4]
8. Explain how the guaranteed insurability option helps policyowners protect themselves against the possibility that they, as insureds, may become uninsurable. [4]

9. When the reduced paid-up insurance nonforfeiture option is elected, what type and amount of coverage is provided? [5]

10. How does the reduced paid-up insurance nonforfeiture provision in a whole life policy differ from a similar reduction under a variable life or a universal life policy? [5]

11. Why is the insurer allowed to assess an interest charge against the amount borrowed? [6]

12. A policyowner intends to surrender her policy with a reported $60,000 cash value. Two years ago she took out a $10,000 policy loan with an 8% fixed policy loan rate. None of the loan has been repaid, and there are no applicable surrender charges. How much will she receive as a result of surrendering the policy? [6]

13. Describe the extended term insurance nonforfeiture option. [6]

14. A policyowner elects the extended term insurance option for a policy having $30,000 cash value, a $100,000 face amount, and indebtedness of $10,000. [6]
How much extended term insurance will be provided?
How much will be available to purchase the extended term coverage?

15. Explain when a spendthrift clause in a settlement agreement is enforceable. [7]

16. List and describe the four fundamental settlement options that have evolved from settlement option concepts. [7]

17. Explain why the interest option is simple and flexible. [7]

18. Define the fixed-period option and the fixed-amount option. [7]

19. Describe the flexibility features available with the fixed-amount option. [7]

20. Explain the underlying principle of a life income option. [7]

21. Describe the following life income options: [7]
Straight life income option
Life income with guarantee (period certain)
Installment-refund option
Cash-refund option

22. Describe the two functions the prospective policyowner plays in the creation of a life insurance contract. [8]

23. Explain the key elements in implementing the plan. [8]

Self-Test Questions

1. The premium for Irene's life insurance policy is still unpaid at the end of the grace period, what action will the insurance company take on her 10-year-old whole life plan with $8,000 cash value and the APL (automatic premium loan) option?
   - (A) cancel the policy
   - (B) surrender it for the $8,000 cash value
   - (C) advance the premium payment automatically as a loan from the $8,000 cash value
   - (D) move the policy to an extended term plan under the settlement options

2. A contract of adhesion is a contract in which
   - (A) both parties contribute to the terms and conditions
   - (B) the values exchanged are not equal
   - (C) both parties make a legally enforceable promise
   - (D) one party has the option of affirming or rejecting

3. If an insured dies during the grace period, the insurance company can
   - (A) consider the death claim invalid
   - (B) deduct overdue premium plus interest from the settlement
   - (C) require new evidence of insurability to reinstate the policy
   - (D) activate the automatic premium loan provision, if selected

4. The nonforfeiture provisions of a policy would be used in which of the following situations?
   - (A) at the death of the insured
   - (B) at the termination of the policy
   - (C) to guarantee dividends
   - (D) in either a term or permanent policy

5. The spendthrift clause is intended to protect life insurance proceeds from attachment or seizure by
   - (A) the insured's creditors
   - (B) the surviving spouse's creditors
   - (C) the beneficiary's creditors
   - (D) both the insured's and the beneficiary's creditors

6. Which of the following statements concerning reduced paid-up insurance is (are) correct?

   I. There is no surrender privilege under reduced paid-up life and endowment policies.
   II. A reduced paid-up policy is payable on the same conditions as the original policy.

   (A) I only
   (B) II only
   (C) Both I and II
   (D) Neither I nor II

7. Which of the following statements concerning life settlement options is (are) correct?

   I. A life income option and an annuity are based on the same principle.
   II. The life income option is flexible and after payments have begun, changes can be made to the income amount and who receives them.

   (A) I only
   (B) II only
   (C) Both I and II
   (D) Neither I nor II

READ THE FOLLOWING DIRECTIONS BEFORE CONTINUING

The questions below differ from the preceding questions in that they all contain the word EXCEPT. So you understand fully the basis used in selecting each answer, be sure to read each question carefully.

---

8. All of the following are typically requirements for reinstating a lapsed policy EXCEPT

   (A) The company may require that any outstanding policy loan be paid.
   (B) Proper evidence of insurability has been submitted and accepted by the company.
   (C) Back and current premiums must be paid, with interest.
   (D) The policy must first be surrendered for cash.

9. All of the following statements concerning the waiver of premium rider are correct EXCEPT

    (A) The waiver will not be granted if the insured's disability begins after a specified age.
    (B) The waiver will not be granted if the insured's disability is self-inflicted or the result of war.
    (C) The typical rider requires that the disability last at least 2 or 3 weeks before premiums will be waived.
    (D) The definition of disability used in the rider determines whether premiums will be waived.

10. All of the following are types of life income settlement options EXCEPT

    (A) pure or straight life annuity
    (B) life annuity with guaranteed installments
    (C) cash-refund annuity
    (D) interest-only annuity

LIFE INSURANCE TAXATION, MARKETING, ETHICS, AND SERVICE

8

Learning Objectives

An understanding of the material in this chapter should enable you to

1. Explain the income, estate, and gift taxation of life insurance.
2. Explain the modified endowment rules.
3. Explain life and viatical settlements and their place in the insurance and investment marketplace.
4. Describe planning concepts using life insurance, including pension maximization, mortgage cancellation, supplemental retirement plan, charitable gifts, estate liquidity, wealth replacement, and the cost of waiting.
5. Discuss the ethical issues associated with being an advisor.
6. Outline the responsibilities and duties the advisor-client and advisor-insurer relationships create.
7. Discuss service activities and responsibilities of the advisor that will improve relationships with clients.

This chapter examines the income, estate, and gift taxation of life insurance and several life insurance marketing concepts. A rapidly developing area in life insurance, life and viatical settlements, is discussed. The chapter then explores the ethical issues associated with the role of an advisor, and the responsibilities and duties the advisor and company have to each other in the insuring process. Finally, the last step of the selling/planning process, Service the Plan, is covered. Methods for servicing clients to improve and build successful, professional advisor-client relationships are presented.

The Income, Estate, and Gift Taxation of Life Insurance

Income Tax Treatment of Life Insurance

We will briefly summarize the income tax treatment of premiums, death benefits, cash values, dividends, loans, withdrawals, surrenders, 1035 Exchanges, and modified endowment contracts (MECs).

Premiums

Premiums paid for individual life insurance policies in the United States are usually considered a personal expense and are not deductible for income tax purposes. However, there are exceptions to this:

- Premiums paid for life insurance in an alimony agreement may be deductible.
- Premiums paid for life insurance that is owned by a charity, and where proceeds are paid to the charity as the beneficiary, may be deductible as a charitable contribution.
- In business situations, employers are allowed to deduct premiums for life insurance protection if paid in the form of compensation or a bonus to an employee. The employer may then deduct the amount of the compensation or bonus as a business expense.
- If life insurance is part of a pension plan, the premiums are deductible as part of a contribution by the employer to a tax-qualified plan.

It must be emphasized that a deduction for premium payments may not be claimed in any case in which the taxpayer is a policy beneficiary.

Death Benefits

Generally, death proceeds from a life insurance policy are exempt from income taxation when paid in a lump sum (Internal Revenue Code Sec. 101). Congress recognizes that life insurance ownership achieves a social purpose, so it writes tax laws to encourage the purchase of life insurance products. There are some exceptions to this general rule, and not all state income tax laws follow the lead of the federal tax laws.

When death proceeds are held by the insurer for future withdrawal or distribution, all interest earned on the proceeds is taxable to the beneficiary as ordinary income.

Accelerated Death Benefits. Amounts received under a life insurance contract covering the life of a terminally or chronically ill insured are excludible from income as amounts payable by reason of the death of the insured if certain conditions are met. Terminal illness must be certified by a physician, and the illness or condition typically must be expected to result in death within 24 months of the certification.

transfer-for-value

Transfer-for-Value. One exception to the general rule for income tax-free death benefits is encountered when a policy has been transferred from one owner to another in exchange for valuable consideration (something of value—usually money). This is known as *transfer-for-value*. A part of the proceeds would be subject to federal income tax. The taxable amount is the difference between the face amount and the amount paid to transfer the policy from the previous owner to the new owner, and the premiums made by the new owner. Keep in mind that this type of transfer could negatively affect income taxation of policy proceeds.

Certain transactions are exempt from the transfer-for-value rule, including situations in which the policy is sold to the insured. Transfer-for-value situations are often found in business applications of life insurance used to insure employees, partners, officers, and others. The following insurance policy transfers are exempt from the *transfer-for-value rules,* so they will not result in a loss of the tax exemption for death proceeds:

1. transfer of the policy to the insured
2. transfer to a partner of the insured
3. transfer to a partnership of which the insured is a partner
4. transfer to a corporation of which the insured is a shareholder or officer
5. a transfer in which the transferee's basis is determined in whole or in part by reference to the transferor's basis (*carryover basis*)

Life Insurance Living Benefits

If a policyowner holds a life insurance policy until death, the cash value buildup within the policy, which has not been taxed during the insured's lifetime, escapes taxation permanently as it passes to the beneficiary without income tax and estate tax, if properly planned.

Cash Values

Tax rules relating to money received from the policy during the lifetime of the insured are discussed next.

cost basis

Cash Surrenders. To determine if income tax is due on the surrender of a policy for cash or at the maturity of an endowment, it must be determined if the amount received from the policy over the life of the contract exceeds the net premiums paid. Net premiums paid means the gross premium less any dividends or cash withdrawals received, and less any outstanding loans. The resulting amount is called the *cost basis*, meaning the amount the policyowner paid with after-tax money. The total net premiums are then subtracted from the amount of cash the policyowner receives upon surrender or maturity. Any amount received in excess of the owner's cost basis is reportable as ordinary taxable income in the year received. Premiums paid for supplementary benefits, such as waiver of premium or accidental death riders are not included in the cost basis.

Matured Life Contracts. An exception to the tax-free treatment of policy proceeds is encountered when a policy's benefit becomes payable during the insured's lifetime because he or she has reached the maturity date. The proceeds are not considered a death benefit, and any gains in the policy would be considered ordinary income for the tax year in which they are distributed. The cash proceeds received will be taxable to the extent that they exceed the policyowner's cost basis in the policy (that is, the after-tax premiums paid).

Most current cash value policies have resolved this issue by offering maturity riders that extend the contract, allowing the policy to continue until the death of the insured. Interest paid is fully taxable to the payee as ordinary income. Electing an interest-only settlement option may also postpone the taxation of gains in the contract. The policyowner should consult with his or her tax advisor in such a situation before the maturity date of the life insurance contract.

LIFO/FIFO

Dividends. The cash dividend is taxable only when all dividends paid exceed the amount of premiums paid into the policy. Dividends are generally taxed on a first-in first-out *(FIFO)* basis; that is, dividends (and withdrawals) are treated as a nontaxable return of capital (refund of premiums) to the extent of premiums paid. Withdrawals in excess of premiums paid are taxable as ordinary income. *LIFO* tax treatment, or last-in first-out, means that gains (interest, profits, earnings) are recovered before contributions. Withdrawals of dividends or cash value are taxed as income first (LIFO) if the policy is classified as a modified endowment contract (MEC), discussed later.

If dividends are withdrawn or the policy is surrendered, a calculation is made to determine if proceeds received are in excess of premiums paid, resulting in ordinary income tax being due in the year received on any excess amount. For this reason, as well as others, paid-up additions is generally the dividend option recommended.

If a policyowner chooses not to receive the dividends in cash, but allows the dividends to accumulate at interest with the insurance company, the interest earned on the dividends is subject to taxation as interest income. Interest payments on the dividends are treated the same as interest on any type of savings account.

Loans. The loan provision gives the policyowner the right to borrow a percentage of the cash value that has accumulated in the policy. Loans are not taxable income while the policy is in force. If a policy is surrendered, or lapses with a loan outstanding, and if that loan, with other cash value, is greater than the cumulative premium payments made, there will be a taxable gain on the difference.

Special attention should be given to policies with loans. As interest rates rise and fall, and loan amounts accrue, the policy could reach a point where it will be depleted of cash value and in danger of lapsing. Monitor the policy to assess its status, and advise the client to repay loans or pay loan interest if the policy loan begins to deplete the remaining policy values. Policy loans should be considered a last source of funds in most circumstances.

Withdrawals. The cash value in a universal life type policy (that is not a modified endowment contract or MEC) can be withdrawn up to the policy cost basis (FIFO) without incurring income tax. Any gain withdrawn after the entire cost basis has been withdrawn will be subject to ordinary income tax. ithdrawal features are associated with universal life policies. Withdrawals of gains from a life insurance policy during the first fifteen policy years that are associated with a reduction in the policy's death benefit will be subject to the LIFO tax treatment, even if the policy is not an MEC.

Sec. 1035

Sec. 1035 Policy Exchanges. Section 1035 Exchange is an exchange of insurance contracts that allows for the deferral of taxes that would be due if the policyowner surrendered one policy and purchased another in two separate transactions. Section 1035 allows the non-taxable exchange of

- An existing life or endowment policy for a new life or endowment policy or qualified LTC policy
- An existing life or endowment policy for a new annuity or qualified LTC policy
- An existing annuity for a new annuity or qualified LTC policy
- An existing LTC policy for a new qualified LTC policy

The Pension Protection Act of 2006 provides tax-free exchange of qualified LTC contracts from one insurer to another, or from an annuity or life insurance contract to a qualified LTC contract without incurring a taxable event. Qualified LTCI riders are eligible as well.

When a policyowner exchanges an existing policy for a new one and does so in accordance with the Internal Revenue Code guidelines of *Sec. 1035*, no gain is attributed on the exchange. The adjusted basis of the old policy is carried over to the new one. Only the newly added premium paid after the exchange will be measured for MEC status. A Sec. 1035 exchange is allowed only when transferring cash values from an annuity to an annuity, life insurance to life insurance, or life insurance to an annuity contract. The new policy must retain the same insured and policyowner as the original policy.

modified endowment contract (MEC)

Modified Endowment Contract. The *modified endowment contract* or *MEC* came into being with the 1988 amendment to the tax code (Technical and Miscellaneous Revenue Act (TAMRA), IRC Secs. 72 and 7702A). Prior to this time, people were putting large sums of money into life insurance contracts so they could accumulate funds on a tax-deferred basis and then take tax-free withdrawals by means of policy loans. This was contrary to the intent of the tax code—that life insurance was to be used primarily to provide a death benefit. TAMRA provided that if a policy was over-funded (whether at issue or at a later date), it would be classified as an MEC, and as such, any distribution from the policy representing a gain would be taxed.

To determine if a policy should be classified as an MEC, the seven-pay test is applied. The seven-pay test limits to the amount of premiums that can be paid into a life insurance policy to that amount of net annual premiums that would make the policy paid up within 7 years using the cash value accumulation test (CVAT).

Material changes that occur to a policy once it is in force will cause the policy to be retested. Examples of a material change include a face amount increase or decrease, the addition of a rider or an increase in its amount, a reduction in rating, a change to nonsmoker status or a policy withdrawal. The rules apply as if the changes existed since the beginning of the policy. Your home office should be able to guide you on the classification of a policy as an MEC in these situations.

If a policy is or becomes an MEC, it is treated the same as any other life insurance policy, with one exception. Distributions or withdrawals any time before death are treated like premature annuity or individual retirement account (IRA) distributions, on a *LIFO* tax basis to the extent there is gain in the policy. Under the interest-first rules, any distributions from an MEC are taxed as income first and a recovery of basis second. In addition, the taxable gain is subject to a 10 percent penalty, unless the distribution is made after age 59½ or death, or as a result of disability or annuitization. Distributions from an MEC include:

- policy loans (including automatic premium loans)
- cash dividends
- withdrawals
- surrenders

If a policy becomes an MEC, it remains an MEC for as long as it exists. The "taint" (MEC status) carries over to any policy that is issued in exchange for a MEC, even if the new contract would not normally be classified as an MEC. This means that care must be taken when making a 1035 exchange of a MEC.

A Sec. 1035 exchange (tax-free exchange in which one policy is exchanged for another if certain rules are met) is a material change for purposes of the MEC rules. According to the IRS, the policy received in exchange will be treated as a newly issued policy with a new 7-year period beginning on the date of exchange. The new policy must be tested under the seven-pay test rules. Cash values transferred from the existing policy does not count as premium. If the policy fails the material change test, it will be classified as an MEC. Once again, look to your home office for guidance in these situations.

Estate Taxation of Life Insurance

Because the federal estate taxation of life insurance is complex, this section provides only a brief review of some of the major issues. Although the death benefits of a life insurance policy are generally free of income taxation, they can become includible in an insured's estate and subsequently subject to federal estate tax and estate administrative expenses. There are three basic situations in which life insurance is included in a decedent's gross estate:

- when it is payable to the insured's estate
- when the insured possessed incidents of ownership in the policy at the time of death
- when the insured transferred incidents of ownership by gift within 3 years of death

probate

Proceeds Payable to the Estate. Life insurance proceeds are not generally part of the *probate* estate, which involves the passing of the will through the local court system where the deceased lived. Life insurance proceeds pass by provision of contract directly to the beneficiary, bypassing probate. Thus, the proceeds can be paid promptly to the beneficiary, without the delay caused by the administration of the estate. There is no public record of the death-benefit amount or to whom it is payable.

The proceeds do become a part of the probate estate if they are paid to or for the benefit of the insured's estate. Life insurance proceeds payable to the executor for the benefit of an insured's estate are also includible in the estate, regardless of who owned the contract or who paid the premiums. There are many reasons (in addition to avoiding federal estate taxation) why insurance advisors should not recommend that life insurance be payable to a decedent's estate:

- Insurance payable to a decedent's estate subjects the proceeds to the claims of creditors (exclusions and amounts vary by state).
- Insurance payable to a decedent's estate subjects the proceeds to the costs and delays of probate administration and possible estate taxation.
- In many states, life insurance proceeds are exempt from state death taxes (either fully or partially) if payable to a named beneficiary. They become subject to such taxes if they are payable to the insured's estate.

incident of ownership

Possession of Incidents of Ownership. A life insurance policy is included in an insured's estate if he or she possessed an *incident of ownership* in the policy at the time of death. An incident of ownership is broadly defined as any right to the policy's economic benefits. When insurance proceeds are paid to a named beneficiary other than the insured's estate, incidents of ownership in the policy at the time of death are the key criterion for inclusion. The regulations provide that incidents of ownership include (but are not limited to) the power to

- change the beneficiary
- assign the policy
- borrow on the policy
- surrender the policy
- exercise any other essential contract rights or privileges

To remove life insurance proceeds from the reach of federal estate tax, the insured must divest himself or herself of all significant rights and privileges under the contract.

Transfers by Gift within 3 Years of Death. Life insurance is included in the gross estate of an insured who transfers incidents of ownership in the policy by gift within 3 years of his or her death. Transfers made more than 3 years before the insured's death are not includible in the insured's estate, assuming the insured has retained no incidents of ownership.

If estate inclusion and tax is a potential issue, a policy on the estate owner should be owned from its inception by a third party. This could be the insured's spouse, adult child, or an irrevocable life insurance trust (ILIT). This third party should pay all premiums, because inclusion may result if premiums are paid from funds provided by the insured. If a trial or preliminary application is used to determine if the prospect is insurable, it is best to have a trust or another third party serve as applicant. The third party should also be the beneficiary for all proceeds. Check with the insurer's procedures and the treatment under the laws of the local jurisdiction.

The purpose of this brief review of federal taxation of life insurance is to alert you to the questions your prospects and clients may ask, and to give you an appreciation for the importance of the proper implementation of an insurance policy. It is not definitive, so you should not give tax advice based on this information. When a client believes that a personal tax problem might result from the use of life insurance, the client should consult his or her own tax advisor. Your company may be able to help you in specific cases. As a service to your clients and as an opportunity to gain prospects from referrals, you should establish a relationship with one or more estate planning attorneys and a CPA familiar with estate taxation.

You may depend upon your life insurance company to provide the client with accurate information when any notice of taxation is sent. Ask your agency or home office for further information regarding the tax reporting and technical support for the products you sell.

Gift Taxation of Life Insurance

The transfer of the policy from one individual to another party (such as a relative or an employee's irrevocable life insurance trust) is a gift subject to tax. In addition, a continuing annual gift results if a person pays premiums on the policy. There is also a continuing annual gift for an employee if their employer pays premiums, because this employer payment represents compensation earned by the employee that is indirectly transferred to the policyowner. Such potentially taxable gifts may avoid taxation if they qualify for the annual gift tax exclusion. Gifts made directly to beneficiaries generally qualify, while gifts to insurance trusts may be considered future interests that do not qualify for the annual gift tax exclusion. For this reason a Crummey trust [or Crummey provisions to an irrevocable life insurance trust (ILIT)] is used to qualify the gift as a gift of present interest, making it eligible for the annual gift tax exclusion.

Life and Viatical Settlements

life settlement

A segment of the industry that is growing rapidly is the life settlement market. A *life settlement* involves the selling of an existing life insurance policy by its owner to a third party. In exchange for a cash settlement, the policyowner transfers ownership and all other rights of the policy to that third party. The sale of the life insurance policy is completed through a broker or financial advisor to a settlement company or other provider, to obtain a sum of money that exceeds the policy's cash value, but which is less than the death benefit. Life settlements are coming to be seen as a new investment asset class by many, and growth and acceptance of this sector are expected to continue.

It is estimated that sales of life settlements experienced a robust growth up until 2007, when it was estimated that $12 billion in face amount of life insurance was sold in life settlements. More recently, the amount sold has declined, largely due to the global financial crisis and the resulting lack of availability of funding, and more stringent underwriting practices. Based on a recent estimate by the U.S. Government Accountability Office, $7 billion of face amount in life insurance was sold in life settlement transactions in 2009

(Life Settlements Task Force, Securities and Exchange Commission, July 22, 2010). The market appears to be rebounding with the economic recovery.

Typically, life settlement offers are made to affluent senior clients over age 65 who have experienced a significant decline in health since the policy was first issued, making the policy more valuable due to the insured's poor health. A life settlement is a way to release dormant cash value in a life insurance policy that is no longer needed or wanted. Seniors who need cash to pay for living expenses, long-term care expenses or other needs, may find this an attractive alternative. Other situations that may lead to life settlements include the following:

- A buy-sell or key person policy is no longer needed.
- A policy is performing poorly.
- There are no heirs to benefit from the coverage of a policy.
- An anticipated estate planning need is no longer present.
- A policy represents insurance on a debt that has been retired.
- A single life contract is being replaced by a second-to-die policy.
- Renewal premiums for a level term policy will be significantly higher.
- A product is no longer suitable.
- Coverage is no longer affordable.

viatical settlements

The life settlement market emerged from the viatical settlement market, in which the insureds generally own smaller policies, have very limited financial resources, and need money. *Viatical settlements* refer to instances in which death is considered imminent, and the insured must be medically certified to be terminally ill with a life expectancy of less than two years. Life settlements focus on policies insuring older individuals with life expectancies greater than two years, typically between two and ten years. These secondary market transactions generally involve wealthy seniors who are not terminally ill and own larger policies. When death is imminent (less than 2 years), most insurers provide policyowners with accelerated benefits for prepayment of death benefits.

It is well established in both practice and case law that the owner of a legitimate, in-force life insurance policy has the right to sell it, even to a third party who has no valid insurable interest in the life of the insured. Through a life settlement, a policyowner can obtain a higher value for their cash value policies than they can achieve if they allow the policies to lapse, or they surrender or borrow from them. The benefit is even greater to the policyowner of term insurance, since surrendering it would generate no cash surrender value and the life settlement company may pay handsomely for it. When used properly, a life settlement offers a valuable alternative to lapsing or surrendering a policy, and helps open doors to more beneficial investment opportunities.

The settlement company serves as a secondary market to facilitate transactions between the original owners of life insurance policies and those who buy policies to speculate on the timing of the insureds' deaths. The settlement provider keeps a policy in force by making subsequent premium payments, and collects the proceeds at the policy's maturity (the earlier of the maturity date or the death of the insured). All types of policies, normally beyond the contestability period, are life settlement candidates. Companies use a variety of criteria to calculate an offering price for a policy, and some of the characteristics of the majority of cases that are selling today are listed here:

- face amount ($500,000 to $5 million)
- anticipated premiums to maintain the policy until maturity
- insured's age (70 or older)
- health status and health conditions
- client's overall situation
- life expectancy (120 months or less)
- policy structure (maturity age 200 or greater, minimum level annual premium less than 6 percent of death benefit)
- loans and money drawn against the policy
- insurance company's rating (A or better)
- policies beyond contestable period

There have been problems associated with life settlements including fraud and misrepresentation of policy values and insureds' life expectancies, lack of competitive bids and bid-rigging, ethical treatment of policyowners, commission irregularities, investors not earning what they anticipated, a lack of confidentiality for the insureds, and lack of insurable interest. Many of these problems have been resolved in today's marketplace, largely due to competition, self-regulation of the industry, licensing requirements, and regulatory oversight. There is currently much legislative debate and activity regarding life settlements, and it is expected that this will continue.

It is very important to carefully evaluate a situation and exercise due diligence in the selection of a settlement company. A reputable and financially sound institutional investor, such as a bank or insurance company, treats settlements much the same way as an insurer underwrites new business, by creating a portfolio using the law of large numbers and pooling settlement contracts. Institutional investors have come to realize that big blocks of properly underwritten policies acquired through life settlements can form a very predictable, very conservative, and very profitable source of income. The settlement provider performs medical and financial underwriting, just like an insurer. Funding is derived from capital markets by major institutions from around the globe. Like individually issued policies, there is no individual interest in any one policy. Private or individual investors may provide unreliable funding, and create a potential problem with privacy concerns in situations in which individuals have a financial stake in the insured's health and longevity.

One of the latest developments is partial settlement; in this case a policyowner receives less cash than under a full life settlement. In return, he or she can name a beneficiary to receive a portion of the death benefits when the insured dies.

Controversies Regarding Life and Viatical Settlements

While most companies recognize that there are cases for which a life settlement is in the best interest of the client, some settlements, particularly investment-oriented settlements, are a cause for concern.

1. First, life insurance policies sold purely for investment can threaten the tax-favored status of life insurance. Life insurance products receive favorable tax treatment based on the social benefit they provide—protecting survivors from financial ruin. Take away the social benefit and you take away the reason for the tax-favored status.
2. Second, insurance companies price products on the assumption that some will lapse. Policies that are settled are not likely to lapse, since it is in the investors' best interest to continue paying premiums. Although the overall effect of life settlements is likely to represent only a small percentage of life insurance in force, a company or product line may be adversely affected if lapse assumptions do not accurately reflect the impact of life settlements.
3. Third, if beneficiaries are not involved in life settlement decisions, they may try legal means to recover what they think should have

been their inheritance. Even if the lawsuits fail, they will consume the beneficiary's and life insurance company's resources.

4. Fourth, life settlements are not always in the best interest of the policyowner or his or her beneficiaries. If the policyowner does not want or need a policy, or has a need for cash, there are other options, such as policy loans, that can be used to meet the immediate needs of the policyowner while still protecting a portion of the death benefit for beneficiaries.

Life settlements have been surrounded in controversy, and there are conflicting views as to their value. While reputable life settlement providers do exist, in the past, this business was largely unsupervised and unregulated. There has been rapid development of the regulatory environment as this business has grown. Carriers have also been involved in efforts to manage the potential effects of life settlements. Many insurance companies discourage or prohibit their agents from engaging in life settlement transactions. Many companies are taking actions to minimize or avoid life settlements before they occur. Most common is a review of forms and requests on in-force policies to identify potential settlements. More than half of all companies ask applicants directly whether they plan to settle the policy for which they are applying.

Proponents of life settlements say they will make life insurance a more attractive product, due to the increased value offered by a secondary market for life insurance. This provides liquidity to an illiquid product, and provides an alternative to what the insurer offers. Life settlements, on average, offer three to four times the cash surrender value of the policy. In at least half of the cases, the proceeds from life settlements are used to purchase additional insurance.

As with any other recommendation you make, proper fact-finding must be done and suitability issues addressed. The need, the product, and the prospect must be correctly matched.

Stranger-Originated Life Insurance (STOLI)

A spin-off of the settlement market and a very controversial development in the life insurance business is stranger-originated life insurance (STOLI). STOLI is defined as a life insurance policy initiated for the benefit of a third party investor who at the time of policy origination has no insurable interest in the insured—the major criticism of these transactions by the industry and state regulators. STOLI practices include cases in which life insurance is purchased with premium financing arrangements, resources, or guarantees from or through a person or entity who, at the time of policy inception, could not lawfully initiate the purchase. At the time of policy inception, there is an arrangement or agreement to directly, or indirectly, transfer the ownership of the policy and/or the policy benefits to a third party, who would expect to receive the death benefits. Some of these transactions are driven by the demand for policies in the life settlement market.

The main characteristic of STOLI arrangements is that insurance is purchased purely as an investment vehicle, not to provide for the insured's beneficiaries. STOLI goes by several names, including investor-initiated life insurance (IILI), zero premium life insurance, investor-owned life insurance (IOLI), "free" life insurance, and non-recourse premium financing, among others. Non-recourse financing is a program that allows an investor to make a loan to the insured that covers the cost of the policy. The loan is repaid through a percentage of the death benefit, or the debt is erased if the policy is transferred to the investor or sold to a life settlement company after 2 years. The insured is promised that he or she can walk away from the arrangement after 2 years with no repayment of the loan and no personal recourse.

There is a great deal of legislative activity regarding STOLI transactions. The NAIC has adopted model state statutes addressing life settlements, including provisions addressing licensing of brokers and providers, policyowner disclosure for those buying policies, and regulators examination and enforcement powers. As of July 2010, more than 45 states have adopted legislation that would amend the states' life/viatical settlements statutes to add consumer protections and address concerns regarding the proliferation of STOLI. Much of the legislation is designed to stop STOLI, and not to restrict or impede legitimate life settlements. With respect to state securities laws, 48 states treat life settlements as securities. The SEC has recommended to Congress that it amend the definition of security under federal securities laws to include life settlements.

Life Insurance Marketing Ideas

A multitude of marketing ideas exist for selling life insurance, for the simple reason that it is such an important financial product and can serve so many purposes in a person's life. Below are just a few of the needs life insurance can address. We are sure you and your colleagues can think of others. **Be sure to get compliance approval from your company before using any sales concept with the public.** Some marketing concepts may not be permitted by your company, or may require specific language or methods of presentation to use with the public.

The Many Uses of Life Insurance—The Swiss Army Knife of Financial Products
• Provide a death benefit • Provide income to survivors • Secure a line of credit • Fund a buy-sell agreement • Guarantee future insurability • Equalize an inheritance • Pay estate taxes • Create an estate • Give to charity • Supplement college, retirement, and other expenses • Pay funeral and last expenses • Pay mortgages and debts • Provide an employee benefit • Protect a business from financial loss

Supplemental Life Insurance Retirement Planning (SLIRP)

Supplemental Life Insurance Retirement Plan (SLIRP)

Have you ever considered life insurance as a potential source of additional funding for retirement? Life insurance is not, and should not be, the first vehicle that comes to mind when considering retirement funding. However, there are many advantages to using permanent life insurance to supplement retirement income. Life insurance, properly structured through the marketing concept known as *SLIRP (Supplemental Life Insurance Retirement Plan),* can provide a preretirement death benefit, tax-deferred cash value accumulation, tax-free withdrawals contingent on certain stipulations, and an ultimate tax-free death benefit to beneficiaries.

Here's how SLIRP works:

- The cash surrender value for universal life and variable universal life policies, and dividend values for whole life, if available, can be withdrawn to supplement retirement income. As long as withdrawals do not exceed the cost basis, there is no taxable distribution. The cost basis is the investment in the contract, and is generally the amount of premiums paid.

- After the cost basis is reached, loans can be made against the policy's cash value. The result is an income tax-free cash flow that can supplement retirement income. Interest will be at current rates, but the loan does not have to be repaid. The interest is simply added to the loan. Keep in mind that although neither the loan nor the interest needs to be repaid, you have to watch the cumulative amount of the loan so that the policy is not in danger of lapsing. The policy should be kept in force; should the policy be surrendered or lapsed, taxes would have to be paid on all policy loans that represent gains. Of course, the amount of any unpaid loan, plus any interest accrued, is deducted from the policy's death benefit before payment to any beneficiaries.

Benefits of SLIRP. SLIRP has the following benefits:

- Generally an income-tax-free death benefit.
- Can be tailored to individual needs.
- Can be structured to avoid the early withdrawal penalties of qualified retirement plans.
- Can be pledged as collateral for a loan.
- Availability of waiver-of-premium rider can continue premium payments upon total disability.
- Government-defined annual contribution limits found in pension plans, IRAs, and other retirement plans do not exist, provided the policy stays within the tax law definition of life insurance.

Risks of SLIRP. SLIRP has the following risks:

- If using a UL policy, the interest rate must be adequate to support a sufficient cash value growth so that supplemental income can be generated. This concept may not work well in lower interest rate environments.
- The earlier this plan is started before retirement, the more effective it will be. It takes time to develop cash value in any permanent policy. Lump sum or excess premium payments in the early years of the policy will also help accelerate cash value growth.
- If loans are used, you must carefully monitor the loan amount and loan interest amount in relation to the cash value growth in the policy. You do not want the loan interest increase to exceed the regular cash value growth in the policy, or the policy will begin to

lose its value and subsequently will not be able to be sustained without increased premium or loan payments.

Pension Maximization

pension maximization

There is a tough decision for those in line for a defined-benefit pension at retirement, one that could cost thousands of dollars. It's called the "pension dilemma," because the retiree must decide whether to take a full pension benefit and expose his or her spouse to a loss of benefits at death, or take less than the maximum single-life benefit in exchange for continuing benefits after death for the spouse. Fortunately, for many couples, there is another alternative, known as *pension maximization.*

As an example, let's say a worker is eligible for a $1,000 monthly pension benefit at retirement. He will receive that amount under the single-life option. The problem is that this benefit will be paid only as long as he lives. At his death, the pension benefits dies with him. This is fine if he's single, but not if he's married. Should he die first, his spouse not only loses her husband, but also $12,000 a year in income.

This is why most married people select a joint and survivor option, which pays benefits as long as either partner is alive. Since the spouse has a legal claim to his or her spouse's benefits, this is the option automatically offered by pension law to married retirees. Before a retiree can elect a single-life option, both husband and wife must agree in writing. However, the cost can be high.

Although the actual number depends on many factors, a typical $1,000 monthly benefit could be reduced significantly. For the sake of discussion, if a joint and full survivor option is selected, the single-life benefit of $1,000 could be reduced by as much as $250. This adds up to $3,000 a year—$30,000 over a 10-year period—in lost benefits.

Pension Maximization Option. The pension maximization concept is reasonably simple. At retirement, the worker and spouse opt to take the single-life benefit option rather than a reduced joint and survivor benefit to receive the maximum pension benefit for as long as the worker lives. The individual eligible for a pension purchases a sufficient amount of permanent life insurance prior to retirement, naming the spouse as beneficiary. The couple uses the difference between the amount for a single versus a joint and survivor benefit to pay the life insurance premiums on the pension candidate.

The death benefit of the life insurance is informally earmarked to replace the lost pension benefit if the retiree dies first.

Target Market for Pension Maximization. The ideal candidate for pension maximization is someone who meets all the following criteria:

- participates in a defined-benefit pension plan
- several years away from retirement
- married
- healthy enough to qualify for life insurance coverage

Risks of Pension Maximization. Pension maximization has the following risks:

- In order to determine whether or not this alternative will work, the employee should first check with his or her pension plan administrator and find out about the projected benefits under the straight life option, and what the decreased amount will be each month to add the spouse under a survivorship option. Ideally, the amount of premium required for a policy that will insure the pension should be no larger than the difference between the amount for a single versus a joint and survivor benefit.
- If the illustration shows out-of-pocket premium payments ceasing because dividends or cash values are used to fund the policy, keep in mind that the premium is due throughout the life of the policy, until the insured dies. Therefore, if the dividend scale or interest crediting rates are reduced, additional out-of-pocket premiums will be necessary in order for the spouse to obtain the proceeds at the insured's death. The life insurance must be able to remain in force at lower projected interest rates, if not guaranteed rates.
- An extremely critical issue to address is whether the pension plan requires the retiree to select the joint and survivor option in order to continue postretirement medical benefits for both the retiree and his or her spouse. It may not be wise to pursue the pension maximization alternative if it means medical coverage will cease for either spouse.
- Making a comparison of different plans requires an advisor to provide the insurance costs and annuity cash flows on an after-tax basis. The advisor should compare these with an after-tax pension benefit. What first appears to favor pension maximization may not hold true on an after-tax basis.

- If a private life insurance plan is purchased, it may have to provide higher benefits if there is a provision for cost-of-living adjustments (COLA) in the pension. COLAs may be included in the pension and must be accounted for in the life insurance plan.
- Some pension plans have a “pop up” provision. If the spouse dies first, the retiree’s benefit pops-up to the higher individual retirement option amount. This benefit would negate one of the benefits of the life insurance plan.
- If an insurance premium is missed on a life insurance policy, it may cause the policy to lapse.
- How will private insurance and annuity costs and benefits be affected by interest rates, inflation, or a change in marital status?
- The pension fund is guaranteed by the pension plan sponsor. If a life insurance policy is purchased, the benefits will depend on the long-term financial strength of the company providing the plans.
- If a pension maximization plan depends on the candidate obtaining a life insurance policy, have all approvals been obtained and will the policy be in full force before it is too late to change your option selection with the pension plan? Certain conditions may prevent the worker from obtaining a life insurance policy on a favorable basis, or at all.
- Life insurance rates are based primarily on age. The younger the insured is when making this decision, the lower the rates. However, pension maximization may work even if the worker is at or near retirement.

Pension Maximization Benefits. The benefits of pension maximization include:

- The retiree receives the maximum pension benefits to which he or she is entitled.
- The spouse shares in the maximum benefits. Should the retiree die first, even though his pension stops, the spouse’s income continues in the form of insurance proceeds, which are received income tax free. In fact, these insurance proceeds can be set up as an annuity, with income benefits guaranteed for life, just like a pension.
- Should the spouse die first, the maximum benefits will continue. The life insurance can be cash surrendered, the beneficiary changed, or the cash value used to purchase paid-up insurance.
- Cash values accumulate tax-deferred in the life insurance policy. If the couple lives well into their golden years, the insurance can

protect other assets for their heirs. In fact, no matter what happens, their estate can be protected, enabling them to pass assets on to their children, grandchildren, or a favorite charity.

- The advisor should *strongly* recommend that the retiree weigh the options *very* carefully before deciding. Sold properly and in the right situation and set of circumstances, this strategy can be very beneficial to the plan participant and his or her family. Sold improperly, this strategy can potentially have adverse financial consequences for the pensioner or his/her spouse.

Mortgage Cancellation

The family home is one of every American's most treasured assets. However, what happens if one of the income producers who support the payment of the mortgage dies? In a dual-income situation, what happens if one person dies? Besides the emotional trauma, a surviving spouse may experience a significant drop in household income and be unable to meet mortgage payments.

Banks and mortgage companies encourage homeowners to purchase mortgage life insurance, which will pay off any mortgage balance in the event of a premature death of the homeowner-insured. In many cases, the bank or mortgage company is the beneficiary on this insurance. The mortgage company receives the life insurance benefits, and the family receives the deed to the house.

However, the surviving spouse may not to want to remain in the home. The daily reminders may be too difficult for the spouse and family to handle, the house may be too big to maintain, the spouse may want to move closer to family and friends, or relocate for a better job. Additionally, it may not be the best financial move or the right time to pay off the home.

Instead, it may be better to purchase a personally owned life insurance policy, which gives the spouse more options and provides them with full control over how the proceeds can be used. The policy would not be tied to the house, so if the family moves, the policy can go with them. It would continue to be available for the many purposes previously discussed. If the policy is whole life, it will have tax-deferred accumulation, a fixed and guaranteed level premium, guaranteed death benefit, and loan values. The cash value can be used to pay off the mortgage early, if that makes sense, based on the interest rate on the mortgage loan and the overall financial situation of the family and their financial options and goals.

Estate Planning

As families age and children mature and move out on their own, there is often a tendency for people to think that their life insurance needs diminish or even disappear. In some cases this may be true, but for most families the need for life insurance, especially permanent insurance, does not diminish; it simply changes.

The Value of Life Insurance. The need for life insurance during retirement cannot be separated from the estate planning process. Although life insurance may serve a lifetime purpose such as supplementing retirement income, its importance for estate planning is the death benefit it provides. Life insurance can be very important for estate planning, which provides many opportunities for new sales for the following reasons:

- ensuring adequate income for a surviving spouse and other dependents
- planning for final expenses, including estate settlement costs and taxes
- enhancing an existing estate or creating an estate where none exists
- equalizing the estate when a family business is involved

Ensuring Adequate Income for Dependents. Ensuring adequate income for surviving family members is the goal of many life insurance purchases. The concept of human life value is common in sales to young families who are dependent on the income earned by the prospect. It appears in older families as well. When wage earners die, their most valuable asset—their ability to earn income—dies with them. If others are dependent on their income, those survivors must either adjust their lifestyles or find a way to replace the lost income. Life insurance is the obvious choice for income replacement.

For most couples, the same situation exists after retirement. Earned income has been replaced by retirement income, but the amount of that income is often tied to the life of the recipient. At the death of one member of a couple, both Social Security benefits and company pension benefits can drop dramatically. Without proper planning, the surviving spouse may find it difficult to maintain his or her lifestyle.

Final Expenses and Estate Settlement Costs. Using life insurance proceeds to pay final expenses makes good financial sense at any age. It is one of the most common applications of life insurance, and it is as valid for estate planning purposes as for any other purpose.

estate liquidity

Life insurance makes cash available when it is needed most—at the time of the insured's death. It ensures that the cash needed to pay funeral costs, debts, probate and administrative costs, and final income taxes will be there. Life insurance can also provide the funds necessary to pay state and federal death and estate taxes. These purposes are generally known as *estate liquidity* needs.

The need for cash to settle an estate increases as the size of the estate increases. Administrative fees are often tied to the size of the estate and, under current law, the federal estate tax is progressive. This means that the tax rate increases as the size of the taxable estate increases. Consequently, the need for life insurance, especially in estates with little liquidity, increases.

On December 16, 2010, Congress passed the Tax Relief, Unemployment Insurance Reauthorization and Job Creation Act of 2010. This legislation provided for a short-term extension of the Estate, Gift and Generation-skipping Transfer taxes for 2010, 2011 and 2012. Provisions included the reunification of estate and gift taxes, and a 35% top rate and $5 million exemption for estate, gift and GST taxes. Additionally any unused exemption could have been transferred to one's spouse. The $5 million exemption amount was indexed for inflation in 2012.

With the American Taxpayer Relief Act of 2012 (ATRA), there is finally legislation reforming the federal wealth transfer tax system that provides some stability and better ability to plan. The key components of the legislation provide:

- *Tax rates*. Congress compromised to set the maximum tax rate at 40 percent. There are lower rates in the table, but the maximum 40 percent rate applies to transfers over $1 million.
- *Exemption amount (applicable exclusion amount)*. The exclusion amount for all wealth transfer tax systems is $5 million, indexed annually for inflation. Because inflation indexing already applied in 2012, the applicable exclusion amount for 2013 was $5,250,000, and may be indexed again for 2014 and subsequent years.
- *Portability of applicable exclusion amount*. The portability provision permits the surviving spouse to inherit and use the unused exclusion amount of the deceased (first-to-die) spouse. For

example, if Harry died in 2013 and left his widow Sally $1 million, she can leave as much as $9,500,000 tax-free when she dies.

- *Estate tax deduction for state estate or inheritance taxes.* The estate deduction for state estate and inheritance taxes is now permanent. The federal estate tax credit for state death taxes paid under prior estate tax law is repealed.
- *Unified estate and gift tax system.* The wealth transfer system treats property transferred by gift during lifetime, or property transferred after death under a unified system. This means all transfers during life or at death are treated the same.

Creating and Enhancing an Estate. Life insurance can create an estate where none exists. It is property bought with a contract and contractual guarantees that will deliver large amounts of money upon the death of the insured. Life insurance is essentially a financial mechanism that guarantees the desired accumulation at the time of death regardless of when that death occurs. For people with limited resources who want to leave something for their spouse, children, or other purposes, life insurance may be the obvious answer.

Equalizing the Estate. Another appropriate use of life insurance in estate planning is to equalize distributions to heirs. Like income continuation, equalizing distributions is a problem common to business owners.

EXAMPLE

Consider the case of Carl Anderson. Carl owns a dairy farm. His estate, including the farm and its equipment, is valued at $680,000, and like many farmers, he is "cash poor." Most of his assets are tied up in farming.

Carl and his wife have two children. His son left the farm and works as an accountant. His goal is to someday save enough money to open his own firm, and his father would like to be able to help him realize his dream. Carl's daughter and her husband live in a house Carl built for them on his property, not far from his own house. Carl's son-in-law works the farm with Carl, and as Carl has gotten older, the son-in-law has taken on more and more responsibilities.

Carl would like very much to leave the farm to his daughter and her husband when he dies, but he is faced with a dilemma. First, he wants to make certain that his wife will be secure. Second, he would like to be able to help his son realize his dream of opening his own accounting practice. How can Carl meet all three of his objectives?

We have already talked about using life insurance to ensure survivor income. Carl can purchase life insurance to provide a stream of income for his wife, and he can arrange the transfer of the farm's ownership in a way that will allow his wife to remain there until her death.

One solution to meeting his objectives for his son is to use life insurance to equalize the benefits. Carl can purchase life insurance with a benefit equal to the value of the farm, equalizing what he leaves behind for each child.

Another solution is to use life insurance to fund a buy-sell agreement with his daughter and son-in-law that will sell the farm to them, returning cash to his estate. The cash in the estate can be used to secure his wife's future and, at her death, the remainder can be divided equally between the children.

There are many other possibilities, and no one way is always applicable. As with all estate planning issues, the property owner's goals are the primary consideration, and the final solution must be the one with which she or he is most comfortable.

Charitable Giving

Life insurance can be used to make charitable contributions. Clients do not have to be wealthy to leave money to a charitable organization, and many people choose to contribute to a charity at their death. An existing life insurance policy, or one purchased specifically for that purpose, makes an excellent device for such planned giving.

While there is no immediate gift or income tax advantage to making a charity the beneficiary of an existing life insurance policy, life insurance is an excellent vehicle for completing the charitable intent of the policyowner. At the donor's death, the proceeds of the policy go directly to the charity without passing through the donor's estate, but the value of the policy is included in the estate if it is owned by the donor. If paid to the charity, it could qualify for an estate charitable deduction.

From an estate tax point of view, a better approach is to make a gift of the policy to the charity, transferring ownership and removing it from the estate. If the value of the policy exceeds the annual gift tax exclusion amount, the excess qualifies as a charitable contribution for gift tax purposes. Gifts of life insurance are considered gifts of present interest as long as the recipient of the policy has all policy rights. To receive the income, gift, and estate tax advantage of making a gift of life insurance, the donor must make a gift of his or her entire interest in the policy. If any right or control over the policy is maintained, the gift will not qualify.

Properly structured, the purchase of new policies may provide income tax benefits to the donor in addition to meeting the charitable intention. Premium payments may be income tax deductible if made to the charity to pay premiums on a policy owned by the charity on the donor's life. If the donor purchases the policy or has any incidents of ownership in it, it will be included in his or her estate. If the charity purchases the policy and the donor has no ownership interests, the policy will not be part of the donor's estate.

Advantages of Life Insurance in Charitable Giving. Many prospects will not initially make the connection between charitable giving and life insurance. Charitably inclined prospects frequently need to be educated about the role and advantages of life insurance in a charitable giving program.

- The face value of life insurance is guaranteed by the insurance company. A definite amount can be earmarked for the charity. Life insurance is not subject to the fluctuations that may affect stocks, bonds, or real estate.
- Life insurance allows a donor to leverage his or her contribution. A substantial bequest can be made for relatively small and manageable premium payments. Premiums can also be paid in advance. On the other hand, an outright gift of the premium amount will cease on the donor's disability or death. Disability waiver of premium can be added to the life insurance policy.
- Proceeds of a policy gifted to charity escape federal estate tax, probate, and other administrative costs. The proceeds go directly to the charity.
- Life insurance can also serve as a wealth replacement vehicle for the donor's heirs, to replace any assets given to the charity.
- An outright gift of a life insurance policy and/or premium payments made subsequently can offer tax advantages to the donor.
- The out-of-pocket costs of the gift are reduced by a current income tax deduction.

The Cost of Waiting

cost of waiting

Another effective sales approach designed to emphasize the need and advantage of beginning a life insurance program today is called the "*cost of waiting*." A comparison between the costs and values of a plan started today and one started 5 or 10 years from now can show a dramatic difference in the face amount of protection a given premium can purchase, as well as the cash value that can accumulate over the years. By waiting, the premium will grow increasingly higher, the cash value growth over the prospect's life will be smaller, the prospect will be without protection while they delay, and they could lose their insurability in the interim. These are all good reasons to buy now.

In today's fast-paced world, many people put off important decisions until some other time. While young people think about their financial future, with the possible changes in the job market, uncertain future of Social Security, and the impact of inflation and taxes, many of them overlook life insurance. If something were to happen to them, someone would have to pay their bills and final expenses. Many have significant debts, such as student loans, credit card debts, car payments, and mortgages. Life insurance can pay these obligations—not leaving them to loved ones to pay.

Ethics for Life Insurance Advisors

Ethics is the cornerstone of our business, upon which our reputation has been built. As our industry and practices evolve, we must build upon this foundation. Ethical behavior must be practiced not only by financial advisors, but also by the companies we represent. Our futures and the futures of all those we advise depend upon it.

Our business is one of unique, long-term promises and commitments made by life insurance advisors on behalf of insurance companies; promises that are often not fulfilled for 40 or 50 years, sometimes longer. As a result, the industry's one and only real product is a *promise to pay*.

We ask our clients to place their faith in us and the companies we represent for delivery on a carrier's promise—a promise that must be honored even when a client is no longer alive to witness its fulfillment. It is clear that trust is the real commodity with which we deal. Without our commitment to ethical integrity to foster trust, our industry will not survive, for without ethics there would be no trust. Without ethics, no one would keep promises.

Trust is the key ingredient in financial products. The agent generally knows far more about the product than the client. The company drafts the contract. Without a sense of trust that (1) the agent is looking out for the client's best interest, (2) the agent is fairly representing the product, and (3) the company will honor its obligations, few consumers would be willing to purchase financial products. With the revelations of the recent financial recession, the need to restore public trust in the industry is urgent and every person working in the financial services has a role in this process.

Pursing Self Interest versus Selfishness

Ethics are a set of principles established to help people resolve disputes rationally without resorting to physical force, so that the relationships affected by the dispute can endure and even flourish. Because most disputes are generated over questions of who is entitled to certain goods, the pursuit of goods and the avoidance of harm are at the core of any moral system.

The study of ethics deals primarily with identifying ways to enhance the quality of life by addressing issues of fairness and justice. The basic ethical rule is that you should pursue your interests fairly and unselfishly. Fair treatment means "the same should be treated the same." Consequently, a difference in treatment is justified only when there are relevant differences. *Selfish behavior* is behavior in which the pursuit of self-interest is without regard for the interests of, or at the expense of, others. This notion of fairness and rational thinking underlies the principle of the Golden Rule—do unto others as you would have them do unto you. This principle reinforces the notion that others are the same as you in most respects.

self-interest

selfishness

The principle of fairness helps us to see the unethical nature of selfishness. Selfishness is different from the pursuit of self-interest. The pursuit of *self-interest* is a perfectly natural and acceptable activity. *Selfishness* is the pursuit of self-interest at the expense of another, when one is not entitled to the good pursued. When a person is being selfish, he or she puts his or her own interest first in a situation where pursuing that interest will hurt another. For example, if there is one piece of cake allotted to each person at a party, and I take two pieces, I have deprived someone of their share of the cake. In such a case, whoever pursues his own interest will do so at the expense of the other. It is for situations such as this that society has created rules of fair distribution. If two people have a desire or need for the good, why should it go to one and not to the other? We need rules to decide. These are the ethical rules of society.

The exchange of goods in a free market requires the informed consent of both parties. A life insurance sale is a market transaction, so if we misrepresent the product, or withhold significant information, informed consent is prevented, which represents a misappropriation of the buyer's money, and as such, is stealing.

Life insurance was originally designed to respond to an ethical belief that people have a moral responsibility to provide support and maintenance for their children during their dependent years. Given that fact, life insurance is an exceptional financial instrument in that the benefit goes to a person other than the one who makes the investment and the sacrifice. Buying life insurance requires the setting aside of one's self-interest for the sake of others and as such, is the very essence of unselfishness. Consequently, a life insurance advisor becomes a promoter of this type of altruistic behavior.

This discussion can be summarized using the American College Code of Ethics. The Code consists of two parts: the professional pledge and the eight canons.

The American College Code of Ethics
"In all my professional relationships, I pledge myself to the following rule of ethical conduct: I shall, in light of all conditions surrounding those I serve, which I shall make every conscientious effort to ascertain and understand, render that service which, in the same circumstances, I would apply to myself."
The eight canons are:
I. Conduct yourself at all times with honor and dignity.
II. Avoid practices that would bring dishonor upon your profession or The American College.
III. Publicize your achievement in ways that enhance the integrity of your profession.
IV. Continue your studies throughout your working life so as to maintain a high level of professional competence.
V. Do your utmost to attain a distinguished record of professional service.
VI. Support the established institutions and organizations concerned with the integrity of your profession.
VII. Participate in building your profession by encouraging and providing appropriate assistance to qualified persons pursuing professional studies.
VIII. Comply with all laws and regulations, particularly as they relate to professional and business activities.

There are at least three groups of people involved in the ethics of insurance: the insurer (the company), the client may be the policyowner, insured or beneficiary), and the advisor. Each has a relationship to the other and carries ethical responsibilities. The following discussion will review the relationships and ethical responsibilities that involve the advisor: (1) the advisor/client relationship, and (2) the advisor/insurer relationship.

The Advisor/Client Relationship

Although consumers have access to more information than ever before, they have increasingly depended on professionals to interpret and provide advice as to how best achieve their financial goals. Consumers rely on professional advice to translate the raw data into information that can be used to make good financial decisions.

The Advisor's Responsibility to the Client. In the advisor/client relationship, an advisor's responsibilities to the client change during the course of the relationship. For example, the client is technically only a prospective client before the policy goes into effect. In the early stages of contact between advisor and client, the client is a customer and the advisor is a salesperson. In that context, the ethics of marketing hold. In a marketing situation, the advisor must adhere to the requirements of honest marketing, such as necessary disclosure and the avoidance of undue pressure, which could limit the client's freedom to buy or not to buy. After the insurance goes into effect, the customer is then an "insured" and a client, and new obligations emerge. The advisor's responsibilities now include servicing, helping with claims, and monitoring policies and updating coverage. The differences can be minimized by the adoption of a general principle to cover all phases of the relationship. Most people would agree that the advisor should follow the Golden Rule and treat clients as they would like to be treated.

The advisor has an obligation to determine a client's needs for life insurance. The attempt to sell a client an unnecessary insurance policy would tend to involve lying and/or deception, practices considered unethical. There might be times when such a sale does not involve deception, but is the result of the advisor's ignorance about the product. The advisor might not have known what the client needed and subsequently recommended an unsuitable product. If the advisor does not know, but could reasonably be expected to know, that advisor has an obligation to divulge the ignorance and to learn more, or call in an advisor who does know. If the advisor thinks he knows, but does not, we might hold the advisor responsible for his ignorance. Whatever the resolution of these issues, we can see that the obligation to analyze needs puts the further requirement of product knowledge on the shoulders of the advisor.

In addition to adherence to the Golden Rule in selling and looking out for the client's best interests, other obligations are inherent in the advisor/client relationship.

Confidentiality. In the course of writing a policy and performing a needs analysis, the advisor acquires a great deal of private information about the client. It is an obligation of the advisor to keep such information confidential, which means it should only be shared with those who have a legitimate right to such information after the client has authorized a release. When financial advisors use this personal information for their own gain, or do not properly protect it, they violate the promise of confidentiality upon which the success of the financial services industry depends.

Obligations Associated with Delivering the Policy. The advisor is responsible for delivering the insurance policy to the policyowner and often also collects any premium that may be due at the time of policy delivery. Since some coverages do not take effect until the policy is delivered, timely delivery is crucial. The advisor should take the time to explain all the policy provisions, including riders and exclusions, to ensure the policy meets the needs of the client and to explain how the agency handles ongoing service. Finally, the advisor needs to explain any changes that have been made to the policy that were not in the original application.

Claims Handling. When the situation arises for the owner or beneficiary to make a claim, the advisor has a responsibility to help in various ways. The advisor should explain what the beneficiary is obliged to do in order to collect on a claim, help the beneficiary expedite the claim settlement, mediate between the beneficiary and the insurer, and explain the final settlement, if the settlement is not what the owner or beneficiary expected.

Other Servicing. The advisor should review the client's policies to see if they are up to date with reference to beneficiaries and, more importantly, to see if they provide the coverages currently needed.

Ethics of Market Conduct. Thus far, we have looked at what the advisor should do. All of the above aside, most of the attention paid to ethics in the insurance industry relates to market misconduct; the most notorious examples of unethical behavior being on the part of advisors involved in unfair trade.

Unfair Trade Practices. One unfair trade practice is misrepresentation, including misrepresenting the benefits or terms of a policy; misrepresenting dividends as guaranteed when they are not; misrepresenting the financial condition of the insurer; misrepresenting a life insurance policy as some other instrument; and, finally, misrepresenting oneself by perhaps claiming to be a financial planner when one is not.

Coercion that restricts free choice of products is also unethical. For example, for a bank to coerce one of its clients into buying the mortgage insurance it is selling rather than a competitor's insurance as a condition of granting a loan is clearly unethical. This violates the conditions of a free market exchange and informed consent as discussed earlier.

twisting

Other well-known types of unethical behavior are twisting and churning. *Twisting* occurs when a policyowner is induced to discontinue and replace a policy through advisor or insurer distortion or misrepresentation of the facts. When a policy is replaced unnecessarily, it is known as churning. These practices are unethical to the extent they exemplify the advisor pursuing self-interest at the expense of the client. If the replacement were beneficial to the client, it would be the ethically correct thing to do.

rebating

There is also the practice of rebating, which is usually considered unethical, although there is some argument and support for it. *Rebating* is defined as any inducement in the sale of insurance that is not specified in the insurance contract. An offer to share a commission with an applicant is an example of such an inducement. Rebating is generally considered unfair discrimination, because it gives one advisor an unfair advantage over other advisors, or is seen as unfair to those clients who are not given a rebate.

It is also generally unethical, as well as illegal, for an advisor to charge fees in addition to a policy premium for services that are not 'truly' extra. There is a good deal of argument concerning the proper way to compensate advisors. As a result of past abuses in the replacement of policies in order to take advantage of front-end-loaded commissions, the question has been raised about the appropriateness of front-end-loaded commission-based selling as opposed to level commissions or fee-based selling. Although more advisors are moving towards fee-based compensation, there has been little headway made in converting life insurance sales towards a level-commission system.

The advisor owes the client the truth. It is unethical to do what is called company bashing. It is clearly unethical to tell lies or to misrepresent the strengths and weaknesses of the competition, whether it is another advisor or another company. Advisors may suggest that another advisor or company is disreputable. If a product is not meeting a client's needs, or if clients are being misguided by another advisor, the first advisor has an obligation to disclose that fact, but it should be based on facts, not the needs and desires of the advisor to replace the business of another advisor.

Insufficient or misleading disclosure occurs when an advisor fails to disclose all of the information necessary for a client to make a purchasing decision. Disclosure is misleading if it confuses or hides the true meaning or relevance of the information disclosed, making it difficult for the client to act in his or her best interest.

Conflicts of Interest. A conflict of interest exists when a party to a transaction can gain by taking actions that are detrimental to the other party to the transaction. In some cases, the advisor finds himself or herself in a conflict due to the nature of the financial services business, such as company policies, commission requirements, or compensation incentives. Others may be a result of the actions of the advisor, such as what he tells the client or the company that may create conflicts. One common standard in professional ethics is that the advisor always act in the best interest of the client, and to put the client's interest before his or her own. One example could be offering biased advice. As the client depends on the advisor for advice, the practitioner could exploit this dependence and made recommendations which benefit himself at the expense of the client or the insurer.

Advisors should make recommendations based on their client's needs, but they need to sell policies to make a living and their company needs to sell policies to stay in business. Consequently, from time to time there can be pressure on the advisor to sell the client what he or she does not need, as a result of the advisor's personal financial situation or from the advisor's company and manager. According to The Market Conduct Handbook for Agents, "the insurer may say it wants the field force to provide a needs analysis but, in fact, the reward system for the advisor is based on sales—not service. If an advisor discovers that less service and needs analysis can result in quicker sales, then the advisor faces the ethical conflict of whether to make more sales and more money at the expense of the clients' needs." Of course, for the advisor to act for reasons of self-interest at the expense of another, is the very core of selfishness and is an attitude universally condemned.

Professionalism. Burke A. Christensen, JD, CLU, former general counsel and vice president of the Society of Financial Service Professionals, suggests that "a *professional* is a person engaged in a field that requires (1) specialized knowledge not generally understood by the public, (2) a threshold entrance exam requirement, (3) a sense of altruism, and (4) a code of ethics." (Burke A. Christensen, *Journal of the American Society of CLU and ChFC*, January 1990) In applying this definition, specialized knowledge in the insurance and financial services field is immediately evident in the complexity and depth of the information that must be mastered by the practitioner. Advisors and others working in this industry also must pass licensing exams, maintain continuing education requirements, and keep up with current state and federal regulations and tax and legislative changes. The third requirement, a sense of altruism, is the characteristic that promotes adherence to the fourth requirement, a code of ethics. *Altruism* is defined as an unselfish regard for the welfare of others. Altruism does not mean working for free, or giving away your services. It does mean acting unselfishly, taking others' needs and concerns into account before your own. Demonstration of altruism can be its own reward; it often wins trust, confidence, and reliance, all of which are important to success as an adviser to others.

Fiduciary versus Suitability Standard. The financial reform legislation (Dodd-Frank Act) passed in July, 2010 includes a provision regarding the necessary degree of care that a financial advisor must provide to clients. The issue of concern in the bill to financial advisors is that currently advisors are held to one of two standards, based on their registration. An advisor may be registered as an agent or broker (registered representative of a broker-dealer), or as a registered investment advisor (RIA). Broker-Dealers and associated persons are regulated under the Securities Exchange Act of 1934 and are held to a “suitability” standard that requires them to make recommendations that are appropriate for a client’s age, risk tolerance, investment objectives, time horizon and financial status. On the other hand, Registered Investment Advisors (investment advisors) are held to a “fiduciary” standard under the Investment Advisors Act of 1940, meaning the advisor must recommend what is in the client’s best interest when providing personalized investment advice. They must place the interests of the customer ahead of their own. They must act with prudence, with the skill, care, diligence and good judgment of a professional. The fiduciary standard imposes the utmost duty of good faith, loyalty, and full and fair disclosure of all material facts, including potential conflicts of interest. Conflicts of interest should be avoided, and unavoidable conflicts must be managed in the client’s favor. The suitability standard does not have these requirements. It requires only that the product sold suits the needs of the consumer. The bill required that the SEC study the situation and make new rules, if necessary, based on its findings. This may have a tremendous impact on the financial services industry and will play out over the next months or years.

These, in brief, are the ethical responsibilities an advisor has toward his or her client. We will now consider the responsibilities the advisor has toward his or her company.

The Advisor/Insurer Relationship

Agency is defined as the relationship that results from the consent by one person or entity (the principal) that another party (the agent) will act on the principal's behalf. The agent is subject to the principal's control, and there must be consent to the agency by the agent. This relationship and meaning of agency exists when an individual is contracted as an agent representing an insurance company.

The Advisor's Responsibilities to the Company. An advisor (and, in some cases, a broker) serves as an agent of the company in accord with agency law. The agent is empowered to act on behalf of the company (the principal) and acts performed by the agent bind the company. Thus, when the agent signs an application or binds an insurance contract, he or she binds the company to that contract. Because an agent is expected to act in the best interest of the company, there are times the agent's interests are subordinated to those of the company. However, an agent is never required to do anything illegal or unethical for the sake of the company.

If the agent is bound to act in the best interest of the principal, defining the responsibilities of the agent to the company will require a review of the interests of the company. Knowledge of the agent is considered to be knowledge of the company. For example, if the agent has knowledge of health matters pertinent to the issuance of life insurance, it is assumed that this knowledge is also available to the insurer. Agents owe a duty of loyalty to their companies, acting in utmost good faith, honesty and integrity in handling all affairs relating to their company. Some believe the primary and only responsibility of for-profit businesses is to maximize profit for the shareholders. Therefore, as an agent for the company, the agent must act in ways that will make money for the company, not cost the company money.

There is a popular hypothetical case in which a husband cancels a life insurance policy covering himself. His wife had encouraged him to purchase the policy, and he had reluctantly agreed. The cancellation took place late on a Friday. The agent did the paper work and gave the client a cancellation slip, but did not send the requisite paperwork to the company because the mail had already been collected for the weekend. The husband was killed in a hunting accident on Saturday and his wife called the agent on Sunday because she was unable to find the policy, all she had found was the cancellation memorandum. This scenario raises many questions. What should the agent do? What obligations does the agent have to the company? What obligations does the agent have to the wife (beneficiary)?

If we concentrate on the obligation to the company, although sympathy favors ripping up the return receipt and the paperwork, that is unfair to the company to whom the agent owes his first loyalty. Giving the money to the wife is tantamount to giving stockholders' or other policyholders' money to her. Of course, considerations of good public relations and a compassionate image might persuade the company to pay the benefit if they knew the truth. However, that raises the question of what obligations companies have to clients or former clients.

Some people would argue that the agent should withhold the information from the company while others would argue that as an agent, committed to looking out for the best interests of the company, he is obliged to inform the company of the cancellation. The law clearly maintains the latter position. The courts hold that a company is aware of all information known by any of its agents. When polled on this issue, agents are likely to be split in their response as to which course of action is ethical.

Not all situations are as difficult to resolve as the one above. In most situations, the obligations are clear. The agent's contract or agency agreement spells out many of the agent's (or broker's) responsibilities to the company.

Compliance and Ethics. Compliance and ethical conduct have taken an increased role in the insurance and financial services industry over the last decade. *Compliance* means following the laws and regulations, including company rules that apply to the sales of insurance and financial products. These are the minimum standards. State and federal laws regulate the insurance and securities industries to protect consumers from unfair sales practices. Company rules are designed to make certain that the company and its advisors are following state and federal requirements. They are also designed to make sure that the company is receiving complete and accurate information from producers on which to base underwriting and claims decisions. Following these regulations and rules is the first step in professional conduct.

Ethical behavior is doing the right thing. Professional *ethics* can be defined as behaving according to the principles of right and wrong that are accepted by your profession. Behaving ethically requires putting the prospect's best interest before your own, maintaining the highest possible standard in all your business dealings. You continue to develop your skills to provide the best service to those with whom you work. Representing the industry, its companies, and its advisors in the best light is the ethical thing to do.

unauthorized entity

Unauthorized Insurance Carrier. A financial advisor has an obligation to make sure the company he or she represents is licensed to do business in the state where he or she solicits the sale of policies. Each state has laws specifying that only admitted carriers may issue policies within its boundaries.

Failure to follow this rule can have serious consequences for both the policyowner and the advisor. Policyowners are jeopardized because state guaranty funds are typically set aside to cover losses only of admitted carriers. This means that the policyowner may lose all benefits of coverage should the unauthorized carrier run into financial difficulties.

The risk to the advisor may come directly from state insurance laws, which hold the advisor personally liable for any client losses arising out of business placed with an unauthorized carrier. The advisor may also face additional legal action by the client based on more generalized concepts of malpractice.

Good ethical and business practice dictates that you investigate the company(ies) with which you place business. If you are uncertain as to whether or not a company is authorized to do business in a state in which you solicit business, call your home office or your state insurance department.

YOUR FINANCIAL SERVICES PRACTICE: UNAUTHORIZED ENTITIES

Regulation of insurance products and services varies from state to state. In Florida, for example, regulations prohibit doing business with an unauthorized insurance entity. An *unauthorized entity* is an insurance company that has not gained approval to place insurance in the jurisdiction where it or a producer wants to sell insurance. These carriers are unlicensed and prohibited from doing business in that state. In most cases, these carriers have characterized themselves as one of several types that are exempt from state regulation. It is the financial advisor's responsibility to exercise due diligence in making sure the carriers for whom they are selling are approved by the department of insurance in that state.

Service the Plan

The primary goal of the selling/planning process is to turn prospects into clients. The intermediate step is creating a customer, someone who has purchased a product from you but with whom you have not yet established a solid client/advisor relationship. In the servicing step, your goal is to turn good customers into client who consistently follow your recommendations and enthusiastically refer you to others. They believe in you and the products and services you provide.

This section looks at the benefits of providing excellent service, starting with the policy delivery, then looking at ways to monitor the plan and deliver promised services to the client. Together, they work to satisfy your present clientele and provide you with referrals and additional business—key ingredients in building a successful practice.

Delivering the Contract

A good policy delivery interview goes a long way toward keeping your policy *persistency* rate high (and lapse ratio low) and strengthening your client base with each new sale. Your persistency rate measures the number of policies that remain in force over a given time, normally measured in yearly periods. Selling a policy is your first challenge; keeping it on the books is the next, and policy service plays a key role in maintaining a high persistency rate.

The delivery of the policy confirms for the client their decision to buy and completes the sales process in their eyes. This is why it is so important to meet with your new policyowner to deliver the contract in person. You establish a pattern of service for the future, and you demonstrate and reinforce your personal approach and philosophy of selling and service.

Explain the kinds of service the client can expect and reinforce the systems you have in place to accomplish the service. Set an appointment for an annual review to express your commitment to these service goals. Then, of course, deliver on your promises.

delivery interview

Delivery Interview Objectives. Often the policy delivery is your first return visit with the client after the sale. To a world accustomed to a "take the money and run" approach to selling, the *delivery interview* can be your chance to excel and stand apart from other salespeople. Conducting an effective and thorough delivery interview and providing ongoing client service will be critical to your long-term success. A polished policy delivery accomplishes the following:

- ***Reinforces the Buying Decision*** —Time has elapsed since you wrote the application. It may be many weeks since you last met. Your policyowner remembers saying yes to your proposal, but may not remember exactly why. You have the opportunity to reemphasize the needs and reasons the prospect bought the policy. It is essential that the client understand why he or she bought the product, the solutions it provides, and the benefits he or she will derive from keeping it. Reaffirm that they made a good decision.
- ***Builds Trust*** —Here you sell the future. By promising future service on this policy and ensuring that the policy and your continued service will meet the client's future needs, you offer your expertise as a financial services professional. Tell the client of your continued support through periodic reviews. The timing of these should be based on a mutually agreeable time interval.
- ***Reopens the Selling/Planning Process***—At policy delivery, you can set the stage for addressing the remaining needs and objectives of the buyer. If a total needs analysis was not done, then an attempt to schedule this type of planning could be made. If the total needs analysis has been performed, additional needs can be addressed.
- ***Obtains Referred Leads***—Some feel that the delivery interview is the best time to ask for referrals, because the buyer's interest is highest at that point. With the purchase completed, the buyer feels that the goals he or she set out to accomplish have been addressed. A satisfied buyer can be your best source of referrals. What better source than a satisfied buyer, to ask for names of people for whom your services and products might also be of value?
- ***Prevents Lapses***—There should be nothing casual about policy delivery. The advisor must treat it seriously. Industry statistics

show that half of all policy lapses occur during the first 6 months after policy issue. The only way to reduce the chances of this customer becoming one of these statistics is to deliver in person every policy you sell. Of equal importance is the need to do it in a way that reinforces the buyer's confidence that the purchase was made for the right reasons. Only the advisor can take this step for the policyowner.

How to Achieve Delivery Objectives.

- ***Reinforcing the buying decision.*** Any symptoms of buyer's remorse must be addressed. At this meeting, you can deal with objections up front and face to face, instead of months later when you hear the policy is about to lapse. Send the client a thank you letter for his or her confidence in you, expressed through the purchase. In the letter, summarize the reasons for the purchase and the benefits provided by the plan. Some advisors include this letter with their policy delivery package, so the client can easily see and review it, or they send it shortly after the sale is made.
- ***Building trust.*** Promise a lot and deliver more. If you told the policyowner you would do something (for example, get an attorney's name, check on another policy, or bring an agency calendar) be sure to follow through and do it in a timely fashion. Not fulfilling expectations can lead to immediate customer dissatisfaction and introduce tension into the relationship. Trust does not develop in a day. It must be nurtured over time. When you deliver what you promise after the sale, clients begin to trust you.
- ***Reopening selling/planning process*** Be sure that the client knows about all the products and services you offer. Even if you have already presented this information, review what you can do again. If you have a personal brochure or resume, be sure that the client has one. Periodically send compliance-approved articles, brochures, or reports based on what you know about the client's interests, business, or company. This will build rapport as well as generate or develop interest in further cross-selling opportunities.
- ***Obtaining referred leads*** Help the client by sharing the specifics on the types of referrals that would be most helpful. Ask the client if he or she would be willing to be a reference for you. If appropriate, socialize with the client, building the relationship and sharing in a common interest (golf, community activities, hobbies, and so on). Volunteer to provide a benefit to the client, such as speaking at the client's meeting, providing services to the client's organization,

or introducing him or her to other clients whom they may benefit from knowing.

- ***Preventing lapse.*** You must keep a customer satisfied in order to fight off competition. You are naive if you think your competitors use different prospecting and relationship building techniques than you. The reason for diligence in maintaining customer satisfaction is to protect your investment from your competitors.

Company and State Requirements at Policy Delivery

The number and complexity of delivery requirements from state insurance departments and companies have grown over the last few decades as regulators and insurers respond to marketing and producer conduct issues and the public's desire to feel protected from fraudulent and unethical practices. The following is a summary of the most common policy delivery requirements.

buyer's guide

Buyer's Guide. The *Buyer's Guide* gives the prospective purchaser a clear explanation of life insurance products and how to shop for them. Generally, the Buyer's Guide must be delivered to the consumer with the policy. Some states require it to be delivered with the application, and there are state variations in the forms themselves and state-specific requirements that must be followed.

policy summary

Policy Summary. Most states require that a policy summary be delivered with the policy. This form, normally produced by the home office with your policy, defines the main features of the currently issued policy and includes specific information on the policy values of the contract (guaranteed and nonguaranteed), including the premium, guaranteed cash values, guaranteed death benefit, and the policy's loan interest rate.

Signed Illustration. The National Association of Insurance Commissioners (NAIC) Illustrations Model Regulation has become law in most states and policy in many companies. This regulation establishes guidelines for companies and advisors regarding the content and presentations of sales illustrations. The regulation covers all life insurance products except those with face amounts under $10,000 and variable life. It requires that an illustration matching the issued policy be presented to the policyowner. The advisor and policyowner must sign this illustration; one copy is given to the policyowner, one is returned to the company, and one is retained in the advisor's client file.

Delivery Receipt. Most companies and some states require that the advisor and policyowner sign policy delivery receipts upon policy delivery. This form typically contains information regarding guaranteed and nonguaranteed elements in the policy and information regarding proper policy delivery. The client and advisor sign and retain a copy, with a copy being returned to the insurer.

Client File. A client file must be kept as long as a policy is in force. Once a policy is no longer in force because it lapsed, was surrendered, or a claim was paid, a file must be kept for 5 to 8 years, depending on jurisdiction. Where litigation or other disputes exist, files should be kept even longer. Inactive files must normally be kept for 2 years. Individual companies and states may have their own rules for documents to be maintained in files, as a routine part of the compliance process, but these are the typical general guidelines:

- complete illustrations, including signed NAIC illustration
- any materials used in solicitation of the sale
- fact-finder and suitability related materials
- copies of applications and related materials
- replacement forms and related materials, if appropriate to sale
- copy of policy delivery receipts
- contact sheet used to keep records of date and content of all client contacts and discussions
- substantive correspondence concerning contractual changes or concerns of the client
- documents required by your company

Normally, no original documents or blank, signed documents should be stored in a file. Original documents should be submitted to the company and blank, signed documents are strictly forbidden. You should keep good, compliant files, not only to meet requirements, but to build a servicing system that will help you develop and maintain satisfied clients.

Servicing the Plan

Good client service separates the best businesses from those that fail. The successful advisor recognizes that each service opportunity is a marketing opportunity, a chance to demonstrate to clients that he or she is reliable, responsive, trustworthy, and empathetic to their needs. When servicing opportunities are seen as marketing opportunities, referrals and more sales follow.

Objectives of Service

The service step is the key to client building, which is the key to long-term success. As one top producer explains, "the essential factor for most of us in transforming a policyowner into a client rests basically with the type of service we provide." By service, we mean two things. First, we mean the monitoring of the insurance plan through annual reviews. Second, we mean responding to policyowners' requests and providing optional personal-touch services. Together, they work to achieve the objectives of client building.

Your success at client building through monitoring and servicing will accomplish four things:

- maintain policyowners' persistency
- invite repeat sales from policyowners
- earn ongoing referrals to new prospects
- lower expenses

Maintain Persistency. A strong client relationship can help prevent competitors from taking your business. In a competitive climate, service is clearly a necessary defensive strategy. Maintaining a high profile with clients through your service activities and other contacts will help clients feel loyal and committed to the business you have done together. A policyowner who feels no such loyalty or commitment is not likely to think twice about accepting the next attractive proposal that comes along. Your persistency will suffer unless you take steps to keep your clients in the fold.

Repeat Sales and Referrals. Client building is also part of a smart offensive marketing and sales strategy. Experienced advisors will tell you that as much as 75 percent or more of their new business comes from existing clients or referrals provided by these clients. If you are relatively new to the business, preoccupied with generating production and first-year premium, or struggling to find a market, consider the difference it would make if most of your sales were to people who had already bought from you or those they referred. People have a tendency to refer those like themselves. If the client values your products and services, there is a good chance that those they refer will as well.

Lower Expenses. Another consideration is the cost of developing clients. What are your marketing and sales costs for finding one qualified prospect and going through a multiple-interview sales process? Factor in the cost of obtaining the lead, sales promotion, telephone, secretarial and mail expenses, other overhead expenses, automobile costs, meals, computer time, and presentation materials. Multiply the total cost by the number of prospects it takes to make a sale. By selling primarily to clients, you will lower your sales and marketing costs. Good service is defined by how well it enables you to achieve these objectives.

Customers versus Clients

All clients are customers, but not all customers are clients. A client is a person who has bought from you, but is also someone with whom you have developed, or are developing, a strong interpersonal business relationship. As a result of this relationship, if the client has any problems in areas relevant to your expertise, he or she will look to you for direction. An advisor finds comfort in knowing that he or she can call or visit the client for a private meeting at almost any time.

How does a customer become a client? Most consumers buy products and never develop an interpersonal relationship with the sales person. They might not even recognize the advisor after they have made the purchase. For advisors representing products and services that depend on client relationships, time spent developing those relationships is very important. To build a lifetime career on client relationships, it is essential to convert customers to clients.

Proactive Service

Service is reactive when it is provided at the client's initiative. It corresponds to the minimum level of required service. Service is proactive when it is provided at the advisor's initiative. With proactive service, the advisor cultivates client service requests in order to create client contact and opportunities to demonstrate reliability and responsiveness. Proactive service sets you apart and is the key to persistency, additional sales, and a regular stream of referrals.

Most successful advisors have an automated contact management system to ensure regular contact and communication with clients and prospects on a year-round basis. This is very personal and individualistic, with much freedom to fit an advisor's personality, his or her clientele, budget, manner of doing business, and a variety of other factors. There is no right or wrong way to do this, but all advisors should devote some attention to this broad area of communications.

Keeping in touch by various methods is an important part of the client service process. Newsletters, birthday and anniversary phone calls, and periodic mailings about topics of interest continue to put you in front of the client, build prestige, and foster the advisor-client relationship.

Brochures. A brochure can resemble a simple resume, or can be a beautiful, multi-colored piece with graphics and high-quality paper. Many companies provide a template that you can complete with your own personal information. There are many business services and printers who do this type of work, for a wide range of charges. In addition to your business card, you should have a descriptive piece that promotes your expertise, products, services, education, business philosophy, community involvement, personal background, and any other combination of information that will help build your relationship with clients. The brochure can be used as part of an initial contact, as a handout at your first meeting, or at policy delivery.

Newsletters. Newsletter are a good way to keep in contact with your clients, keep your name in front of them, and provide interesting items of financial interest which may also serve as prospecting ideas. You can write your own. Some companies provide subscription services that offer options on a continuum from full-service direct delivery to clients to do-it-yourself delivery of the newsletters. There are also numerous industry services and associations that offer them. The newsletter should have your name, address, and phone number, and possibly your photo.

Greeting Cards. Birthday cards are a way of saying, "I'm thinking of you and I care about you." Calendars and greeting cards at the holidays also help you to stand out and put your name in front of the prospect or client. Many advisors use other gifts, such as calendars, pocket diaries, and pen sets as a technique to keep in contact with clientele.

Handwritten Notes. A handwritten note is an especially personal touch in this day of technology and rapid-pace life. It is such a rare occasion when we receive something someone has cared enough to write in his or her own hand that it creates an impression as being something special.

Hand address the envelope, and use a commemorative postage stamp, if possible. Your note will certainly stand out from the onslaught of mass-produced computer-generated envelopes, flyers, magazines, and newspapers.

Consider having your note cards or stationery imprinted with your company's name and logo, your name, and business information. Work on developing the message you want to convey. For example, when writing a note to a new client, you can communicate much more than a simple "thank you."

EXAMPLE
Thank you for giving me the opportunity to do business with you. My goal now is to continue to offer you excellent follow-up service, so that you'll have no reservations about referring others who have similar needs.

Make Regular Phone Contacts. Stay in touch with your clients periodically; regular phones calls can ensure that you do. The appropriate interval between calls is typically based on the value of that client. Often, these stay-in-touch calls are intentionally unrelated to business. Some advisors actually refuse to discuss business. This is all a part of creating a relationship with your clients. In addition, you should always contact clients to let them know the results of any meetings you had with referrals they gave you. Be sure to thank your clients for their support.

Monitoring the Plan

Monitoring is the servicing aspect that separates a life insurance policy from a life insurance plan. A policy gets thrown into a drawer and never reviewed. Too frequently, an advisor does not follow up and an active advisor-client relationship and client-building process is deserted. Conversely, an insurance plan is monitored and revised to ensure that it is doing what the client intends. Taking into account this important distinction, we have considered monitoring as a separate topic from the other servicing aspects of an insurance plan. It is the backbone of the client-building service activity.

Periodic Reviews

If you are not doing policy reviews, or have convinced yourself they are not necessary, you are making a major mistake, both for yourself and your clients. If you want to be accepted as an advisor, the policy review is the best way to develop this reputation, since it is an opportunity to discuss real life issues and not just products. Your clients' personal circumstances undergo changes, and if you are not current with them, you are irrelevant. Someone else will come along and capture them.

Although most clients prefer annual reviews, ask the client how frequently they would like to meet. Everyone should have a review, but find out your client's preferences for timing. Some clients may want to meet every 6 to 9 months, while others may feel 18 to 24 months is fine. By asking for your client's input on the timing of reviews you will be contacting them when they want to hear from you.

Set the Appointment. Build your client's expectations about the value of your proactive service. Lay the groundwork early on in the process, preferably at the initial interview, when you explain how you work and the services you offer. Position yourself as an advisor who helps people uncover their insurance and financial goals, creates and implements plans to achieve them, and continues to monitor their plans and make adjustments as needed.

Prepare for the Appointment. If you have kept good records, preparing will be easy. Refresh your memory by reviewing the needs analysis and the financial information that the client provided you. Reexamine the information you gathered on your client's attitudes, values, and goals. Keep notes on personal information to help foster individualized relationships. Review plan recommendations, giving attention to those recommendations that were implemented, and those that were not. Put together a game plan of areas in which you feel client needs may exist.

Conduct the Review. Review the client's insurance and/or financial plan, and evaluate its progress in relation to the client's needs and goals. If appropriate, recalculate needs and note any shortfalls. Inquire about any changes in the client's current or future financial situation. Listen carefully and note any planning opportunities. Implement any plan changes and set any necessary follow-up appointments.

Ask for Referrals. An annual review is the perfect time to ask your client if he or she knows anyone who might share the same values and goals. There is a high probability that your client values and trusts you; otherwise, the client would not have let you review his or her financial plan. Thus, the client is likely to want to refer you to family members and friends.

Here are some strategies to consider:

Relate one to one. Realize that all business is personal and no relationship is static.

Reinforce relationships. Seize every opportunity to learn about your client's needs, dreams, and realities. Communicate and reinforce the reason your client chose you. People do business with people, not companies.

Exceed expectations. Meeting clients' expectations is the price of admission into today's market. Strive to exceed expectations to create customer commitment and loyalty. Expect to lose business if you deliver merely what the customer needs, since they probably have many avenues to get it. Instead, discover and deliver what they want. If you do not add value, you are no longer necessary.

Be an expert listener. Demonstrate your knowledge and gain customer loyalty by asking the right questions and listening closely to the answers.

Differentiate yourself. Do not compete on price, but rather on policy benefits and the value of your expertise and your products. Differentiate your services in your client's mind by adding choice, specialization, research, responsiveness, technology, and knowledge. Most clients do not buy on price alone. Your job is to offer the best overall value, not the lowest price. Educate clients about the value of your products.

Establish strategic alliances. Look to suppliers, clients, and even competitors for joint opportunities that will add value for your clients. Introduce clients to each other and to those who can build value in their situation. Find advisors in related fields, such as attorneys, accountants, bankers, insurance specialists in other lines of insurance in which you are not involved, and community leaders and business leaders for whom you can become a client and with whom you can develop joint work opportunities and share referrals. The key is developing relationships in your community.

Become referable. To get referrals you need to be referable. That means you must offer more than a product. You have to offer a process, and even better, a memorable experience. You have to earn the trust of your clients.

Monitor Changing Needs and Circumstances

A person's personal and financial situation change over time. Age, marriage, births, divorce, deaths and other life events cause a person's insurance and other financial needs to change. We will review some of the more common changes here.

Coverage Amount. First, check that the amount of coverage is adequate to protect the needs the client desires to protect. This will include products other than life insurance.

Policy Values. For permanent insurance, track cash values and policy dividends (if applicable) to ensure they are going to achieve any anticipated cash goals for retirement and other future goals.

Type of Need. Sometimes the amount needed does not change. It might be that the type of solution needed changes. This might include term conversions, universal life death-benefit options, premium levels, and so on.

Automatic Transactions or Changes. The greatest client-building tool is honest communication. When automatic changes occur, communication with the client can help them adjust or perhaps take advantage of the changes. For example, natural contact points would include policy changes such as children's term rider changes, term premium increases, or guaranteed insurability option dates.

Law Changes. Sometimes the concepts used to sell the policy may change due to law changes. This would require monitoring to be sure that the plan performance will take place as anticipated; otherwise, changes may need to be made. Tax law changes also often provide new sales opportunities. The most common areas impacted are income tax planning, retirement planning, and estate planning. Keep in mind is that tax law changes are constantly being made and you want to keep abreast of them for opportunities and threats to yourself and your clients.

Chapter Eight Review

Key Terms and Concepts

- transfer-for-value
- cost basis
- LIFO/FIFO
- Sec. 1035
- modified endowment contract (MEC)
- probate
- incident of ownership
- life settlement
- viatical settlements
- Supplemental Life Insurance Retirement Plan (SLIRP)
- pension maximization
- estate liquidity
- cost of waiting
- self-interest
- selfishness
- twisting
- rebating
- unauthorized entity
- delivery interview
- buyer's guide
- policy summary

Review Questions

1. Summarize the income, estate, and gift tax rules relating to life insurance. [1]

2. Explain life and viatical settlements and the issues that make life settlements controversial. [3]

3. Briefly summarize the following life insurance marketing concepts:
   Supplemental life insurance retirement plan (SLIRP)
   Pension maximization
   Estate planning
   Charitable giving
   [4]

4. Discuss the differences between selfish behavior and self-interest with regard to ethical behavior. [5]

5. List examples of unethical market conduct that the advisor should avoid. [5]

6. Discuss the responsibilities the agent has towards the client. [6]

7. Discuss the objectives of the delivery interview, and how to achieve them. [6]

8. Explain what you should do to prepare for the delivery interview. [6]

9. Discuss the common state and company requirements for policy delivery. [7]

10. Discuss how to provide high-quality service and how this can enhance your business. [7]

Self-Test Questions

1. A man purchases a $100,000 whole life policy. Many years later, he surrenders the policy for its cash value of $50,000. At that time, he had paid $45,000 of premiums and received dividends of $10,000. What were the income-tax consequences upon receipt of the cash surrender value?

   (A) He received the entire $50,000 tax-free.
   (B) He received $45,000 tax-free and $5,000 as long-term capital gains.
   (C) He received $15,000 tax-free and $35,000 as ordinary income.
   (D) He received $35,000 tax-free and $15,000 as ordinary income.

2. The booklet prepared by the National Association of Insurance Commissioners that provides objective advice and comprehensive cost comparison for those purchasing life insurance is called

   (A) the Insurance Guide
   (B) the Consumer's Resource Book
   (C) the Buyer's Guide
   (D) Choosing the Policy that Fits

3. Any inducement in the sale of insurance that is not specified in the insurance contract is known as

   (A) churning
   (B) rebating
   (C) company bashing
   (D) twisting

4. Dividends paid to the policyowner are generally

   (A) taxed on a FIFO (first in, first out) basis
   (B) taxed on a LIFO (last in, first out) basis
   (C) taxed at capital-gains rates because they represent a return of capital
   (D) never subject to tax because they are a return of premium paid

5. The document given to the buyer at policy delivery that illustrates the premiums, the guaranteed death benefit, the policy's loan interest rate, and other specifics on the policy purchased is called the

   (A) policy summary
   (B) buyer's guide
   (C) policy receipt
   (D) prospectus

6. Which of the following statements regarding ethics is (are) correct?

   I. Ethics deals primarily with enhancing, not diminishing, the quality of life.
   II. Summarized, the basic ethical rule states that you should pursue your interests fairly and unselfishly.

   (A) I only
   (B) II only
   (C) Both I and II
   (D) Neither I nor II

7. Which of the following statements regarding ethics is (are) correct?

   I. Selfish behavior is behavior in which self-interest is pursued without regard for, or at the expense of others.
   II. By "selfishness" we mean just the amount of self-interest, which is ethically unacceptable.

   (A) I only
   (B) II only
   (C) Both I and II
   (D) Neither I nor II

READ THE FOLLOWING DIRECTIONS BEFORE CONTINUING

The questions below differ from the preceding questions in that they all contain the word EXCEPT. So you understand fully the basis used in selecting each answer, be sure to read each question carefully.

---

8. If a policy becomes a modified endowment contract (MEC), taxation of all of the following may be affected EXCEPT

   (A) withdrawals
   (B) loans
   (C) surrenders
   (D) death benefits

9. All of the following statements concerning “agency” are correct EXCEPT
   (A) The agent represents the client and his or her primary loyalty must be to the client.
   (B) The consent by one person or entity (the principal) that another party (the agent) will act on the principal’s behalf.
   (C) The agent is subject to the principal’s control, and the agent must consent to the agency.
   (D) The term “agent” specifically means “one who acts for another.”

10. Premiums paid for individual life insurance policies in the United States are usually deductible for income tax purposes in all of the following circumstances EXCEPT
    (A) life insurance in an alimony agreement
    (B) life insurance that is owned by and that is paid to a charity as beneficiary
    (C) premiums paid in the form of a bonus (salary) to an employee
    (D) premiums for individually owned life insurance on a family member

APPENDIX A: ANSWERS TO QUESTIONS

Chapter 1

Answers to Review Questions

1. Life insurance provides a tool for risk management, a process for dealing with the risk of loss of life. Insurance substitutes certainty for uncertainty, through pooling of groups of people who share the risks to which they are exposed. Uncertain risks of individuals are combined, making the possible loss more certain, and providing a financial solution to the problems created by the loss. The essence of insurance is the principle of indemnity, that the person who suffers a financial loss is placed in the same financial position after the loss as before the loss occurred. The law of large numbers states that as the size of the sample (insured population) increases, the actual loss experience will more and more closely approximate the true underlying probability. Insurance relies on the law of large numbers to minimize the speculative element and reduce volatile fluctuations in year-to-year losses.
2. In risk pooling or group sharing of losses, persons exposed to loss from a particular source combine their risks and agree to share losses on some equitable basis. The risks may be combined under an arrangement whereby the participants mutually insure each other, called "mutual insurance," or they may be transferred to an insurer that, for a consideration called the "premium," is willing to assume the risks and pay the resulting losses. Risk pooling is a basic principle that makes insurance possible.
3. All life insurance products are actuarially created by calculating the relationships of mortality, interest, and expense and the financial values resulting from each based on time. The assumptions made concerning these three factors will determine the premium at which a policy is sold, the structure of the policy, and over time the performance of the policy and the profitability and solvency of the life insurance company. All life insurance policies, regardless of type, are based on these same elements. Mortality rates project the cost of covering death claims as they occur. Interest earnings reflect the income the company expects from the investment of premiums over time that will be added to the reserves, or held aside for the future, to pay claims. Expenses include the cost of creating, offering, and maintaining the product to pay all promised benefits. These factors must also provide profit to the insurer.

4. *Yearly Renewable Term (YRT) insurance* is the simplest form of insurance offered by life insurance companies. It provides insurance for a period of one year but permits the policyowner to renew the policy for successive periods of one year without furnishing evidence of insurability. The policyowner can renew the policy simply by paying the renewal premium. The premium for yearly renewable term insurance is determined by the death rate for the attained age of the individual involved. To calculate the premium, the company takes the mortality rate for age/gender group, determines the number of deaths from the group, and multiplies by the face amount of the policy (measured by number of thousands).
5. *Level premium insurance* has premiums that remain constant throughout the premium-paying period. Premiums that would otherwise increase with each passing year are leveled out; the premiums paid in the early years of the contract will be more than sufficient to meet current death claims, while those paid in the later years will be less than adequate to meet incurred claims. The redundant premiums in the early years of the contract create an accumulation that is held by the insurance company for the benefit and to the credit of the policyowners. This accumulation is called a *reserve* and is sufficient to pay all claims as they come due.
6. Life insurance is concerned with the *economic* value of a human life, which is derived from its earning capacity and the financial dependence of other lives on that earning capacity. The *human life value approach* is based on the proposition that a person should carry life insurance in an amount equal to the capitalized value of his or her net future earnings. The potential estate, or the earnings and savings that can be received and accumulated, is far more substantial than the existing estate. The family's economic security lies in the earning capacity of each wage earner. The earner's economic value relating to income diminishes each year as potential income is converted to actual income, and the income earner gets closer to retirement.
7. A cleanup fund or funds for final expenses are those expenses associated with the death of an individual. Some people undergo a lengthy period of hospital treatment and incur large medical bills. The cleanup fund is used to liquidate all current outstanding obligations, which include: the costs of daily living for survivors; final expenses, such as funeral costs, cemetery plot, and burial; repairs and replacements associated with events surrounding the family member's death; state and federal estate taxes; and the cost

of estate administration including executor's or administrator's fee, appraisers' fees, legal fees, and probate court expenses.

8. The types of income needs include the following:
   - Readjustment income—the income needed by the family during the readjustment period following the insured's death, which is approximately equivalent to the family's share of income the producer provided prior to death.
   - Income during dependency period—income may need to be provided to support children until they are self-sufficient.
   - Life income for surviving dependent spouse—income that will allow the surviving spouse to maintain a desired standard of living.

9. Answers:
   - Cash needs—needs that may not be found in every situation, but which require attention according to specific family goals and lifestyle demands.
   - Mortgage redemption needs—A common desire is to have the surviving family have a rent- or mortgage-free home that will give peace of mind, adequate and comfortable living, and reduce monthly income requirements.
   - Educational needs—If college or other educational goals are desired, additional funds or income will be needed.
   - Emergency needs—A liquid fund should be set up from which additional income can be provided if and when it is needed.
   - Retirement needs—This need can provide funds in the event of death during retirement. In the event of a long life, a cash-value policy can provide funds to supplement retirement income.

10. The eight steps in the selling/planning process are:
    a. **Identify the prospect**—Identify whom you are going to approach and why.
    b. **Approach the prospect**—Contact the prospect by telephone, by mail, or face-to-face and ask for an appointment, stating the reason why you are interested in meeting.

c. **Meet the prospect**—In the initial interview you establish rapport and explain your business purpose.
d. **Gather information and establish goals**—Using a fact-finder, ask questions that will uncover the prospect's situation.
e. **Analyze the information**—Based on the fact-finder, analyze the prospect's present financial situation.
f. **Develop and present the plan**—The next step is to devise a realistic plan for bringing the prospect from his or her present financial position to the attainment of those objectives. A good plan must reflect the prospect's needs, attitudes and goals. The plan must be the prospect's plan, not the advisor's plan.
g. **Implement the plan**—You must motivate the prospect to act and help him or her acquire the financial products required to put the plan into action. You must answer concerns that may prevent him or her from implementing the plan.
h. **Service the plan**—Deliver the policy and reaffirm the decision to buy and the problems that can be solved by having this product. Reinforce the benefits you are providing. Get referrals.

Answers to Self-Test Questions

1. B
2. B
3. C
4. C
5. A
6. D
7. C
8. B
9. A
10. D

Chapter 2

Answers to Review Questions

1. The multiple-of-income approach for determining the life insurance amount needed uses a *multiple-of-annual income*, which is easy to explain and requires few calculations. This simplistic approach ignores the financial and personal situation of the individual. It does not take into account the important differences in people's lives that actually determine what amount of life insurance they should have, such as family size, living expenses, and stage of life. It also ignores information about assets the client has already accumulated and any external financial resources such as trusts and inheritances.
2. The *human life value approach* is based on the concept that a person should carry life insurance in an amount equal to the *capitalized value* of his or her net future earnings.

    a. Estimate the individual's average annual earnings from personal efforts over the remaining years of his or her income-producing lifetime.
    b. Deduct federal and state income taxes, life insurance premiums, and the cost of self-maintenance.
    c. Determine the number of years between the individual's present age and the contemplated age of retirement.
    d. Select a reasonable rate of interest at which future earnings will be discounted.
    e. Multiply (1) minus (2) by the present value of $1 per annum for the period determined in (3), discounted at the rate of interest selected in (4).

3. Post-death financial needs are separated into two main categories: cash (lump-sum) needs at death and ongoing income needs. First, project future cash flow income needs and find the present value of all those needs. Then identify and deduct all of the existing sources of income (Social Security, investments, employee benefits, and so on) to determine the income deficit. This amount equals the unfunded amount that can be made up with life insurance. Future income payments can be comprised solely of investment earnings on a capital sum, or they can be a combination of investment earnings and liquidation of part of the capital sum. Within the life insurance industry, the liquidating approach is referred to as a

financial needs analysis, and a nonliquidating approach is often referred to as a *capital needs analysis*.

In the *financial needs analysis* approach, both principal and interest are used to provide income and capital for a certain period into the future, at which point all capital is spent. This is also known as the *capital distribution method* or *liquidating approach*, since all funds are expected to be distributed over time. Since the principal is used as income, this method requires a smaller amount of initial principal to provide the desired income than in the capital conservation method, which preserves principal.

A serious shortcoming of the liquidating approach is that the fund may eventually be totally consumed. The *capital needs analysis* follows the same approach, but satisfies the income needs using only the earnings on a principal sum, which is not liquidated. The capital-needs analysis method uses the *capital conservation method*, where capital is preserved rather than spent. This method uses only interest generated from investments to provide the desired income.

4. A business can take a business expense deduction for premium paid for group term (Sec. 79) plans. If the plan is nondiscriminatory, the first $50,000 of coverage is tax free to all plan participants. Taxable amounts of coverage above $50,000 are taxed at Table 1 rates. With groups of 10 or more employees, the coverage test requires the plan to do one of the following: (1) cover at least 70 employees, (2) have no more than 15 percent in the key employee group, or (3) benefit a reasonable classification of participants. Participants with less than 3 years of service, who work part-time, or who are subject to collective bargaining may be excluded. The benefits test requires a flat amount or a uniform percentage of compensation.
5. One advantage to executive bonus is its ability to avoid the nondiscrimination rules applicable to other fringe benefits. In a Sec. 162 plan, shareholder-employees and executives who participate in the plan apply for, own, and name the beneficiary on permanent life insurance policies covering their lives. The premiums for such policies are provided through a bonus payment by the employer-corporation. The corporation pays the premium directly to the insurer, or bonuses the premium to the employee. The premium amount paid directly to the insurer (or bonused to the employee) is treated as gross compensation income to the

employee. This compensation is treated as ordinary income subject to the employee's individual income tax rate. If the bonus, along with the employee's other compensation represents reasonable compensation, the corporation deducts the amount of the bonus as an ordinary business expense under Sec. 162.

6. Split-dollar splits the premium, death benefits, and cash value between an employer and an employee, under a number of different arrangements, to satisfy the goals of those parties. For example, the executive may need life insurance for family protection or estate liquidity, or may need assistance in affording the premiums. Perhaps the employer wishes to reward the employee and provide tax-advantaged benefits or additional compensation. Policy ownership is very important. In the endorsement method, the employer owns the policy and an endorsement is attached, indicating that after the premiums paid by the employer are reimbursed, the employee's beneficiary receives the balance of any death proceeds. With the collateral assignment method, the employee owns the policy, which is collaterally assigned to the employer to the extent of indebtedness on employer contributions to the policy. The taxation under the new regulations follows two mutually exclusive methods determined by policyownership. Under the economic benefit method, the participant reports income based on the value of pure insurance coverage under Table 2001 or equivalent. Under the loan method, the non-owner (employer) is treated as loaning premium payments to the owner. Loan interest must be paid, or the interest will be treated as compensation and taxed accordingly.

7. Deferred-compensation plans can be categorized as either *qualified* or *nonqualified*. Under a deferred-compensation plan, part of the employee's compensation over the employee's working years is deferred until a later period, such as the employee's retirement. This deferral meets two goals. First, the deferred compensation will provide income for the employee during his or her retirement. Second, the deferred compensation plan is tax-deferred until the income is received.

   Nonqualified plans provide a similar deferral of the employee's receipt of ordinary income. However, nonqualified plans also cause a deferral of the employer's tax deduction until such benefits are paid. Although employees are generally not taxed on the promised benefits from a qualified plan until they are received, death benefits provided by life insurance are currently taxable. The current cost of "pure insurance" protection is subject to taxation, determined by the rates supplied by IRS Table 2001—One-Year Term Premiums.

8. A qualified plan must generally purchase life insurance in order to provide any substantial pre-retirement death benefit. This gives the plan significant funds at a participant's death, which is particularly important in the early years of his or her employment when the amount contributed on the participant's behalf is still relatively small. An insured preretirement death benefit can be provided in either a defined-benefit or defined-contribution plan. Contributions to the plan by the employer may be used to pay life insurance premiums as long as the amount qualifies under the tests for *incidental benefits.* In general, the IRS considers that nonretirement benefits in a qualified plan (e.g., life, medical, or disability insurance) will be incidental and therefore permissible as long as the cost of providing these benefits is less than 25 percent of the cost of providing all the benefits under the plan. The 25 percent rule is applied to the portion of any life insurance premium that is used to provide current life insurance protection. Any portion of the premium that is used to increase the cash value of the policy is considered a contribution to the plan fund to pay retirement benefits, and it is not considered in the 25 percent limitation.

   Qualified plans must meet federal nondiscrimination and administrative compliance standards. These standards increase the cost of such plans. A broad base of employees must be included and significant administrative fees must be paid. The corporation gets an immediate income tax deduction for contributions to the plan, while the employee's tax on plan benefits is deferred until the benefits are received. Qualified plans will include pension plans, IRAs, profit-sharing plans, and Sec. 403(b) plans. Nonqualified plans provide a similar deferral of the employee's receipt of ordinary income. Nonqualified plans also cause a deferral of the employer's tax deduction until such benefits are paid. Because closely held corporations often want to maximize the benefits for shareholder-employees, the goal of their retirement plans is to discriminate in favor of shareholder-employees and key executives to the fullest extent of the nondiscrimination rules. Since discrimination is permitted in nonqualified arrangements, these plans are often more favorable to the closely held corporation. The employer can finance its obligation in a nonqualified plan through corporate-owned life insurance. This type of financing is attractive, since life insurance as a corporate asset is a good match for the type of liabilities created by nonqualified arrangements. The accumulation in an ordinary life insurance policy can be useful in the participant's retirement years to provide for any salary continuation benefits offered by the plan. The primary benefit of the life insurance financing is its ability to meet the employer's death benefit obligation should the participant die prematurely. Nonqualified plan policies are owned by and payable to the employer. As such, they avoid constructive-receipt or economic-benefit problems, because the general creditors have access to the funding policies. The premiums are nondeductible. The cash surrender value builds up tax free, and the proceeds will be nontaxable when received. The corporation receives a deduction when the benefits are actually paid to the participant.

9. Key employee life insurance indemnifies a business concern for the loss of earnings caused by the death of a key officer or employee. In many business concerns, there is one person whose capital, technical knowledge, experience, or business connections make him or her a valuable asset of the organization and a necessity to its successful operation. Insurance is purchased on the life of the key employee by the business and is made payable to the business as beneficiary. In most cases, some form of permanent insurance, usually ordinary life, is purchased, and the accumulating cash values are reflected as an asset on the business's books. If key person protection is needed for only a temporary period, term insurance is normally used. Premiums paid for key person insurance are not deductible as a business expense, but in the event of death, the proceeds are received free of federal income tax.

10. A buy-sell agreement binds the surviving parties to purchase the business interest of the first owner to die at a price set forth in the agreement and obligates the deceased owner's estate to sell his or her interest to the surviving owners. The various interests are valued at the time the agreement is drawn up and revised from time to time thereafter. Each owner is insured for the amount of his or her interest, and either the business or the other owners own the insurance. Upon the first death among the owners, the life insurance proceeds are used by the survivor(s) to purchase the deceased's interest. Thus, the business continues in operation for the benefit of the surviving owners, and the deceased's heirs receive the going value of his or her business interest in cash.

Under a stock-redemption agreement, the corporation is the "purchaser" of the stock at the death of a shareholder. Each shareholder subject to the agreement binds his or her estate to transfer the stock to the corporation in exchange for the required purchase price. A cross-purchase agreement is a contract in which each shareholder agrees to purchase a specified percentage of the shares of stock held by a deceased shareholder at the time of death. Each shareholder must also agree to bind his or her estate to sell the stock owned at his or her death.

Answers to Self-Test Questions

1. A
2. B
3. D
4. B
5. C
6. A
7. C
8. C
9. B
10. D

Chapter 3

Answers to Review Questions

1. Term insurance provides life insurance protection for a limited period only. The face amount of the policy is payable if the insured dies during the specified period, and nothing is paid if the insured survives. The period may be as short as one year, or it may run to age 65 or above. Such policies may insure for the agreed term only, or they may give the insured the option of renewing the protection for successive terms without evidence of insurability. Term insurance may be regarded as temporary insurance. The premium for term insurance is initially relatively low, despite the fact that it contains a relatively high expense loading and an allowance for adverse selection. The reason premiums can be low is that most term contracts do not cover the period of old age when death is most likely to occur and when the cost of insurance is high.
2. Variations of term insurance include the following:

- Renewable term—contains an option to renew for a limited number of additional periods of term insurance, usually of the same length, without evidence of insurability.
- Convertible term—contains a provision that permits the policyowner to exchange the term contract for a contract on a permanent plan without evidence of insurability.
- Reentry term—a term insurance policy intended to charge a higher premium to those in poorer health when they renew their term insurance, thereby reducing the degree of adverse selection.
- Long-term contracts—term contracts designed to provide insurance over a long period, such as term to age 65.
- Nonlevel term—the amount of insurance may either increase or decrease throughout the term of the policy.

3. Renewable term insurance contracts contain an option to renew for a limited number of periods of term insurance, usually of the same length. The key to the renewable feature is the right to renew the contract without providing evidence of insurability. Where the term policy contains no renewal privilege, or where evidence of insurability is required, the insured may find it difficult or impossible to continue a contract, or obtain any other form of life insurance, due to poor health, dangerous occupation or hobby, or some other reason. Renewability prevents this. Its chief function is to protect the insurability of the insured.
4. If a term policy is converted as of the current date, conversion is referred to as an *attained-age method*, because the current age determines the premium. A conversion using the original date of the term policy is referred to as the *original-age method* or a *retroactive conversion*. Advantages of original-age conversions include (1) a lower premium and (2) the possibility that the contract being issued at the original date contains actuarial assumptions or other features more favorable than those being offered in current policies. A major disadvantage is the financial adjustment involving a payment by the insured to the company, which may be quite substantial if the term policy has been in effect for a number of years. The payment is calculated as the larger of (1) the differences in the reserves (or cash values) under the policies being exchanged or (2) the differences in the premiums paid on the term policy and those that would have been paid on the permanent plan, with interest on the difference at a stipulated rate.

5. The purpose of a time limit on term conversions is to minimize adverse selection. As the time limit on conversion approaches, those insureds in poor health are more likely to convert and pay the premium than those who believe they are in good health. Typically, a policy will require conversion within 10 years of the policy date, or before age 60 or 65.
6. Select and ultimate term (reentry) insurance is a policy subject to two different premium schedules. The lower premium rate is based on select rates given to those who have recent, favorable evidence of insurability. Select rates are available at renewal if the insured submits satisfactory evidence of insurability. The higher-premium rate schedule is based on ultimate rates, which are those rates applicable after 10–20 years of previously providing evidence of insurability. The insured who cannot or wishes not to show good health to the insurer when required will pay considerably higher rates to renew their coverage.
7. Term-to-65 policies (1) are designed to provide long-term protection, (2) often give prospective policyowners the option to purchase waiver-of-premium and accidental death benefits, and (3) customarily provide for cash and other surrender values.
8. Term insurance is useful and suitable when either the need for protection is temporary or the insured cannot afford the premiums for permanent insurance. Temporary needs can and should be solved through term insurance. Examples of a suitable use of term insurance include younger adults with limited income, families with dependent children, covering a loan, mortgage redemption, to protect a speculative investment or business venture, or key person insurance on a person instrumental to the success of a business or similar venture.
9. Marketing is the planning and implementation of a process dedicated to identifying specific consumer needs, isolating groups of people who have those needs, and then producing and customizing the products and services that satisfy those needs. Much of marketing does not involve interaction with a buyer for making a sale. Selling is a part of marketing and is the result of successful marketing. It is the transaction resulting from the encounter between buyer and seller, the exchange of the product or service for the buyer's cash. Any effective marketing strategy you create should accomplish four things: (1) create a perpetual qualified prospect machine; (2) decrease your appointments-to-sales ratio (efficiency in creating clients); (3) decrease your contacts-made-to-appointments ratio (decrease the

amount of time and energy devoted to prospecting); and (4) help you focus and specialize to create a higher value for your services.

10. There are three sources of names: people who know you favorably, people recommended by those who know you favorably, and people who do not know you at all. The most common prospecting methods include: referrals, networking, centers of influence, speaking to groups, social mobility, and direct mail.

Answers to Self-Test Questions

1. B
2. A
3. A
4. C
5. D
6. C
7. B
8. D
9. B
10. C

Chapter 4

Answers to Review Questions

1. The general features of whole life include the following:

    - Permanent protection—provides for the payment of the face amount upon the death of the insured, regardless of when death occurs.
    - Reserve and cash value—increases over the duration of the policy and eventually equals the face amount at the end of the policy period (usually age 100).
    - Policy loans—gives the policyowner access to the cash value that accumulates inside the policy without having to terminate the policy. Policy loans create interest charges on the borrowed funds. The policyowner has the option of paying the policy loan interest in cash or having the unpaid interest charge added to the balance of the outstanding loan(s) so that additional interest charges will be applied to the unpaid interest amount. If the policy loan

and accrued interest are not paid in cash, the life insurer can recover the outstanding balance of the loans and accrued interest in the following ways: (1) from the death benefits if the insured dies or (2) from the cash surrender value if the policy is terminated. In fact, the policy will automatically terminate if the policy loan balance plus unpaid interest ever exceeds the policy cash value.

A policy loan reduces the death benefit that a beneficiary would receive on the death of the insured by the amount of the loan and accrued interest. It reduces the cash surrender value by the amount of the loan and accrued interest for the policyowner, if the policy is surrendered or terminated. The outstanding loan would also reduce the extended-term insurance or reduced paid-up insurance benefits available upon lapse.

- Automatic premium loan—when this option is selected, a delinquent premium will be paid automatically by a new policy loan. This will keep the policy in force as long as there is adequate cash value to cover each delinquent premium. However, the policy will terminate if the cash value is exhausted.
- Nonforfeiture or surrender options—the surrender value may be taken in cash, a reduced amount of paid-up insurance, or paid-up term insurance.
- Annuity or retirement income—the surrender value can be used to purchase an annuity or retirement income.
- Participating versus nonparticipating—can be purchased on a participating (pays policyowner dividends) or nonparticipating (does not provide for policyowner dividends) basis.

2. Unlike whole life policies for which premiums are paid until the insured's death, limited-payment life insurance is a type of whole life insurance for which premiums are limited by contract to a specified number of years. The limitation may be expressed as a number of annual premiums (for example, 20-pay life) or as the age beyond which premiums are not required (for example, life paid up at 65).
3. A joint life policy is one written on the lives of two or more persons. There are two types of joint life policies, depending on when the death benefits are paid. First, a joint life policy pays the death benefit upon the death of the first insured to die. These policies might fund business buy-sell agreements, or be used by married

homeowners as mortgage insurance. The second type, called *survivorship life* or a *second-to-die policy*, pays the death benefit upon the death of the last of two or more lives insured under a single policy. These policies have become popular to provide funds to pay estate taxes and settlement costs for wealthy couples that wish to maximize deferral of estate taxes at the first death.

4. The key uses of whole life are to provide protection against long-range or permanent needs, and to accumulate a savings fund that can be used for general purposes or to meet specific needs or objectives.

5. Long-term care insurance (LTCI) combination plans have been a niche market in the life insurance industry for many years. In today's marketplace, there are two basic approaches to life insurance with long-term care benefits. In the "integrated or hybrid" design, single-premium whole life or universal life policies are sold with both life insurance and long-term care coverage. The second approach uses an optional rider on a whole life, universal life, or variable universal life policy for which premium is paid on an on-going basis.

   Under both designs, the death benefit is accelerated to cover qualifying long-term care expenses, typically after a 90-day elimination period. For an additional cost, the policyowner may be able to elect an extension-of-benefits option that provides for continuation of long-term care coverage to several times the life policy death benefit. Inflation protection is also offered. The long-term benefits are tax-qualified, so benefit triggers and covered expenses are uniform across companies and mirror tax-qualified stand-alone LTCI plans. Covered expenses include home health care, assisted living, nursing home care, and adult day care. The policyowner chooses a desired total LTC available fund and a period of time over which that fund will be paid out (24, 36, or 48 months are common, with a few carriers offering 60 months or lifetime payouts).

6. While a whole life insurance contract provides a survivorship benefit at age 100 that is equal to the death benefit that would have been payable prior to the insured's age 100, endowment contracts make the same full-survivorship benefit payable at younger ages. Among the wide variety of endowments that have been sold are 10-, 15-, 20-, 25-, 30-, 35-, and 40-year endowments (or longer). Alternatively, the maturity date can be a specific age of the insured, such as 55, 65, 70, or older. Endowment policies have nearly

disappeared from new policy sales, because changes in the federal income tax laws in the mid-1980s took away the tax preference for newly sold endowments. Interest earned on the cash value of a newly sold endowment would now be taxed annually rather than tax deferred as with other life insurance policies.

7. The *adjustable life policy,* which can be positioned anywhere along the spectrum from short-duration term insurance through single-premium whole life insurance, gives the policyowner the right to request and obtain a reconfiguration of the policy at specified intervals.

   Adjustable life insurance contains all of the same guarantees regarding cash values, mortality, and expenses as whole life insurance, but has the flexibility to allow the policyowner to adjust the plan of insurance, the premiums, and/or the face amount after it is in force. This allows changes to be made within the original policy instead of issuing a new policy each time needs change. It appeals to purchasers who want the ability to restructure their coverage without assuming any of the investment or mortality risks.

   Adjustable life is a whole life policy with fixed premiums. Although premiums can be changed, such a change requires a formal adjustment agreed to in writing by both insurer and policyowner before it can be made. The premium remains fixed and inflexible between formal adjustments. The elements subject to change are the premium, face amount, and cash value. Most changes can be made without evidence of insurability, but the insurer can require such evidence if the proposed change increases the amount at risk.

8. A current assumption whole life policy has a guaranteed death benefit and a premium that must be paid by the end of the grace period or the policy will lapse. Premiums paid are charged for mortality and expense and credited with interest to produce the policy cash value. In low premium plans, premiums are guaranteed for several years and then *redetermined* periodically (every 2 or 5 years). Depending upon current assumptions and the amount already accumulated in the cash value, premiums for the next period may go up or down. In the high-premium version of CAWL, favorable experience may increase the cash value to a level where the policy becomes self-supporting. There is no guarantee that premiums will ever vanish, or if they do, that they will not have to be paid again in the future if experience worsens. There are still many guaranteed elements in current assumption whole life

policies. There is a guaranteed death benefit and a minimum guaranteed interest rate to be credited on policy cash values. Beyond this, there are design variations that lead to different names in the marketplace. Some companies guarantee the mortality charge and the expense charges. Those policies are referred to as an interest-sensitive whole life policy, because excess interest (credited interest minus guaranteed interest) credited to the cash value becomes the only nonguaranteed element in the contract. Most CAWL policies have some degree of flexibility in the expense elements. Because many of these designs periodically recast the premium amount based on recent experience, some of these policies are referred to as indeterminate premium whole life policies. There is a guaranteed maximum premium that can be charged, but the actual mortality, interest, and expenses result in lower premium amounts being charged if there is favorable experience under the policy. The high premium version of current assumption whole life insurance uses favorable experience to increase the cash value and as a result, the policy may become self-supporting.

9. Most arguments against permanent (whole life) insurance focus on two allegations: (1) whole life overcharges for the premium, and (2) the accumulation and protection elements should be separated. The first argument is only true if a person dies within a short time of purchasing the policy. We do not know when we will die. Permanent insurance protects the insured against living too long as well as dying too soon. In a long-life term, premiums can exceed the policy death benefit payable. By paying a level premium, the policyowner shifts the financial risk of death to the insurance company, preventing the need to pay prohibitive premiums in old age for term insurance. The argument that the cash value (reserve) is paid out with the face amount as a death benefit, and not in addition to it, is because the reducing risk amount is part of the assumption made initially in calculating the premium. The second argument that the accumulation and protection elements should be separated is based on the proposition of "buying term and investing the difference" of the two premiums. This argument assumes that the individual can invest more wisely and with a greater return than the insurance company. When looking at the investment objectives of safety, yield, and liquidity, the insurance industry is difficult to outperform. Yield and safety are inverse, and as one increases, the other decreases. Whole life also offers a number of tax advantages and loan privileges that enhance its value.

10. The principal objectives of insurance companies' general investment portfolios, and the whole life insurance product specifically, are safety of principal, yield, and liquidity, based on a portfolio of conservative and diversified investments. Whole life cash values never go down unless withdrawn. Regarding safety of principal, the life insurance industry has compiled a solvency record over the years that is unmatched by any other type of business organization. It has survived wars, depressions, and inflation; composite losses to policyowners have been relatively rare. Even the few companies seized by the regulators in recent years have been able to rescue most of their policyowners' contracts.

    Whole life follows a conservative investment strategy. Its investment goals are safety of principal and a steady flow of income in order to guarantee future benefits. Investments must be safe and predictable. The dollars backing whole life are invested in the insurance company's general portfolio. The general portfolio of the insurance company is composed primarily of high-grade, long-term corporate and government bonds and mortgages. The quality of a company and its investments vary, so it is important to study how a company invests its money.

11. The objective of the initial interview for the advisor is to establish rapport, get the client's agreement to do fact-finding, and continue the selling/planning process. In the sales process, the advisor must help the prospect with a life insurance need understand the nature and extent of the problems that may develop by not having adequate life insurance. The potential problems must be clearly identified and understood by the buyer before he or she will be motivated to take action. The buyer must have a strong desire to solve these problems and the advisor must present compelling reasons to act now rather than later if the sale is to be made and the problems resolved.

    This process takes form in the initial interview. There are four basic objectives to the initial interview. Whether you use a sales track supplied by your company or create your own compliance-approved presentation, the purposes are essentially the same. Your objectives are as follows:

    a. Create a sense of rapport and credibility, and build trust.
    b. Uncover insurance and other financial needs and determine priorities.
    c. Establish your ability to help.

d. Obtain your prospect's permission to proceed, and ge their commitment to work with you.

Answers to Self-Test Questions

1. B
2. C
3. A
4. D
5. C
6. C
7. D
8. D
9. B
10. A

Chapter 5

Answers to Review Questions

1. A variable life insurance policy provides no guarantees of either interest rate or minimum cash value. In order for policyowners to gain the additional benefit of better-than-expected investment returns, they also have to assume all of the downside investment risk. The SEC requires variable life policies to be registered with the SEC and all sales to be subject to the following requirements applied to other registered securities:

    - Policy sales can be made only after the prospective purchaser has a chance to read the policy prospectus.
    - An insurance company issuing a variable life insurance policy must be registered as an investment company and all sales agents must be registered with the SEC for the specific purpose of variable life insurance policy sales.
    - Agents who sell variable life insurance policies must be licensed as both life insurance agents and securities agents.

2. Because the primary reason for life insurance is to provide death benefits, it makes sense to link superior investment performance with increases in the death benefit level. A variable life insurance policy has a minimum death benefit equal to the initial face

amount when the policy was first purchased. If the policy's actual investment performance exceeds a target level of investment performance, the excess investment return is used to purchase additional life insurance under either the level additions method or the constant ratio method. Under both methods, the amount of additional coverage in excess of the initial face amount will fluctuate depending on actual investment performance. If investment earnings are negative (actual earnings are lower than the target rate), then downward adjustments are made from any previously attained levels above the policy's initial face value. If investment earnings are positive (actual earnings are above the target rate), the adjustments will be upward.

3. Life insurance companies are now offering many more investment fund options than they made available in the early stages of the VLI product's development. Most insurance companies have more than a dozen funds from which to choose in their current product offering. There are usually a variety of stock funds, including growth stock funds, income stock funds, balanced stock funds, and international stock funds. Bond fund offerings are likewise more robust and include different durations and different types of issuers (large corporations, small corporations, state governments, and the federal government) as well as Government National Mortgage Association funds (GNMAs) and collateralized mortgage obligations (CMOs). Many insurance companies offer a managed fund as one of their portfolio choices, and have formed alliances with large mutual fund groups that make their entire range of mutual funds available.
4. Unlike a whole life policy, in which the cash value increases over time due to the crediting of at least the guaranteed interest rate, the cash value of a variable life policy fluctuates daily based on the net asset value of the separate account funds that make up the policy portfolio.
5. The prospectus is a full disclosure of the provisions of the contract, including expenses, investment options, benefit provisions, and policyowner rights under the contract. The prospectus provides a very thorough overview of all expense charges levied by the insurance company against VLI contracts. This includes commissions paid to soliciting agents, state premium taxes, administrative charges, collection charges, and fees for specific future transactions. The prospectus explains how charges are made against the asset account to cover the cost of insurance under the contract. It also explains the manner in which charges

are levied against the separate account itself—the fees associated with managing the various mutual fund type of accounts from which the policyowner can choose. Part of the charges are always some specified percentage (usually less than one full percent) of the assets in the separate accounts. The prospectus explains the surrender charge applicable to policy surrenders. This information is often set forth in a table, giving the policy year and the applicable percentage for the surrender charge in that year. Surrender charges are commonly levied during the first 10 to 15 years of the contract. The prospectus describes the investment objectives of each of the available investment funds and a record of their historical performance. Any investment restrictions applicable to these portfolios are fully disclosed. There are also projections of future performance under the contract if portfolio funds generate a fixed level of investment earnings over the projected interval. Under SEC regulations, the permissible rates of return that can be projected are the gross annual rates after tax charges, but before any other deductions at 0, 4, 8, 10, or 12 percent. The insurance company can decide the permissible rates it chooses to project.

6. With a VLI policy, the policyowner assumes the investment risk and participates in favorable investment returns. The fixed-premium provision does not allow the policyowner to increase or decrease the death benefit as an option; favorable results automatically translate into increased death benefit amounts. The policy does guarantee a minimum death benefit level equal to the original face amount of the contract, regardless of how negative the investment performance. If all required premiums are paid, the insurance company guarantees a death benefit equal to the original face amount of the policy will be paid, even if the investment funds are otherwise inadequate to support the policy. The variable feature of this contract can provide additional coverage if warranted by investment experience, but the policyowner will never be required to pay more or permitted to pay less than the guaranteed premium.
7. Section 7702 of the Deficit Reduction Act of 1984 (DEFRA) defines life insurance for income tax purposes, requiring a certain amount of the death benefit to be at risk (insurance amount), depending on age. For life insurance to qualify for the income tax benefits afforded by the U.S. Congress, there must be a statutory amount of death benefit in excess of the cash value. These rules were created to limit how much money can be put into a life insurance policy, and therefore prevent abuse of the true purpose of granting tax benefits to life insurance, which is to encourage citizens to

purchase it for the protection of family and business interests. The definition in the law is expressed in terms of the net amount at risk: "only the excess of the amount paid by reason of the insured's death over the contract's net surrender value should be deemed to be life insurance" .

8. Universal life insurance was introduced in 1979 as a revolutionary new product. It was the first variation of whole life insurance to offer truly flexible premiums. The policy death benefit can be adjusted upward (sometimes requiring proof of insurability) or downward to meet the policyowner's needs. Two other features were also initiated with universal life policies: (1) the policyowner's ability to withdraw part of the cash value without having the withdrawal treated as a policy loan, and (2) the choice of either a level death benefit design or an increasing death benefit design.
9. The true innovation of UL insurance was the introduction of completely flexible premiums after the first policy year, the only time a minimum level of premium payments for a universal life policy is required. The first year's premium can be arranged on a monthly, quarterly, semiannual, or annual basis. The insurance company requires only that a minimum specified level of first-year premium payments be equaled or exceeded. After the first policy year, it is up to the policyowner to decide the amount of premium to pay (limited by the maximums contained in the income tax definition of life insurance) and even whether or not to pay the premiums. Premiums can only be skipped altogether if the policy cash value is at least adequate to cover the next 60 days of expense and mortality charges. Otherwise, the policy would lapse by the end of the grace period if no additional premium was paid.
10. A UL policy permits the policyowner to make partial withdrawals from the policy's cash value without incurring any indebtedness. Money can be taken out of the policy cash value, but no interest is charged on the amount withdrawn, as there would be with a policy loan. Withdrawals do affect the policy's future earnings, because the fund still intact to earn interest for future crediting periods is reduced by the amount of the withdrawal. Its effect on the death benefit depends on the type of death benefit in force. Partial withdrawals do not reduce the death benefit amount under the level death benefit design. They do, however, decrease the amount of the policy's cash value and correspondingly increase the amount at risk. Partial withdrawals under the increasing death benefit design will reduce the death benefit payable, because the

withdrawal decreases the cash value that constitutes part of the death benefit amount.

11. Nearly every UL policy is issued with a target-premium amount. The target amount is the suggested premium to be paid on a level basis throughout the contract's duration or for a shorter period if a limited-pay approach was originally intended to fund the policy. The target premium amount is merely a suggestion and carries no liability if it is inadequate to maintain the contract to any duration, much less to the end of life. Some insurance companies have introduced a secondary guarantee associated with their target premium. These companies have pledged contractually to keep the policy in force for, say, 15 or 20 years and to pay the full death benefit as long as the premium has been paid in an amount equal to or greater than the target premium at each premium-payment interval. The target premium is also the amount companies use to determine the maximum full first-year commission rate of new sales.
12. UL insurance gives policyowners a choice between level death benefits and increasing death benefits. The level death benefit design is much like the traditional whole life design. When the death benefit stays constant and the cash value increases over the duration of the contract, the amount at risk or the protection element decreases. The one new aspect of a level death benefit design under UL policies results from a tax-law definition of life insurance that was added to the Code shortly after the introduction of UL insurance policies. This required that a specified proportion of the death benefit be derived from the amount at risk. Whenever the cash value in the contract gets high enough that this proportion is no longer satisfied, the UL policy starts increasing the death benefit with a level death benefit option. This is known as the corridor test. The increasing death benefit design is a modification that was introduced with UL policies. Under this approach, there is always a constant amount at risk that is superimposed over the policy's cash value. As the cash value increases, so does the total death benefit. A reduction in the cash value will reduce the death benefit. This design pays both the policy's stated face amount and its cash value at the insured's death. A higher portion of the premium is needed for the larger amount at risk under this design.
13. Most UL policies credit current interest rates on the cash value as long as there are no outstanding policy loans. Once the policyowner borrows funds from the cash value, the insurance company usually credits a lower interest rate, or earnings rate, to the portion of the cash value associated with the policy loan. Many universal life

policies sold today credit the cash value with the current rate for nonborrowed funds and a lower rate, which is often two percentage points lower than the current rate, for borrowed funds. Any outstanding debt will reduce any death-benefit proceeds or cash value proceeds otherwise payable under a universal life policy.

14. UL policies cover expenses through front-end loads and/or back-end loads (surrender charges). Early UL policies were front-end-loaded products. They took a significant proportion of each premium dollar as administrative expenses, and the remaining portion was then credited to the policy cash value. As UL insurance policies evolved, more of them moved to a back-end loading design. They lowered or eliminated the up-front charge levied against incoming premium amounts and instead imposed surrender charges to the cash value of a policy surrendered during the contract's first 7 to 15 years. Surrender charges are highest during the first policy year and decrease over the remaining years until the year in which the insurance company expects to have amortized all excess first-year expenses. At that point, the surrender charge is reduced to zero and will not be applicable at later policy durations. After the premiums (less any front-end load) reach the policy cash value, they are subject to a mortality charge based on the amount at risk. The current mortality rate charged is often considerably less than the guaranteed maximum mortality rate set forth in the policy for each attained age of the insured. After deductions for expenses and mortality, the UL cash value is then increased at the current crediting rate to reflect investment earnings on that cash value. The actual rate credited is a decision made by the insurance company, and it reflects current economic conditions. Competitive pressures have caused insurance companies to minimize front-end loading in order to emphasize that nearly all premium dollars go directly into the cash value. The actual expenses are deducted internally, but are not easily discernible by the consuming public. For example, expenses can be embedded in the spread between actual mortality costs and actual mortality charges or in the spread between investment earnings and the interest rate credited to the cash value accounts.

15. Secondary guarantees keep the policy in force for a set number of years or to a certain age. They guarantee to pay the full death benefit as long as the premium is paid in an amount equal to or greater than the premium amount required at each premium-payment interval. These plans function like a term-to-age-100-and-beyond, with minimal cash value build-up (the

cash value is used to pay the premium), and an emphasis on death benefit protection. These plans keep the death benefit in force even when the policy cash values are depleted. Accumulation under these riders is secondary, trading off the cash accumulation for the death benefit guarantee. Interest rate crediting may be lower, and the charges for mortality and expenses may be higher, than a policy without the no-lapse guarantee. The lower crediting and higher mortality and expense charges are an indirect, but additional cost of the guarantee that allows the company to lower the premium.

16. Indexed universal life (IUL) is permanent life insurance that offers all the benefits of UL with accumulation values tied to a stock market index. An IUL policy has a fixed-interest-rate component, as well as an indexed-account option. Whereas traditional ULs may credit 4 percent–6 percent, an IUL has the ability to receive index-linked gains as high as 18 percent today. In years for which the index does well, interest-crediting rates will rise, and in years where the index performs poorly, interest crediting will fall. The policyowner reaps the rewards of stock market-type gains, but is also protected with minimum guaranteed interest rates in case of stock market losses. IUL otherwise has all of the typical features of traditional universal life and operates under the same policy mechanics. The major difference with an IUL is the option to participate indirectly in the upward movement of a stock index without accepting the normal risk associated with investing in the stock market. The actual interest credited to a policy's cash value is determined by the changes of an equities index. Most insurance companies use the S & P 500 Index® as the underlying index for their IUL product. This combination of the potential to realize higher upside returns without the downside risk makes the IUL policy a unique and attractive cash accumulation vehicle.
17. Variable universal life insurance (VUL) incorporates all of the premium flexibility and policy adjustment features of the universal life policy with the policyowner-directed investment aspects of variable life insurance.

    - VUL differs from UL in providing no minimum interest rate guarantee. Premium net of mortality and expense charges are invested in separate accounts chosen by the policyowner and the VUL cash value depends solely on the investment results achieved. Like VLI, VUL policies are classified as securities and are subject to regulation by the SEC. The SEC requires registration of agents marketing the product, the separate accounts supporting the contracts, and the contracts themselves. Policies must conform with SEC requirements that the investment funds be separate accounts that are segregated from the insurance company's general investment portfolio and, therefore, not subject to creditors' claims applicable to the insurer's general portfolio in times of financial difficulty. Because VUL is a registered investment product, policies must be accompanied by a prospectus, which is governed by the same rules applicable to prospectuses for variable life policies.

- VUL discards the fixed-premium features of VLI and offers a choice of level or increasing death benefits.

18. The primary objective of the information-gathering process is to uncover meaningful information about the prospect by asking questions. This enables the advisor to have a discussion with the prospect about the prospect's goals, attitudes, priorities, current situation, and any changes anticipated for the future. As a result, recommendations can be made from an informed exchange of ideas. The following are the objectives of the information-gathering interview for the advisor:

    - Gather relevant factual and objective information about the client's current situation, including important personal and employment information, assets and liabilities, financial information, and other related data.
    - Gather subjective data, including important values, feelings, and attitudes towards financial issues. Most importantly, determine the client's goals, objectives, and needs. This includes prioritizing goals in terms of importance and completion target date(s). One important piece of information is risk tolerance, the client's attitude towards risk. Another is the expectations the client has for the process.
    - Gain a dollar commitment for the amount the client is willing and able to spend to accomplish the identified goals.

19. Review the list of your prospect's needs, concerns, and desires identified in the information-gathering interview. This process determines the facts of the prospect's current financial situation—where they are now. Next, review the prospect's goals to define where they want to be. You will then be in a position to calculate the amount of any additional insurance or investments

needed to close the gap between their present situation and their desired situation. Finally, design a solution, with alternatives, to present to your prospective client to achieve this task.

Answers to Self-Test Questions

1. C
2. A
3. B
4. A
5. D
6. B
7. B
8. A
9. C
10. D

Chapter 6

Answers to Review Questions

1. The net cost method is a flawed method for comparing policies. It looks at a period of coverage, takes the aggregated net premiums paid under the policy, and then subtracts any cash value accumulated at the end of the period and all dividends paid over the period. It does not consider time value of money (interest and timing of payments), and is therefore misleading, because it does not take into account when the money was paid or received, the opportunity cost, or the alternative-use value of the money.
2. There are two interest-adjusted cost indices: the *surrender cost index* and the *payment cost index*. The interest-adjusted indices take into account the time value of money. The interest-adjusted methods take all payments for premiums and treat them as if they had been put into interest-bearing accounts to accumulate interest (assumed to be 5 percent) until the end of the interval for evaluation (10 and 20 years). Similarly, all dividend payments are carried as if they are deposited in an interest-bearing account, and that account balance is calculated for the end of the interval of evaluation. For the surrender cost index, the policy cash value at the end of the evaluation period and the amount of accumulated dividends are subtracted from the accumulated value of all the premiums paid.

The result is divided by the future value of an annuity due of $1 for the length of the evaluation period at the assumed rate of interest. Determining the payment cost index is the same as calculating the surrender cost index, except that there is no recognition of the end-of-period cash value.

3. The cash accumulation comparison method involves accumulating the premium differences between the policies being compared, while holding the death benefits of both policies constant and equal. For example, to compare a cash value contract with a term contract, set the death benefits equal at the beginning of the period, and use the yearly premium difference between the cash value contract and the term policy to determine the amount to deposit into a side fund to accumulate at interest. The calculation is a buy-term-and-invest-the-difference approach to comparing the policies. At the end of the interval being evaluated, the side fund accumulation can be compared to the whole life cash value. The policy with the greater accumulation at the end of the comparison interval is considered the preferable of the two contracts. One of the strengths of the cash-accumulation method is that it allows comparison of permanent insurance policies with term policies. It can also be used for evaluation of replacement proposals. The method has several weaknesses: The cash-accumulation comparison method is much more complex than the net cost and interest-adjusted methods and requires a computer to make the calculations. A significant amount of data must be entered into the computer program in order to calculate the results accurately.

4. The equal-outlay method is similar to the cash-accumulation method. The same amount of premium is expended for a cash value contract and a term policy. The amount by which the premiums of a cash value policy exceed the term premiums is deposited into a side fund, and the difference in premium amounts is accumulated at specified interest rates. Then the death benefit of the term insurance, plus the accumulated side fund amounts are compared with the death benefit under the cash value contract in which dividends, if any, have been used to purchase paid-up additions. Under this type of comparison the policy producing the greater death benefit is considered the preferable contract.

5. There is an inverse relationship between the interest rate and the accumulated values in policy illustrations. That is, higher interest rates result in lower present values, and lower interest rates produce higher present-value amounts.

6. Ledger statements and policy illustrations that do not include interest adjustments are really based on an implicit assumption that the interest rate is zero and the inflation rate is zero.
7. The major elements of the NAIC Life Insurance Illustrations Model Regulation are:
   - The regulation applies to all nonvariable group and individual *life insurance* policies and certificates for more than $10,000 of death benefit.
   - The regulation requires the insurance company to declare to the state insurance department for each policy form whether or not it intends to use illustrations to market that form of coverage. A copy of each illustration the insurer intends to use must be forwarded to the state insurance department.
   - Each illustration used in the sale of a life insurance policy covered by the regulation must be clearly labeled "life insurance illustration" and must include certain specified pieces of information about the company, the agent, the proposed insured, the policy, and its benefit features.
   - The NAIC Model Regulation prohibits insurers and their agents from misrepresenting various specified types of information to the client.
   - The illustration must clearly indicate what elements are guaranteed and what elements are nonguaranteed.
   - Any amount illustrated as being available upon surrender will be the amount after deduction of surrender charges.
   - Each illustration must be accompanied by a narrative summary that describes the policy premiums and features and defines column headings used in the illustration.
   - The summary should also state that actual results may be more or less favorable than those shown in the illustration.
   - The regulation states that illustrations for UL policies must comply with the regulation requirements and that the insurance company must issue annual reports to policyowners after the policy is issued. It also specifies the content of those annual reports.
   - The regulation further stipulates that policyowners have the right to request an in-force illustration annually, without charge.

- Each insurer's board of directors must appoint at least one illustration actuary, who will certify that the illustrations are in compliance with the illustration regulation and are insurer-authorized. The regulation states the qualifications of an illustration actuary, including membership in good standing of the American Academy of Actuaries.
- The model regulation sets forth limits on the methodology for calculating illustrations.

8. The illustration actuary must certify that the illustrations are in compliance with the illustration regulation and are insurer-authorized. The illustration actuary must annually certify the method used to allocate overhead and expenses for all illustrations and file such certification with the insurance commissioner and with the insurer's board of directors. Further, the illustration actuary is required to report any mistakes found in previous certifications to both the commissioner and the board of directors.
9. The plan must be the prospect's plan, not yours, meaning it must reflect the prospect's goals, needs and so on. It must reflect the prospect's risk tolerance level and be suitable in every way to their time horizon, goals, and overall financial situation. It must be affordable, so the best plan is the one that remains in force. You should review the fact-finding highlights and prepare a plan based on the information you have collected and analyzed. In presenting the plan, you should reestablish the prospect's need, review the facts and planning assumptions, and the prospect's objectives. Emphasize relevant facts and features to the prospect. Keep the prospect involved in the presentation.

Answers to Self-Test Questions

1. A
2. C
3. C
4. B
5. A
6. C
7. C
8. D
9. B

10. D

Chapter 7

Answers to Review Questions

1. The prospective policyowner performs only these two functions in the creation of a life insurance contract:

    a. He or she applies for the policy (the contract) by filling out the application and supplying any medical information required by the insurer.

    b. The applicant is then asked to accept or reject the contract as offered by the insurer. The applicant accepts the offer by paying the initial premium. If a partial premium is paid and the insurer's agent issues a premium (conditional) receipt, only temporary coverage under the terms of the receipt is in effect. The contract is accepted by the applicant and binding on the insurer under the particular terms of the receipt and the policy. Even after the applicant accepts the insurer's offer of coverage and a contract is binding on the insurer, the policyowner may, in effect, reject the contract and get a full refund based on the 10-day free-look provision.

2. The face page of the contract usually has the following information:

    - Name of the insurance company
    - Specific details for that policy
    - General description of the type of insurance provided by that policy contract
    - Statement about the policy's free-look provision
    - Insurer's promise to pay
    - Signatures of the officers of the company (usually the president and the secretary), which bind the company to the terms of the contract

3. The standard policy provision laws require that life insurance policies include certain provisions, but allow the insurance companies to select the actual wording. However, the wording must be submitted to and approved by the state insurance department. The state insurance codes generally impose a requirement that unless specifically exempted from the law, all life insurance policies delivered or issued for delivery in the state must contain language

substantially the same as certain specified provisions. Insurers are also generally given the option to insert different provisions than those specified in the statute if the language in the insurer's provisions is more favorable to policyowners. The insurance department determines whether an alternative provision is more favorable to consumers.

4. As a result of the provision, a policy that would have lapsed for nonpayment of premiums continues in force during the grace period. The premium remains due, however, and if the insured dies during the grace period, the insurer may deduct one month's premium from the death benefit.

5. The policyowner is expected to pay interest on the "loan" because he or she has withdrawn assets from the insurer intended to support the level premium concept. If the policyowner withdraws those assets, it is fair to expect him or her to pay an interest rate that would approximate what the insurer would earn if the money were left with the insurer to invest.

6. The goals of the entire contract statutes are

    - to assure that the policyowner is given a copy of all documents that constitute the contract,
    - to preclude any changes in the contract after it has been issued.

7. The typical requirements that must be met for a policyowner to reinstate a life insurance policy are as follows:

    - The reinstatement must occur within a specified period from the date of lapse—for example, three or five years.
    - The policyowner must provide evidence of insurability satisfactory to the insurer.
    - The policyowner must pay or reinstate any other policy indebtedness with interest at a specified rate. This includes back premium due and policy loans if required by the insurer.
    - Normally, insurers do not permit reinstatement of a policy that has been surrendered for its cash value.

8. Rather than voiding the contract based on misrepresentation of age, the practice is to adjust the policy's premium or benefits to reflect the truth after discovering the inaccuracy. Because Jim is already dead, the benefits would be adjusted. Adjustments in the policy's premiums or benefits based on misstatements of age or sex are not precluded by the incontestable clause. This is because

incontestability clauses preclude contests of the validity of the policy. The typical policy provides that if the age of the insured has been misstated, the insurer will adjust all benefits payable under this policy to that which the premium paid would have purchased at the correct age or sex. In this case, the death benefit would be reduced from $100,000 to approximately $90,000 [that is, $100,000 x ($1,500/$1,667)].

9.

$10,000	loan
+ 800	first-year interest ($10,000 x 0.08)
+ 864	second-year interest ($10,800 x 0.08)
$11,664	policy indebtedness

$60,000	cash value
–11,664	indebtedness
$48,336	cash upon surrender

10. When the reduced paid-up option is elected, the policyowner receives a reduced amount of paid-up cash value insurance, payable upon the same conditions as the original policy. The amount of paid-up insurance provided under the reduced paid-up option is the sum that can be purchased at the insured's attained age by the net surrender value. This amount is derived by the cash value, less any policy indebtedness, plus the cash value of any dividend additions or deposits. It is applied as a net single premium, computed on the mortality and interest bases specified in the policy for the calculation of the surrender value.
11. The reduced paid-up option is provided by a benefit provision in a whole life policy and is a guaranteed option upon lapse. There is no option providing for reduced paid-up insurance for a VUL policy or UL policy. The policyowner has to request a death benefit reduction to create the equivalent of a reduced paid-up surrender option. Because the policyowner bears the investment risk with VUL insurance, further adjustments may be needed if the earnings on the cash value drop below the level anticipated when the policy benefit was reduced.
12. The extended term insurance option provides paid-up term insurance in an amount equal to the original face of the policy, increased by any dividend additions or deposits and decreased by

any policy indebtedness. The length of the term is that which can be purchased at the insured's attained age by the application of the net surrender value as a net single premium.

13.

   a. $90,000 of extended term ($100,000 – $10,000)
   b. $20,000 as a net single premium purchase ($30,000 – $10,000)

14. The automatic premium loan clause provides that any defaulted premium will be automatically paid and charged against the cash value without request from the policyowner, unless he or she elects to surrender the policy for cash or one of the paid-up insurance options. The effect of the automatic premium loan clause is to extend the original plan of insurance for the original face amount, decreased by the amount of premiums loaned with interest. Such extension will continue as long as the cash value at each premium due date is sufficient to cover another premium.
15. The advantage of backdating is that the insured will pay lower annual premiums for each increment of the policy, because the premium will be based on the younger age. The disadvantage is that the insured must pay the premium applicable to the length of the backdating. This means that the insured will have paid for insurance protection during the time before the policy was issued when no coverage was provided.
16. Under the typical provision, the policyowner receives the right to acquire additional insurance in specified amounts at specified times or ages. Typically, this provision allows additional purchases every three years and after marriage or the birth of a child, provided the events occur before the insured reaches the specified maximum age (often 45). This right to purchase additional insurance may be very valuable, because the insured does not have to provide evidence of insurability in order to exercise the option.
17. When either the policyowner or beneficiary elects the settlement option, and the settlement option is to benefit the party who elected it, a spendthrift clause (if included in the settlement agreement) will not be enforced. A spendthrift clause is generally enforceable when the party procures the life insurance policy or settlement agreement for the benefit of someone else.
18. The four fundamental settlement options are: the interest option, the installment time option or fixed-period option, the installment amount option or fixed-amount option, and the life income option.

19. The interest option is a simple option, because the insurance company maintains the proceeds intact until a stated period has expired or a stated occurrence has taken place. Afterwards, a method of ultimate disposition of the proceeds commences. The interest option is flexible, because of the varying degrees of control over proceeds held by the company that a primary beneficiary can be given. For example, if a policyowner wants the beneficiary to have access to money for emergencies, he or she may give the primary beneficiary a limited right of withdrawal. The policyowner may also give the primary beneficiary the right to elect a liquidating option if additional flexibility is desired.
20. The fixed-period option provides payments over a stipulated length of time, while the fixed-amount option provides payments of a stipulated amount. The two options are based on the same mathematical principles and differ only as to whether emphasis is attached to the *duration* of the payments or to the *level* of payments.
21. The fixed-amount option offers a great deal of flexibility. The beneficiary can be given the right to indicate when the liquidation payments are to begin. In the meantime, the proceeds will be held at interest, with the interest payments going to the primary beneficiary. Unlike the fixed-period option, the beneficiary can be given either a limited or an unlimited right of withdrawal. Under this option, withdrawals will merely shorten the period of installment payments and will not necessitate recomputing benefit payments. The beneficiary can also be given the right to accelerate or retard the rate of liquidation. He or she can be given the privilege of varying the amount of the monthly payments, subject to limitations the policyowner might impose. The beneficiary can be given the privilege of discontinuing payments during particular months of the year or from time to time. Finally, this option can include a provision for transferring the remaining proceeds to another liquidating option.
22. The principle underlying a life income option is identical to that of an annuity. A life income option is the annuity principle applied to the liquidation of insurance proceeds. At a minimum, all life income options guarantee benefit payments as long as the primary beneficiary (or beneficiaries) lives. Other guarantees can be added, such as a minimum number of benefit payments (payments for at least a specified period) or return of at least the amount of proceeds placed under the option. With a life income option, the annuity principle works as follows: If the primary beneficiary is willing to pool his or her death proceeds with the proceeds of others in the same situation. The insurer, relying on the laws of probability

and large numbers, can provide each of the participants with an income of a specified amount as long as he or she lives, regardless of longevity. No one would outlive his or her income. Such an arrangement implies a willingness on each participant's part to have all or a portion of his or her unliquidated principal and/or interest at the time of death used to supplement the exhausted principal of those who live beyond their expectancy.

23. There are several life income options available in a life insurance policy:

    a. The straight life income option is equivalent to a pure immediate annuity. The first payment is due one payment period (usually, one month) after maturity of the policy or after election of the option, whichever is later. The monthly income provided per $1,000 of proceeds depends on the age and sex of the beneficiary and the insurer's assumptions as to mortality and interest. The monthly income benefit is paid as long as the primary beneficiary lives, but ceases upon his or her death.

    b. The life income option with a specified period of guaranteed payments is a mathematical combination of a fixed-period installment option of appropriate duration and a pure deferred life annuity. For example, a life income option that promises to provide payments of a specified amount to a beneficiary aged 45 throughout his or her remaining lifetime, and in any event for 20 years, is a combination of a fixed-period installment option running for 20 years and a pure life annuity deferred to the beneficiary's age 65. If the beneficiary does not survive to age 65, the portion of the proceeds allocated to the deferred life annuity is retained by the insurance company without further obligation. The primary beneficiary receives a monthly income benefit as long as he or she lives. If the primary beneficiary were to die during the 20-year period certain, the monthly income benefit would be paid during the 20-year period certain, so the monthly income benefit would be continued to the contingent beneficiary for the remainder of the period certain.

    c. The installment refund option is a combination of a pure immediate life annuity and decreasing term insurance in an amount sufficient to continue payments until the proceeds, without interest, have been paid out in full. (In addition to promising monthly benefit payments as long as the primary beneficiary lives, this option promises to continue the monthly payments beyond the primary beneficiary's death until the proceeds of the life insurance policy have been returned.) At the inception, the term insurance is in an amount equal to the proceeds, less the first payment due immediately, but it decreases with each periodic payment and expires altogether when the cumulative benefit payments equal or exceed the life insurance proceeds committed to the installment-refund option.

Like the installment refund option, the cash-refund option is a combination of a pure immediate life annuity and decreasing term insurance. Because the refund is payable in cash, rather than payable in installments, a slightly larger amount of term insurance is required.

24. In preparing for the closing interview, you should review the information gathered previously and highlight key areas. Refresh your memory on the details discussed so you are very familiar with the client's information when you meet again. Review their needs, goals, and priorities, making note of factual and subjective information. Review issues and concerns raised by the client in your conversations. Review your recommendations and the reasoning behind the decisions you have made regarding the solutions you have designed. Analyze the alternative plans you may have prepared, and be ready to discuss the benefits and drawbacks of each option. This will give your client the information he or she needs to decide what is best for them. Mentally walk through the presentation, anticipating objections, concerns, and points of resistance that the client may present. Be prepared to respond to objections by listening, summarizing, and addressing the prospect's concerns. Use checking questions to focus on the prospect's response. Watch for buying signals.

Answers to Self-Test Questions

1. C
2. D
3. B
4. B
5. C
6. B

7. A
8. D
9. C
10. D

Chapter 8

Answers to Review Questions

1. **Income Taxation**

   Premiums paid for individual life insurance policies are considered a personal expense and are not deductible for income tax purposes. Premiums are deductible when they are paid in an alimony agreement or paid for a policy owned by a charity and the charity is the owner and beneficiary (i.e., a charitable contribution). In business, premiums are paid as a bonus to an employee, as a business expense. If life insurance is part of a pension plan, the premiums are deductible as part of a contribution by the employer to a tax-qualified plan.

   Generally, death proceeds from a life insurance policy are exempt from income taxation when paid in a lump sum. Any interest paid on proceeds left with the insurer, such as under settlement options, is taxable as ordinary income.

   To determine a taxable on surrender, it must be determined if the amount received from the policy over the life of the contract is in excess of the net premiums paid. Net premiums paid means the gross premium, less any dividends received, less any outstanding loans. This is the cost basis, the amount the policyowner paid with after-tax money. The total net premium is then subtracted from the amount of cash the policyowner receives upon surrender or maturity. Any excess is reportable as ordinary taxable income in the year received.

   Policy loans give the policyowner the right to borrow a percentage of the cash value that has accumulated in the policy. If a policy is surrendered with a loan outstanding, and if that loan, with other cash value, is greater than the cumulative premium payments made, then there will be a taxable gain. Loans are otherwise not taxed when taken. Interest paid is personal and not deductible.

The cash dividend is taxable only if and when it exceeds the amount of premiums paid into the policy. Dividends are generally taxed on a first-in, first-out (FIFO) basis; that is, withdrawals are treated as a nontaxable return of capital to the extent of premiums paid. Withdrawals in excess of premiums paid are taxable.

Estate Taxation

The death benefits of a life insurance policy can become includible in an insured's estate and subsequently subject to federal estate tax. There are three basic instances when life insurance is included in a decedent's gross estate:

- When it is payable to the insured's estate
- When the insured possessed incidents of ownership in the policy at the time of death
- When the insured transferred incidents of ownership by gift within 3 years of death

Gift Taxation

The transfer of the policy from one individual to another party (such as a relative or the employee's irrevocable life insurance trust) is a gift subject to tax. In addition, there is a continuing annual gift if the person pays premiums on the policy. There is also a continuing annual gift to the employee if the employer pays premiums, because this employer payment represents compensation earned by the employee that is indirectly transferred to the policyowner.

2. Typically used by senior clients, the life settlement is a way to release dormant cash values in a life insurance policy that is no longer needed or wanted. Seniors who need cash to pay for living expenses, long-term care expenses and other needs, may find this an attractive alternative. Through a life settlement, a policyowner can obtain a higher value for their policies than if it were allowed to lapse, be surrendered, or borrowed against. A life settlement is a transaction in which an existing life insurance policy is sold by its owner to a third party. In exchange for a cash settlement, the policyowner transfers ownership and all other rights of the policy to that third party. The sale of the life insurance policy is completed through a broker or financial advisor to a settlement company or other provider, to obtain a sum of money that exceeds the policy's cash value. The provider keeps the policy in force by making subsequent premium payments, and collects the proceeds

at the policy's maturity (the earlier of the maturity date or the death of the insured). All types of policies, as long as they are out of contestability, are life settlement candidates.

3. Answers:

   a. Properly structured life insurance, structured through the marketing concept known as SLIRP (Supplemental Life Insurance Retirement Plan), can provide a preretirement death benefit, tax-deferred cash value accumulation, tax-free withdrawals contingent on certain stipulations, and an ultimate tax-free death benefit to beneficiaries.

   b. Pension maximization addresses the "pension dilemma," because the retiree must decide whether to take a full pension benefit and expose his or her spouse to a loss of benefits at death, or take less than the maximum single life benefit in exchange for continuing benefits after death for the spouse.

   c. The areas of consideration for life insurance in estate planning include:

      - ensuring adequate income for a surviving spouse or other dependents;
      - planning for final expenses, including estate settlement costs and taxes;
      - enhancing an existing estate or creating an estate where none exists;
      - equalizing the estate when a family business is involved.

   d. Life insurance is an excellent vehicle for completing the charitable intent of the policyowner, because the proceeds are guaranteed to be paid directly to the charitable beneficiary at the insured's death. At the donor's death, the proceeds of the policy go directly to the charity without passing through the donor's estate; however, the value of the policy is included in the estate if it is owned by the donor. If paid to the charity, it could qualify for an estate charitable deduction. Many prospects will not initially make the connection between charitable giving and life insurance. The advantages of life insurance in a charitable giving program include the following:

- The face value of life insurance is guaranteed by the insurance company. A definite amount can be earmarked for the charity.
- Life insurance allows a donor to leverage his or her contribution. A substantial bequest can be made for relatively small and manageable premium payments.
- Proceeds of a policy gifted to charity escape federal estate tax, probate, and other administrative costs. The proceeds go directly to the charity.
- Life insurance can also serve as a wealth replacement vehicle for the donor's heirs, to replace any assets given to the charity.
- An outright gift of a life insurance policy and/or premium payments made subsequently can offer tax advantages to the donor.
- The out-of-pocket costs of the gift are reduced by a current income tax deduction.

4. Summarized, the basic ethical rule is that you should pursue your interests fairly and unselfishly. Selfish behavior is behavior in which the pursuit of self-interest is without regard for the interests of, or at the expense of, others. Reflecting on the principle of fairness helps us see the unethical nature of selfishness. By "selfishness" we do not mean just the pursuit of self-interest. The pursuit of self-interest is a perfectly natural and acceptable activity. Selfishness is the pursuit of self-interest *at the expense of another* when one is not entitled to the good pursued. When a person is being selfish, he or she puts their own interests first in a situation where pursuing that interest will hurt another.
5. Most people would agree that the advisor should follow the Golden Rule and treat clients as he or she would like to be treated. This rule exists and needs to be followed because insurance advisors, like everyone else, are subject to conflicts between self-interest and the interests of others. Advisors should make recommendations based on their client's needs. It is unethical to sell a client an unnecessary insurance policy. To attempt to sell a client an unnecessary policy would tend to involve lying and/or deception, practices universally considered unethical. The advisor has an obligation to keep personal and private information confidential. The advisor is responsible for delivering the insurance policy to the

insured and explaining all the policy provisions. The advisor is also responsible for handling clients and providing good service.

6. Misrepresenting the benefits or terms of a policy, misrepresenting dividends as guaranteed when they are not, misrepresenting the financial condition of the insurer, misrepresenting a life insurance policy as other than what it is, and finally, misrepresenting oneself by perhaps claiming to be a financial planner when one is not are all examples of unethical market conduct. Coercion that restricts free choice of products is also unethical. Twisting occurs when a policyowner is induced to discontinue and replace a policy through advisor or insurer distortion or misrepresentation of the facts. When a policy is replaced unnecessarily it is known as churning. These practices are obviously unethical to the extent they exemplify the advisor pursuing self-interest at the expense of the client. Rebating is defined as any inducement in the sale of insurance that is not specified in the insurance contract. An offer to share a commission with an applicant is an example of such an inducement, and is illegal in most states except California and Florida. Rebating is generally considered wrong, because it gives one advisor an unfair advantage over other advisors, and is seen as unfair to those clients who are not given a rebate. Company bashing is telling lies or misrepresenting the strengths and weaknesses of another advisor or another company. Unethical discrimination is exclusion committed based on some unjustified bias or hatred toward a person or group.
7. The objectives of a policy delivery are to reinforce the buying decision, build trust, reopen the selling/planning process, obtain referred leads, and prevent lapses. Reemphasize the needs and reasons the prospect bought the policy. The client must understand why he or she bought the product, the solutions it provides, and the benefits he or she will derive from keeping it. Educate the policyowner about the policy. Send the client a thank you letter for his or her confidence in you. Summarize the reasons for the purchase and the benefits provided by the plan. When you deliver service after the sale, the client's trust in you will grow. Be sure that the client knows about all the products and services you offer. Even if you have already presented this information, review what you can do again. If you have a personal brochure or resume, be sure that the client has one. Periodically send compliance-approved articles, brochures, or reports based on what you know about the client's interests, business, or company. This will build rapport and develop interest in cross-selling opportunities. Help the client by sharing the

specifics on the types of referrals that would be most helpful. Ask the client if he or she would be willing to be a reference for you. If appropriate, socialize with the client, building the relationship and sharing in a common interest. You must keep a customer satisfied in order to fight off the competition.

8. The policy delivery should not be an afterthought or a casually dismissed step in the sales process. This interview should be taken as seriously as any other part of the selling/planning process. You must prepare and practice for the interview as you would with any other sales technique or it will not be as effective as it could be. Work to accomplish all the objectives to maximize your effectiveness and efficiency. Alert the client to future contact points at the delivery interview. If you use a client newsletter, show the client a sample or deliver an issue. Set the expectation of a mutually agreed upon review timetable.

   Check the policy when you receive it, before you call the applicant for delivery. Make sure it is exactly as applied for. Ask for an appointment that will give you time to review the contract, ask for referrals, and set the stage for your continuing relationship. This meeting will reinforce the benefits of this purchase, so do not allow yourself to be rushed through it. You want to review all of the ideas you talked about in the past. Give your policy a professional appearance by delivering it in an attractive policy wallet. Review the policy contract, pointing out its key features.

9. Generally, a Buyer's Guide must be delivered to the consumer with the policy. Some states require its delivery with the application. There are state variations in the forms themselves and state-specific requirements. The Buyer's Guide is designed to give the consumer and prospective purchaser a clear explanation of products and how to shop for them. Most states require delivery of a policy summary with the policy. This form gives the main features of the currently issued policy and includes specific information on the policy values (guaranteed and nonguaranteed) of this particular contract.

   The National Association of Insurance Commissioners (NAIC) drafted an Illustrations Model Regulation, which establishes guidelines for companies and advisors regarding the content and presentations of sales illustrations. The regulation covers all life insurance products except face amounts under $10,000 and variable life. It requires that an illustration matching the issued policy be presented to the policyowner. The advisor and policyowner must sign this illustration; one copy is given to the policyowner, one is returned to the company, and one is retained in the advisor's client file.

Most companies and some states require the advisor and policyowner to sign policy delivery receipts. The delivery receipt contains information regarding guaranteed and nonguaranteed elements in the policy and information regarding proper policy delivery. A client file must be kept as long as a policy is in force. Once a policy is no longer in force because it lapsed, was surrendered, or a claim was paid, a file must be kept for five to eight years, depending on jurisdiction. Where litigation or other disputes exist, files should be kept longer. Documents to be maintained in files generally include a signed NAIC illustration, any sales materials used in the sale, a fact-finder and suitability materials, replacement forms if appropriate, copies of policy delivery receipts, records of dates and general content of all client contacts, and substantive correspondence concerning contractual changes or concerns of the client.

10. The delivery of the policy confirms for the client their decision to buy and completes the sales process in the eyes of the policyowner. This is why it is so important to meet with your new policyowner to deliver the contract in person. You establish a pattern of service for the future and demonstrate your personal approach and philosophy of selling and service. Explain the kinds of service the client can expect and reiterate the systems you have in place to accomplish it. Set an appointment for an annual review to express your commitment to these service goals and the goals of this meeting.

    Broaden the product portfolio you offer to customers and develop strategic alliances with other producers who offer products and services you do not, including attorneys, accountants, bankers, and specialists in other lines of insurance. Broaden your areas of expertise. Pursue professional designations, add additional licenses, and generally improve your expertise and the skills that make you more valuable to clients. Be sure to frequently tell your prospects and clients about your total product and service portfolio. Go back to every client for regular review, and explain your total portfolio. In planning reviews, the advisor and the client need to agree on how involved the reviews should be and how frequently they should occur. They may include identifying changes in conditions that would affect the current plan, obtaining information from the client to determine changes in personal circumstances, reviewing work done by other professionals and providers of financial services, and reviewing the client's progress toward financial goals.

Answers to Self-Test Questions

1. D
2. C
3. B
4. A
5. A
6. C
7. A
8. D
9. A
10. D

GLOSSARY

accelerated benefits • a provision in a life insurance policy that allows death benefits to be paid to the policyowner prior to the insured's death when the insured is terminally ill and has a limited life expectancy

accidental death • an unexpected death caused directly, unintentionally, and apart from any other cause and that occurred within a specified period after the event

accidental death benefit • a life insurance rider that increases the death benefit, usually doubling it, when the insured dies accidentally

adjustable life • life insurance that can be configured anywhere from short-duration term insurance through single premium whole life and that gives the policyowner the right to request and obtain a reconfiguration of the policy at specified intervals

adverse selection • the tendency of persons with a higher-than-average chance of loss to seek insurance at standard (average) rates. Because this is selection against the insurer, it will result in higher-than-expected losses if it is not controlled by underwriting.

amount at risk • the difference between the face amount of an insurance policy and its reserve

annuity • the annual payment of an allowance or income for a lifetime or a specified number of years

annuity certain (fixed-period annuity) • an agreement under which periodic payments are made for a definite period of time without being linked to the duration of a specified human life, such as a mortgage or bank loan or as period-certain guarantee for an annuity pay out

annuity due • an annuity with payments at the beginning of the period

assignment provision • a life insurance policy provision that specifies the conditions under which a policyowner can transfer some or all of his or her rights in the policy to another

attained age • the number of years a person has already lived

attained-age method of conversion • an insurance policy conversion method that uses the insured's age at the date of exchange as the effective age for future premiums

automatic premium loan provision • an insurance contract provision that stipulates that any defaulted premium will be automatically paid and charged against the cash value without request from the policyowner unless he or she elects to surrender the policy for cash or one of the paid-up insurance options

back-end withdrawal penalties • surrender charges that apply during the early years of life insurance and annuity contracts as well as federal income taxes applicable to annuity contracts up to age 59-1/2

backdating • issuing the policy as if it had been purchased when the insured was younger. The advantage is that the insured will pay lower annual premiums for each increment of the policy, because the premium will be based on the younger age. The disadvantage is that the insured must pay the premium applicable to the length of the backdating.

benefit • is what the prospect gets from a feature. It is what the product does for the prospect and why he or she wants it. Benefits are value-laden and subjective

blackout period • the period of time from whenever the youngest child of a deceased worker reaches age 16 (or is no longer disabled in certain cases) until the surviving spouse is aged

60. It is called the blackout period because the surviving spouse of a deceased worker is not eligible for monthly benefits during this time.

broker • a full-time insurance producer who works independently and has no primary relationship or minimum production requirements with any company

Buyer's Guide • gives the prospective purchaser a clear explanation of life insurance products and how to shop for them. Generally, the Buyer's Guide must be delivered to the consumer with the policy. Some states require it to be delivered with the application, and there are state variations in the forms themselves and state-specific requirements that must be followed.

buy-sell agreement • a contract binding the owner of a business interest to sell the business interest for a specified or determinable price at his or her death or disability and a designated purchaser to buy at that time

capital conservation method • the method used in a capital-needs analysis to determine post-death budgetary needs of an income producer's survivors. This method uses only interest from a survivor fund, which should not be depleted if invested conservatively.

capital distribution method • the method used in a financial-needs analysis to determine post-death budgetary needs of an income producer's survivors. Because it uses both principal and interest from a survivor fund that may eventually be depleted, it is also known as the liquidating approach.

capitalized value • the monetary value of the future earnings and total economic values of a human life to others that can be created to replace the economic value of that life to that person's dependents.

capital needs analysis • a method of computing a desired income level that can continue indefinitely. All income is derived from income earned on a principal sum, which is preserved.

cash accumulation comparison method • a method of comparing life insurance costs. The technique is to accumulate the premium differences between the policies being compared while holding the death benefits of both policies constant and equal. The calculation is a buy-term-and-invest-the-difference approach. At the end of the interval being evaluated, the side fund accumulation can be compared to the whole life cash value. The policy with the greater accumulation at the end of the comparison interval is considered the preferable choice.

cash needs • the lump-sum monetary needs at death to pay for expenses that a person would like to have taken care of for his or her survivors. These may include funds for final expenses, debts, mortgage cancellation or a rent fund, estate administration and taxes, if applicable, an emergency fund, and any prefunding of future anticipated needs, such as children's education.

cash refund annuity • a type of refund annuity that promises that upon the death of the annuitant it will pay to the annuitant's estate or a contingent beneficiary a lump sum that is the difference, if any, between the purchase price of the annuity and the sum of the monthly payments already distributed

cash surrender value • the cash values provided under nonforfeiture law, based on the level premium concept that creates a prefunding of death benefits and cash value.

cash value • the amount of equity in a policy against which a loan can be made. The savings element results when premiums during the early years of a whole life policy exceed what is necessary to pay death claims. This excess is set aside and accumulates for the benefit of the insured.

cash value accumulation test (CVAT) • a procedure by which the cash value of a policy is generally limited to the net single premium that would be needed to fund the policy's death benefit

centers of influence • influential people you know, who know you favorably and agree to introduce or refer you

churning • the process of generating brokerage commissions through unnecessary securities transactions; advising a client to make unnecessary transactions is also considered churning.

cleanup fund • a source of money to meet final expenses resulting from an insured's death and to liquidate all current outstanding obligations; also known as a probate fund or estate clearance fund

collateral assignment method • the technique used with split-dollar life insurance whereby the employee owns the policy and is responsible for paying the premium. The employers' share of the policy proceeds is secured by an assignment.

Commissioners Standard Ordinary (CSO) Morality Tables • Developed by the NAIC to serve as the standard (statutory) mortality tables for calculating minimum policy reserves, surrender values, and company assets and liabilities. The 1980 tables were the first to establish separate male/female and smoker/non-smoker rates. The 2001 tables are currently being introduced and approved for use throughout the states and will take full effect by 2009.

commutation • applied to proceeds distributed under a liquidating option, the present value of remaining installment payments are withdrawn in a lump sum. This does not apply to proceeds held under the interest optionand is identical to an unlimited right of withdrawal. It must be specifically authorized in the settlement agreement.

company bashing • an unethical practice in which lies are told or facts are purposely misrepresented concerning the strengths or weaknesses of the competition whether it is another agent or another company

comparative-interest-rate method • a modification of the cash-accumulation method of comparing life insurance costs This method calculates the interest rate that would make a term insurance policy side fund exactly equal to the difference between a cash value policy death benefit and a term insurance death benefit; often referred to as the Linton yield method.

compound interest • interest earnings that are not distributed but are instead added to the original principal and reinvested at the same interest rate or at a different rate of interest; thus, it is interest on interest

contestability • an insurance company's right to refuse payment of a claim, often due to fraud or misrepresentations on an insured's application

contract of adhesion • a contract that is not negotiated. It is drafted entirely by one party (insurance company). The other party can only accept or reject the contract. Ambiguities will be interpreted in favor of the policyowner.

contract rates • a specified rate of income per $1,000 of proceeds guaranteed in a policy

convertibility • a feature in term life insurance that allows the insured to replace the term coverage with permanent individual life insurance without having to show evidence of insurability. .

cost basis • the amount a policyowner paid on their policy with after-tax money. It is used to determine if income tax is due on the surrender of a policy for cash or at the maturity of an endowment, and to determine if the amount received from the policy over the life of the contract exceeds the net premiums paid.

cost of insurance • the amount a policyowner must pay for protection; the sum that each policyowner must contribute as their pro rata share of death claims in any particular year

cost of waiting • provides a comparison between the costs and values of a plan started today and one started 5 or 10 years from now to show the dramatic difference in the face amount of protection a given premium can purchase, as well as the cash value that can accumulate over the years. By waiting, the premium will grow increasingly higher, the cash value growth will be smaller, the prospect will be without the protection by delaying, and could lose their insurability in the interim.

cross-purchase plan • a contract that provides that the surviving partners are obligated to buy a prearranged share of the deceased partner's interest from his or her estate

cumulative right of withdrawal • a right of withdrawal that does not expire at the end of the period to which it pertains Any withdrawal amounts that are not taken out during a particular year can be withdrawn in any subsequent year, in addition to any other sums that can be withdrawn under the terms of the agreement

current assumption whole life • nonpar whole life policies under which premium rates or cash values are redetermined periodically based on current assumptions as to mortality, interest, and expenses

current rates • rates that are applicable to contracts currently being issued, or the rate that is being paid on an existing policy.

death benefit options • universal life insurance gives policyowners a choice between level death benefits and increasing death benefits. The level death benefit design is much like the traditional whole life design. When the death benefit stays constant and the cash value increases over the duration of the contract, the amount at risk, or the protection element, decreases. Under the increasing option, there is a constant amount at risk that is superimposed over the policy's cash value. As the cash value increases, so does the total death benefit payable. The amount at risk is always the face amount.

decreasing term insurance • term insurance that provides systematic decreases in the amount of insurance from year to year

delay clause • a legally sanctioned postponement of payment of the cash surrender value for a period of 6 months after demand thereof and surrender of a life insurance policy.

delivery interview • confirms for the client their decision to buy and completes the sales process in their eyes. This is why it is so important to meet with your new policyowner to deliver the contract in person. You establish a pattern of service for the future, and you demonstrate and reinforce your personal approach and philosophy of selling and service.

dependency period income • the income required during the expanse of time that extends from the date of the insured's death until the youngest child is self-sufficient or perhaps completes the desired level of education

direct recognition • an attempt to increase the equity (fairness) of dividend distributions reflects the "contribution" principle; that is, that policy choices made by a policyowner are reflected in the dividend. This is commonly found in cases in which a policy with a loan may receive a lower dividend.

discounting • a process by which today's value (present value) is calculated at a specific rate of interest, based on a given sum due at a designated time in the future

dividend (policyowner) • a refund to the policyowner of a portion of a life insurance premium after the company meets such obligations as claims, expenses, and reserves (not to be confused with a dividend to stock owners of stock insurance companies)

divisible surplus provision • that portion of insurance company surplus that is available for distribution to participating policyowners as policyowner dividends

economic benefit method • under the *economic benefit method* the owner of the life insurance contract is treated as providing economic benefits to the non-owner of the contract. The value of the life insurance coverage or other benefit provided to an employee under a split-dollar plan is valued and taxed to the employee as additional taxable income.

economic value of a producer • the future earning capacity (dollar value) of an individual income producer represented by native ability and acquired skills

educational fund • an amount set aside to provide for educational/training needs

emergency fund • an amount set aside to cover unexpected financial needs

endorsement method • the technique used with split-dollar life insurance whereby the employer owns the policy and has the primary responsibility for paying the premium. The beneficiary designation provides for the employer to receive a portion of the death benefit equal to its premium outlay (or some alternative share), with the remainder of the death proceeds going to the employee's designated beneficiary.

endowment life insurance • a variation of whole life insurance that provides level death benefits and cash values that increase with duration so a policy's cash value equals its death benefit at maturity, and allows the purchaser to specify the policy's maturity date

entire contract provision • in life and health insurance, a provision that specifies that the policy and the attached application constitute the entire agreement between the parties

entity plan • a business buy-sell agreement in which the business itself is the designated purchaser of the deceased's business interest. The business buys life insurance on the owners and in the event of an owner's death, purchases that owner's share of the business from his or her heirs.

equal outlay method • a method of comparing life insurance costs, a buy-term-and-invest-the-difference approach. The amount by which the cash value contract premiums exceed the term premiums is deposited into an interest-bearing side fund. The term insurance plus the side fund is compared to the cash value policy, including any paid-up additions. Under this type of comparison, the policy producing the greater death benefit is considered the preferable contract.

equity split dollar • an arrangement in which the employer's interest is limited to the actual premiums the employer paid and the excess cash surrender value vests in the employee. Current life insurance protection as well as any other benefit received by the employee during the year, including any increase in the employee's vested interest in the policy's cash value, are taxable income under the IRC regulations.

estate clearance fund • a source of money to meet final expenses resulting from an insured's death and to liquidate all current outstanding obligations; also known as a probate fund

evidence of insurability • the basic purpose of underwriting, or evaluating the insurance risk to the insurer

exclusion • for income tax purposes, an item of value that the taxpayer receives that is not includible in his or her gross income under a specific provision of tax law

executive bonus (Section 162) • shareholder-employees and executives apply for, own, and name the beneficiary on permanent life insurance policies covering their lives. The corporation provides the premiums through a bonus payment. Premiums are treated as income to the employee, subject to the employee's normal individual income tax rate.

extended term insurance • a nonforfeiture option that provides paid-up term insurance in an amount equal to the original face of a policy, increased by any dividend additions or deposits and decreased by any policy indebtedness; The length of the term is determined by how long it can be purchased at the insured's attained age by applying the net surrender value as a net single premium

fact finding • the objective of the information-gathering process is to uncover meaningful information about the prospect by asking questions. This will enable the advisor to have a discussion with the prospect about the prospect's goals, attitudes, priorities, current situation, and any changes anticipated for the future.

feature • a characteristic about a product—what it is and what it does; a fact about the product

feeling finding • involves identifying the goals, attitudes, and values that are the rationale and background for the factual data. It is critical to understand the subjective aspect of a prospect's life as thoroughly as possible.

FIFO/LIFO • Dividends and cash values are generally taxed on a first-in first-out (FIFO) basis; that is, they are treated as a nontaxable return of capital (refund of premiums) to the extent of premiums paid. Withdrawals in excess of premiums paid are taxable as ordinary income. LIFO tax treatment, or last-in first-out, means that gains (interest, profits, earnings) are recovered before contributions.

Financial needs analysis • a method of determining budgetary needs based on income and cash needs. Because it uses both principal and interest from a survivor fund that may eventually be depleted, it is also known as the liquidating approach or the capital distribution method.

fixed-amount option • provides that proceeds of a life insurance policy may be liquidated in payments of a stipulated amount; also known as an installment amount option

fixed-period option • provides that proceeds of a life insurance policy may be liquidated in payments over a stipulated period of time; also known as an installment time option

free-look provision • gives a policyowner a period of time, usually 10 days, to return the policy after acceptance

future interest • the postponed right of use or enjoyment of the property

future value • the amount to which any given principal sum will accumulate at a later date

gift tax • a tax imposed on transfers of property by gift during the donor's lifetime

grace period • the period of time between the date the policy's premium is due and the date the policy will lapse. Most policies have a 31-day grace period. This means that the premium can be paid any time within the 31-day period after it is due, and during this period the policy will remain in force.

gross premium • the premium actually paid by the policyowner; it is the net premium increased by an allowance for the insurer's expenses and contingencies

group term insurance • insurance protection provided to a specific group for a limited period of time, for example, employer-provided group health insurance

group term life insurance (IRC Sec. 79) • insurance protection provided to a specific group for a limited period of time, for example, by an employer. Section 79 allows a tax deduction for employer-paid group term premiums and provides up to $50,000 of coverage tax-free to participants

guideline premium/cash value corridor test (GPT) • is really two tests combined. The guideline premium test requires that the sum of the premiums paid under the contract do not exceed, at any time, the greater of the guideline single premium or the sum of the guideline level premiums. The GPT also defines the relationship between the cash value and the death benefit, limiting the permissible cash value based on the corridor percentage test. The policy must meet the death benefit, or corridor, test at all times. The corridor refers to the percentage that the death benefit must exceed the cash value, or the amount at risk that must exist at any age.

guaranteed insurability (purchase) option • an option to acquire additional increments of coverage at future dates or upon future events without further evidence of good health or insurability

human life value • the capitalized present value of net future earnings of an individual

human life value approach • a method for determining how much life insurance a person should carry based on the proposition that a person should carry life insurance in an amount equal to the capitalized value of his or her net earnings until retirement

illustrated scale • a scale of nonguaranteed elements currently being illustrated that is not more favorable to the policyowner than the lesser of (1) the disciplined current scale or (2) the currently payable scale

illustration selling • involves an emphasis on the product "looking for a need," rather than a need looking for a solution (product). Illustration selling focuses on the numerical values of an illustration, rather than conducting a fundamental financial planning process, uncovering the client's needs based on fact-finding, and designing solutions to financial problems and concerns.

immediate annuity • an annuity that must be purchased with a single premium because it begins to pay periodic benefits at the end of the first payment period (such as one month) following the purchase date

immediate annuity with guaranteed payments • an annuity contract that starts paying benefits the next payment interval after it is purchased (for example, one month after purchase if paid out monthly) that guarantees to pay some specified amount even if the annuitant does not live long enough to collect that amount during his or her lifetime. Benefit payments will cease at the later of the annuitant's death or the end of the guaranteed payments.

incident-of-ownership • any right to the economic benefits of a piece of property, such as a life insurance policy

income needs • the ongoing income needs of the surviving dependent family members that continues until those members become self-supporting. These include readjustment period income, dependency period income, and income for the surviving spouse.

incontestable clause • a provision in the life insurance contract that gives the insurance company up to 2 years to void the contract on the basis of material misrepresentation, concealment, or fraud in applying for coverage. After that 2-year period, the insurer will not be able to void the coverage on those grounds unless the insured died during that period.

increasing term insurance • term insurance that provides systematic increases in the amount of insurance from year to year

indemnity • the principal of insurance that states that the person who suffers a loss that is covered by insurance is placed in the same financial position after the loss as before the loss occurred.

indeterminate premium whole life • a policy under which there is a periodic recasting of the premium amount based on recognition of the most recent interval of experience

indexed UL • permanent life insurance that offers all the benefits of universal life with accumulation values tied to a stock market index. An IUL policy has a fixed interest rate component as well as an indexed account option that has the ability to receive index-linked gains as high as 18 percent or more. The policyowner can reap the rewards of stock market-type gains, yet is protected with minimum guaranteed interest rates in case of stock market losses.

installment refund annuity • a type of refund annuity that promises that if the annuitant dies before receiving monthly payments equal to the purchase price of the annuity, the payments will continue to a contingent beneficiary or beneficiaries until the full cost has been recovered

initial interview • the first meeting the advisor has with a prospect. The objective of the initial interview for the advisor is to establish rapport and get the client's agreement to do fact-finding and continue the selling/planning process.

interest • represents the difference between the principal—the value of the original capital invested—and the amount that must be repaid by the borrower after a specified term. To an insurer it is the income from invested capital; to a borrower it is the price paid for the use of money.

interest-adjusted indices • a method that takes all payments for both premiums and dividends and treats them as if they had been put into interest-bearing accounts to accumulate interest until the end of the interval for evaluation. Essentially, this is the net-cost method refined to recognize interest earnings.

interest option • a life insurance settlement option under which the death proceeds are retained by the insurer temporarily, with only the interest earnings thereon distributed to the beneficiary

interest-sensitive whole life • a contract in which mortality and expense charges are guaranteed because excess interest (credited interest minus guaranteed interest) credited to the cash value becomes the only non-guaranteed element in the contract

IRC Sec. 7702 (DEFRA) • defines life insurance for income tax purposes, requiring a certain amount of the death benefit to be at risk (insurance amount), depending on age. For life insurance to qualify for the income tax benefits, there must be a statutory amount of death benefit in excess of the cash value.

joint life • an insurance contract written on the lives of two or more persons and payable upon the death of the first person to die; also known as a first-to-die-joint-life policy

key persons • those individuals whose unique talents and experiences are crucial to the success of a business entity

key person life insurance • insurance designed to protect a business firm against the loss of income that results from the death or disability of a key employee

lapse • the termination of coverage in a policy when the renewal premium is not received by the insurance company within the grace period

law of large numbers • a concept that embodies a mathematical principle stating that as the number of independent trials or events (that is, exposures) increases, the more closely will actual results approach the probable results expected from an infinite number of trials or events (exposures)

legal reserve • a fund maintained by a life insurance company for future claims; subject to state regulation

level premium insurance • a plan of insurance under which premiums do not increase from year to year but, instead, remain constant throughout the premium-paying period

life annuity • *See* life-only annuity.

life annuity certain • a type of refund annuity that provides a certain number of annuity payments whether the annuitant lives or dies, and payments continue for the whole of the annuitant's life if he or she lives beyond the guaranteed period

life annuity due • a contract under which the first payment is due at issue or contract date and payments continue as long as the annuitant lives

life annuity immediate • a contract under which the first payment is due at the end of one payment interval and payments continue as long as the annuitant lives

life event • often a motivator to purchase life insurance. Life events are key life milestones, such as having a child, getting married, buying a home, or changing jobs

life expectancy • the average number of years a person is expected to live; it is an average future lifetime for a representative group of persons of the same age

life income option • any settlement option based on a life contingency. Payments cease when the specified person(s) die(s)

Life Insurance Illustrations Model Regulation • standards for policy illustrations set by the National Association of Insurance Commissioners (NAIC) in 1996. This regulation applies to all non-variable group and individual life insurance policies and certificates for more than $10,000 of death benefit.

life settlement • life settlements are typically offers made to affluent senior clients over age 65 who have experienced a significant decline in health since the policy was first issued; the policy is more valuable due to the insured's poor health. A life settlement is a way to release dormant cash values in a life insurance policy that is no longer needed or wanted.

limited right of withdrawal • the right of a beneficiary under a deferred-settlement agreement to withdraw all of the proceeds at any one time, subject to restrictions

limited-payment life • a type of whole life insurance for which premiums are limited by contract to a specified number of years; thereafter, the policy is fully paid up

loading • the amount added to the net premium to cover expenses of operation, to provide for contingencies, and to allow any profit

loan • a transfer of money (or other property) with an obligation to repay the money plus interest (or to return the asset transferred) at a certain time

loan method • under the *loan method,* the non-owner of the life insurance contract is treated as loaning premium payments to the owner. The loan method is the default treatment for split-dollar plans that don't meet the specified requirements for the economic benefit regime. Thus, loan treatment will apply to plans of the type that have been referred to as "collateral assignment plans" where the employee or the employee's trust or beneficiary is the owner of the contract.

market conduct • how an insurer and its advisors operate in relation to the insurance-consuming public as to products sold and prices charged, particularly with regard to compliance with insurance regulations and ethical codes of behavior.

marketing • the planning and implementation of a process dedicated to identifying specific consumer needs, isolating groups of people who have those needs, and then producing and customizing the products and services that satisfy those needs. It is the art of planning when, where, why, how, and to whom to sell. Successful marketing focuses on the needs of the consumer and produces a mutually beneficial relationship between a buyer and seller.

Medical Information Bureau (M.I.B.) • an organization sponsored by its member life insurance companies to gather and maintain principally medical information disclosed by applicants for life insurance

misstatement of age-or-gender provision • a life insurance policy provision that specifies that, if the insured's age or sex has been misstated, the benefits payable under the policy will be adjusted to what the premium paid would have purchased at the correct age or sex

model regulation • various insurance regulations promulgated by the National Association of Insurance Commissioners intended for adoption by each state insurance department. They promote uniform regulation of insurance in all states.

modified endowment contract (MEC) • special tax treatment applies when a life insurance policy is characterized as a MEC. A policy will be treated as a MEC if it fails the so-called 7-pay test.

modified premium whole life • a premium that has been changed from the regular premium for a similar policy, reduced in early years and increased to a stepped-up amount in later years

Monte Carlo analysis • a technique that randomizes actual monthly investment returns over the past, to project the probability of achieving targeted outcomes based on certain premium levels

mortality expectations • an insurance company must establish a range of *mortality expectations* within which applicants will be regarded as average risks and entitled to insurance at standard rates or applicants will be considered either preferred or substandard and subject to a discount or surcharge. After the limits for the risk categories are established, the company adopts selection and classification procedures to place applicants into the proper categories.

mortality, interest, expense • the main factors in the design of a life insurance policy that determine the premium, the performance of the policy, and the profitability of the policy for the life insurance company

mortality rate • a ratio of deaths within a total population. This ratio can be refined by such factors as age, cause, or gender.

mortality table • a list of mortality experience used to estimate longevity and the probability of living or dying at each age; it is used to determine the risk factors in calculating a gross premium rate

mortgage cancellation fund • money provided to liquidate the mortgage upon an insurer's death so the family can continue to occupy the home. This can be provided through a special mortgage redemption policy, which embodies the decreasing term insurance principle.

multiple of income approach • a method of determining the life insurance need of an income producer, based on a multiple of annual income. Income multiples vary greatly in the industry and the financial press. This simplistic approach ignores the financial and personal situation of the individual. It does not take into account the important differences in people's lives that actually determine what amount of life insurance they should have, such as family size, living expenses, and stage of life.

NASD/FINRA • National Association of Securities Dealers and Financial Industry Regulatory Authority are the non-governmental self-regulatory agencies that regulate and oversee operation securities dealers. Financial advisors must be licensed through this organization to sell securities (variable products and mutual funds).

National Association of Insurance Commissioners (NAIC) • membership organization of insurance commissioners whose goal is to promote uniformity of state regulation and legislation as it relates to insurance. The NAIC often drafts model legislation that is eventually adopted by individual states.

needs analysis approach • a way of determining how much life insurance a person should carry by analyzing the various needs a family or other dependents would experience if the income producer died

net-cost method • a way of comparing life insurance policies in which all net premiums paid under the policy are added together, then the cash surrender value for the interim under consideration and all dividends paid over that period are subtracted from the total. This method does not consider the time value of money (interest).

net payment index • helps to compare costs at some future point in time if premiums continue to be paid and cash values are not withdrawn; it is especially useful when the main concern is that benefits are to be paid at death

net premium • life insurance premium based only on mortality and interest, ignoring the costs of company operations. It is used for calculating reserve .

net single premium • the sum of the present values of all the expected benefits of an insurance contract based on mortality and interest only (ignores operational expenses). It is the amount needed today for all insureds in a classification, together with future investment earnings, to pay all claims within that class of insureds

new-money method • with the new-money method, the return earned on money invested in the insurance policy depends on when the investment is made. The rate of return is determined by the rate the company is able to secure at the time the policyowner purchases the policy. Different blocks of policies will receive different interest crediting and dividend amounts under the new-money method.

noncumulative right of withdrawal • a right of withdrawal, whether exercised or not, that expires at the end of the period to which it pertains; most limited rights are noncumulative

nonforfeiture laws • statutes that define the minimum amount that must be returned upon surrender of a policy to prevent forfeiting equity accumulated in level premium policies

nonforfeiture options • a set of choices available to a policyowner regarding how a life insurance policy's cash value can be used, including cash surrender value, reduced paid-up insurance, and extended term insurance

nonlevel term insurance • refers to insurance policies in which the amount of insurance may increase or decrease throughout the term

nonparticipating policy • an insurance contract under which a policyowner does not share in the profits experienced by the insurer; also called a guaranteed cost policy

nonqualified deferred compensation • qualified plans must meet federal nondiscrimination and administrative compliance standards. Nonqualified plans allow a deferral of the employer's tax deduction until such benefits are paid. Closely held corporations often want to maximize benefits for shareholder-employees, so the goal of their retirement plans is to discriminate in favor of shareholder-employees and key executives to the fullest extent of the nondiscrimination rules. Since discrimination is permitted in nonqualified arrangements, these plans are often more favorable to the closely held corporation.

nonlevel term • term insurance for which the face amount may either increase or decrease

nonrefund annuity • a contract that provides a fixed life income with payments ceasing at an annuitant's death

OASDI • Old-Age, Survivors and Disability Income (commonly called Social Security)

one year term • also known as yearly or annually renewable term (YRT or ART)

optional provisions • in addition to the required provisions and the prohibited provisions, there are numerous other provisions that are neither required nor prohibited. These include suicide, ownership, assignment, plan change, and accelerated benefits.

ordinary life insurance • a type of whole life insurance for which level premiums are based on the assumption that they will be paid until the insured's death; also known as continuous premium whole life insurance

original age • the age of the insured when the policy was originally taken. When a conversion is effective as of the original policy date at the original age, the premium rate for the permanent insurance is that which would have been paid had the new contract been taken out originally, and the contract is that which would have been issued originally

ownership provision • in life insurance, a provision that specifies that the insured is the owner of the policy, unless the application states otherwise, and that the owner can exercise ownership rights, such as changing the beneficiary (unless irrevocable), assign the policy, take a policy loan, and so on.

paid-up insurance • a policy that has been paid in full but has not yet matured

participating policy • life insurance that pays a return of premium as a dividend. The policy is eligible for dividends.

payor benefit • available as a rider to a policy insuring a juvenile; this is an example of a decreasing term rider. This rider provides a death benefit and waiver-of-premium benefit on the life of the premium payor, usually a parent. The decreasing death benefit on the payor's life is sufficient to pay all the premiums that would be due on the juvenile's policy from the payor's death to the insured's age 21.

pension maximization • At retirement, the worker and spouse opt to take the single-life benefit option rather than a reduced joint and survivor benefit to receive the maximum pension benefit for as long as the worker lives. The individual eligible for a pension purchases a sufficient amount of permanent life insurance prior to retirement, naming the spouse as beneficiary. The couple uses the difference between the amount for a single versus a joint and survivor benefit to pay the life insurance premiums on the pension candidate. The death benefit of the life insurance is informally earmarked to replace the lost pension benefit if the retiree dies first.

permanent insurance • refers to whole life, universal life, and other cash value types of insurance, as distinguished from the temporary protection afforded by term insurance; also called *permanent plan insurance*

policy face page • contains the name of the insurance company, specific details of the policy, the name of the insured and the policyowner, the face amount, the policy number, and the policy date or issue date (some include both dates). There is a general description of the type of insurance provided, the free-look provision, the insurer's promise to pay (the insuring clause), and signatures of the officers of the company, which binds the company to the terms of the contract.

policy illustration • a numerical spreadsheet projecting what could happen under a policy if actual experience mirrored all the assumed factors used to calculate the illustration. The NAIC model regulation strictly defines what and what cannot be shown in an illustration.

policy loan • an advance of money available to a policyowner from a policy's cash values

policy summary • most states require that a policy summary be delivered with a life insurance policy. This form, normally produced by the home office with the policy, gives the main features of the issued policy, such as premiums, cash values and guarantees and non-guaranteed elements

preferred risk • an individual whose health, occupation, and life style indicate an above-average life expectancy, who should experience a lower rate of mortality than that among insured lives generally because of more rigorous underwriting requirements

present interest • a present right to use or enjoy property

present value • what something is worth today; the value today that is equivalent to a given sum due at a designated time in the future

present value of $1 per annum • the current value of a series of an annuity (or annuity due) if the payments are discounted at an appropriate interest rate

probate • involves the passing of the will through the local court system where the deceased lived

prohibited provisions • most states prohibit insurers from including certain provisions in their policies. For various reasons, courts or state legislatures have determined that these prohibited contract provisions violate public policy.

prospectus • a document that provides the complete details of the product, including investment features, options, fees, other costs, death benefits, and payout options

PS 58 cost • the pension service term insurance rates used to value the economic benefit of life insurance offered as an employee benefit, used in traditional split-dollar plans. These rates were replaced by the 2001 Table.

qualified prospect • The prospect selection process requires qualifying your prospects, moving them from being "suspects" to "prospects." To do this you will have to establish the four characteristics of a qualified prospect. Qualified prospects display certain characteristics that make them potential customers for life insurance:

- They need protection from loss of life.
- They can afford to pay the premiums for the protection.
- They can be approached by you.
- They are insurable.

qualified retirement plan • retirement plans that are eligible for favorable tax status under Internal Revenue Code Sec. 401(a). There are eight types of qualified plans including defined-benefit pension plans, cash-balance plans, money-purchase pension plans, target-benefit plans, profit-sharing plans, 401(k) plans, stock bonus plans, and ESOPs.

rabbi trust • a trust, usually irrevocable, established by a corporate employer to finance payment of deferred-compensation benefits for an employee

rate • a number that equates to the value of benefits under an insurance contract

rate making • the process by which the promises of an insurance contract are valued

readjustment income • an amount closely equivalent to the family's share of the producer's earnings at the time of his or her death. The length of the financial readjustment period depends largely on the magnitude of the change(s) the family will have to make in living standards.

readjustment period • the time following the death of a wage earner during which a person or family needs to become acclimated to the changes in their finances

rebating • a reduction of an insurance premium or gift of some other valuable consideration not specified in a policy to the buyer as an inducement to purchase insurance

redetermination • a process in which an insurance company reviews the actual experience for a block of policies compared to the previous review and decides what adjustments, if any, are necessary based on the assumption that past experiences are indicative of what to expect in the period before the next review. The level of premiums influences the frequency of redetermination.

reduced paid-up insurance • a surrender option that allows the insured to take a reduced amount of coverage payable upon the same conditions as the original policy. The protection continues in the reduced amount until the insured's death unless the reduced policy is surrendered for cash, and no further premiums are called for under this plan.

reentry term insurance • a term insurance policy intended to charge higher premiums to those in poorer health when they renew their term insurance

refund annuity • any type of annuity that promises to return (in one manner or another) a portion or all of the purchase price of the annuity

reinstatement • a provision that requires the insurer to restore coverage to its original premium-paying status. Usually it requires evidence of good health and payment of past-due premiums. This provision requires the insurer to reinstate the policy if the policyowner provides proof that the insured was cognitively impaired at the time the premium was due and the policy lapsed within 6 months of the due date.

renewability • a feature commonly found in individual term life insurance that allows the policyowner to renew (extend) the policy for another period of protection, up to a stated point in time, without having to show evidence of insurability

replacement • a transaction in which a new life insurance or annuity contract is to be purchased and it is known, or should be known, by the proposing agent or company that, because of such transaction, an existing life insurance or annuity has been or will be terminated, converted, or otherwise reduced in value

reserve • the present value of future benefit payments (surrender and death) minus the present value of future incoming premiums. It is an amount that must be maintained by the insurer in order to meet definite future obligations

"results" war clause • limits an insurer's obligation only if the insured's death is the result of military service

retirement needs • funds that will be sufficient to take care of the post-retirement needs of the insured and the spouse, if applicable

retroactive conversion (original age) • an insurance policy conversion method that uses the insured's age on the original date of the term policy as the effective age for future premiums

return-of-premium (ROP) term • Under return-of-premium life insurance, if you live to the end of the policy period, your premiums are returned. If the policy is terminated, a few companies offer a partial return of premium. If the policy is surrendered, there may be no refund, and there may be a surrender charge in the early years. The longer premium payments are made, the higher the percentage of return will be.

revocable contingent beneficiaries • alternate beneficiaries named by the policyowner to cover the possibility the primary beneficiary predeceases the insured; the beneficiary can be changed by the policyowner without the beneficiary's permission

right of withdrawal • The beneficiary may be given the right to withdraw all or a portion of the proceeds held by the insurer under a deferred-settlement arrangement. If the beneficiary can withdraw all of the proceeds at any one time, he or she has an unlimited right of withdrawal. If the privilege is subject to restrictions, it is identified as a limited right of withdrawal.

risk management • the process for dealing with risk of loss

risk pooling • group sharing of losses on an equal basis by persons exposed to similar risk

risk tolerance • is the degree to which a client is willing or reluctant to accept the risk that his investment may decline in value and that the premium may increase over time

secondary guarantee (no lapse) • the purpose of a no-lapse guaranteed product is to provide the largest amount of permanent insurance coverage for the least amount of cost. Although this product will eventually have no cash or surrender value, it will have a death benefit guaranteed to stay in force for life, assuming the contract owner has paid the planned premiums as agreed.

Section 1035 exchange • when a policyowner exchanges an existing policy for a new one in accordance with Internal Revenue Code Section 1035, no gain is attributed on the exchange. The adjusted basis of the old policy is carried over to the new one. Only the newly added premium paid after the exchange will be measured for MEC status. A Sec. 1035 exchange is allowed only when transferring cash values from an annuity to an annuity, life insurance to life insurance, or life insurance to an annuity contract. The new policy must retain the same insured and policyowner as the original policy.

Section 7702 of the Internal Revenue Code (extended the corridor test) • a test for flexible-premium life insurance developed by Congress—applicable to all life insurance policies, including fixed-premium endowments, entered into after October 22, 1986

select and ultimate term insurance • a term insurance policy intended to charge higher premiums to those in poorer health when they renew their term insurance, thereby reducing the degree of adverse selection. The product is commonly called *reentry term insurance.*

select mortality table • a presentation of data that shows the rate of mortality not only by age but also by duration of insurance; it recognizes the experience of recently selected lives evaluated to be in good health. It reflects the effects of selection.

self-interest • the pursuit of self-interest is a perfectly natural and acceptable activity. The basic ethical rule can be summarized: pursue your interests fairly and unselfishly.

selfishness • is behavior in which the pursuit of self-interest is without regard for the interests of, or at the expense of, others. Selfishness is the pursuit of self-interest at the expense of another when one is not entitled to the good pursued. When a person is being selfish, he or she puts his or her own interest first in a situation where pursuing that interest will hurt another.

selling • selling is the end result of successful marketing. It is the transaction resulting from the encounter between buyer and seller, the exchange of the product or service for the buyer's cash.

selling/planning process • The selling/planning process involves eight steps culminating in satisfying the needs and wants of the buyer. Those needs and wants must be matched with the appropriate product or service as a solution. The advisor guides the prospect through each step of the selling/planning process. If any step is omitted or inadequately completed, a sale will not be made, or will be on an unstable foundation. By following the selling/planning process systematically, better results will be obtained for both the client and the advisor, because a more complete process will be achieved. If the sale is not successful, it provides you with an opportunity to analyze what took place between you and the prospect, and identify the areas that need strengthening and improvement.

separate account assets • assets segregated from those of the general account for the purpose of funding variable life insurance, variable universal life insurance, variable annuities, pensions, and other benefits

separate accounts • funds managed and invested separately for use in variable life and annuity products. These funds are separate from the other company assets.

settlement agreement • a document provided when the insurance company retains the proceeds under one of the optional methods of settlement because its liability has continued beyond the maturity of the policy. This agreement contains the designation of the various classes of beneficiaries and a detailed description of the manner in which the proceeds are to be distributed.

settlement options • periodic income choices available to beneficiaries and policyowners for payout of death benefits, including the interest option, fixed-amount option, fixed-period option, and life income option

seven-pay test • one of two tests applied to a life insurance policy to determine if it is a modified endowment contract (MEC). If the premium paid at any time during the first 15 years of the policy exceeds the level premium necessary to fully pay up the policy in 7 years with level payments, the policy will be an MEC. Tax law discourages single premium and other highly funded variations of life insurance.

single life insurance • a life insurance policy on a single life, as opposed to insurance on two or more persons as in joint life

single-premium life • the ultimate limited-pay life. Under this plan the number of premiums is limited to one, so the policy is paid-up from inception.

special needs of surviving spouse and family • certain needs not found in every family situation, such as care and therapy for disabled family members, specially equipped vehicles, medication, and so on

spendthrift clause • trust provision restricting beneficiaries from assigning trust income or principal interests prior to distribution

split-dollar life insurance • a plan that splits a life insurance policy's premium obligations and policy benefits between two individuals or entities, normally between an employer and an employee. This arrangement went through significant tax-law changes in 2001 and 2002.

standard nonforfeiture law • a law requiring life insurance surrender values to be at least as large as those that would be produced by the method the law prescribes. Each policy must contain a statement of the method used to fund the surrender values and benefits provided under the policy at durations not specifically shown. This law does not require specific surrender values.

standard provisions • certain specified items that states require in their life insurance contracts, either as set forth in the statute or whose effect is the same in substance to those in the statute

"status" war clause • limits an insurer's obligation to return of premium if the insured should die while in military service outside the territorial boundaries of the United States, whether or not the cause of death can be attributed to military service

stock redemption plan • a buy-sell agreement that binds a corporation to purchase a shareholder's interest at the occurrence of certain events, such as death or retirement

straight life annuity • *See* life-only annuity.

suicide provision • a life insurance policy provision that specifies that if an insured, whether sane or insane, commits suicide during the first 1 or 2 years of the policy, the insurer will be liable only for a return of the premium

suitability • deals with the appropriateness of the product for the client based on their overall need, financial situation, ability to pay the premium, and risk tolerance

supplemental life insurance retirement plan (SLIRP) • life insurance can provide a host of retirement benefits, such as a preretirement death benefit, tax-deferred cash value accumulation, tax-free withdrawals contingent on certain stipulations, and an ultimate tax-free death benefit to beneficiaries

surplus • an amount that results when an insurance company's assets are greater than its liabilities

surrender • a full surrender provision in a deferred annuity contract allows the policyowner total withdrawal of funds prior to maturity of the contract. Compare partial surrender.

surrender charge • charge imposed by an insurance company to encourage purchasers to make long-term commitments. The charge penalizes premature withdrawals.

surrender cost index • compares the costs of surrendering an insurance policy and withdrawing the cash value at some future point in time. It is especially useful when the main concern is the level of the cash values.

surrender options • a set of insurance contract provisions increasingly used to adapt policy coverage to changing circumstances and needs, also known as nonforfeiture options. Most policies stipulate that the surrender value may be taken in one of three forms: cash, a reduced amount of paid-up life insurance, or paid-up term insurance.

survivorship life (second-to-die) • a type of life insurance policy that covers two or more persons in which the proceeds are payable on the death of the last person to die

Table 2001 • A new transitional table adopted in IRS Notices 2001-10 and 2002-8 for split-dollar arrangements. Table 2001 replaces the PS 58 table for valuing economic benefit. The Table 2001 rates are much lower than the PS 58 rates.

target marketing • you look for a group of people (a segment) which is large enough that you will never run out of contact names and small enough that the members are interrelated to the degree that your reputation will precede you. The group is identifiable and accessible, with members who have common characteristics and needs and communicate with one another.

target premium • a suggested premium to be paid on a level basis throughout a universal life contract's duration or for a shorter period of time if a limited-pay approach was originally intended to fund a policy. It is merely a suggestion and carries no liability if it is inadequate to maintain the contract to any duration, much less to the end of life. It also sets the maximum amount of full commission to be paid.

term insurance • a contract that pays death benefits only if the insured does not survive the specified period

three-factor contribution plan • a distribution plan that recognizes only three major sources of surplus: mortality savings, excess interest, and loading savings

time value of money • the concept that a specific amount of money received (paid) in a specific time period has a different value than the same amount received (paid) in a different time period. This concept is expressed as an interest rate that represents or creates these different values.

transfer-for-value • a rule that specifies that, subject to certain exceptions, if a life insurance policy is transferred from one owner to another for valuable consideration, the death proceeds will be subject to federal income taxation

twisting • occurs when a policyowner is induced to discontinue and replace a policy through an agent's distortion or misrepresentation of the facts

ultimate mortality table • a presentation of data that excludes the effects of selection and reflects only the rates of mortality that can be expected after the influence of selection has worn off

unbundling • the specific cost of insurance charges, expense charges, cash values, death benefits, and interest crediting are itemized and available to the policyowner through annual reports

universal life • a variation of whole life insurance that offers truly flexible premiums and includes provisions similar to those contained in the adjustable life contract. The policyowner has the right to withdraw part of the cash value without having the withdrawal treated as a policy loan; the policyowner also has the choice of either a level-death benefit or an increasing-death benefit design.

unlimited right of withdrawal • the right of a beneficiary under a deferred-settlement agreement to withdraw some or possibly all of the proceeds at any one time, subject to restrictions

variable life insurance (VLI) • a market-driven life insurance policy that provides a guaranteed minimum death benefit, but the actual death benefit or cash value is dependent upon investment fluctuations of the funds selected by the policyowner

vanishing premium • a situtation in which the premium will "disappear," or not need to be paid out of pocket (the premium must be paid). The premium is paid through policy values, either by dividends in a whole life type policy, or by excess interest in a universal life type policy. This concept is different from paid-up status, where the premium no longer needs to be paid.

variable universal life (VUL) • a variation of whole life insurance, this policy incorporates all of the premium flexibility and policy adjustment features of the universal life policy with the policyowner-directed investment aspects of variable life insurance. This policy eliminates the direct connection between investment performance above or below some stated target level and the corresponding formula-directed adjustment in death benefits. Then it adopts the death benefit designs applicable to universal life policies: either a level death benefit or an increasing death benefit design for which a constant amount at risk is paid in addition to the cash accumulation account.

viatical settlement • refer to instances in which death is considered imminent, and the insured is terminally ill with a life expectancy of less than two years. The policyowner can receive cash in excess of the cash surrender value, or the fair market value of the policy in the secondary market.

waiver-of-premium • if the insured becomes totally disabled as defined in the life insurance contract, the insurance company will waive payment of premiums on the policy during the continuance of the insured's disability

whole life • traditional whole life insurance policies have fixed and guaranteed premiums, cash values, and death benefits. Whole life is characterized by guarantees. Coverage can never be cancelled and premiums can never be increased. Premiums are to be paid throughout the insured's lifetime.

yearly renewable term insurance (YRT) • insurance provided for a period of one year only that permits the policyowner to renew the policy for successive periods of one year without having to furnish evidence of insurability

INDEX

M

N

O

P